AF478159

Social Security Programs and Retirement around the World

A National Bureau of
Economic Research
Conference Report

Social Security Programs and Retirement around the World
Working Longer

Edited by **Courtney C. Coile, Kevin Milligan, and David A. Wise**

The University of Chicago Press

Chicago and London

The University of Chicago Press, Chicago 60637
The University of Chicago Press, Ltd., London
© 2019 by the National Bureau of Economic Research, Inc.

Published 2019
Printed in the United States of America

28 27 26 25 24 23 22 21 20 19   1 2 3 4 5

ISBN-13: 978-0-226-61929-3 (cloth)
ISBN-13: 978-0-226-61932-3 (e-book)
DOI: https://doi.org/10.7208/chicago/9780226619323.001.0001

Library of Congress Cataloging-in-Publication Data

Names: Coile, Courtney, editor. | Milligan, Kevin, editor. | Wise,
    David A., editor.
Title: Social security programs and retirement around the world :
    working longer / edited by Courtney C. Coile, Kevin Milligan,
    David A. Wise.
Other titles: National Bureau of Economic Research conference report.
Description: Chicago : The University of Chicago Press, 2019. | Series:
    National Bureau of Economic Research conference report | Includes
    index.
Identifiers: LCCN 2019024387 | ISBN 9780226619293 (cloth) |
    ISBN 9780226619323 (ebook)
Subjects: LCSH: Post-retirement employment—Western countries. |
    Retirees—Employment—Western countries. | Age and
    employment—Western countries.
Classification: LCC HD6279 .S64 2019 | DDC 368.4/300918—dc23
LC record available at https://lccn.loc.gov/2019024387

♾ This paper meets the requirements of ANSI/NISO Z39.48-1992
(Permanence of Paper).

Relation of the Directors to the
Work and Publications of the
National Bureau of Economic Research

1. The object of the NBER is to ascertain and present to the economics profession, and to the public more generally, important economic facts and their interpretation in a scientific manner without policy recommendations. The Board of Directors is charged with the responsibility of ensuring that the work of the NBER is carried on in strict conformity with this object.

2. The President shall establish an internal review process to ensure that book manuscripts proposed for publication DO NOT contain policy recommendations. This shall apply both to the proceedings of conferences and to manuscripts by a single author or by one or more co-authors but shall not apply to authors of comments at NBER conferences who are not NBER affiliates.

3. No book manuscript reporting research shall be published by the NBER until the President has sent to each member of the Board a notice that a manuscript is recommended for publication and that in the President's opinion it is suitable for publication in accordance with the above principles of the NBER. Such notification will include a table of contents and an abstract or summary of the manuscript's content, a list of contributors if applicable, and a response form for use by Directors who desire a copy of the manuscript for review. Each manuscript shall contain a summary drawing attention to the nature and treatment of the problem studied and the main conclusions reached.

4. No volume shall be published until forty-five days have elapsed from the above notification of intention to publish it. During this period, a copy shall be sent to any Director requesting it, and if any Director objects to publication on the grounds that the manuscript contains policy recommendations, the objection will be presented to the author(s) or editor(s). In case of dispute, all members of the Board shall be notified, and the President shall appoint an ad hoc committee of the Board to decide the matter; thirty days additional shall be granted for this purpose.

5. The President shall present annually to the Board a report describing the internal manuscript review process, any objections made by Directors before publication or by anyone after publication, any disputes about such matters, and how they were handled.

6. Publications of the NBER issued for informational purposes concerning the work of the Bureau, or issued to inform the public of the activities at the Bureau, including but not limited to the NBER Digest and Reporter, shall be consistent with the object stated in paragraph 1. They shall contain a specific disclaimer noting that they have not passed through the review procedures required in this resolution. The Executive Committee of the Board is charged with the review of all such publications from time to time.

7. NBER working papers and manuscripts distributed on the Bureau's web site are not deemed to be publications for the purpose of this resolution, but they shall be consistent with the object stated in paragraph 1. Working papers shall contain a specific disclaimer noting that they have not passed through the review procedures required in this resolution. The NBER's web site shall contain a similar disclaimer. The President shall establish an internal review process to ensure that the working papers and the web site do not contain policy recommendations and shall report annually to the Board on this process and any concerns raised in connection with it.

8. Unless otherwise determined by the Board or exempted by the terms of paragraphs 6 and 7, a copy of this resolution shall be printed in each NBER publication as described in paragraph 2 above.

Contents

Acknowledgments

Funding for this project was provided by the National Institute on Aging, grant number P01-AG012810, to the National Bureau of Economic Research. We thank two anonymous reviewers for detailed and thoughtful comments. The views expressed herein are those of the authors and do not necessarily reflect the views of the National Institute on Aging, the National Institutes of Health, or the National Bureau of Economic Research.

Introduction

Courtney C. Coile, Kevin Milligan, and David A. Wise

Project Overview

Through the coordination of the work of a team of analysts in 12 countries for nearly 20 years, the ISS project has used the vast differences in social security programs across countries as a natural laboratory to study the effects of retirement program provisions on the labor force participation (LFP) of older persons. The project's first several phases (Gruber and Wise 1999, 2004, and 2007) documented the strong relationship across countries between social security incentives and older men's LFP, confirmed this relationship in microeconomic analysis, and estimated the labor market and fiscal implications of social security reform. Later volumes have examined the relationship between disability insurance program provisions, health, and retirement (Wise 2012, 2016) and explored whether older employment affects youth unemployment (Gruber and Wise 2010) and whether older workers are healthy enough to work longer (Wise 2017). This analysis is the eighth phase of the ongoing project, and it is focused on recent trends in LFP and potential explanations for these changes in behavior.

Courtney C. Coile is professor of economics at Wellesley College and a research associate of the National Bureau of Economic Research.

Kevin Milligan is professor of economics at the University of British Columbia and a research associate of the National Bureau of Economic Research.

David A. Wise is the John F. Stambaugh Professor of Political Economy, Emeritus, at Harvard Kennedy School and a research associate of the National Bureau of Economic Research.

This chapter is part of the National Bureau of Economic Research's International Social Security (ISS) project, which is supported by the National Institute on Aging (grant P01 AG012810). We thank the members of the other country teams in the ISS project for comments that helped shape this chapter. For acknowledgments, sources of research support, and disclosure of the authors' material financial relationships, if any, please see https://www.nber.org/chapters/c14040.ack.

The results of the ongoing project are the product of analyses conducted for each country by analysts in that country. Researchers who have participated in this phase of the project are listed first below; those who have participated in prior phases are listed second in italics.

Belgium: Alain Jousten, Mathieu Lefebvre, *Arnaud Dellis, Raphaël Desmet, Sergio Perelman, Pierre Pestieau,* and *Jean-Philippe Stijns*

Canada: Kevin Milligan, Tammy Schirle, *Michael Baker,* and *Jonathan Gruber*

Denmark: Paul Bingley, Nabanita Datta Gupta, Peder J. Pedersen, and *Michael Jørgensen*

France: Didier Blanchet, Antoine Bozio, Corinne Prost, Muriel Roger, *Luc Behaghel, Thierry Debrand, Ronan Mahieu, Louis-Paul Pelé, Melika Ben Salem,* and *Emmanuelle Walraët*

Germany: Axel Börsch-Supan, Irene Ferrari, *Tabea Bucher-Koenen, Hendrik Jürges, Simone Kohnz, Giovanni Mastrobuoni, Johannes Rausch, Reinhold Schnabel, Morten Schuth,* and *Lars Thiel*

Italy: Agar Brugiavini, Giacomo Pasini, Guglielmo Weber, and *Franco Peracchi*

Japan: Takashi Oshio, Satoshi Shimizutani, Emiko Usui, *Mayu Fujii, Akiko Sato Oishi,* and *Naohiro Yashiro*

Netherlands: Adriaan Kalwij, Arie Kapteyn, and Klaas de Vos

Spain: Pilar García Gómez, Sergi Jiménez-Martín, Judit Vall-Castelló, *Michele Boldrín,* and *Franco Peracchi*

Sweden: Lisa Laun, Mårten Palme, *Per Johansson,* and *Ingemar Svensson*

UK: James Banks, Carl Emmerson, Gemma Tetlow, *Richard Blundell, Antoine Bozio, Paul Johnson, Costas Meghir,* and *Sarah Smith*

US: Courtney Coile, *Kevin Milligan, David Wise, Jonathan Gruber,* and *Peter Diamond*

An important goal of the project has been to present results that are as comparable as possible across countries. Thus the chapters for each phase are prepared according to a detailed template that we develop in consultation with country participants. In this introduction, we summarize the collective results of the country analyses and borrow freely from the country chapters. In large part, however, the results presented in the introduction could only be conveyed by a combined analysis of the data from each of the countries. The country chapters themselves present much more detail for each country and, in addition to the common analyses performed by all countries, often present country-specific analysis relevant to each particular country.

Introduction

At the turn of the 20th century, a majority of men in developed economies worked even at the oldest ages. As Costa (1998) documents, the LFP rate of men aged 65 and older in 1900 was 65 percent in the United States, 61 percent in Britain, 58 percent in Germany, and 54 percent in France.[1] Given the relatively short life expectancies of the time, many men of this era would have spent few, if any, years in retirement.

By the late 20th century, however, work past age 65 had become the exception rather than the rule. The share of men aged 65–69 in the labor force in 1995 was only 4 percent in Germany, 5 percent in France, 15 percent in the United Kingdom, and 27 percent in the United States. Including men aged 70 and older (to match the earlier figures) would drive these values lower still. With life expectancies at older ages rising quickly over the same period—by 4.3 years for men at age 65 in the United States during the 20th century (Bell and Miller 2002), for example—retirement emerged as a distinct and important phase of life.

The growth of public pension programs has long been a leading candidate to explain this decline in older men's participation. Germany introduced the world's first old-age social insurance program in 1889, and other developed countries followed suit over the next several decades. Over time, many countries expanded their programs to cover more of the workforce, provide benefits for new categories of individuals such as survivors and the disabled, and offer more generous benefits.

The ISS project was started in the mid-1990s against this backdrop of decades of decline in older men's work and the growth of public pension programs in many developed countries. The project sought to use the vast differences in social security programs across countries as a natural laboratory to study the effects of retirement programs on the LFP of older persons.

As it turns out, the launch of the ISS project coincided with the end of the century-long decline in men's LFP. Not only was the declining trend arrested, but the employment rates rose tremendously in many countries. This is illustrated for men aged 60–64 in figure I.1. While the exact year of the trough varies across the country, the LFP has risen by an average of 17 percentage points in the 12 ISS countries between its lowest point and 2014, as noted on table I.1. Participation rose in every country, but the magnitude of the increase varied, from 7 points in Japan and Spain to 35 points in Germany and 44 points in the Netherlands.

Why did so many countries experience a substantial increase in men's LFP at this particular time, following a century of earlier withdrawal from the labor force? Why was the increase larger in some countries than others? The answers to these questions are pivotal as countries seek solutions to the fiscal and retirement security challenges posed by the expansion in life-spans and may want to encourage further increases in elderly labor supply. If the turnaround in labor supply is driven by demographic or global economic trends,

---

1. These data are for the years 1895–1901, depending on the country; see Costa (1998) for details.

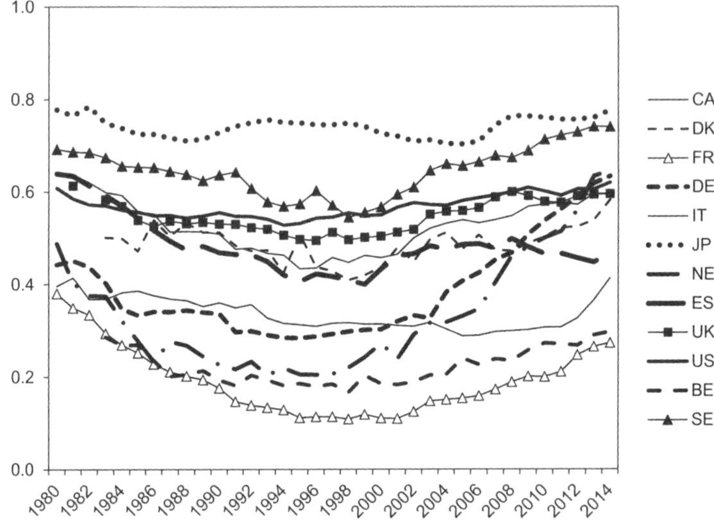

Fig. I.1   LFP of men aged 60–64, 1980–2014

Table I.1   Increase in LFP of men aged 60–64, trough to 2014

Country	Year of minimum LFP	Minimum LFP	2014 LFP	Difference
Belgium	1998	0.167	0.297	0.130
Canada	1995	0.434	0.596	0.162
Denmark	1998	0.409	0.582	0.173
France	1998	0.109	0.273	0.164
Germany	1995	0.284	0.633	0.349
Italy	2005	0.288	0.413	0.125
Japan	2005	0.703	0.776	0.073
Netherlands	1993	0.204	0.644	0.440
Spain	1999	0.400	0.466	0.066
Sweden	1998	0.545	0.740	0.195
UK	1996	0.495	0.595	0.100
US	1994	0.528	0.619	0.091
Average		0.381	0.553	0.172

then any one country's direct policy choices will change little. On the other hand, if policy changes around social security programs have contributed significantly to the turnaround in LFP, then further direct policy measures might be effective in prolonging work lives.

The goal of this phase of the ISS project is to begin to answer these questions by documenting the changes in the LFP and employment of older men and women from 1980 to the present and exploring the factors that may have contributed to these changes. The methods we use are primarily descriptive, as we examine trends over time in the labor supply and in those factors that may affect it. By investigating these issues in a cross-country context, we can gauge whether trends observed in individual countries hold true in other countries. We can also potentially build a stronger case that a certain factor—say, improving health or education—may be contributing to changes in participation if we observe larger changes over time in participation in those countries where the factor also changed more rapidly. In some cases, we highlight interesting case studies from individual country chapters that suggest a role for a particular factor, although the individual chapters offer much more of this as well as additional analyses undertaken by the authors to shed light on questions of particular interest in their context. In future work with the ISS project, we will explore the individual factors in microdata and simulations for each country, which will contribute to making a stronger causal case.

Our analysis here in this introductory chapter shows that countries have had diverse experiences and reveals some indication of which factors may have played a more consistent role across countries. For health and education, we find little evidence that these are strong contributing factors. Health and education generally improved both in times when LFP rates were falling and when they were rising. Further, countries experiencing greater improvements in health and education over time did not see bigger increases in the older worker labor market participation in general. Turning to the expansion of women in the workforce over the last generation, we find that this factor may have had an impact on not just the work behavior of older women but also the work behavior of older men. Countries with a larger expansion of female LFP (measured at midcareer rather than in old age to avoid correlation with other factors affecting older women and older men's participation) saw larger increases in the participation of older men. Finally, institutional factors embedded in social security programs seem very important in explaining the older-age working patterns in some individual countries. While no one factor appears to explain the experience of all countries, examining what has happened in different countries enriches our understanding of why men and women are working longer and provides a path for future research.

Trends in LFP and Employment

We begin by describing trends in LFP and employment for men and women aged 55–69 in the 12 ISS countries from 1980 to the present. Figures I.2 and I.3 illustrate these trends for men and women, respectively. While for men there are not strong differences across cohorts in the share of the population working at age 55, for women in many countries, younger cohorts have been working more. For women, it is therefore harder to distinguish what part of the trend in elderly LFP is due to delayed retirement (which might relate to

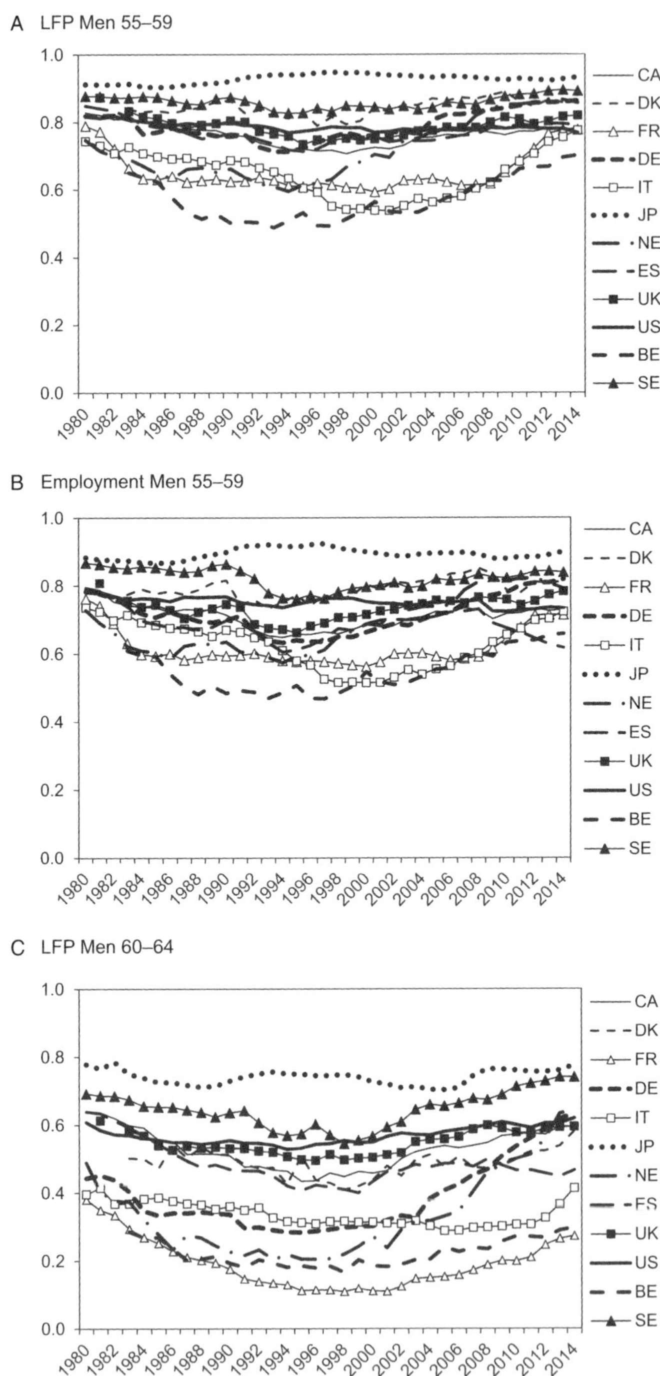

Fig. I.2 **LFP and employment, men aged 55–69, 1980–2014**

D Employment Men 60–64
CA
DK
FR
DE
IT
JP
NE
ES
UK
US
BE
SE

E LFP Men 65–69
CA
DK
FR
DE
IT
JP
NE
ES
UK
US
BE
SE

F Employment Men 65–69
CA
DK
FR
DE
IT
JP
NE
ES
UK
US
BE
SE

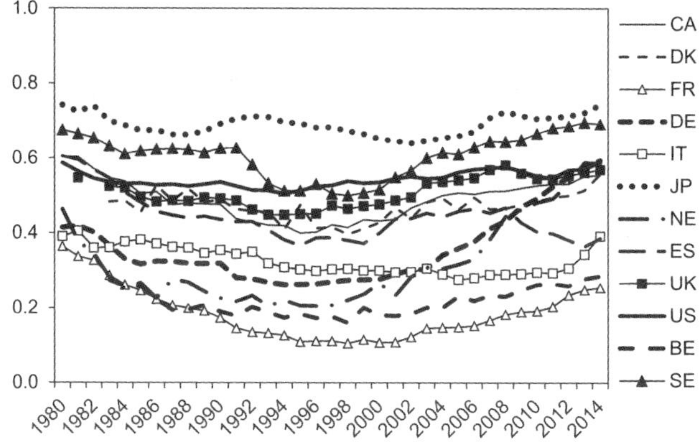

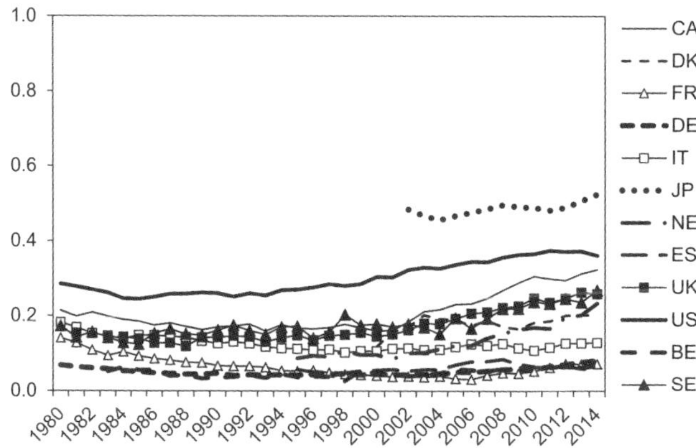

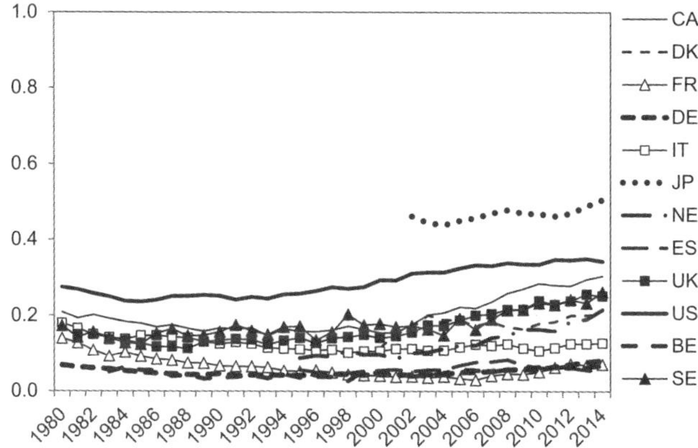

Fig. I.2   (cont.)

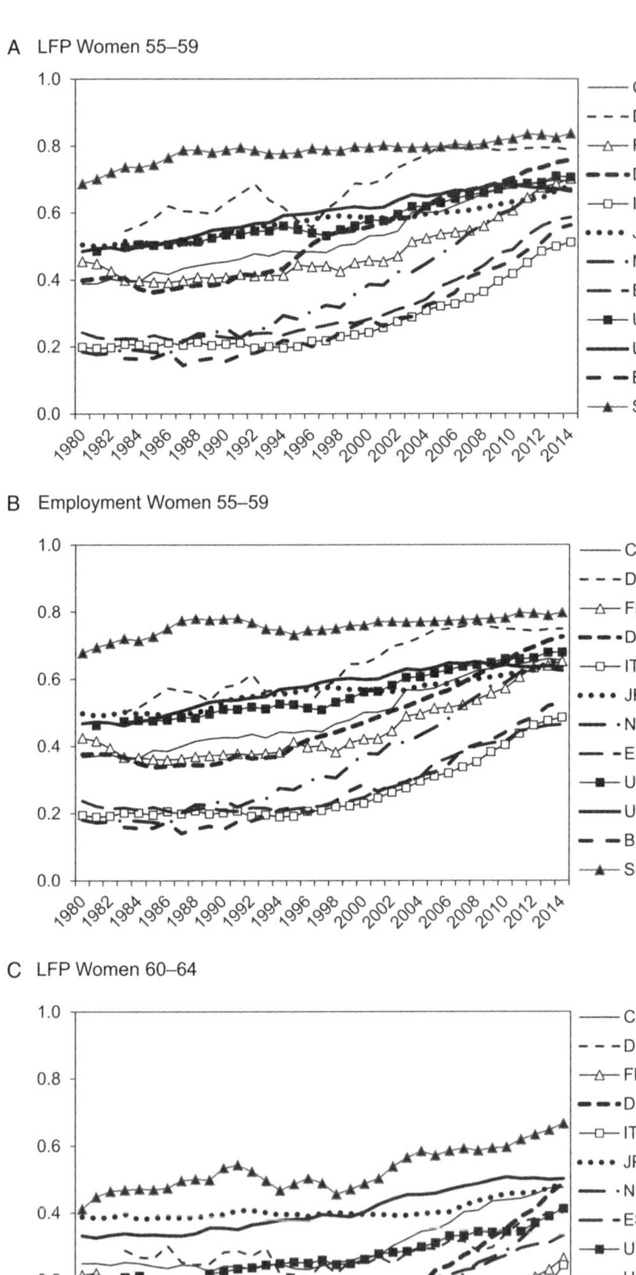

Fig. I.3   LFP and employment, women aged 55–69, 1980–2014

D Employment Women 60–64
1.0
0.8
0.6
0.4
0.2
0.0
1980 1982 1984 1986 1988 1990 1992 1994 1996 1998 2000 2002 2004 2006 2008 2010 2012 2014
CA
DK
FR
DE
IT
JP
NE
ES
UK
US
BE
SE

E LFP Women 65–69
1.0
0.8
0.6
0.4
0.2
0.0
1980 1982 1984 1986 1988 1990 1992 1994 1996 1998 2000 2002 2004 2006 2008 2010 2012 2014
CA
DK
FR
DE
IT
JP
NE
ES
UK
US
BE
SE

F Employment Women 65–69
1.0
0.8
0.6
0.4
0.2
0.0
1980 1982 1984 1986 1988 1990 1992 1994 1996 1998 2000 2002 2004 2006 2008 2010 2012 2014
CA
DK
FR
DE
IT
JP
NE
ES
UK
US
BE
SE

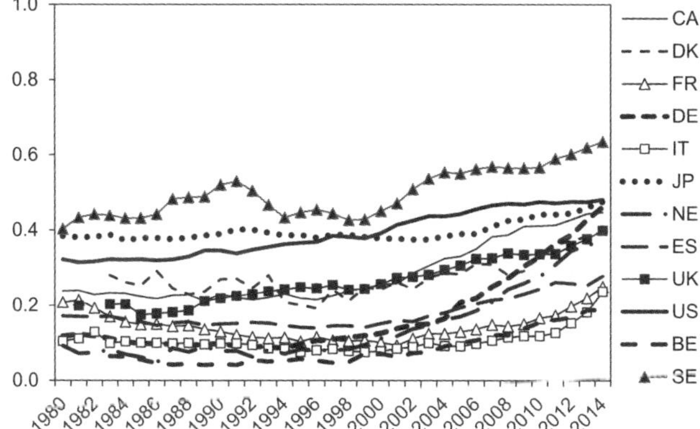

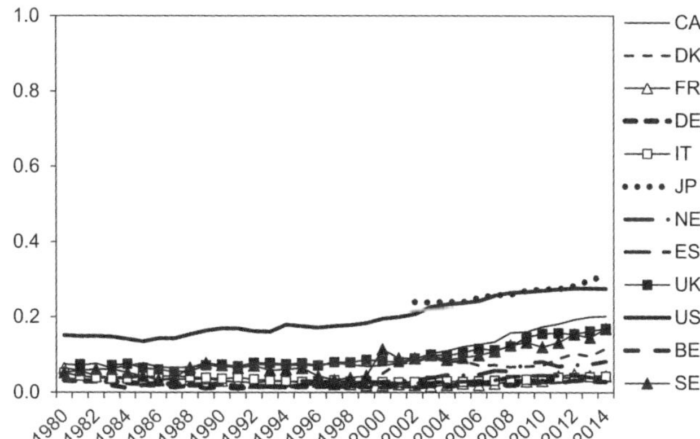

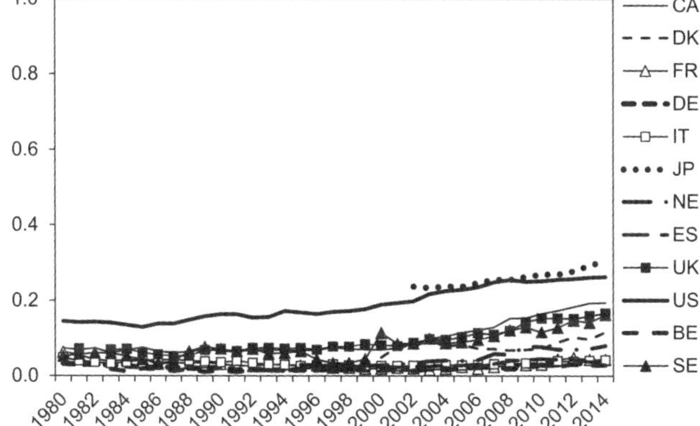

Fig. I.3   (cont.)

Table I.2   Increase in LFP, trough to 2014

Country	Men			Women		
	55–59	60–64	65–69	55–59	60–64	65–69
Belgium	0.214	0.130	0.041	0.418	0.159	0.019
Canada	0.075	0.162	0.164	0.304	0.250	0.138
Denmark	0.070	0.173		0.242	0.210	
France	0.184	0.164	0.042	0.310	0.170	0.027
Germany	0.150	0.349	0.041	0.395	0.296	0.024
Italy	0.237	0.125	0.026	0.316	0.166	0.016
Japan	0.029	0.073		0.182	0.107	
Netherlands	0.261	0.440	0.148	0.494	0.355	0.061
Spain	0.078	0.066	0.008	0.367	0.181	0.015
Sweden	0.064	0.195	0.128	0.148	0.254	0.135
UK	0.084	0.100	0.140	0.220	0.229	0.114
US	0.000	0.091	0.116	0.179	0.176	0.140
Average	0.126	0.172	0.085	0.298	0.213	0.069

Notes: Denmark and Japan are omitted for the 65–69 age group because the data series start after 2000. Data series for Spain and the Netherlands are included but begin only in 1995.

changes in health at older ages or in public pension provisions, for example) rather than these underlying cross-cohort differences. We present women alongside men in this analysis while emphasizing this different context and encourage readers to bear this point in mind with respect to the LFP rates presented in the individual country chapters as well.

Patterns in participation for men aged 55–59 are broadly similar to those for men aged 60–64, discussed above, though the magnitudes of the changes are somewhat smaller. As before, most (8 of 12) countries reached the trough of participation during the 1993–98 period. The average increase in participation from the trough to 2014 is 13 percentage points, an increase about three-quarters as large as that seen for men aged 60–64 (17 points). As before, the size of the change varies across countries, as seen in table I.2. There was no change in the United States, as participation remained relatively constant between the mid-1990s and 2014, and an increase of only 3 points in Japan, which consistently has the highest participation rate of all the countries. By contrast, participation rose by 7–8 points from the trough to 2014 in Canada, Denmark, Spain, and the UK and by 15–26 points in Belgium, France, Germany, Italy, and the Netherlands.

For men aged 65–69, there is a somewhat different pattern across countries. The largest increases are in Canada, the Netherlands, Sweden, the UK, and the US. Except for Sweden and the Netherlands, these countries had relatively small increases in participation in the two younger age groups. The average increase among all the countries from trough to 2014 for this age group is 8.5 points, smaller than the average increase in the other age groups.

Finally, we can add the increases across the three age groups in each country as one way to gauge the overall rise in participation at age 55–69. The Netherlands experienced by far the largest increase in participation (85 points), followed by Germany (54 points). The US and Spain had the smallest total increases (21 and 15 points), while the other countries fell in the middle (30–40 points).

Another finding from these figures is that while the employment rate is (unsurprisingly) slightly lower than the participation rate, trends over time in the two series are very similar. This is particularly true for the older age groups. The one exception is after the recent recession (2007 and beyond), where there is a bigger divergence between employment and participation for men aged 55–59, particularly in Spain. This suggests that normal cyclical trends in unemployment (which is the difference between the employed group and the labor force group) are unlikely to be an important factor. Because trends in LFP and employment are largely similar, we focus on participation in the remainder of the analysis.

Patterns in women's LFP are quite different from those of men. For women aged 55–59, the trough year is in the 1980s in all countries—in fact, it is 1980 or 1981 for about half the countries, which is essentially the beginning of our sample period. Thus, unlike the men's pattern of a U shape that reaches the bottom in the mid-1990s, here there is often no *U*, or only a shallow one with a trough in the mid-1980s. The average increase in women's LFP from the trough to 2014 in this age group is also much larger, 30 points versus 13 points for men. As noted above, increases in older women's participation may reflect both an increased propensity to delay retirement and the effect of rising participation (at all ages) across cohorts. For women, it seems likely that any tendency to retire earlier over the first half of our sample period that might arise from the same factors that are affecting men is being swamped by ever-increasing LFP among successive cohorts of women.[2]

There are notable differences across countries in the magnitude of the increase in participation over time, as seen in table I.2. Increases appear to be inversely proportional to initial participation rates, leading to a converging trend across countries. Denmark, Japan, the UK, and the US had participation rates of around 50 percent in 1980, and all experienced increases of less than 25 percentage points by 2014. Meanwhile, Belgium and the Netherlands had participation rates below 20 percent in the early 1980s and experienced increases of 40–50 percentage points.

At ages 60–64, there is similarly either no U shape or one that appears relatively shallow compared to the pattern for men. The average increase in participation from trough to 2014 for this age group is 21 percentage points, which is still very large but smaller than the 30 point increase at ages 55–59.

---

2. See Goldin (2006) for an overview of the changes in women's employment, education, and family roles during the 20th century.

The increase at ages 65–69 is smaller still, averaging 7 points. However, Canada, Sweden, the UK, and the US experienced increases about twice as large as the average in this oldest group, as was the case for men. Overall, LFP among women in all three age groups is now at an all-time high, and there is little suggestion in the figures that it has yet reached its peak.

Factors That May Affect LFP

Next, we turn to exploring those factors that may help to explain the changes in LFP. In the discussion below, we consider a number of potential factors, including changes in mortality and health, education and occupation, unemployment, social security program provisions, and women's LFP (which may affect men's participation).

Mortality and Health

Health is a critically important factor in individuals' retirement decisions, as established in early studies such as Diamond and Hausman (1984) and confirmed in more recent studies such as Wise (2016). It stands to reason that changes over time in the health of the older population may have had an impact on LFP.

Mortality rates offer a number of advantages as a measure of health. They can be measured consistently across countries and over long periods of time, generally quite precisely because they are typically based on vital statistics records for the full population rather than survey data. A clear disadvantage is that they may be an imperfect measure of work capacity at older ages, which is what is relevant for retirement decisions.[3] Also, the relationship between mortality and more subtle indicators of health does vary across countries, as can be seen in the individual country chapters in Wise (2012) and Wise (2017). However, Milligan and Wise (2012) find that there is a strong within-country relationship between changes over time in self-assessed health and changes in mortality. To the extent that self-assessed health may be a better measure of work capacity, this is reassuring. Time series on self-assessed health are unfortunately available for only about half of the ISS countries, so we do not use these data directly here, though some countries make use of them in their own chapters.[4]

---

3. A number of recent papers have explored the question of whether people are living healthier as well as longer lives. While studies such as Crimmins and Beltran (2011) have found that people are spending more years living with disease, studies such as Cutler, Ghosh, and Landrum (2014) and Chernew et al. (2016) find that disability-free life expectancy is rising faster than life expectancy, indicating that disability is increasingly being compressed into a shorter period before death. It seems possible if not likely that disability would matter more for labor supply than disease, as some diseases may not interfere with work or can be managed with medication or lifestyle changes.

4. In a majority of the countries for which data on self-assessed health is available, the share of older individuals reporting themselves to be in fair or poor health is declining over time—this

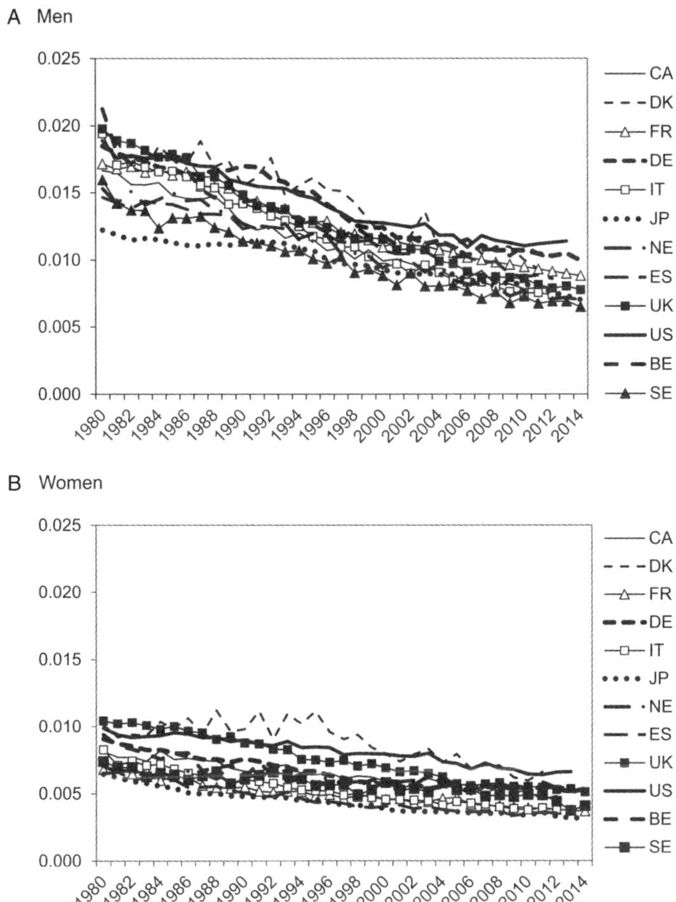

Fig. I.4 Mortality at age 60, men and women, 1980–2014

Mortality rates at older ages have declined substantially during the past several decades, as shown in figure I.4. For men, the average mortality rate at age 60 in 1980 was 1.7 percent. By 2011, this had dropped roughly in half, to 0.9 percent.[5] Mortality improved notably and continuously throughout

is the case in Denmark, Germany, Spain, Sweden, and the US (1980–95), though the share in fair or poor health is essentially flat over time in Canada, the UK, and the US (after 1995). As discussed below with respect to mortality, there is little evidence that trends over time in self-assessed health are driving trends in LFP, as there is no U-shaped trend in health (like there is in men's participation).

5. The year 2011 is used here because it is the last year for which all countries (except Germany) have data; Germany is excluded from these calculations because its data series ends earlier.

the period for all countries, with a somewhat smaller absolute decrease in Japan, which had the lowest initial mortality rate. Mortality rates in 1980 for women were far lower than those for men, averaging 0.9 percent. By 2011, this value had fallen to 0.5 percent.

In establishing changes in mortality rates as a possible driver of changes in LFP, one is immediately confronted by the difficulty that LFP for men exhibits a U shape with a trough in the mid-1990s, while mortality has improved continuously throughout this period. Thus the hypothesis that rising participation since the mid-1990s has been driven by improving health would appear to be undercut by the fact that health was also improving during the earlier part of our sample period when participation was falling. For women, the lack of a U shape in participation (or the presence of a shallower *U*) makes this problem a bit less glaring. Nonetheless, even for women, this constitutes weak evidence at best that changes in health may be driving changes in participation.

To continue to probe the plausibility of a causal relationship between mortality and LFP, in the left panel of figure I.5, we plot the change in participation for men aged 60–64 from 1995 to 2011 against the change in the mortality rate at age 60 over the same period. The slope is expected to be negative, as those countries in which the mortality rate fell more are expected to have a larger increase in participation. The figure shows that the slope is in fact negative, although the result is sensitive to the outlier observations. For women, the slope is negative, as seen in the right panel of the figure. The magnitude of the effect for women indicates that moving from being the country with the smallest mortality improvement (no improvement) to that with the largest improvement (a drop of 0.4 percent over the 16-year period) is associated with an increase in participation of about 5 percentage points (roughly one-third of the average increase of 14 points during this period). However, the lack of a robust effect for men casts doubt on the notion that this reflects a causal effect, as one would expect improvements in health to affect both genders in a similar way.

Overall, we find little evidence that improvements in health—as measured by mortality rates—are a driving force behind the increases in LFP over the past few decades. We base this assessment on the fact that there has been continuous improvement in mortality rates since 1980, whereas participation among men was falling for the first half of the sample period and rising for the second. Likewise, there is inconsistent evidence for the hypothesis that countries with faster improvement in mortality rates since 1995 also experienced faster growth in LFP. Of course, we cannot rule out the possibility that the results would differ if we were able to examine other health measures beyond mortality that might be more directly tied to work capacity; unfortunately, the lack of a consistent time series for such health measures in enough of the countries prevents us from exploring this further.

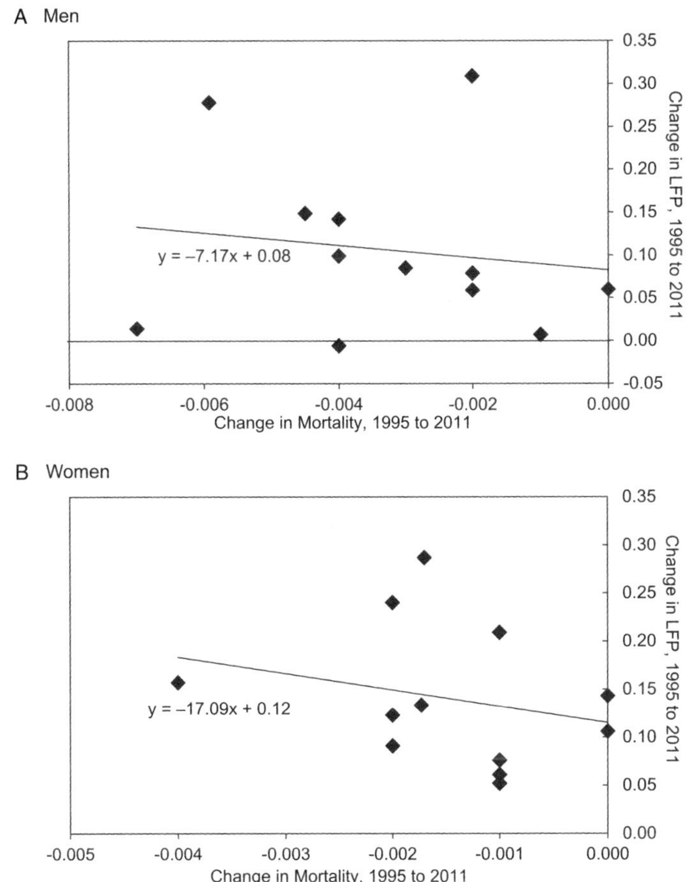

Fig. I.5   Change in LFP at ages 60–64 versus change in mortality rate, 1995–2011

Nonetheless, this analysis suggests that we need to look to other factors to explain recent increases in participation.

Education and Occupation

Education and occupation also offer promise as potential explanatory factors for changes in participation, especially with the shifts in labor demand induced by increased globalization and technical change. LFP rates at older ages tend to differ sharply by education—Coile, Milligan, and Wise (2016) report that for men aged 55–64 in all ISS countries, those in the highest education group have participation rates 20–40 percentage points higher than those in the lowest education groups. Occupation is a closely related factor, since one reason for the strong relationship between education and partici-

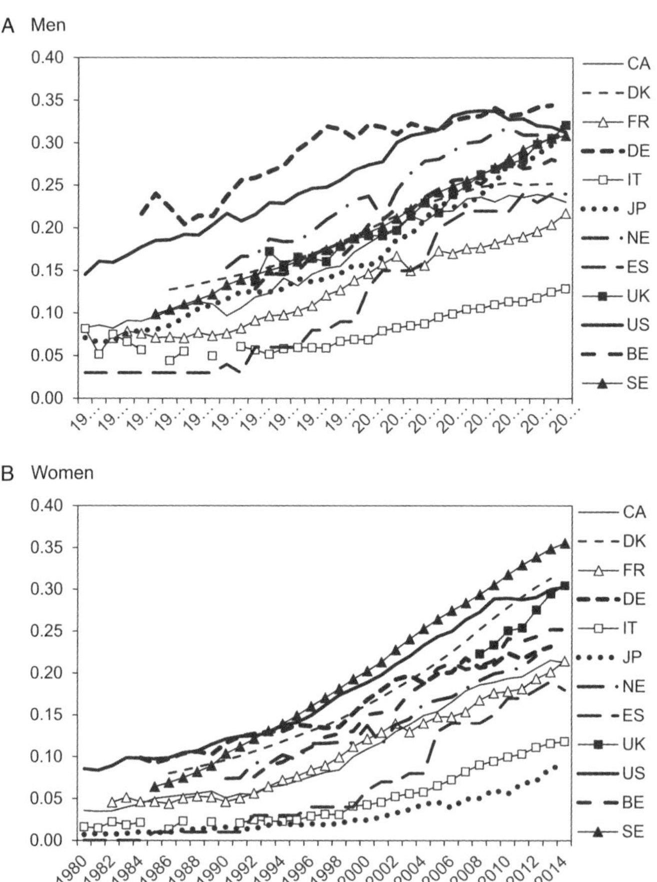

Fig. I.6   Share of men and women aged 55–64 with a college education, 1980–2014

pation may be that people with more education tend to have jobs that are less physically demanding, making it easier for them to work to older ages.[6] If successive cohorts nearing retirement age have higher levels of education and are more concentrated in white-collar occupations, this may tend to increase participation at older ages.

Figure I.6 shows the share of men and women aged 55–64 who have a college education. Over the period of 1980–2016, the share of men with a college education rises by 15–20 percentage points in virtually all countries, with the exception of Italy, where the increase is about 5 points. Compared

6. Belbase et al. (2016, p. 5) argue that the notion that it is difficult for blue-collar workers to remain on the job at older ages and easy for white-collar workers to do so is too simplistic and that it is "important to consider the particular abilities required by an occupation and whether these abilities decline significantly by the time workers reach typical retirement ages."

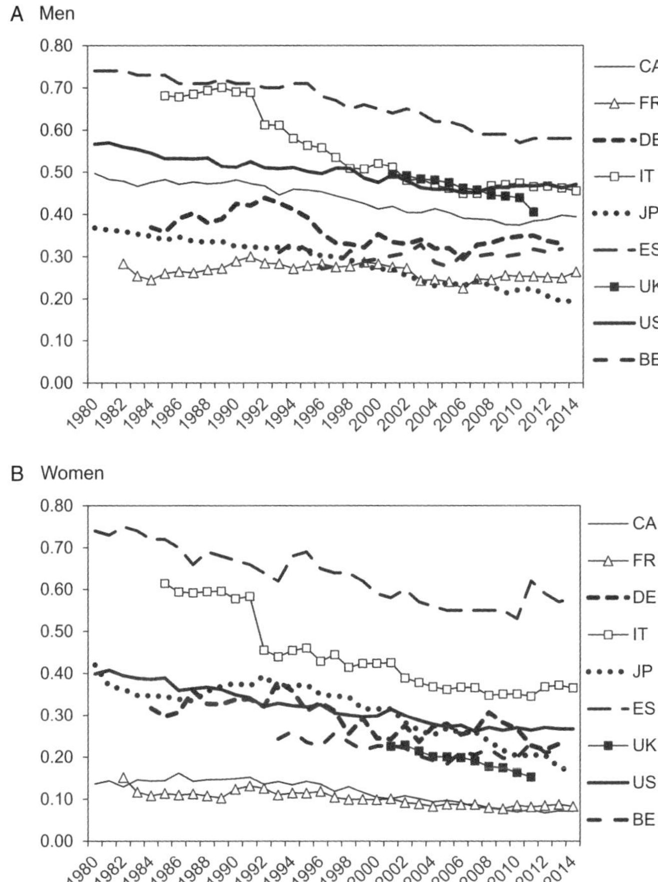

Fig. I.7   Share of men and women aged 55–64 in blue-collar work, 1980–2014

to men, women have a lower share initially in 1980, but the rate of growth over time is quite similar. By 2012 (the last year for which we have complete data), the average share of men and women with a college degree across all the ISS countries is 26 and 21 percent, respectively.

The share of men and women in blue-collar occupations is shown in figure I.7 for countries where these data are available.[7] There are large differences across countries at any point in time, which likely result as much from differences in the definition of blue collar in each country as from differences in the occupational composition of the workforce. The changes

7. The country chapters for Belgium, Denmark, Sweden, and the UK (chapters 1, 3, 10, and 11, respectively) provide a more detailed analysis of how the nature of work has changed over time (e.g., sector shifts, changes in physical demands).

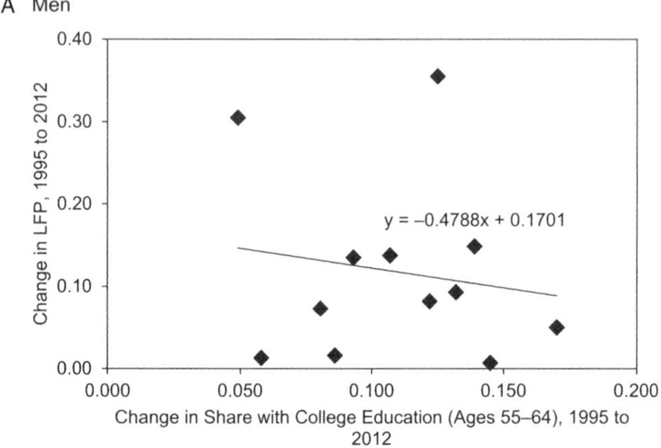

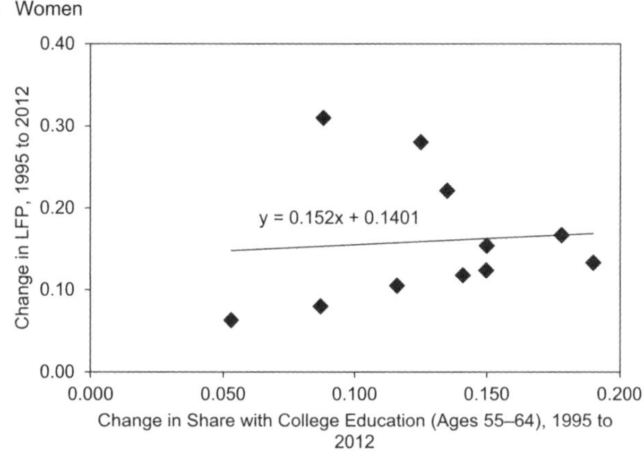

Fig. I.8   Change in LFP at ages 60–64 versus change in share with college, 1995–2012

over time within countries are of greater interest for our purposes. There are declines over time for men in most countries; France and Belgium, which have among the lowest rates of blue-collar work as defined here, have only minimal declines. If we compare countries that have a similar share of blue-collar work in 1980 in order to control for differences in definition, we see that the magnitude of changes over time varies by country. Italy and Spain, for example, have similarly high rates of blue-collar work at the beginning of the sample period, but the decrease is larger in Italy; Japan experiences a larger decrease than Germany. Results for women are largely similar, though the share of blue-collar work for women is substantially lower than for men in some countries, including Canada, France, and the US.

Could the rise in education and the decline in blue-collar employment be driving changes in LFP over the past several decades? As with mortality, one challenge to this hypothesis is that the share of men with a college education continuously increases during this period (and the share in blue-collar employment continuously falls), while participation exhibits a U shape. Put differently, while the data from the mid-1990s to the present is consistent with this theory—men are reaching retirement with more education and more likely to be in white-collar employment and so are working longer—the data from the first half of the sample period is at odds with it. For women, the U shape is muted, so the conflict is less evident, but it remains difficult to draw any causal conclusion from this analysis.

We probe this relationship further by exploring whether countries that experienced a more rapid increase in the share of people with a college education also tended to have larger increases in participation since 1995. Here the expected slope is positive, but the actual slope for men is slightly negative. For women, the slope is positive; the magnitude suggests that if the change in the share with a college education were 10 percentage points higher, participation would rise by an additional 1.5 points.

Overall, the results for education are much the same as for health. The simple time-series data do not support the hypothesis that changes in health and education are driving changes in participation for men because they cannot explain the U shape in men's participation. And there is inconsistent evidence as to whether larger changes in these factors since 1995 are associated with larger changes in participation. In sum, we find little evidence to support some of the most frequently suggested explanations for why workers are retiring later—namely, that they are healthier and better educated.

Unemployment

We now turn to unemployment rates to explore what role, if any, differences in unemployment across countries or over time may have played in labor trends. Labor demand is cyclical, as firms respond to expansions and contractions to the demand for their products and services, and these fluctuations in labor demand may affect retirement behavior (Coile and Levine 2007). If there were a mismatch between labor demand and labor supply underlying the shifts in employment, we expect it would be evident—at least transitorily—in the unemployment rates. We graph the unemployment rates for men and women aged 55–64 in figure I.9 from 1980 to 2014.

In 10 of the 12 countries, the unemployment rate for older workers follows a more-or-less cyclical trend within a fairly narrow range over this time period. The case of Spain also follows this pattern—except the business-cycle pattern was simply much stronger. As can be seen in figure I.10, taken from chapter 9, the unemployment rate for older workers in Spain mirrored the trends for all workers over most of this period.[8] This elevated unemployment rate for older workers in Spain may help explain why the peak-to-trough LFP change in Spain is among the lowest in any of our countries for

8. The unemployment rate is defined as the number of unemployed individuals divided by the sum of employed and unemployed individuals.

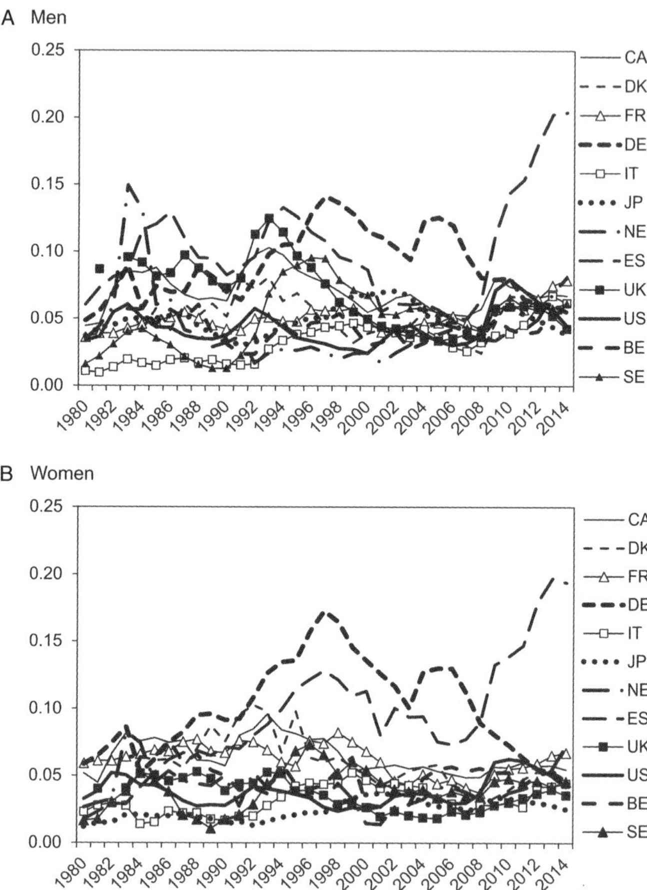

Fig. I.9   Unemployment for ages 55–64, men and women

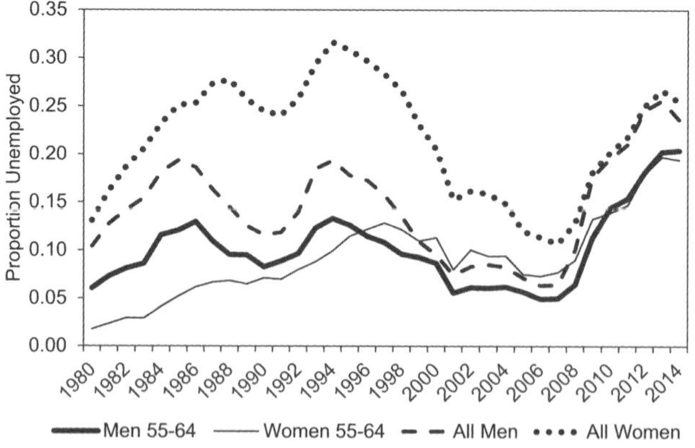

Fig. I.10   Unemployment in Spain

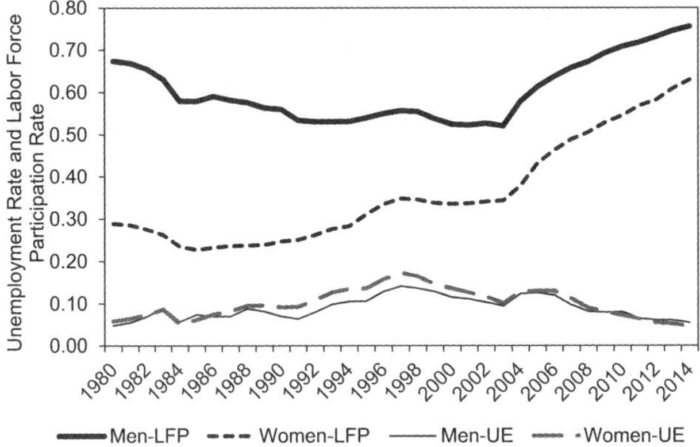

Fig. I.11   German labor force participation and unemployment for ages 55–64

both sexes in table I.2, as some discouraged job seekers may have exited the labor force early rather than continuing to look for jobs.

The other exception to the general pattern in figure I.9 is Germany, but there is a policy influence at play in this country. We graph data for Germany on its own in figure I.11 to investigate this case. As explained in chapter 5 in this volume, the enlarged unemployment episode of the 1990s in Germany has its roots in policy, as early retirement through extended unemployment benefits became available and popular. This new "bridge to retirement" led to higher reported rates of unemployment among older workers in Germany until 1997, when a new system of actuarial adjustments was phased in, making this option less attractive. Since that time, the rebound in LFP for both men and women is among the highest of any of our countries, as documented in table I.2. This inverse relationship between the unemployment rate and the LFP rate is most clear for men, as shown in figure I.11. For women, the story is more complicated by the continued increase of female LFP across cohorts.

Overall, unemployment does not seem to be a major driver of LFP trends. Over all of the remaining years and countries (omitting Spain and Germany, the case studies just discussed), the average unemployment rate at ages 55–64 is 5 percent for men and 4.5 percent for women. Naturally, there are fluctuations in this rate with the business cycle as well as some differences across countries, but they appear unrelated to the sustained increases in participation over the past 20 years. However, unusually high levels of unemployment in Spain in recent years may have dampened the increase in participation there, while a German early retirement scheme tied to unemployment appears to have had an impact on participation in that country.

Social Security

Another explanation for the turnaround in LFP over the last 20 years comes from the structure of social security benefits. As explored in previous rounds of the ISS project (most directly, Gruber and Wise 2004), the structure of social security benefits can induce a behavioral labor supply response among those entering the age range of retirement. This can happen through many channels, ranging from explicit pension eligibility ages to actuarial penalties and bonuses for retirement timing to minimum years of contributions, which may be affected by recessions and time out of the labor market.[9] If social security reforms over the past several decades have increased the financial incentives for continued work at older ages, this may be responsible for some or even much of the rise in LFP since the mid-1990s.

In addition, for some countries, it is the rules for disability insurance that matter more. Many countries have made changes to their disability insurance programs over the past several decades, including tightening eligibility requirements—for example, by eliminating provisions that exempted workers of a certain age or in certain industries from medical screening requirements. Previous ISS work in Wise (2012) gives a full account of the changes in disability insurance rules by country, while Wise (2016) examines the importance of disability insurance empirically, concluding that changes in the stringency of access to disability insurance can have a substantial effect on work at older ages.

In this round of the ISS project, we have not simulated the full dynamic social security or disability insurance incentives—including the timing and the accrual of benefits—that our previous research has shown to be important for retirement decisions. However, we can capture a sense of the importance of these incentives by looking at some simple examples. For ease of exposition, we focus here on three changes in eligibility ages for public pensions, although there are useful discussions of other changes to social security provisions in many of the individual chapters.

In Italy, eligibility ages for retirement benefits for men have increased substantially. As described in more detail in chapter 6, a series of reforms first introduced a minimum age (52) for the receipt of early retirement benefits in 1996 (previously, eligibility depended only on having a certain number of contribution years) and then increased it steadily over time, reaching age 63 in 2012. There were also changes to the normal retirement age for men over this period, going from age 60 to 66.

In figure I.12, we graph these statutory retirement ages (right-hand axis) and the LFP rates (left-hand axis) for the relevant age ranges for Italian men. At the top, the LFP rate at ages 50–54 begins to rise almost exactly when the minimum age for early retirement benefits is introduced in 1996. In the last 10 years of our graph, when the early retirement age is already far older

---

9. Countries in which workers may have special access to old-age pension (or other) benefits based on a minimum number of contribution years include Belgium, France, Germany, Italy, and Spain. More details on these provisions and (where applicable) the potential effect of changes in these provisions on participation are available in chapters 1, 4, 5, 6, and 9.

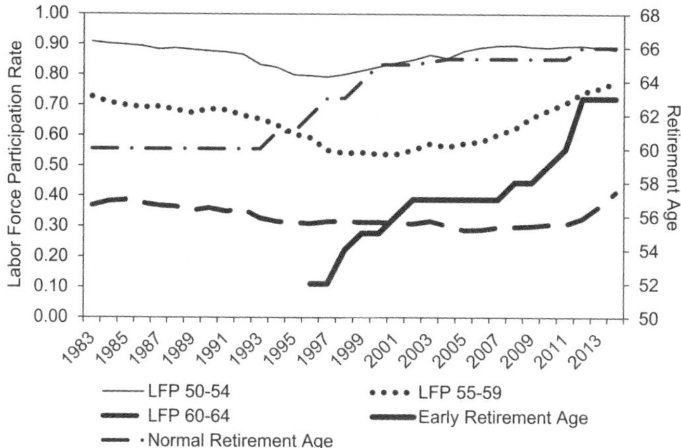

Fig. I.12   LFP and retirement ages for Italian men

than age 54, there is little more increase in the LFP rate for ages 50–54. For ages 55–59, there is a strong increase in participation from 54 percent in 2001 to 78 percent in 2014. Of note, the early retirement age started affecting this age range in 2000, almost exactly when the LFP rate began increasing. Finally, the LFP rate for ages 60–64 begins increasing in 2012, just as the early retirement eligibility age jumped from age 60 to age 63. Taken together, the timing of the changes in the LFP rate for Italian men moves in tight synchronicity with the upticks in the early retirement age. This suggests a strong relationship between social security incentives and the upswing in the LFP for older men in Italy.

A similar story can be told in the case of Japan. For women, the eligibility age for both the flat-rate and wage-based components of the pension rose from age 55 to 60 in a series of steps, starting in 1987, in order to match the eligibility age for men. There was a further increase in the eligibility age for the flat-rate benefit only starting in 2006 that affected both men and women. Figure I.13 juxtaposes the employment rates for women aged 55–59 (top panel) and those aged 60–64 (bottom panel) with the change in eligibility age. As the figure illustrates, the employment rate at ages 55–59 began to rise in the late 1980s, along with the rise in the eligibility age. For women aged 60–64, who were not directly affected by the initial increase in the eligibility age, employment remained flat until the mid-2000s and then began to rise once the eligibility age for the flat-rate benefit began to increase from age 60 to 64. Results for men, shown in chapter 7, reflect a similar increase in employment at ages 60–64, starting in the mid-2000s, which is also very likely related to the increase in the eligibility age during this period.

A final example comes from the UK, which has increased the state pension age for women from 60 to 65 in a series of steps. Figure I.14 shows the

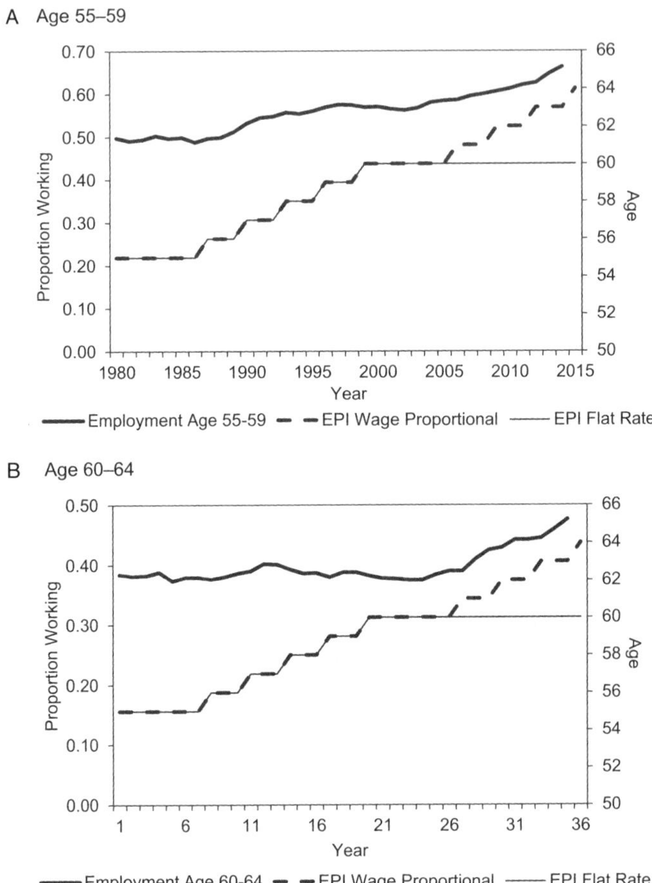

Fig. I.13   Employment and retirement ages for Japanese women

employment rate for women at single ages from 56 to 63 over the period of 2003–15. A striking pattern emerges. When the pension age was raised from 60 to 61 in 2010, employment at age 60 rose by 10 percentage points over the next two years. A similarly large and rapid increase in employment was seen at age 61 once the pension age was raised to 62 in 2012 and at age 62 once the pension age was raised to 63 in 2014. Aside from these three sharp increases, employment rates remained flat or rose only slowly throughout this period. The simultaneity of the eligibility age increases and surges in employment makes a strong case that pension reform is a key driver of higher employment among UK women. More generally, these three examples clearly indicate that social security provisions such as the eligibility age can exert an important influence on employment rate at older ages.

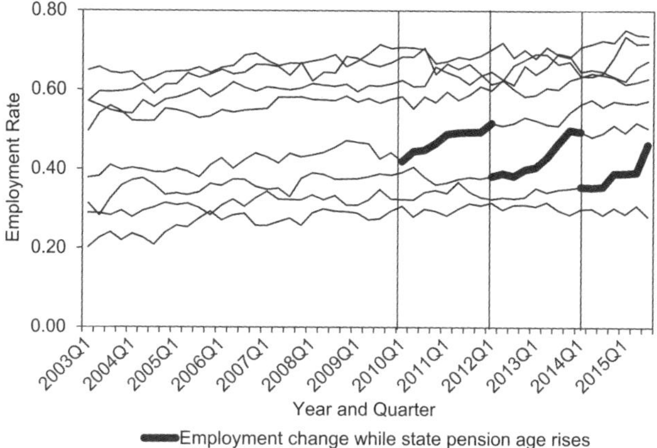

Fig. I.14   Employment for UK women by exact age (ages 56–63)

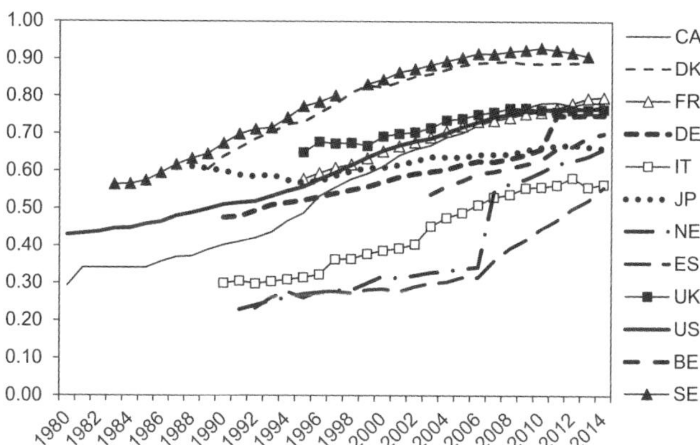

Fig. I.15   LFP of females aged 35–44, lagged 20 years

Women's LFP

The next factor to consider is the impact of the increasing LFP by women. While this increase is important on its own, the increase in work by older women over the last 20 years also has a potential impact on men. If married couples prefer to retire at the same time, women working later into their lives might keep men later in the workforce. This hypothesis was explored in depth for the cases of Canada, the US, and the UK by Schirle (2008), who finds that it explained between one-quarter and one-half of the change in the LFP by married men.

This channel is potentially important for explaining the upswing in male LFP after 1995, because the men arriving at ages 55–64 in the mid-1990s

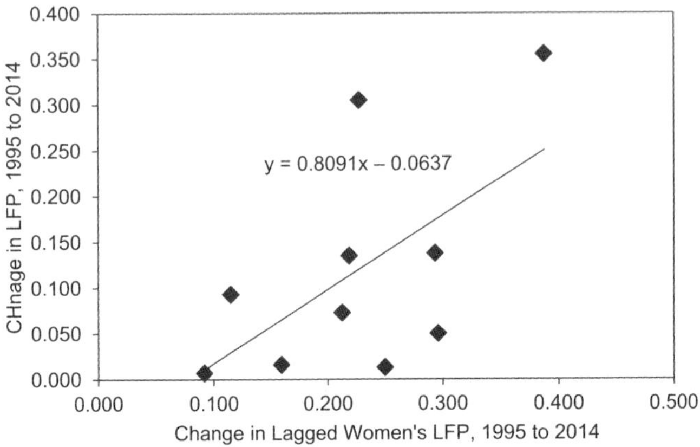

Fig. I.16   Change in LFP for men aged 60–64 versus change in lagged women's LFP, 1995–2014

were married to women who had much greater LFP throughout their lives than earlier cohorts. This is shown in figure I.16, where we graph the LFP of women aged 35–44 lagged by 20 years. These women were ages 55–64 in the year shown, and so these numbers give an indication of the proportion of men in the age range of 55–64 who were married to women with substantial lifetime labor force attachment. We focus on this measure rather than on the current participation of women aged 55–64 because the latter may be influenced by other factors—such as changes in social security provisions—that are also affecting older men's participation. Over the period of 1995–2014, the average LFP of women (using ages 35–44, or a 20-year lag) across our 12 countries grew dramatically, from 50 to 72 percent. It is also worth noting the vast difference across countries, with Sweden and Denmark showing very large shares of women working and Italy and Spain showing very low shares.

To explore the potential impact of this trend on men's participation, in figure I.16, we provide a scatter plot of the changes between 1995 and 2014 in the male LFP at ages 60–64 compared to the changes in female LFP, lagged 20 years. There is a clear and strong positive relationship evident here, with a coefficient on the trend line of 0.81. The magnitude of this coefficient suggests that having the participation of women (at a younger age) increase by an additional 10 percentage points over time is associated with an 8-point increase in the participation of older men. This provides additional support for the Schirle (2008) hypothesis about the male LFP and working spouses.

To show how the impact of women working may matter in a specific country, we bring up the case of Canada.[10] In figure I.17, we re-create the analysis

10. While the Canadian analysis is the most thorough investigation of this hypothesis, the country chapters for Germany, the Netherlands, Spain, and the US (chapters 5, 8, 9, and 12,

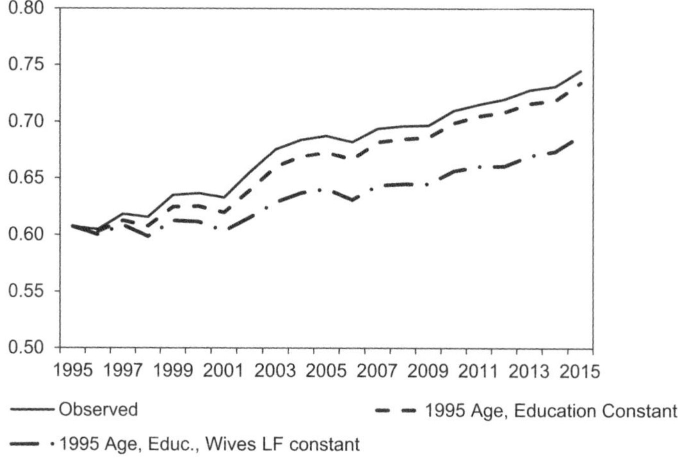

Fig. I.17   LFP of Canadian males, ages 55–64

presented in chapter 2 based on the methods of Schirle (2008). The analysis takes the observed LFP of males aged 55–64 from 1995 to 2015 and makes some adjustments. In the middle line, the adjustment accounts for changes in the age and education structure of the male population over this period. The bottom line makes a further adjustment by imposing the counterfactual that the LFP of wives stayed constant at the 1995 rate instead of increasing like it actually did. The results are striking. The increase in actual men's LFP is 13.8 percentage points from 1995 to 2015. This increase would have been 1.1 points smaller (12.7 points) if there had been no changes in men's education and age composition. Keeping wives' LFP constant at the 1995 level would have reduced the growth in men's participation by a further 4.6 percentage points. This suggests that the working wife effect alone accounts for 33 percent of the increase in male LFP during these two decades, while changes in men's education and age explain only 8 percent of the increase.

Cross-Country Regressions

To summarize our findings, we run some cross-country regressions incorporating all the contributing factors we discuss above. The dependent variable for the regression analysis is the LFP rate in the 55–64 age range, for a given year and country. Regressions are estimated separately by sex and include a full set of year and country dummies. We progressively add explan-

---

respectively) consider the effect of increasing women's participation on the participation of older men as well and find suggestive evidence that it played a role; by contrast, the chapter for Sweden (chapter 10) concludes that this "does not seem to be a dominating factor." The other countries do not take up this hypothesis in any significant way.

Table I.3   Cross-country regressions for men. Dependent variable: Share in the labor force aged 55–64.

	(1)	(2)	(3)	(4)	(5)	(6)
Normal retirement age	0.011	0.013	–0.038	0.006	–0.005	–0.008
	(0.007)	(0.007)	(0.029)	(0.007)	(0.015)	(0.017)
Early retirement age	–0.002	–0.004	–0.004	–0.002	0.001	0.004
	(0.005)	(0.006)	(0.014)	(0.004)	(0.007)	(0.005)
Log mortality		–0.048		–0.022	–0.054	0.088
		(0.142)		(0.120)	(0.074)	(0.061)
Self-assessed health as fair–poor			0.226			
			(0.283)			
College share				0.001	0.002	0.002
				(0.002)	(0.002)	(0.001)
Women LFP, lagged 20 years					0.244*	0.169***
					(0.120)	(0.036)
Blue-collar share						0.151
						(0.209)
Unemployment rate						–0.353***
						(0.088)
Year dummies	Yes	Yes	Yes	Yes	Yes	Yes
Country dummies	Yes	Yes	Yes	Yes	Yes	Yes
R^2	0.917	0.922	0.900	0.940	0.937	0.979
Observations	324	312	160	278	228	173

Notes: Data are drawn from our 12 countries over the time period of 1980–2014, although not all data are available for all countries in all years. Each column reports results from a separate regression. We report the coefficient for each variable listed, with the standard error in parentheses below. The standard errors are robust-adjusted and clustered by country. All specifications include both year and country dummies.

atory variables including the social security normal and early retirement age, the log of the mortality rate, the proportion with college education, lagged female LFP rates, the blue-collar share, and the overall unemployment rate. The number of observations changes across specifications because of missing data for some of the explanatory variables in certain years and countries. The time period covered here is 1980–2014.

The goal of this analysis is descriptive, with the aim being to assess whether there is a common story across countries about which factors may play a role in explaining the increase in work at older ages. Of course, each individual country has its own experience, and the individual country chapters in this book provide this country-specific detail. In future work with the ISS project, careful microdata-based regression analysis of each country will examine the role of these factors—and of changing public pension incentives in particular—in a level of detail not possible here. We view this simple aggregate analysis as a setup for that future work.

The results are presented for men in table I.3 and for women in table I.4. In

Table I.4   **Cross-country regressions for women. Dependent variable: share in the labor force age 55–64.**

	(1)	(2)	(3)	(4)	(5)	(6)
Normal retirement age	0.009	0.006	–0.014	0.005	0.000	–0.001
	(0.005)	(0.006)	(0.019)	(0.004)	(0.006)	(0.009)
Early retirement age	–0.009*	–0.009**	–0.006	–0.010**	–0.002	0.001
	(0.004)	(0.004)	(0.011)	(0.003)	(0.004)	(0.003)
Log mortality		0.102		0.045	0.055	0.048
		(0.060)		(0.046)	(0.046)	(0.029)
Self-assessed health as fair–poor			0.120			
			(0.211)			
College share				0.000	–0.001	0.000
				(0.001)	(0.001)	(0.001)
Women LFP, lagged 20 years					0.408***	0.371**
					(0.057)	(0.112)
Blue-collar share						0.162
						(0.202)
Unemployment rate						–0.321**
						(0.105)
Year dummies	Yes	Yes	Yes	Yes	Yes	Yes
Country dummies	Yes	Yes	Yes	Yes	Yes	Yes
R^2	0.941	0.946	0.937	0.952	0.961	0.979
Observations	324	312	144	262	215	166

Notes: Data are drawn from our 12 countries over the time period of 1980–2014, although not all data are available for all countries in all years. Each column reports results from a separate regression. We report the coefficient for each variable listed, with the standard error in parentheses below. The standard errors are robust-adjusted and clustered by country. All specifications include both year and country dummies.

the first column, we just include the statutory retirement ages, along with the country and year dummies. There is no clear statistical relationship apparent here for men or women. This is at some contrast to the experience of the individual cases of countries discussed above where there was a clear relationship between changes in the statutory ages and older worker LFP. Using a broad age range may explain the lack of significant results here—a more granular age-by-age analysis (as suggested by the Italy and UK examples) and the more detailed modeling of financial incentives that characterized previous ISS research may be better suited to picking up the influence of social security rules.

In column 2, we add a control for health through the log mortality rate. Again, there is no clear relationship available to be seen. In column 3, we use the share of respondents reporting fair or poor health, which results in a large drop in the sample size because many countries are missing data for this variable. There is no evidence of a strong relationship with this alternative measure of health. To maintain a larger sample, we continue with the log mortality measure in the subsequent columns. We add the share with college education in column 4. There is not a clear relationship for either men or women.

In column 5, we add the female LFP rate, lagged 20 years to account for differences in cohort labor market participation by women over the years. We examined this explanatory factor earlier in the case of Canada. Here there is a statistically significant positive relationship for both men and women. For men, the estimated impact is 0.244, meaning that for every 1 percentage point increase in the female cohort LFP, the male LFP increases by about a quarter of a point. For females, the effect is stronger at 0.408, as might be expected given that this captures the effect of higher past participation on the women themselves rather than the spillover effect on their spouses.

In the final column, we include the share in blue-collar occupations and the (all-age) unemployment rate. We lose many countries here because of lack of data for the blue-collar occupations, and as noted earlier, this variable may capture different swaths of the population in different countries. The blue-collar rate does not have a statistically significant effect for either men or women. In contrast, the unemployment rate is strongly significant for men and women, embodying the strong procyclical pattern between elderly LFP and unemployment rates seen earlier.

This regression evidence is meant to summarize the discussion of the individual factors in this introductory chapter and provide motivation for future work. The clearest cross-country impacts seem to come from trends in female LFP and general business-cycle effects. There is no evidence for health or occupational impacts on broad LFP. For the institutional factors, we do not find evidence of an effect based on a fairly crude analysis that only includes eligibility-age variables. It remains for future work to undertake a more detailed analysis looking more deeply at the full range of institutional incentive effects—as was done in previous analyses of the ISS project— which may well uncover a stronger relationship.

Conclusion

This volume continues the work of the ISS project by documenting and investigating the upswing in LFP among older workers over the last two decades. We show that the rise in participation for both men and women is substantial and evident in all 12 countries that are a part of the project. The nature and timing of these changes are surprisingly similar across countries, with a U-shaped pattern for men that generally reaches its minimum in the mid-1990s and a much shallower U or continuously rising pattern for women. There are important differences across countries in the magnitude of the increase as well as in whether the largest change occurred at relatively young (55–59), middle (60–64), or older (65–69) ages.

We also examine different potential explanations for the upswing, including changes in health, education, occupational mix, unemployment, and social security rules and incentives. All these factors have changed substantially over the past two decades, making it important to assess their role in explaining labor force trends. Perhaps surprisingly, despite the well-known association between health or education and retirement at the individual level, we find little evidence that improvements in these factors are key drivers of the increases in participation over time. We base this conclusion on the fact that these factors have tended to improve during times when participation has been rising as well as falling; further, those countries with the largest improvements in health or education have not necessarily experienced the largest increases in participation. While our analysis does not rule out the possibility of a role for these factors, it does suggest that they alone almost certainly cannot explain the large increases in participation over the past two decades. We similarly conclude that unemployment is not a major part of the story, though it may have been important in a few of our countries.

We find more evidence that the increase in female LFP across generations has had an important pull on male LFP. While we are naturally cautious about drawing causal implications from our simple analysis, this variable is significant in our cross-country regressions, and there is a strong positive association between changes in lagged women's LFP and in older men's participation across countries. Past work such as Schirle (2008) supports the conclusion that this factor has likely played a role, at least in some countries.

Finally, and perhaps most importantly, in particular country examples throughout this volume, some of which we discuss above, there is strongly suggestive evidence that social security rules like statutory retirement ages can also change labor market attachment. While we fail to find significant effects of these eligibility ages in our cross-country regressions, we attribute this finding to the simplicity of our aggregate analysis. Past studies in this project (notably, Gruber and Wise 1999, 2004; Wise 2016) as well as the work of many others have consistently found that social security incentives matter for retirement. In our past work, we have relied on differences across countries at a point in time (Gruber and Wise 1999) and on differences across individuals within countries (Gruber and Wise 2004) to uncover this relationship. In the two decades since this project began, many countries have enacted social security reforms. This offers a rich opportunity to make use of these reforms, which generate differences in social security incentives within countries over time, to revisit the role of social security program provisions on retirement behavior.

In sum, many important questions remain to be answered. How much of the reversal in LFP that we document here may be attributable to changes in social security rules? What are the relative roles of statutory retirement ages versus other program changes, such as those to actuarial adjustments and benefit formulas? Future work of the ISS project will examine these questions directly.

References

Belbase, Anek, Geoffrey Sanzenbacher, and Christopher Gillis. 2016. "How Do Job Skills That Decline with Age Affect White-Collar Workers?" Center for Retirement Research, Boston College, Issue Brief No. 16-6, April.

Bell, Felicity, and Michael Miller. 2002. "Life Tables for the United States Social Security Are 1900–2100." Social Security Administration Actuarial Study No. 116.

Chernew, Michael, David Cutler, Kaushik Ghosh, and Mary Beth Landrum. 2016. "Understanding the Improvement in Disability Free Life Expectancy in the U.S. Elderly Population." NBER Working Paper No. 22306, National Bureau of Economic Research, Cambridge, MA.

Coile, Courtney, and Phillip Levine. 2007. "Labor Market Shocks and Retirement: Do Government Programs Matter?" *Journal of Public Economics* 91 (10): 1902–19.

Coile, Courtney, Kevin Milligan, and David Wise. 2016. "Introduction." In *Social Security Programs and Retirement around the World: Disability Insurance Programs and Retirement*, edited by David A. Wise, 1–44. Chicago: University of Chicago Press.

Costa, Dora. 1998. *The Evolution of Retirement: An American Economic History, 1880–1990.* Chicago: University of Chicago Press.

Crimmins, E. M., and H. Beltran. 2011. "Is There Compression of Morbidity?" *Journal of Gerontology: Social Sciences* 66B (1): 75–86.

Cutler, David, Kaushik Ghosh, and Mary Beth Landrum. 2014. "Evidence for Significant Compression of Morbidity in the Elderly U.S. Population." In *Discoveries in the Economics of Aging*, edited by David A. Wise, 21–80. Chicago: University of Chicago Press.

Diamond, Peter, and Jerry Hausman. 1984. "The Retirement and Unemployment Behavior of Older Men." In *Retirement and Economic Behavior*, edited by Gary Burtless and Henry Aaron, 97–132. Washington, DC: Brookings Institution.

Goldin, Claudia. 2006. "The Quiet Revolution That Transformed Women's Employment, Education, and Family." *American Economic Review* 96 (2): 1–21.

Gruber, Jonathan, and David A. Wise, eds. 1999. *Social Security and Retirement around the World.* Chicago: University of Chicago Press.

———, eds. 2004. *Social Security Programs and Retirement around the World: Micro-Estimation.* Chicago: University of Chicago Press.

———, eds. 2007. *Social Security Programs and Retirement around the World: Fiscal Implications of Reform.* Chicago: University of Chicago Press.

———, eds. 2010. *Social Security Programs and Retirement around the World: The Relationship to Youth Employment.* Chicago: University of Chicago Press.

Milligan, Kevin, and David Wise. 2012. "Introduction and Summary." In *Social Security Programs and Retirement around the World: Historical Trends in Mortality and Health, Employment, and Disability Insurance Participation and Reforms*, edited by David A. Wise, 1–40. Chicago: University of Chicago Press.

Schirle, Tammy. 2008. "Why Have the Labor Force Participation Rates of Older Men Increased since the Mid-1990s?" *Journal of Labor Economics* 26 (4): 549–94.

Wise, David A., ed. 2012. *Social Security Programs and Retirement around the World: Historical Trends in Mortality and Health, Employment, and Disability Insurance Participation and Reforms.* Chicago: University of Chicago Press.

———. 2016. *Social Security Programs and Retirement around the World: Disability Insurance Programs and Retirement.* Chicago: University of Chicago Press.

———. 2017. *Social Security Programs and Retirement around the World: The Capacity to Work at Older Ages.* Chicago: University of Chicago Press.

1
Older Men's Labor Force Participation in Belgium

Alain Jousten and Mathieu Lefebvre

1.1 Introduction

The Belgian labor market has undergone profound changes over the course of the last four decades. Changes have been particularly noticeable for the age group 50 and older. While for women, the country has witnessed a steady increase in labor force participation (LFP) since the early 1980s (and even beyond), the picture is wholly different for men of the same age cohorts (e.g., see figure 1.2). Empirically, male LFP has transited through three stages: a first period of strongly declining LFP rates in the 1980s (and partly the early 1990s), followed a second period of relative stability at low levels—from both historical and cross-country points of view (see, for example, Gruber and Wise 2004 for the latter). Finally, as of the early to mid-1990s, there has been a steady upward trend in male LFP, first starting at younger ages and then progressing upward through age groups.

What are the factors that explain these rather profound changes in terms of labor market outcomes in Belgium? This is the issue that we are investigating in the present chapter. The questioning is by no means new: Dellis et al. (2004) already used administrative data covering the years 1993–95

Alain Jousten is professor of economics at the University of Liège and a research fellow of Institute for the Study of Labor (IZA) and of Network for Studies on Pensions, Aging and Retirement (Netspar).

Mathieu Lefebvre is professor of economics at the University of Strasbourg.

The authors acknowledge financial support from the Belspo project EMPOV (TA/00/45). This chapter uses data from the European Union Labour Force Survey (Eurostat, European Union). Eurostat has no responsibility for the results and conclusions, which are the authors' only. Research assistance by Anne-Lore Fraikin and Fanny Voisin is gratefully acknowledged. For other acknowledgments, sources of research support, and disclosure of the authors' material financial relationships, if any, please see https://www.nber.org/chapters/c14041.ack.

to compute various retirement incentive measures (financial and option value), estimate retirement probit models, and simulate the effects of stylized reforms in terms of effective retirement ages.[1] However, given the period being studied, these authors only captured the first two of the three stages that we described above. The main contributions of the chapter to the literature are therefore twofold: First, we extend the study period beyond the early 1990s to the year 2013. Second, we take a step back from individual retirement incentive analysis to explore more broadly the factors that have changed over the course of the period of analysis with an influence on employment at older ages.

The chapter's structure is as follows. Section 1.2 provides an overview of the institutional framework in Belgium that is of relevance for labor market participation and retirement processes at older ages. Section 1.3 describes key labor market indicators using data from the Labour Force Survey (LFS) over the period of 1983–2013—such as the rates of LFP, employment, and unemployment—and also presents trends in participation in (early) retirement routes. Section 1.4 explores how the types of jobs in the country have changed over time in terms of both their "quality" and the "quantity" of work involved. Section 1.5 concludes and sketches pathways for future research.

1.2   Institutional Framework and Recent Reforms

The Belgian labor market is segmented into three main components: the civil servant regimes, the scheme for the self-employed, and the main (and at the same time, residual) contractual wage-earner scheme.

Civil servants benefit from a special regulatory environment, in the sense that both their professional work life and their retirement are organized under a separate set of rules from other workers. Key characteristics include the quasi-complete layoff protection (and the associated noneligibility for unemployment benefits), a "career break" system (also allowing part-time retirement at older ages with full maintenance of pension accrual), a defined benefit disability pension system (no rollover occurs at the retirement age), extensive defined benefit retirement pension rights encompassing some types of early retirement benefits (either formally called this way or acting as such), retired worker benefits (reference full-retirement age of 65, early claiming age of 62), and survivor benefits. No dependent spouse or household benefits are available. All inactivity benefits are essentially general-budget financed, except for survivor benefits, where a special 7.5 percent contribution is levied on all active workers belonging to the respective scheme.

---

1. Further follow-up work extended the analysis to other dimensions, such as the fiscal cost of these early retirement schemes as well as their impact on health and well-being (Desmet et al. 2007; Jousten and Lefebvre 2013; Jousten et al. 2005; Jousten, Lefebvre, and Perelman 2012, 2016; Maes 2011).

The civil servant regime is often considered to be the most generous of the three regimes, though this does not always have to be true. On the one hand, key elements contributing toward its relative generosity are (1) the layoff protection and the traditional (quasi-mechanical) progression through the pay scales, (2) the short wage-averaging period used when computing pensions (increased from 5 to 10 last years of earnings as of January 1, 2012, for regular civil servants born after January 1, 1962, with some categories of civil servants such as railway staff still benefiting from a more favorable 4-year averaging period up from even lower levels before January 1, 2012), (3) the shorter career requirement than the Belgian "reference" of 45 years for some professional groups (policemen, teachers, judges, railway staff, military) and the sometimes rather low full retirement age (as low as 55 years for some railway workers, 56 for large groups of military personnel, 58 for the police, etc.), (4) the indexing of pensions that follows wages (of active workers in the rank and pay scale) rather than the usual price indexing using the slowed-down "health index" (a modified consumer price index widely used for indexing purposes in the country). On the other hand, this generosity is not benefiting everyone in the same way, as many of the above advantages only accrue to specific categories of civil servants, leaving others ineligible for these special favors. Similarly, some distinctive features of the civil servant system can render benefits substantially lower than those accruing in the other schemes. This is, for example, the case in instances of permanent disability occurring earlier in life, where the short reference period and the early stage of progression through largely seniority-based pay scales combine toward generating low pension levels. Also, dependent benefits under the retirement section do not include benefits for divorced partners, for example, as in some of the other schemes.[2]

The regime for the self-employed is the smallest and least generous of the three in absolute terms.[3] Self-employed workers are entitled to disability benefits as well as to retirement benefits, but they have no access to unemployment or special early retirement schemes (such as career breaks, etc.). Disability benefits are a flat rate and payable until the full retirement age—when the rollover into the earnings-related retirement pension occurs. Retirement (and extensive dependent) benefits are based on an earned-income averaging period of 45 years for both men and women—with earned income corresponding to taxable earnings to which a floor and a ceiling are applied.[4] An

---

2. More details at Service fédéral des Pensions (2019).

3. When considering its generosity with respect to the contributions paid into the system, it ranks second after the civil servant scheme given the rather low individual contributions toward the scheme—with general budget financing occurring for the residual (unlike all other systems, taxable wages are subject to a floor and a ceiling). For a detailed description of the system, visit "Pensions," L'Institut national d'assurances sociales pour travailleurs indépendants (INASTI), 2019, http://www.inasti.be/fr/pensions.

4. According to data from the self-employed pension administration, the distribution of pensionable wages for the self-employed is heavily skewed toward lower income levels. Accord-

average wage-to-pension conversion rate of 60 percent for "single" benefit claims and 75 percent for "household" claims (mostly one-earner couples) is applied, with pensions (and disability allowances) indexed to the health index. As of January 1, 2016, the full retirement age is currently set at 65, and earlier claiming is allowed as early as age 62 with a career of 40 years. Until January 1, 2014, early claiming of the self-employed was subject to actuarial corrections. Originally of a linear 5 percent per year of anticipation, they were brought to 3, 4, 5, 6, and 7 percent for 1, 2, 3, 4, and 5 years of anticipation as of January 1, 2007. On January 1, 2013, adjustments for those aged 63 and 64 were dropped before the total removal of actuarial penalty factors a year later.

The third and largest scheme (by both enrollment and scope of coverage) is the contractual wage-earner scheme, encompassing the wide majority of private-sector workers as well as the contractual staff of the public sector.[5] In terms of its design, it resembles rather closely the system applicable to the self-employed. Actually, numerous reforms over the past years have either explicitly or implicitly made changes to the two systems that render them more and more akin to each other in the way benefits are computed and granted. While the full retirement age of 65 and the early claiming age of 62 with 40 years of career as of January 1, 2016 (or 61 and 60 years with 41 and 42 years of career, respectively), are akin to those prevailing and having prevailed in the self-employed system, the actuarial adjustments for early claiming had already been fully abolished in the system as of January 1, 1991.

The wage-earner scheme has several key extra features that differ from the self-employed scheme: (1) it provides for earnings-related disability, unemployment, and conventional early retirement benefits that are not subject to any explicit time limit; (2) generous "time credit" schemes are available, allowing part-time retirement (reductions to 50 or 80 percent of a full-time job) at older ages while largely maintaining full pension accrual. While the threshold age for old-age time credit is currently set at 56, part-time exits are sometimes possible at ages as low as 50, especially for workers affected by industrial restructuring or who have worked in "difficult" jobs.[6]

Several major reforms have affected the work and retirement incentives of all three regimes over time.[7] Five key dimensions have been affected. First,

---

ing to data from the Self-Employed Pension Administration quoted in appendix 2.2 of Vandenbroucke (2014), 40 percent of self-employed workers have incomes below or just above the floor, whereas less than 5 percent earn more or just below the ceiling.

5. This system is the best documented and has been the focus of the last waves of the ISS project—for example Jousten, Lefebvre, and Perelman (2012, 2016)

6. For a complete overview of the old-age time credit regulations, see ONEM Info sheet T151, http://www.onem.be/fr/documentation/feuille-info/t151.

7. The Intergenerational Solidarity Pact that was passed into law in December 2005 represents a major milestone. Though not the first reform targeting the tightening eligibility conditions for social benefits, it is the first comprehensive attempt toward increasing LFP at younger

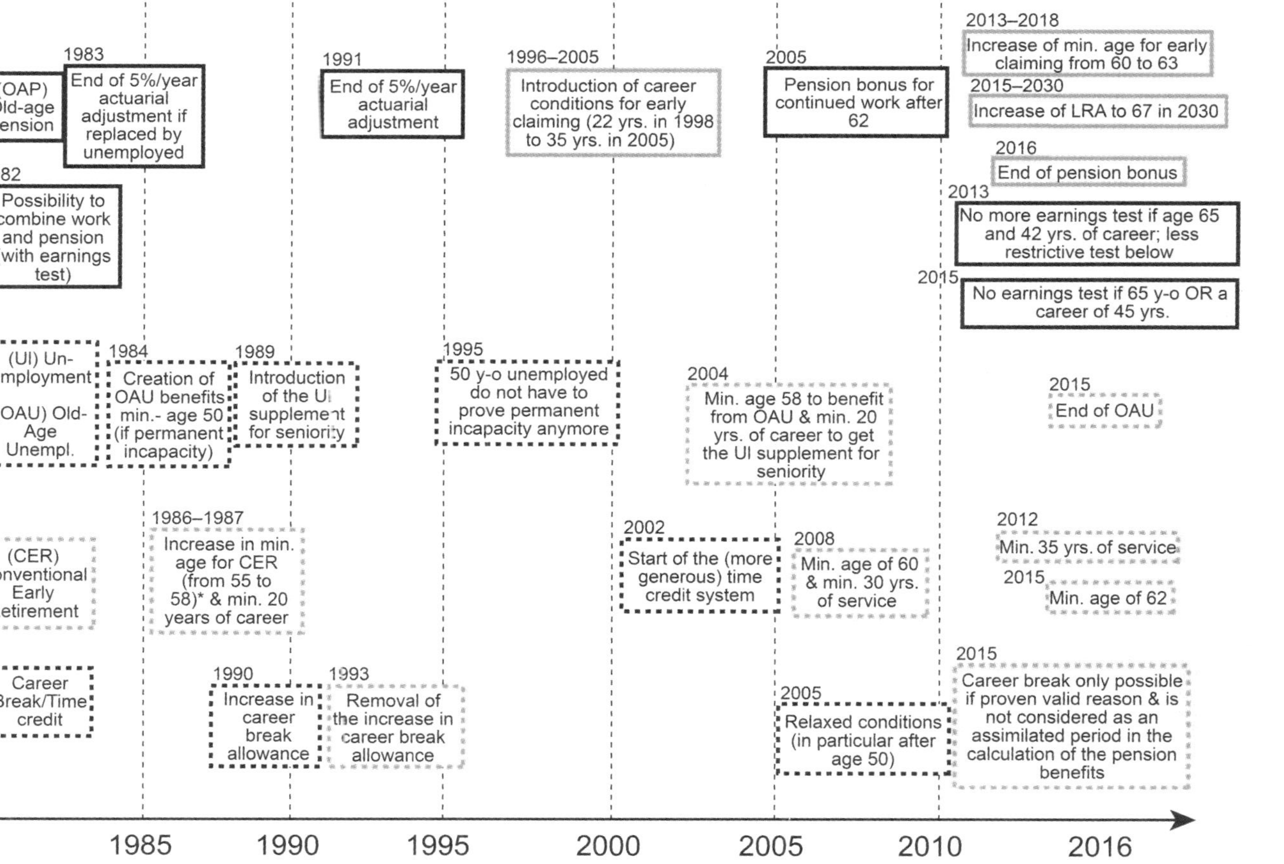

Fig. 1.1   Timeline of reforms, 1983–2016, male wage earners

the female retirement age and career requirement have been progressively aligned from age 60 and 40 years of career toward those prevailing for men (65 and 45, respectively) during a transition phase that started on July 1, 1997, and ended on January 1, 2009.[8] Second, the age for early claiming of retirement benefits has been increased from the long-standing age condition of 60 in half-year increments starting on January 1, 2013, and reaching 63 on January 1, 2018. In parallel, career requirements for early claiming of retirement benefits and for eligibility of early retirement benefits have been progressively tightened to current levels—and are actually projected to tighten further (broadly adding another 2 years on top of current career requirements as of January 1, 2019). Third, conditions for older unemployed workers have progressively been tightened and benefits rendered less generous. Fourth, in 2016, further legislative action was taken to increase the full retirement age to 66 in 2025 and to 67 in 2030. The full retirement age also no longer constitutes a forced retirement age in most situations—with individuals increasingly having the right to continue working. Finally, the rules regarding the retirement pension systems' earnings tests have been substantially loosened—with their complete elimination upon reaching the full retirement age. However, while pension legislation has progressively been adapted to reflect this paradigm change, the same does not necessarily hold true of other social legislation, making the age of 65 a more pivotal age than one could think based on pension laws.

The following timeline provides a visual summary of the main changes to the wage-earner scheme for men over the period of 1983–2016. It documents the increases in generosity (green) and decreases of generosity (red) associated with the main effective (early) retirement routes.

1.3   Labor Market Trends

1.3.1   Data

We use data from the European Union LFS for the years 1983–2013. The data contains information on self-declared labor market status as well as information on self-declared inactivity status from 1992 onward. The information provided by individuals may obviously differ from administrative classification; hence there is no strict correspondence between the institutional environment and reforms thereof as summarized in section 1.2 and the self-declared status of an individual. For example, the conditions for being categorized as unemployed for LFS purposes are substantially

---

ages, reducing labor costs, increasing the effective retirement age, and permitting a smoother transition into retirement. For a recent evaluation of its effects on older workers' employment, see Dejemeppe, Smith, and Vander Linden (2015).

8. In 1987, the previously applicable early claiming age of 55 for women had already been aligned to that of 60 for men.

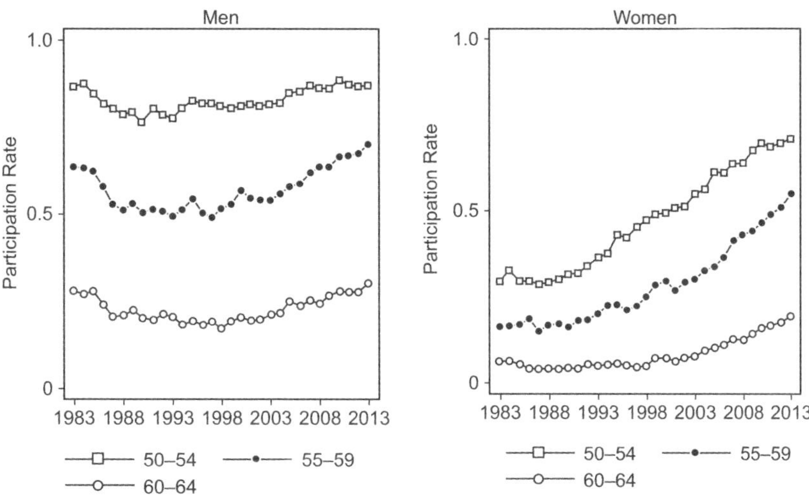

Fig. 1.2   LFP, ages 50–64
Source: Authors' calculations based on LFS data.

different from those for unemployment benefit receipt. Similarly, in case of any kind of self-declared activity, there is no information on simultaneous benefit receipt (pension, unemployment, time credit, etc.).

1.3.2   Headline Indicators

Figure 1.2 documents that the LFP of the Belgian population has undergone profound changes. The strong upward trend in female LFP is the reflection of several factors: First, a seminal increase in the labor market activity of women has progressively reduced the gap between male and female LFP levels. Second, a nonnegligible role in the observed pattern can be attributed to changes in benefit structures. For example, the LFP curve for women in the age group 60–64 is largely tributary to the fact that, as of 1998, an ever-larger share of this group finds itself below the full retirement age—and hence potentially active—resulting in the latter's progressive increase. Third, no doubt female labor market performance is also affected by the same general trends as male labor market performance, which we now discuss in more detail.

Male LFP has undergone a three-stage process across time, as already pointed out in the introduction to this chapter. Figure 1.3 reveals that this trend is to a large part the reflection of an increase in the employment rate—with overall time patterns of LFP and employment largely overlapping. The changes have been the most pronounced for the age group 55–59, where both the initial decrease and the later increase have by far been the strongest, with decreases and increases of as much as 15–20 percentage points.

The unemployment rate has not played a major role in the above trends,

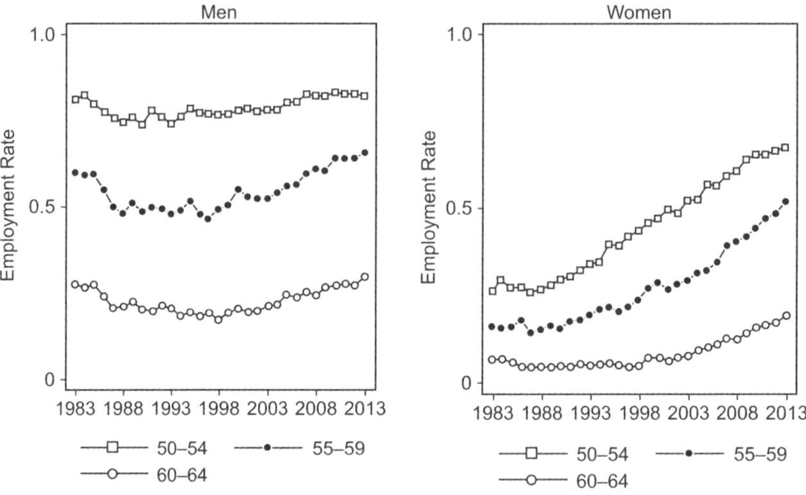

Fig. 1.3   Employment rate, ages 50–64
Source: Authors' calculations based on LFS data.

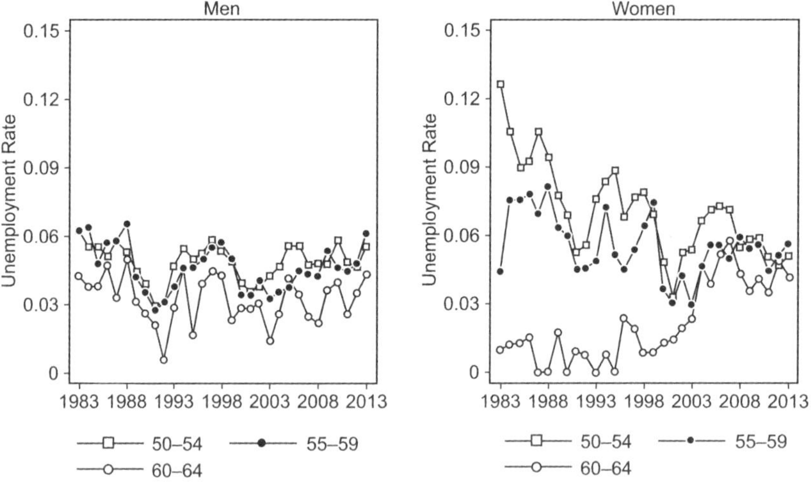

Fig. 1.4   Unemployment rate, ages 50–65
Source: Authors'calculations based on LFS data.

as illustrated in figure 1.4. For ages 50–59, female unemployment rates have undergone a profound transformation, as they have come down from previous heights to reach levels akin to those of their male counterparts. Also, as a result of the increase in the full retirement age, the unemployment statistics for women aged 60–64 also aligned with those of other age groups. Figure 1.5 documents that male and female unemployment rates have remained rather

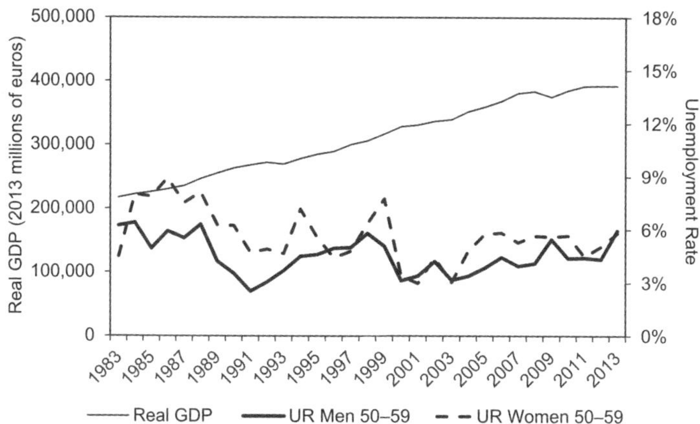

Fig. 1.5   Real GDP and unemployment rate
Source: Authors' calculations based on LFS and Eurostat National Account data (2016).

stable over the entire period, with year-on-year variation likely the reflection of the economic environment faced by these specific sex/age cohorts rather than the overall economic performance as proxied by the trend in real GDP.[9]

1.3.3   Inactivity Patterns

Where do extra workers come from? Given the above patterns, the only possible answer is from various inactivity statuses. LFS data only contains data on inactivity statuses as of the year 1992—and hence only for the second half of the period previously discussed.

Figure 1.6 illustrates the trend in the number of people who declare themselves early retired or retired.[10] It is noticeable that there is a strong downward trend in all age and sex groups considered except for the 60–64-year-old females at the beginning of the observation period when their full retirement age was still 60. This downward trend is consistent with the pattern of reforms discussed in section 1.2, which have overall led to a tightening of eligibility conditions for some early retirement routes (though generosity has sometimes been reformed in an opposite direction).

A second group of inactives who could explain the upward trend in the LFP rate are the disabled. Figure 1.7 plots the time trend over the period of 1992–2013. While for men the overall trend is downward-sloping (par-

9. Figure 1.5 focuses on ages 50–59 to prevent bias relating to the increase of the full retirement age for women.

10. Given the survey nature of the LFS, the statistics can differ from those based on administrative data. For example, a worker on part-time time credit or a career break could appear as employed and active in the LFS, whereas administratively he would possibly show up as early retired. Similarly, a retiree working with earnings below the earnings test would likely be categorized as employed and not retired.

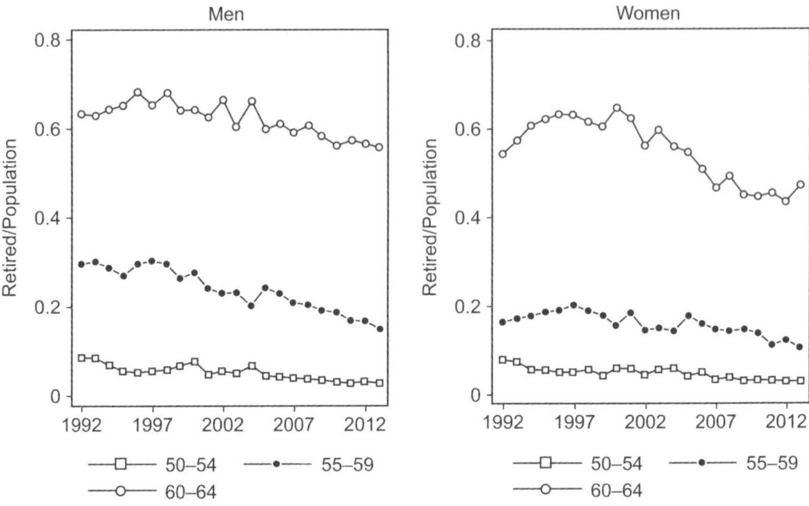

Fig. 1.6   Early retired and retired persons, ages 50–64 by sex
Source: Authors' calculations based on LFS data.

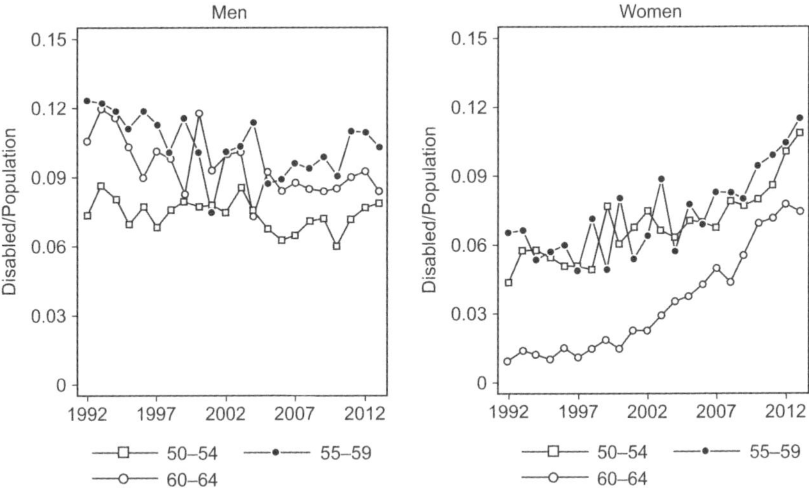

Fig. 1.7   Disabled as a share of the population, ages 50–64
Source: Authors' calculations based on LFS data.

ticularly above age 55), the opposite is true for females. The LFS data thus confirm the observation of a steep increase in the number of female disabled that Jousten et al. (2016) identified using administrative data. These authors argued that while some of the upward trend for women could be explained by the increase in the full retirement age, other factors had to be at play.

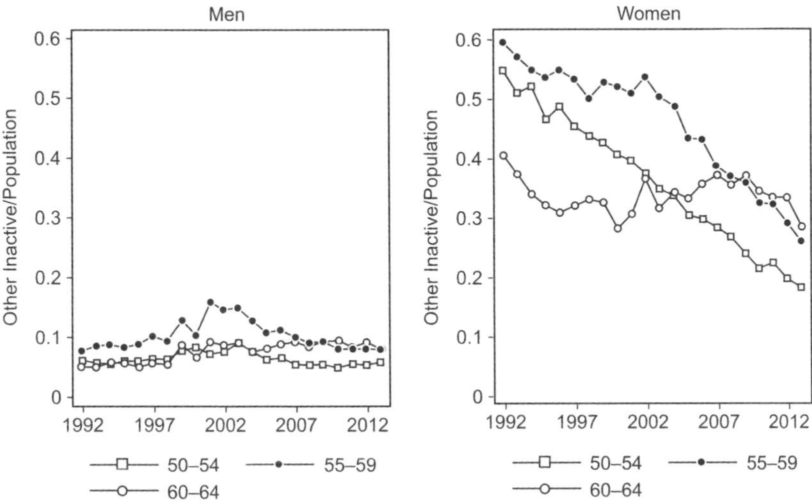

Fig. 1.8   Other inactive as a share of the population, ages 50–64
Source: Authors' calculations based on LFS data.

Figure 1.8 plots the third and residual group—the "other inactives," including those that fulfill domestic tasks. Two key features stand out: levels that are substantially larger for women than for men and a sharp drop for women over the course of the last two decades—shaving off a massive two-thirds of initial levels for age groups 50–59. For the age group 60–64, the drop is less pronounced because of a slowdown in the middle of the observation period, likely corresponding to a slowdown in transitions from inactivity to retirement as a result of the progressive increase in the retirement age over the period of 1997–2009.[11]

Our analysis of inactivity patterns thus identifies two main findings: (1) a strong reversal of male activity and employment patterns as of the 1990s, whose mirror image is a decrease in the people declaring themselves as retired or disabled, and (2) a sustained increase for women's activity over the entire observation period, going hand in hand with a very sharp decrease in the rate of female inactivity.

1.4   The Changing Nature of Employment

Beyond the shifts in the activity and employment rates—the extensive margin that the Belgian and European public debate often focuses on—it is

---

11. Using a unique administrative panel data set, Fraikin and Jousten (2016) document that even for those "other inactives," most transitions out of the "other inactivity" status occur toward retirement pensions, often accrued based on some form of labor market attachment at earlier stages of their career.

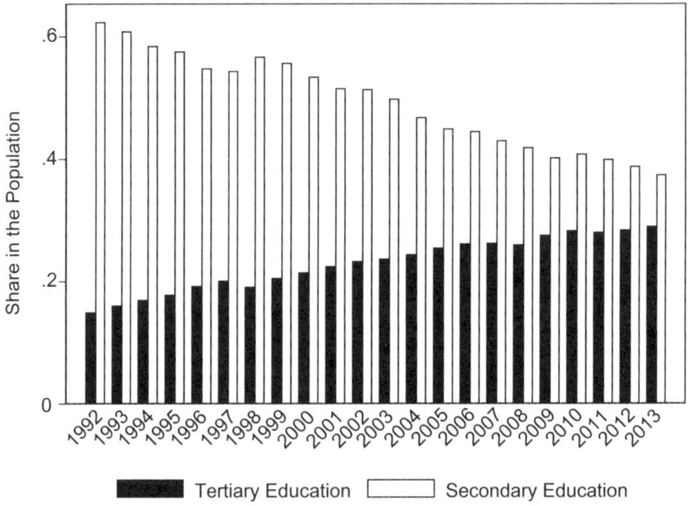

Fig. 1.9   Percentage of males aged 50–64 with a given education level
Source: Authors' calculations based on LFS data.

important to investigate changes in the quantity of work along the intensive margin as well as other qualitative characteristics of these jobs.

Figure 1.9 displays the profound changes in educational attainment across the population aged 50–64, with an increasing prevalence of higher education.

Figure 1.10 displays the shares of the industrial and service sectors among all workers for the age group 50–64. While the role of the service sector has been trending up over the entire time span, major differences subsist across genders, with female employment being close to 90 percent service-based, while male employment is nowadays split approximately two-thirds/ one-third.

Figure 1.11 presents the share of part-time jobs in total employment. Consistently with the increasing availability and popularity of the time credit and career break legislation as well as the greater ease of combining work with retirement, there has been a strong upward trend in the role of part-time work in the Belgian population. For older women, more than half declare themselves in some kind of part-time arrangement, while for men the level is close to 20 percent for ages 55–64. Combined with the employment trends of figure 1.3, figure 1.11 documents that part-time work has been the fastest-growing status among people aged 55–64.[12]

12. Though not reported here, part-time arrangements are substantially less prominent among the self-employed than for wage earners and civil servants—a reflection of both the less-generous early and part-time retirement routes and the fact that the analyzed LFS data refers to the main job (and not secondary jobs).

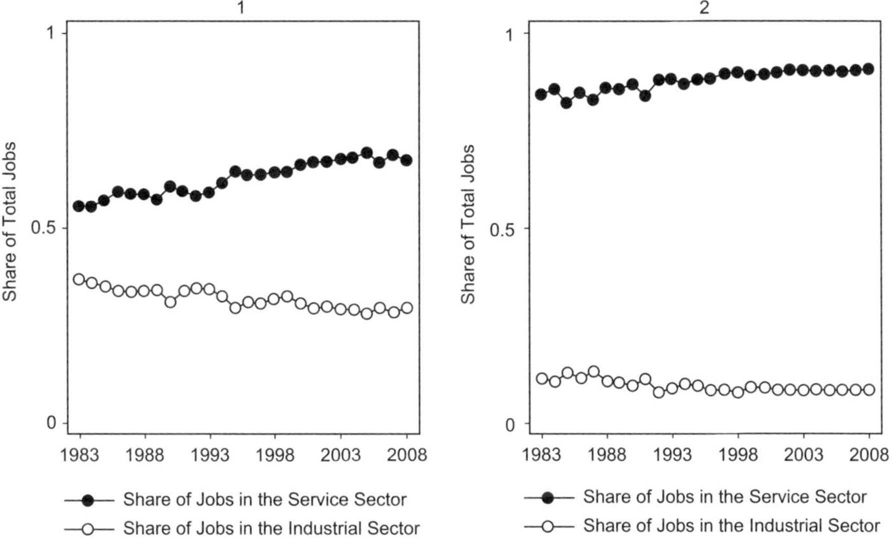

Fig. 1.10   Percentage of jobs in the service and industrial sectors, ages 50–64

Source: Authors' calculations based on LFS data.

Note: Sum does not necessarily correspond to 100 percent, as the primary sector is not included.

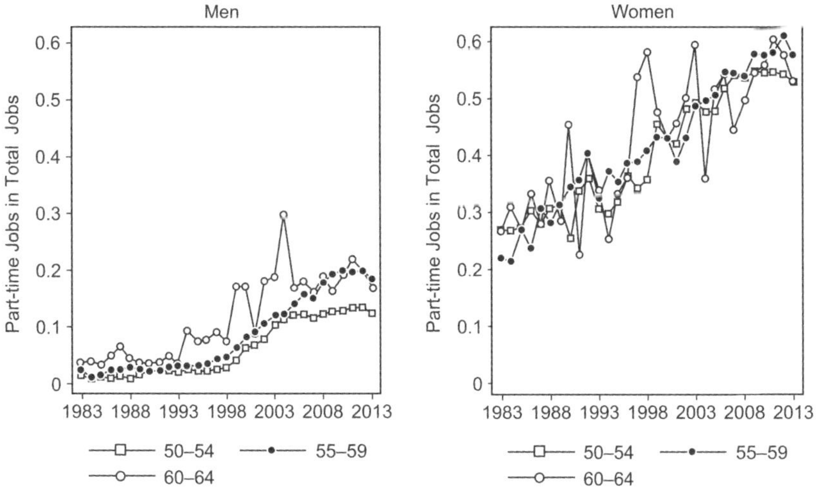

Fig. 1.11   Percentage of part-time jobs in total employment, ages 50–64

Source: Authors' calculations based on LFS data.

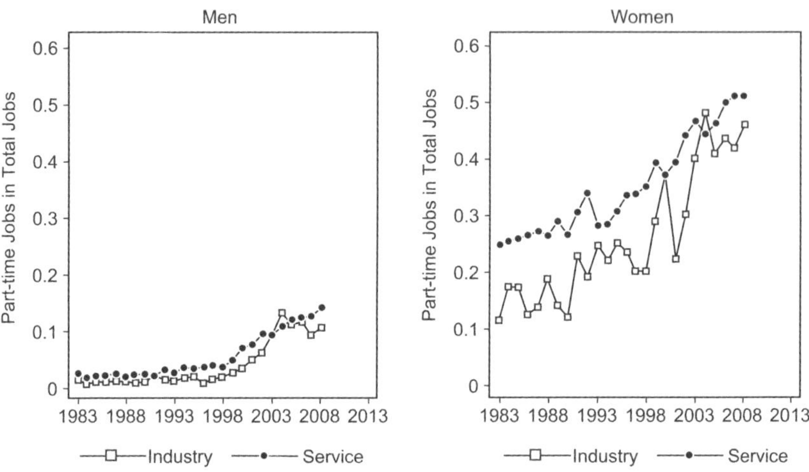

Fig. 1.12   Percentage of part-time jobs in total sectoral employment, ages 50–64
Source: Authors' calculations based on LFS data.

Fig. 1.13   Percentage of part-time jobs in total employment, ages 35–49
Source: Authors' calculations based on LFS data.

Figure 1.12 documents that the gender differences in part-time work in figure 1.10 are not exclusively due to the different sectoral composition, as substantial gender differences prevail all across the period of analysis. Another reason for these differences has to be sought in very different part-time prevalence at much lower ages. Figure 1.13 shows that the share of part-time jobs at ages 35–49 differs even more markedly between genders—

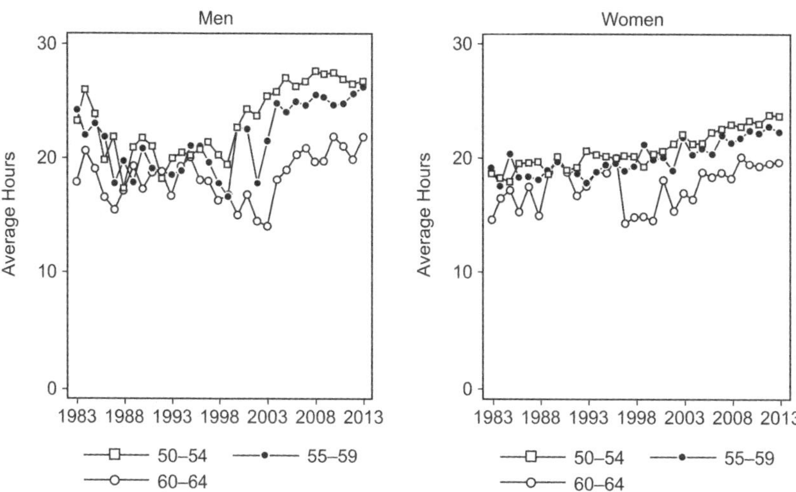

Fig. 1.14   Average number of hours in part-time jobs, ages 50–64
Source: Authors' calculations based on LFS data.

with part-time work almost exclusively being a female phenomenon until the end of the 1990s and still displaying a heavy gender bias thereafter. Part-time patterns later in life are hence a reflection of incentives for older workers and reveal a stock of workers who have been working part time for a long part of their career. While for men the former elements clearly prevail—given the quasi absence of part-time work at younger ages—the latter plays a more prominent role for women.

Figure 1.14 illustrates that average hours of work for part-time workers have a positive long-term trend over the period of observation—currently settling in the vicinity of 20 hours a week for women and 25 for men. In combination with figure 1.11, it confirms the findings of Aliaj et al. (2016). These authors propose a decomposition of total hours of work trends in the economy into an employment and hours-of-work effect. Their analysis shows that while the average hours per worker in the economy have decreased—notably because of an increase of part-time arrangements—total work hours have increased due to the dominance of the growth in the employment rate. Expressed differently, there is some degree of offsetting of positive employment effects through reduced work hours, shedding a somewhat dubitative light on some strongly encouraged part-time work arrangements.

Figure 1.15 presents the changing hours of work attributes of part-time workers across time. First, changes along this dimension seem to be more profound for men than for women. Second, the category of part-time workers displaying the strongest increase are those working more than 30 hours a week, likely corresponding to workers reducing their weekly work sched-

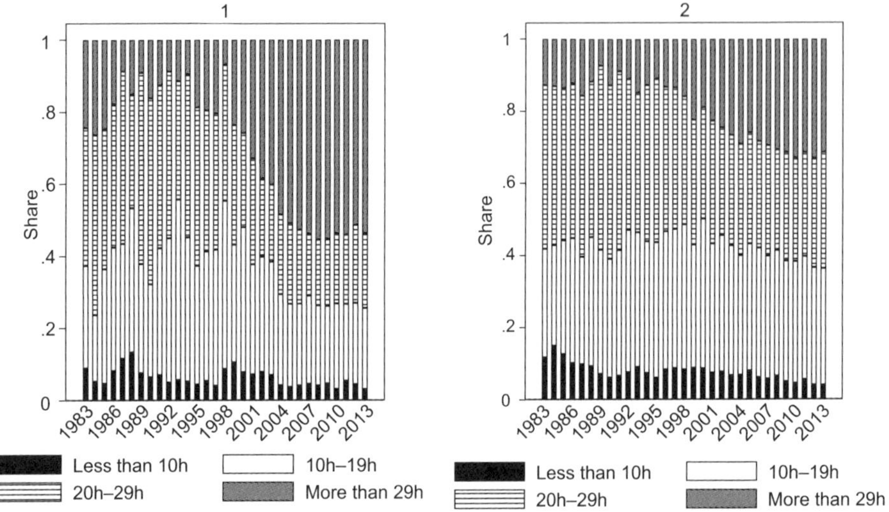

Fig. 1.15   Distribution of hours of work for part-time workers, ages 50–64
Source: Authors' calculations based on LFS data.

ule by one day—in line with old-age time credit and career break legislation. Third, it is precisely the share of the category of workers with 20 to 29 hours—hence those close to the observed averages of figure 1.14—that drops most significantly over the time span.

Our results show that interpreting data on average work hours (such as those of figure 1.14) as representative of a "typical" part-timer is becoming ever less accurate. We further show that a rather persistent 30 percent of male part-timers and 40 percent of female part-timers have a work intensity corresponding to less than a half-time position (less than 19 hours of work). Given the growth of the overall population of part-timers of figure 1.11, it also means that a nonnegligible number of extra workers contribute little toward the financing of social security schemes (through social insurance contributions and/or taxes), while at the same time, they might accrue minimum benefits (e.g., time credit or career break) or already be claiming a pension or other social benefits (e.g., work after retirement). Finally, the increase in the category of part-time workers with more than 29 hours raises more general questions regarding the part-time career break and time credit regimes that cannot be answered with LFS data: How many of these individuals working 30 or more hours in part-time arrangements would have continued working anyhow, and how many are "additional" workers? Depending on the answer to this question, the considerable current (and future) expenditures associated with both schemes could and should be evaluated as to their efficiency.

1.5 Concluding Remarks

We have described the Belgian institutional landscape that workers are facing when deciding to join the labor force or work. Major institutional differences exist between the three social protection regimes for wage earners of the private and public sectors as well as the self-employed—rendering the Belgian context an extremely rich one for economic analysis.

Using data from the European Union LFS, we are able to identify trends in activity and inactivity across both time and gender. Complementary analysis also reveals that the Belgian economy has undergone major sectoral reallocations, though we are not able to identify shifts between the three regimes because of lack of data.

We further document a sharp increase in the prevalence of part-time work for both men and women, with the male component mostly occurring closer to retirement, while females are already working part-time in large numbers at much lower ages.

Our results also illustrate the potential for further analysis. One promising avenue could be to link these survey data with administrative data on benefit entitlements to get a better understanding of the precise activity and exit patterns of the Belgian population—including their use of career break and time credit arrangements. Another avenue would be to revisit the models of work incentives as in Dellis et al. (2004)—integrating the latest labor market and institutional developments.

References

Aliaj, Arjeta, Xavier Flawinne, Alain Jousten, Sergio Perelman, and Lin Shi. 2016. "Old-Age Employment and Hours of Work Trends: Empirical Analysis for Four European Countries." IZA Discussion Paper No. 9819, IZA, Bonn, Germany.

Dejemeppe, M., C. Smith, and B. Vander Linden. 2015. "Did the Intergenerational Solidarity Pact Increase the Employment Rate of Older Workers in Belgium? A Macro-econometric Evaluation." *IZA Journal of Labor Policy* 4:17. https://doi.org/10.1186/s40173-015-0040-y.

Dellis, A., R. Desmet, A. Jousten, and S. Perelman. 2004. "Micro-modeling of Retirement in Belgium." In *Social Security Programs and Retirement around the World: Micro-Estimation*, edited by J. Gruber and D. A. Wise, 41–98. Chicago: University of Chicago Press.

Desmet, R., A. Jousten, S. Perelman, and P. Pestieau. 2007. "Microsimulation of Social Security Reforms in Belgium." In *Social Security Programs and Retirement around the World: Fiscal Implications for Reform*, edited by J. Gruber and D. A. Wise, 43–82. Chicago: University of Chicago Press.

Fraikin, A.-L., and Alain Jousten. 2016. "Work and Retirement Patterns in Belgium: Lessons from a Panel Dataset." Mimeo.

Gruber, J., and D. Wise. 2004. "Introduction and Summary." In *Social Security*

Programs and Retirement around the World: Micro-Estimation, edited by J. Gruber and D. A. Wise, 1–40. Chicago: University of Chicago Press.

Jousten, A., and M. Lefebvre. 2013. "Retirement Incentives in Belgium: Estimations and Simulations Using SHARE Data." *De Economist* 161 (3): 253–76.

Jousten, A., M. Lefebvre, and S. Perelman. 2012. "Disability in Belgium: There Is More Than Meets the Eye." In *Social Security Programs and Retirement around the World: Historical Trends in Mortality and Health, Employment, and Disability Insurance Participation and Reforms*, edited by D. Wise, 251–76. Chicago: University of Chicago Press.

———. 2016. "Health Status, Disability and Retirement Incentives in Belgium." In *Social Security and Retirement around the World: Disability Insurance Programs and Retirement*, edited by D. Wise, 179–209. Chicago: University of Chicago Press.

Jousten A., M. Lefebvre, S. Perelman, and P. Pestieau. 2005. "Social Security in Belgium: Distributive Outcomes." IZA Discussion Paper No. 1486, IZA, Bonn, Germany.

Maes, Marjan. 2011. "Will the Dismantlement of Early Retirement Schemes Increase Older Unemployment? A Competing-Risk Analysis for Belgium." *Labour* 25 (2): 252–67.

Service fédéral des Pensions. 2019. "Pensions de retraite du régime des fonctionnaires," January. http://sdpsp.fgov.be/sdpsp/pdf/publications/retirement_pension_201605.pdf.

Vandenbroucke, Frank, ed. 2014. "Un contrat social performant et fiable: Commission de réforme des pensions 2020–2040." Brussels: SPF Sécurité Sociale. http://pension2040.belgium.be/fr/.

2

The Labor Force Participation of Older Men in Canada

Kevin Milligan and Tammy Schirle

2.1 Introduction

With few exceptions, the labor force participation (LFP) rates of older men in Organisation for Economic Co-operation and Development (OECD) countries have followed a common trend—after declining steadily for decades, the participation rates of older men started to increase after the mid-1990s (Coile et al., introduction to this volume). In Canada, the participation rates of older men reached record lows in 1995 and have increased steadily since. The purpose of this chapter is to document these trends for older men in Canada and review various factors that might underlie these trends.

In what follows, we begin by documenting recent trends in older men's labor force participation rates as well as the participation rates of older women. We then investigate various factors that we might expect to affect the participation and retirement decisions of older men. We consider Canada's public and employer-sponsored pensions, the Canadian business cycle, improvements in Canadian health and mortality, the rising educational attainment of Canadian men, and finally the importance of joint retirement decisions of married couples and the greater labor force attachment of recent cohorts of older women.

Kevin Milligan is professor of economics at the University of British Columbia and a research associate of the National Bureau of Economic Research.

Tammy Schirle is professor of economics at Wilfrid Laurier University.

This chapter is a part of the National Bureau of Economic Research's International Social Security (ISS) project, which is supported by the National Institute on Aging. The authors thank the members of the other country teams in the ISS project for their comments and suggestions. For acknowledgments, sources of research support, and disclosure of the authors' material financial relationships, if any, please see https://www.nber.org/chapters/c14042.ack.

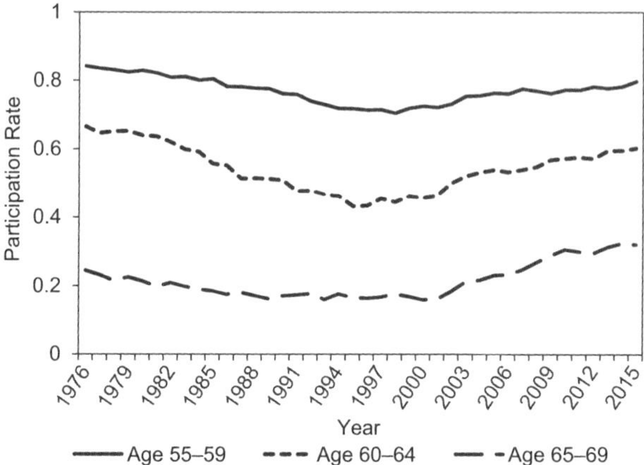

Fig. 2.1   Men's labor force participation rates
Source: Authors' tabulations from the LFS.

Each of these factors will play an important role in individuals' retirement and labor force participation decisions. However, there have been relatively few substantial changes to the setting in which older men are making these decisions. Most key parameters in Canada's public pensions have not changed over the time period we focus on here, and employer-sponsored pension coverage among older cohorts seems to have improved despite the declining coverage for younger cohorts. Recovery from the recession after the early 1990s may have played a small role in increasing participation rates; however, the more recent recession did not result in greater departures from the labor force.

Other factors appear more important. Improvements in health and mortality at older ages as well as higher educational attainment have likely improved the opportunities to remain employed when older. We also suggest that greater labor market attachment among more recent cohorts of older women has driven some of the recent increase in older men's participation as they delay retirement until such time as their wives will join them.

2.2   Trends in Participation Rates

As in many OECD countries, the participation rates of older men and women followed very different trends before the 1990s and have since increased. In figures 2.1 and 2.2, we present the labor force participation rates of older men and women aged 55–64 in Canada since 1976. From 1976 into the early 1990s, the participation rates of older men steadily declined. The decline is most substantial for men aged 60–64, whose participation rate declined from 67 percent in 1976 to only 43 percent in 1995. Thereafter, participation rates have steadily increased, reaching 60 percent in 2015 among

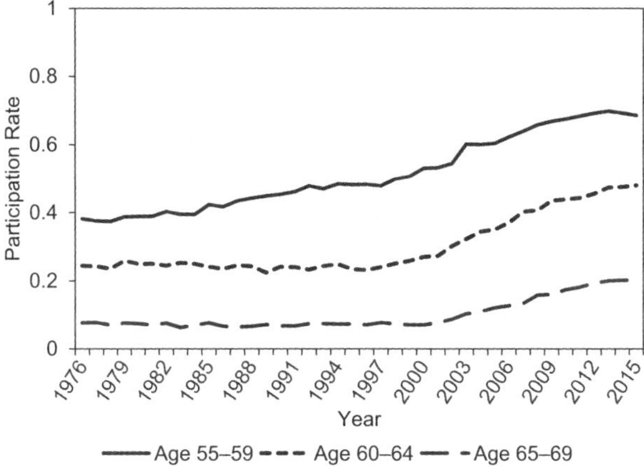

Fig. 2.2   Women's labor force participation rates
Source: Authors' tabulations using the LFS.

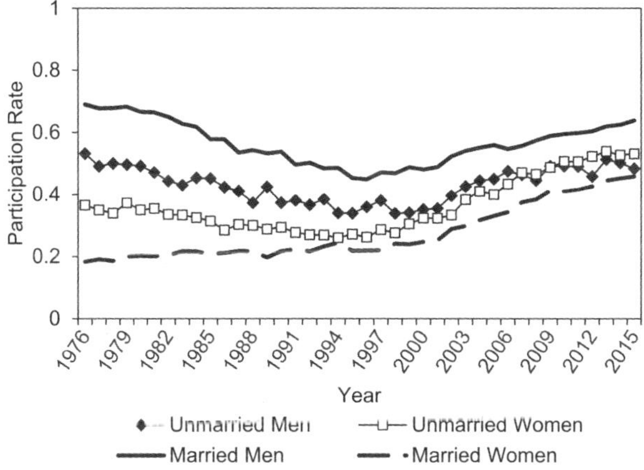

Fig. 2.3   Men's and women's participation rates at ages 60–64 by marital status
Source: Authors' tabulations using the LFS.

60–64-year-old men. The increase in men's participation after the 1990s is most remarkable for those aged 65–69, whose participation rates were only 16 percent in 1993 and reached record levels of 32 percent in 2014 and 2015.

In figure 2.2, we see that trends are quite different for older women, in that their participation rates did not decline before the 1990s as men's did. Participation rates of women aged 55–59 have steadily increased after the early 1980s. Those of older women were stable and then increased substantially after the mid-1990s. In 1996, the participation rate of women aged 60–64 was 23 percent; this rose to 48 percent by 2015.

In figure 2.3, we highlight the fact that trends for older women's participation rates appear related to marital status. Among married women (which includes women in common-law relationships) aged 60–64, we see the general increase in participation rates over time, with a sharp increase after the mid-1990s. For unmarried women (which includes never married, divorced, separated, and widowed women), we see the U-shaped trend similar to that for men. However, the decline in participation rates before the 1990s is not as steep for women as it was for men. The later increase in participation is much steeper for women than men.

In the next section, we consider various factors that might have driven the observed increase in men's participation rates since the mid-1990s. We first consider the roles of public and private pensions. Next, we explore the importance of the business cycle. We then consider changes in individuals' health and education, as these may influence the opportunities one has to participate in the labor force. Finally, we further consider the joint retirement decisions of couples in light of the differential trends presented for married women.

2.3   Factors Potentially Driving Men's LFP

2.3.1   Canada's Public Pensions

The importance of public pension incentives for retirement in Canada has been studied in past literature. For example, Baker, Gruber, and Milligan (2003) show how the financial incentives for retirement embedded in the Canadian public pension system affect individuals' decisions to retire. Schirle (2010) further examines these incentives and finds corroborating evidence. Baker (2002) examined the introduction of an early income-tested benefit (the spouse's allowance) available to those aged 60–64 whose spouses are aged 65 or older and found a reduction in labor force participation in response. Baker and Benjamin (1999), however, examined the introduction of early retirement provisions to Canada's contributory public pensions and found little immediate effect on labor market behavior despite an immediate effect on pension receipt. Compton (2001) also finds that the parameters of Canada's contributory pensions did not have a significant effect on retirement decisions. Overall, the available evidence suggests we should expect the parameters of the public pension system to affect the timing of retirement among those over age 55.

In figure 2.4 we plot the age of eligibility for Canada's main public pension programs. The eligibility age for Old Age Security (OAS, a near-universal benefit) has remained at age 65 since 1967.[1] The Guaranteed Income Supplement (GIS, an income-tested benefit) has the same eligibility age as the OAS

---

1. In 2012, the federal government announced plans to increase the OAS eligibility age to 67, phased in after 2023. In 2016, the government reversed this decision. OAS is clawed back at a rate of 15 percent for relatively high incomes.

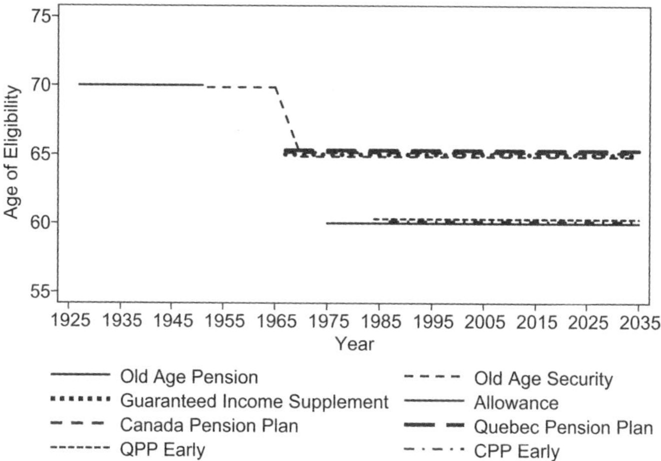

Fig. 2.4   Age of eligibility for public pensions in Canada
Source: Authors' tabulations.

at age 65, and this has not changed over time. A spousal income-tested benefit (the allowance) was introduced for individuals aged 60–64 (if their spouse was aged 65 or older) in 1975. The Canada and Quebec pension plans (CPP and QPP) are contributory pensions intended to replace 25 percent of covered earnings (referred to as the year's maximum pensionable earnings, or YMPE). Both the CPP and QPP set the normal retirement age at 65 (since 1967) and allow for early benefit take-up at age 60 (since 1985 in Quebec and 1987 in the rest of Canada). What is very clear from figure 2.4 is that one of the most important parameters of Canada's public pensions—the age of eligibility—has not changed in the past three decades.

There have been a few small changes to the public pension programs. First, in 1997, the CPP benefit formulas were altered slightly. Prior to 1997, CPP formulas were such that the maximum benefit amount for the CPP had represented 25 percent of a three-year moving average of the YMPE. Changes were phased in so that after 1999, the maximum benefit would represent 25 percent of a five-year average of the YMPE. This reduced only slightly the pension wealth accumulated in the plan and did not significantly alter incentives to retire at each age. Second, eligibility requirements became much more stringent for disability benefits associated with the CPP in 1995. As discussed in Milligan and Schirle (2016), the disability insurance program does not itself have a large effect on retirement decisions in Canada. Third, in 2012, changes to OAS were made so that individuals could choose to defer OAS benefits for up to five years in exchange for a higher monthly benefit. The adjustment is considered actuarially fair. Finally, the income-tested GIS has been made slightly more generous over time, allowing for a larger earnings exemption after 2008 and offering a small top-up benefit (with a higher clawback rate) to the lowest-income seniors since July 2011. Overall,

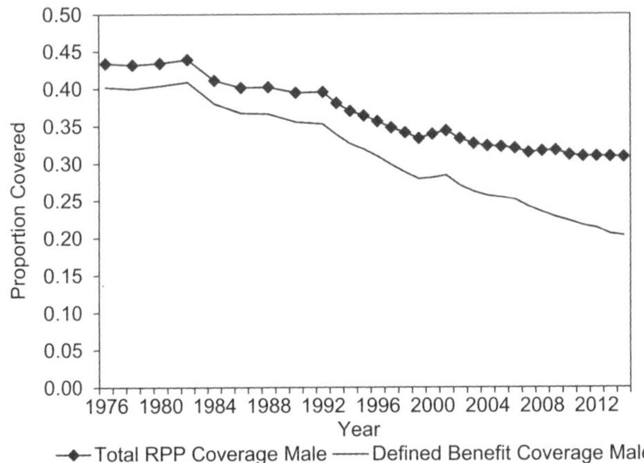

Fig. 2.5   Portion of male labor force participants aged 15 and older who are members of registered pension plans

Source: Authors' tabulations based on CANSIM tables 282–0002 and 280–0008.

we expect that each of these changes may have altered the labor market choices of a small number of individuals; however, policy changes and the expected effects on labor supply would not be large enough to account for the large increases in older men's participation rates.

2.3.2   Employer-Sponsored Pensions

Canada's employer-sponsored pensions are administered independently of the public pension programs, and employers are not required to offer coverage. Among men, the number covered by a registered pension plan (RPP), relative to the number of men aged 15 and older in the labor force, has declined substantially over time. As presented in figure 2.5, the portion of men covered by an RPP declined from 44 percent in 1982 to only 31 percent in 2014. There has also been a shift away from employer-sponsored, defined-benefit pension plans toward defined contribution plans.

It is not clear, however, that this lower coverage among all men reflects the experience of older men during the later 1990s. In fact, among older men, there appears to be greater coverage after the mid-1990s: using data from Canadian tax records, we see that in 1996, 46 percent of men aged 65–69 received "other pensions and superannuation" (CRA 1998).[2] In 2013, 52 percent of men aged 65–69 were receiving pensions (CRA 2015). Despite the increase in pension income receipt, the participation rates of men aged 65–69 increased steadily over this period. We are left with the impression

2. This refers to pension income reported on line 115 of the Canadian federal income tax form and generally represents employer-provided pension income. It will also represent some private savings converted to annuities, which is required for some tax-sheltered savings by age 71.

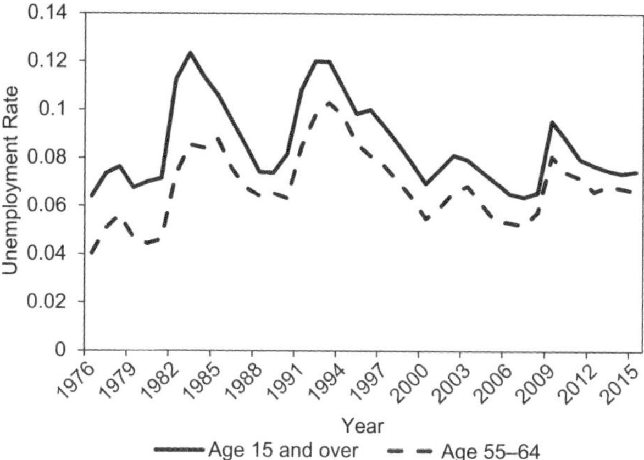

Fig. 2.6   Unemployment rates of men
Source: Authors' tabulations using the LFS.

that declining RPP coverage in the general population of men is not a major factor driving increases in older men's participation after the 1990s.

2.3.3   Business-Cycle Considerations

The initial increase in older men's participation rates coincides with Canada's slow recovery from the recession of the early 1990s. In figure 2.6, we see that the unemployment rates of all men aged 15 and older declined from the early 1990s until 2008. While the unemployment rates of older men (aged 55–64) are generally lower than those of younger men, the trends follow the same pattern. To the extent that this reflects an improvement in men's labor market prospects, we might expect this to be an important factor driving increases in older men's participation after the mid-1990s.

However, when we consider the recession in 2008–9, we see substantial increases in all men's unemployment rates. We do not see a corresponding decline in the participation rates of older men. To the contrary, in figure 2.1, we see the participation rates of older men—particularly those aged 65–69—continue to increase through the recession and up to 2015.

Overall then, we might expect that the improved labor market opportunities of the later 1990s supported the increase in men's LFP rates. However, it is clear that factors independent of the business cycle are also at play.

2.3.4   Health and Mortality

Following the work done in Milligan and Schirle (2017), we explore the relationship between improvements in health over time and increases in employment. In figure 2.7, we see that the life expectancy of older men and women at age 60 has risen dramatically since the 1970s. Between 1970 and 2011, men's life expectancy at age 60 increased by six years. Similarly,

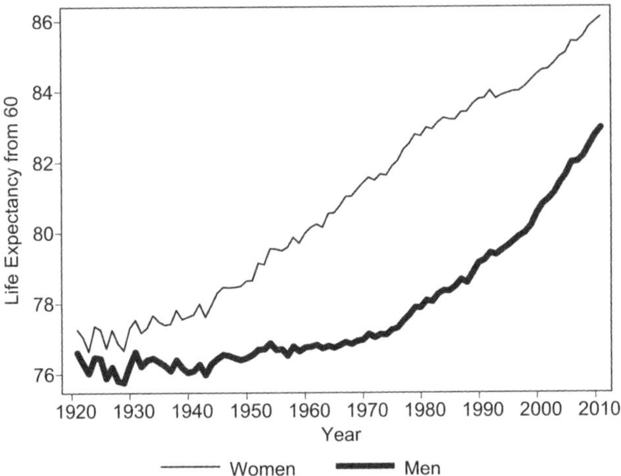

Fig. 2.7   Life expectancy at age 60

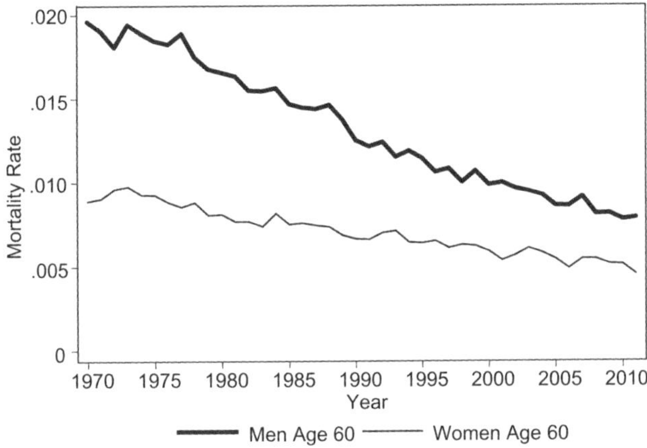

Fig. 2.8   Mortality rates at age 60

in figure 2.8, we see the mortality rates of men and women at age 60 have declined steadily over time.

While we expect improvements in mortality to reflect improvements in health, it is not entirely clear the extent to which this is true. Recent estimates of healthy life expectancy appear to increase at approximately the same rate as life expectancy (Statistics Canada 2012). If we look at self-reports of health among older men (figure 2.9), we see the portion of men reporting fair or poor health did not change over the 1995–2011 period. It is not clear, however, that these self-made reports are comparable over time. The survey question underlying the self-made reports asks respondents to describe their

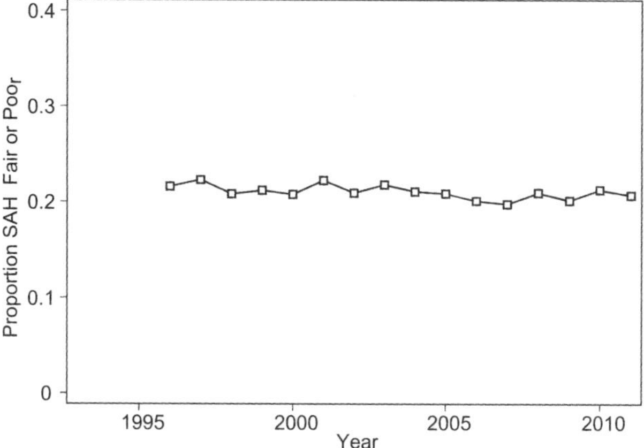

Fig. 2.9   Men aged 55–64 reporting fair/poor health

"state of health" (Statistics Canada 2011), and respondents' reference point is not clear. If the average health of older men is improving over time, and older men are reporting health relative to that average, it would make sense to see no change in this measure.

Clearly, improvements in life expectancy are not going to be the only important factor determining older men's participation rates. If it were, we would have seen increases in participation alongside improvements in mortality over the 1970s, 1980s, and early 1990s. Since the mid-1990s, increases in participation have aligned fairly closely. Milligan and Schirle (2017) have suggested that employment has not quite kept pace with mortality improvements. If they had, older men would be working longer than observed in the data. Specifically, Milligan and Schirle (2017) suggest that if older men in 2011 had remained employed as long as men in 1995 with the same mortality rates, they would be working 1.44 years longer.

Overall we suggest that improvements in health and mortality have facilitated increases in employment among older men since the mid-1990s.

2.3.5   Education

In figures 2.10 and 2.11, we describe how the educational attainment of older men and women has increased over time, specifically the likelihood of having attended high school or completed a university degree (which in Canada is typically a three- or four-year degree and is considered separately from one- to two-year college programs). Older men's likelihood of completing a university degree increased substantially, from 7 percent in 1976 to 13 percent in 1995 and 23 percent in 2015. Women's likelihood of completing university increased at a higher rate, from 3.5 percent in 1976 to 22 percent in 2015.

On one hand, an increase in education should result in higher lifetime

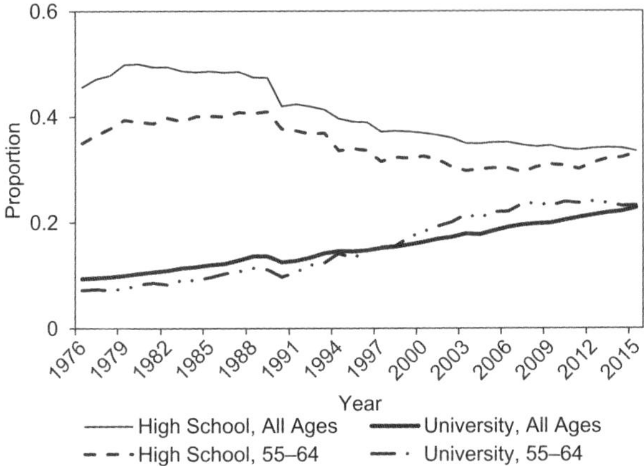

Fig. 2.10   Educational attainment of men
Source: Authors' tabulations using the LFS.

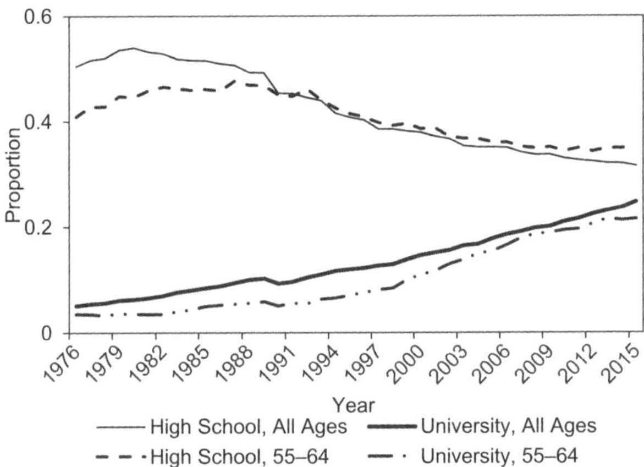

Fig. 2.11   Educational attainment of women
Source: Authors' tabulations using the LFS.

incomes among more recent cohorts of older men and women. We'd expect that to result in earlier retirements, as individuals use their wealth to enjoy more leisure time in retirement. On the other hand, improvements in educational attainment may result in a change in the types of occupations available to older workers—possibly less physically demanding occupations that are more accommodating to worsening health at older ages. In figure 2.12, we present the portion of men working in blue-collar occupations.[3] This has

3. Our definition of blue collar includes contractors and supervisors in trades and transportation, construction trades, other trade occupations, transport and equipment operators,

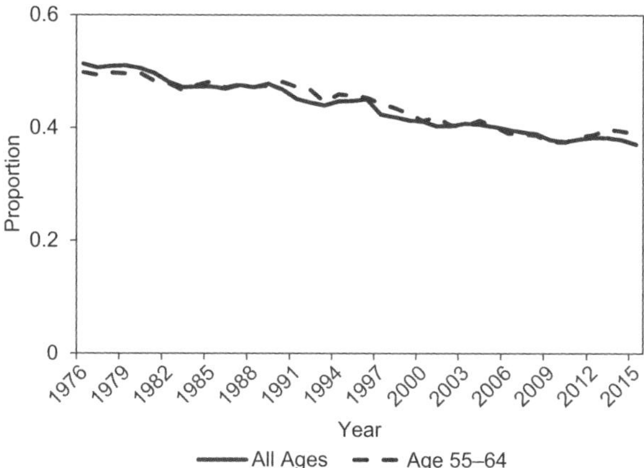

Fig. 2.12   Portion of men employed in blue-collar jobs
Source: Authors' tabulations using the LFS.

steadily declined over time, from 50 percent of all working men in 1976 to 39 percent in 2015.

Schirle (2010) considered the role of education in her examination of older (age 55–64) married men's participation rates since the mid-1990s. However, the role of education was not accounted for separately from other characteristics of men, including age and the number of children in the family. The changes in men's characteristic accounted for 15 percent of the total change in men's participation from 1995 to 2005.

2.3.6   Joint Retirement Decisions and Recent Cohorts of Women

Among the factors affecting the labor force participation decisions of men, we should expect the participation decisions of women—their wives—to be an important factor in the decision-making process. As described in Schirle (2010), there are two routes through which a wife's participation decision might affect a husband's. First, there is an income effect whereby a wife's employment income would reduce a husband's likelihood of participating in the labor force. Second, husbands and wives may have a preference for shared leisure time, especially at older ages. As such, husbands may be more likely to participate in the labor force when their wives are participating in the labor force. Schirle (2010) provides evidence suggesting that the preference for shared leisure time dominates in the retirement decision, in that a husband's participation is positively and significantly influenced by a wife's participation in the labor force. Moreover, a substantial portion (42–46 per-

---

trade helpers, construction and transportation laborers and related occupations, occupations unique to a primary industry, machine operators and assemblers in manufacturing including supervisors, and laborers in processing, manufacturing, and utilities.

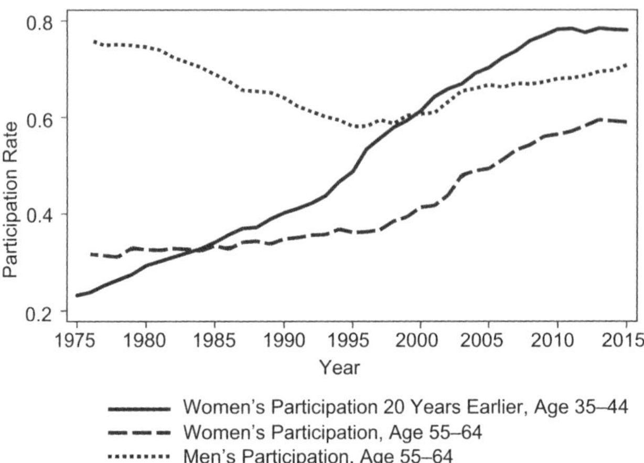

Fig. 2.13   Participation rates of men and women by age

Source: Authors' tabulations using the LFS (1975–2015) and historical documents from Canada's Women's Bureau.

Note: Women's participation 20 years earlier at ages 35–44 depicts for the year in the graph what the participation rates of women aged 35–44 was 20 years prior.

cent) of the increase in older men's participation since the mid-1990s was driven by the response of older men to their wives' increased participation in the labor force.

In figure 2.13, we present the participation rates of men and women at ages 55–64, aligned with the participation rates of the same birth cohort of women 20 years earlier (when they were 35–44 years old). Women's participation rates at ages 35–44 had been rising steadily, with each new cohort of women being more likely to participate in the labor force. For women aged 55–64 in the mid-1990s, rising participation at younger ages (35–44 in the mid-1970s) had accelerated, reflecting greater career attachment that coincided with easier access to birth control and resulting increases in education (see Bailey 2006; Goldin and Katz 2002). This acceleration in women's participation from the 1970s corresponds to the same cohort's increase in participation in the mid-1990s.

With greater career attachment among the cohorts of older women appearing in the mid-1990s, we would expect their husbands (whose wives are typically a bit younger) to have a higher likelihood of participating in the labor force than earlier cohorts of men, as they postpone retirement in the interest of sharing the leisure time with their wives. To characterize the extent to which this matters, we construct estimates using the methods similar to those presented in Schirle (2010).[4] We present a counterfactual

4. Our measures, including age groups, are defined a bit more coarsely given the availability of public-use data files, and we do not account for the number of children.

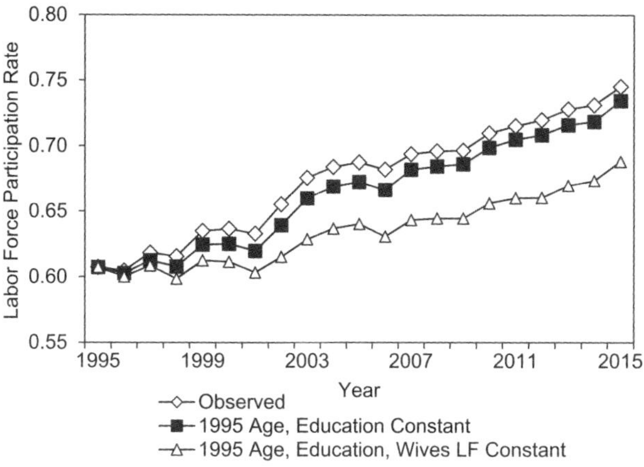

Fig. 2.14   Counterfactual participation rates of men
Note: Authors' calculations based on LFS.

time series for married men's (age 55–64) LFP rates—specifically a counterfactual in which the participation rates of wives did not increase after 1995. We also consider the effects of age structure and education in our procedures. The results are presented in figure 2.14.

Among married men aged 55–64, participation rates increased by 14 percentage points over the 1995–2015 period. Increasing levels of education and changes in the age structure (as the baby boomers moved from being aged 55–59 toward 60–64) explain a small portion of the increase in participation over the 1995–2015 period (only 8 percent of the total increase, or one percentage point). The increase in wives' LFP appears to be an important factor. If the participation rates of wives had not increased over this period, we might expect the participation rates of older married men to be nearly 5 percent lower. In other words, the estimates here suggest that the increase in wives' participation rates over time can explain one-third of the total increase in married men's participation rates since 1995. Despite using the relatively unrefined methods used here, the results align well with those found in Schirle (2010).

2.4   Conclusion

In this study, we have reviewed recent trends in older men's LFP rates and various factors that may have driven these trends. While public and employer-sponsored pensions are an important determinant of the retirement decision, these pensions have not changed substantially for older men over the past two decades. We expect that the recovery of the Canadian economy over the mid to later 1990s contributed to the increase in older men's participation rates but was not a central element driving trends.

Improvements in health and education may have played a larger role in recent trends in older men's participation rates. As education levels increase, there has been a shift away from blue-collar jobs, which tend to be more physically demanding. Combined with improvements in health, older men may now face better opportunities to continue with employment at older ages.

Finally, we expect that continued increases in the LFP rates of older wives have played an important role. The observed increase in participation of older wives reflects long-run trends in women's attachment to the labor market that intensified for younger women in the 1970s. As husbands reveal preferences for sharing leisure time with their (typically) younger wives and their wives are increasingly likely to work at older ages, the labor force attachment of older husbands has increased as well.

References

Bailey, M. J. 2006. "More Power to the Pill: The Impact of Contraceptive Freedom on Women's Life Cycle Labor Supply." *Quarterly Journal of Economics* 121 (1): 289–320.

Baker, M.. 2002. "The Retirement Behavior of Married Couples: Evidence from the Spouse's Allowance." *Journal of Human Resources* 37:1–34.

Baker, M., and D. Benjamin. 1999. "Early Retirement Provisions and the Labor Force Behavior of Older Men: Evidence from Canada." *Journal of Labor Economics* 17 (4): 724–56.

Baker, M., J. Gruber, and K. Milligan. 2003. "The Retirement Incentive Effects of Canada's Income Security Programs." *Canadian Journal of Economics* 36 (2): 261–90.

Compton, J. 2001. "Determinants of Retirement: Does Money Really Matter?" Working Paper No. 2001-02, Department of Finance, Ottawa.

CRA. 1998. Income Statistics 1996 Tax Year, 1998. Revenue Canada. http:// library.queensu.ca/madgic/free/cra/income-tax-stats/1998_for%201996_TaxYr _IncomeStatistics.pdf.

———. 2015. "Final Statistics (T1 Data) 2015 Edition (for the 2013 Tax Year)." Canada Revenue Agency. http://www.cra-arc.gc.ca/gncy/stts/t1fnl/2013/menu-eng .html.

Goldin, Claudia, and Lawrence Katz. 2002. "The Power of the Pill: Oral Contraceptives and Women's Career and Marriage Decisions." *Journal of Political Economy* 110 (4): 730–70.

Milligan, K., and T. Schirle. 2016. "Option Value of Disability Insurance in Canada." In *Social Security Programs and Retirement around the World: Disability Insurance Programs and Retirement*, edited by David A. Wise, 137–78. Chicago: University of Chicago Press.

———. 2017. "Health Capacity to Work at Older Ages: Evidence from Canada." In *Social Security Programs and Retirement around the World: The Capacity to Work at Older Ages*, edited by David A. Wise, 59–84. Chicago: University of Chicago Press.

Schirle, T. 2010. "Health, Pensions, and the Retirement Decision: Evidence from Canada." *Canadian Journal on Aging / La revue canadienne du vieillissement* 29 (4): 519–27.

Statistics Canada. 2011. "Survey of Labour and Income Dynamics (SLID): Preliminary, Labour and Income Interview Questionnaire for Reference Year 2011." Statistics Canada Income Research Paper Series, Cat. No. 75F0002MIE. http://www23.statcan.gc.ca/imdb-bmdi/instrument/3889_Q6_V6-eng.pdf.

———. 2012. *Table 102-0122—Health-Adjusted Life Expectancy, at Birth and at Age 65, by Sex and Income, Canada and Provinces, Occasional (Years)*, CANSIM (database). Accessed February 9, 2015. http://www5.statcan.gc.ca/cansim/a26.

From Early Retirement to Staying in the Job
Trend Reversal in the Danish Labor Market

Paul Bingley, Nabanita Datta Gupta,
and Peder J. Pedersen

3.1 Introduction

Until the 1970s, Denmark was a country with fairly late retirement from the labor force. The normal social security retirement age was 67. The only early retirement possibility was disability insurance, mostly on medical criteria, and some very small social security programs. An early retirement program without any medical criteria, the so-called Post-Employment Wage (PEW) was introduced in 1979 as a reaction to the steep increase in unemployment following the oil crisis. The program became quickly very popular, with the consequence that labor force participation (LFP) went down strongly in the 60–66 age group.

Considering the expected future aging of the population, a controversial point on the agenda in economic policy discussions and analyses later became the question of how to roll this program back and adapt the overall pension system to a demography with an increasing share of the population in the older age groups. In the policy arena, a number of changes and

Paul Bingley is a research professor at VIVE—The Danish Centre of Applied Social Science.

Nabanita Datta Gupta is a professor in the Department of Economics and Business Economics at Aarhus University; a research fellow of the Institute for the Study of Labor (IZA) in Bonn and DIW Berlin; and an alumni affiliate of Cornell Institute on Health Economics, Health Behaviors, and Disparities.

Peder J. Pedersen is an emeritus professor of the Department of Economics and Business Economics at Aarhus University, a research professor at VIVE—The Danish Centre of Applied Social Science, and a research fellow of IZA.

We are grateful for research assistance from Nikolaj Hansen and for advice and references from Anders Holtermann regarding the survey results from the National Research Center for the Working Environment. For acknowledgments, sources of research support, and disclosure of the authors' material financial relationships, if any, please see https://www.nber.org/chapters/c14043.ack.

reforms were enacted in the years 1999–2012, with most of the reforms to be phased in over a quite long period.

At the same time, a surprising turnaround began in the LFP among older workers, in Denmark as well as in most other Organisation for Economic Co-operation and Development (OECD) countries. In this chapter, we discuss the factors behind this turnaround in Denmark. While policy reforms were introduced at the same time as the turnaround in LFP, they are only part of the explanation of the change. First, as mentioned, the reforms were mostly to be phased in over a long period. Second, a number of other factors with an impact on the LFP among older workers were changing. New cohorts of workers 60 years and older were better educated. By many indicators, they were also in better health. Both factors are assumed to have a positive gradient in LFP. Further, the nature of jobs could be changing, making it more realistic to continue working at higher ages due to a reduction of physically demanding job functions. Finally, sectoral changes in the economy could favor older workers, as could other factors on the demand side.

In section 3.2, we summarize briefly the changes in LFP in Denmark between 1980 and 2014 separately for women and men age 60 and older. At the same time, we look into the impact of the Great Recession, beginning in 2008, on different age groups in the Danish labor market.

Section 3.3 surveys the factors expected to have an impact on LFP among older workers. We include policy changes trying to identify the eventual impact on different cohorts of women and men. Further, we relate LFP in the 60 and older group to the big changes in education and health coinciding with the turnaround. We likewise look at the simultaneous effects from education and—self-assessed—health by regressing LFP on these factors for the 60–69 age group using data from the fifth wave of the Survey of Health, Ageing and Retirement in Europe (SHARE), collected in 2013. Section 3.3 also presents indicators of changes in physically demanding jobs with a potential impact on working at older ages. Finally, this section summarizes indicators for the demand side of relevance for older workers.

In section 3.4, we summarize some conclusions relative to the changes in the Danish labor market since the turn of the century, with special emphasis on the developments among older workers since the onset of the Great Recession. Finally, section 3.4 has a (preliminary) conclusion about the nature of the turnaround—that is, is it a specific occurrence with LFP among older workers quickly stabilizing on a somewhat higher level, or is it a process we can expect will continue as longevity continues to increase?

3.2   Recent Changes in LFP among Older Workers

Annual data for LFP by age are available for the whole population from 1980. Before 1980, census data are available along with labor force and

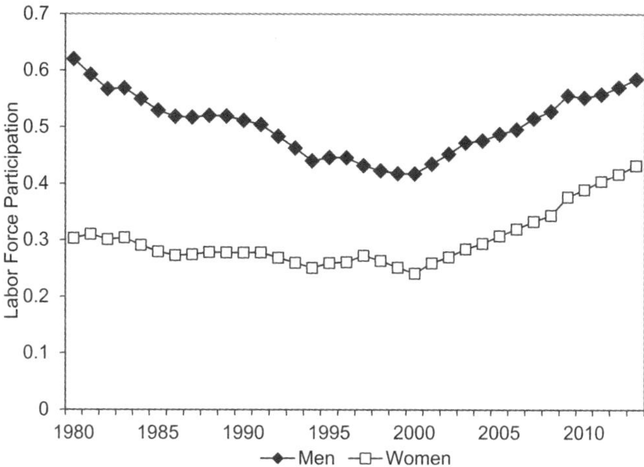

Fig. 3.1   LFP rates for men and women, ages 60–64, 1980–2013
Source: Statistics Denmark.

employment surveys for a number of years in the 1970s. For men aged 60–64, the LFP was nearly 90 percent at the census in 1960. The decade of the 1960s was characterized by comprehensive changes in the Danish economy, with a steep decline in the relative importance of agriculture. These structural changes were accompanied by a decline of some 10 percentage points in LFP to a level of about 80 percent in the 1970s. The introduction in 1979 of the non-health-related early retirement program PEW, mentioned above, was a main factor behind the decline over the next 20 years to a level of 40 percent at the turn of the century. Since then, the turnaround has resulted in an increase to 60 percent LFP among men aged 60–64. The details over time from 1980 are shown in figure 3.1. For women, figure 3.1 shows a turnaround also from around 2000, with an increase of the same 20 percentage points as men. The fairly flat profile of the LFP for women aged 60–64 before 2000 is most probably the net outcome of a cohort effect, tending to increase LFP, and the introduction of PEW, tending to reduce it. However, eligibility for PEW was conditional on a long tenure as a member of an unemployment insurance fund. As the female LFP was less than half the level of men— although increasing strongly in the 1970s—a much lower share of women were able to enter PEW.

For the 65–69 age group, LFP since 1980 is shown in figure 3.2. The turnaround for this age group is predictably weaker than for those aged 60–64 and begins about five years later in 2005. Before having annual data available from 1980, the LFP for men aged 65–69 was 60 percent at the census in 1960, declining about 10–15 percentage points until the beginning of the 1970s. For women aged 65–69, the LFP was flat around 10 percent until the increase beginning in 2005.

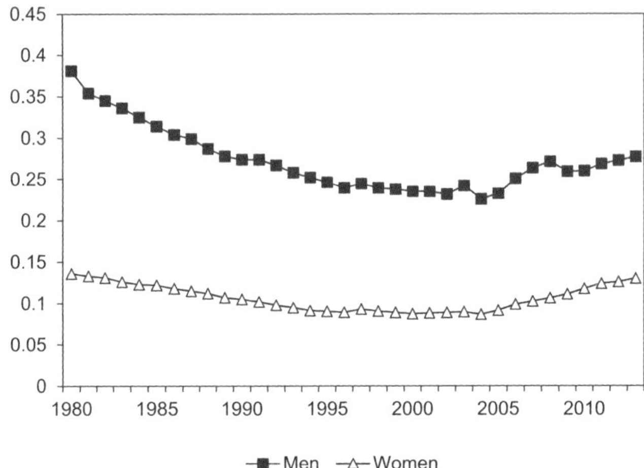

Fig. 3.2   LFP rates for men and women, ages 65–69, 1980–2013
Source: Statistics Denmark.

As mentioned above, the turnaround has occurred in nearly all OECD countries but with great variation. It is interesting that the turnaround has continued in most OECD countries in the years since the onset of the Great Recession. The cross-country variation for men aged 60–64 from 2007 to 2014 lies between an increase of 20 percentage points in the Netherlands and a decline of 13 percentage points in Greece, with increasing LFP in the great majority of countries according to OECD labor force statistics (Larsen and Pedersen 2015, 2016). In an OECD "ranking," the Danish labor market is in eighth place for both men and women, with increases around 8–9 percentage points.

When we compare the turnaround in LFP among older workers since the beginning of the Great Recession with the situation for other age groups, a quite different picture emerges. In figure 3.3, we show the change in LFP in percentage points by age from 2008 to 2014 using register data covering the whole population. Figure 3.3 shows not only a steep positive gradient in age but also that the 60–64 age group is the only one with increasing LFP during the crisis years, with younger age groups experiencing big declines in LFP. While a part of the decline for the youngest groups is likely replaced with ongoing education, there remains the surprising impact during the years of the Great Recession of the increasing LFP in the 60 and older group and the decline for the core working-age groups.

A number of factors that may contribute to an explanation of the profile in figure 3.3 are discussed in the next section. There is, however, a risk that the increase in LFP for the 60–64 age group reflects higher unemployment more than employment. In figure 3.4, we show—for a slightly longer period,

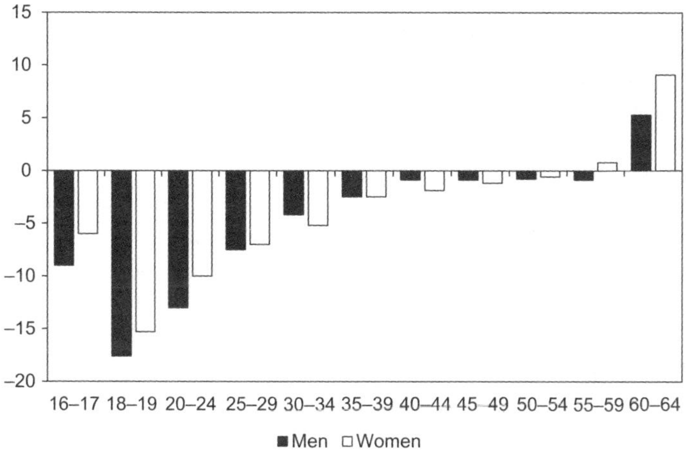

Fig. 3.3   Change in LFP in percentage points by age during the Great Recession, 2008–2014

Source: Authors' calculations on data from Statistics Denmark.

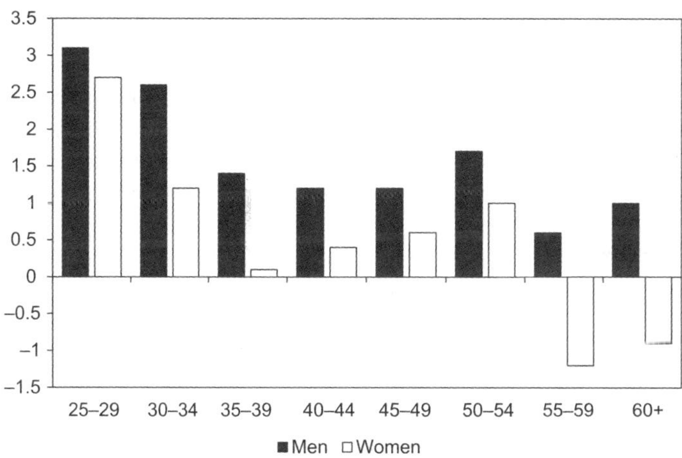

Fig. 3.4   Change in unemployment in percentage points by age and gender, 2008–2014

Source: Authors' calculations on data from Statistics Denmark.

2007–15—the change in unemployment in percentage points by age. For men aged 60–64, unemployment increases, but figure 3.3 shows that this is only a small part of the increase in LFP. For women, employment increases a fortiori, as LFP goes up at the same time that unemployment goes down. To conclude, the next section goes into a number of factors that might explain this change in the situation for older workers.

3.3   Some Factors behind the Turnaround

Important factors behind the turnaround in most OECD countries are summarized and discussed in OECD (2013). As a reflection of many policy changes, the economic incentives to remain longer in the labor force have become stronger. Further, each new cohort of older workers is better educated and seems to be in better health, factors that make longer working lives possible. Another important factor is the changes in many functions at work, where strenuous physical activity has become less important as a consequence of technological change and sectoral shifts in the economy. While those changes have increased the possibility of continuing in a job at older ages, other work-related factors—like the experience of stress and rapid changes in technology with resulting changes in job functions—may work in the opposite direction.

Pension programs have been reformed a number of times. Introduced in 1979, PEW was first available, conditional on eligibility, at age 60, and Old Age Pension (OAP) was first available at age 67, with individuals transferring from PEW to OAP upon turning 67. A reform announced in 1999 and implemented 2004–6 reduced the OAP age of first eligibility to 65, with individuals transferring from PEW to OAP at this younger age. Regarding PEW, there have been a number of smaller changes tightening requirements of unemployment insurance tenure and changing the profile of benefits to create incentives to delay entry to the program. A survey can be found in OECD (2015).

In the OAP program, some minor policy changes have been introduced in recent years with the purpose of increasing the incentive to continue working after the normal retirement age of 65. An option to defer take-up of OAP on actuarial terms between ages 65 and 75 was introduced in 2006, conditional on working at least 1,500 hours per year (then reduced to 1,000 hours per year in 2008 and to 750 hours in 2014). Means testing of a supplementary part of OAP against income from work was reduced in 2008, at the same time as the mandatory retirement at age 70 was abolished for most groups of public-sector employees. For most occupational pensions, first receipt can be delayed until age 75 with actuarial adjustments. Evidence of the so-far minor impact from these changes in the 65 and older group can be found in Amilon and Nielsen (2010), Larsen, Bach, and Ellerbæk (2011), and Larsen and Ellerbæk (2012).

Two major policy reforms announced in 2006 and 2012 will result in future reductions in the maximum number of years in the PEW program along with increases in the age of eligibility to OAP from 65 to 67. Increases in the age of eligibility for PEW began with an increase of 0.5 years in 2014, and eligibility will increase to age 63.5 in 2022. For OAP, the age of eligibility will be raised to age 67, and after 2022, both ages will be indexed to changes in expected longevity.

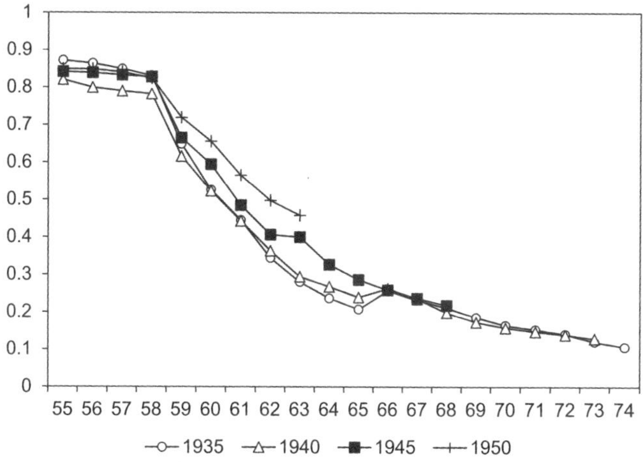

Fig. 3.5   LFP rates, men by cohorts 1935, 1940, 1945, and 1950, at ages 55–74
Source: Authors' calculations on register data.

For the period of turnaround in LFP analyzed here, the minor reforms
of the PEW program are relevant in a cohort setting along with changes in
education and health. In figure 3.5, we show the LFP rates for four cohorts
of men aged 55–74. Only small differences appear between the 1935 and the
1940 cohorts. However, when comparing the 1940 with the 1945 cohort, the
impact of the financial incentives to delay entry until age 63 is clearly seen.
For the 1950 cohort, the LFP is higher at all ages from 60 until 63.

In figure 3.6, we show in more detail for the annual cohorts 1945–49
that the turnaround is found in all cohorts but most strongly in the earliest
cohorts. The kink at age 63 is also still visible for the later cohorts. However, at younger ages, we find a steep increase in LFP—for example, an
increase of nearly 10 percentage points at age 62 between cohorts 1945 and
1949.

For women, the profiles for the same cohorts are shown in figures 3.7 and
3.8. In figure 3.7, we find a decline in LFP at nearly all ages above 54 for
cohorts between 1935 and 1940. This pattern is followed by a steep increase
in LFP from 1940 to 1945 for people in the second half of their 50s. Long-
term unemployed workers ages 50–59 were entitled to enter a transitional
benefits program open between 1992 and 1996.[1] Those who entered the
program left the labor force, and this is presumably part of the explanation
of the big gap for cohorts between 1940 and 1945 at ages below 60. In figure
3.7, we find also the 63-year kink for the 1945 cohort and a steep increase

---

1. This program was taken up by significantly more women than men.

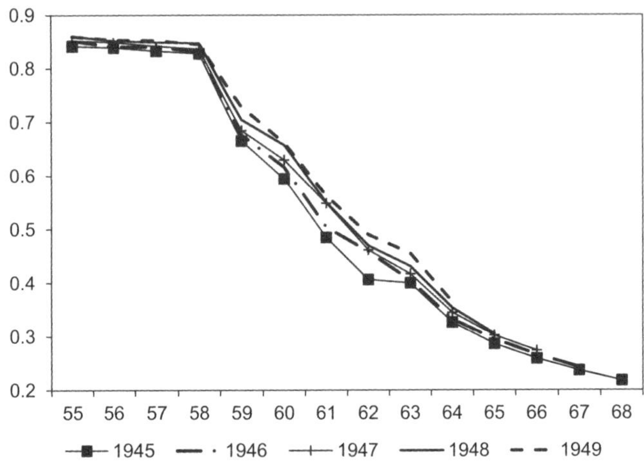

Fig. 3.6   LFP rates, men by cohorts 1945–1949, at ages 55–74
Source: Authors' calculations on register data.

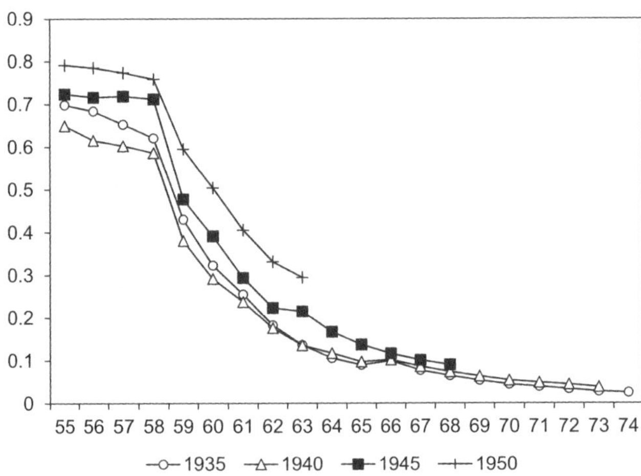

Fig. 3.7   LFP rates, women by cohorts 1935, 1940, 1945, and 1950, at ages 55–74
Source: Authors' calculations on register data.

in LFP until cohort 1950, which we can follow until age 63. In figure 3.8, we show in more detail the changes in LFP between 1945 and 1949 cohorts. As for men, in figure 3.6, we find an increase in LFP around 10 percentage points at age 62 between 1945 and 1949.

While some of the minor policy changes implemented so far clearly play a role in the turnaround, other factors are also expected to be important. Next, we look into changes in education for the cohorts reaching age 60

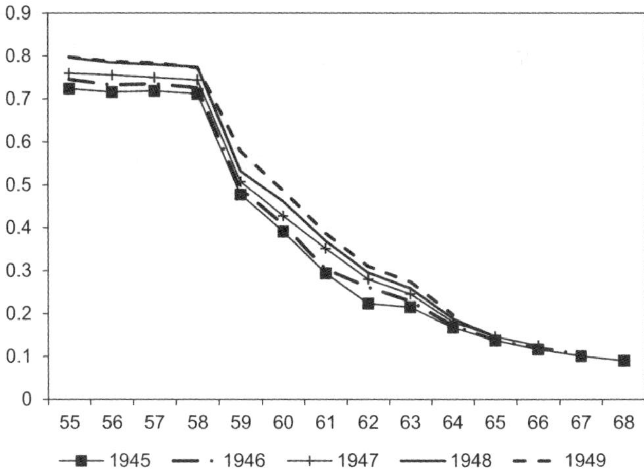

Fig. 3.8   LFP rates, women by cohorts 1945–1949, at ages 55–74

Source: Authors' calculations on register data.

around the turn of the century. In relative terms, the strongest increase is found regarding the share completing a medium-duration or long theoretical education. According to the Ministry of Education (1998), the enrollment to universities increased dramatically between 1936 and 1946—that is, when the 1936 and 1946 cohorts were, respectively, 20 years old. People in these two cohorts—and the cohorts in between—entered the first half of their 60s precisely at the time of the turnaround. For later cohorts, the increase in university enrollment continues but is much slower in relative terms.

Overall, completing a medium-duration or long theoretical education was still of minor relative importance at the time of the turnaround for people around age 60. In quantitative terms, the biggest change is the decline in the share of people without any postcompulsory schooling, roughly corresponding to the group of blue-collar workers. For men as well as women, this group was more than half the individuals in the age interval of 55–64 back in 1980. By 2013, this was down to 25 percent among men and 30 percent among women. The changes in composition by education are shown in figures 3.9 and 3.10 for men and women, respectively.

It is well established that LFP has a positive gradient in education. Relative to the turnaround, however, figures 3.9 and 3.10 do not obviously identify any dramatic shift in education for the relevant age group at the same time as the turnaround in LFP. If education was the only "driver" for LFP, we would expect to observe a smooth increase over the whole period from 1980, not a steep decline until the increase in the late 1990s.

For the years 1995–2012, figure 3.11 shows the results from a shift-share analysis of the change in LFP among men and women aged 60–64, the

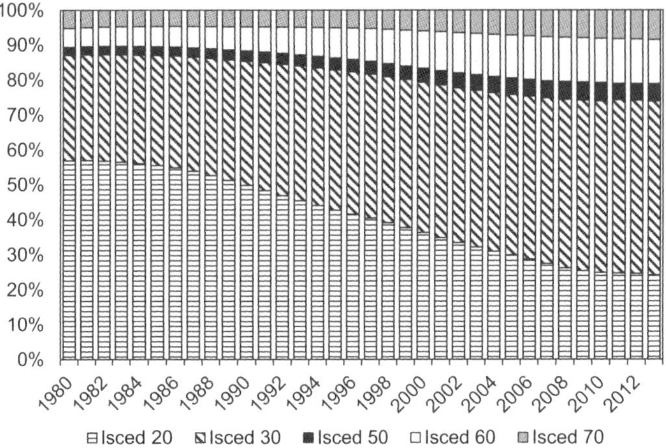

Fig. 3.9   Men aged 55–64 by educational level, 1980–2013

Source: Authors' calculations on register data.

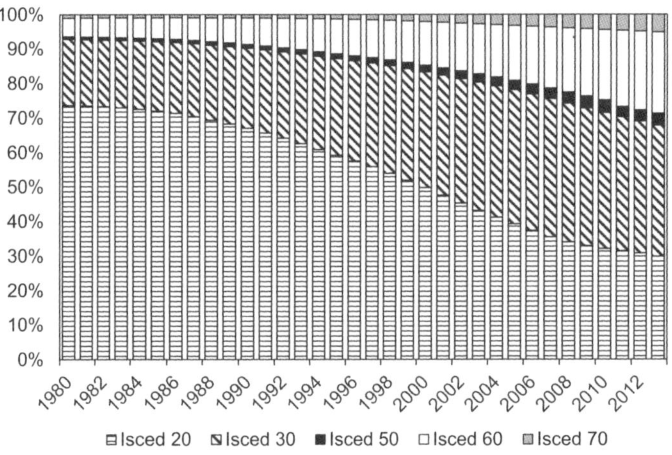

Fig. 3.10   Women aged 55–64 by educational level, 1980–2013

Source: Authors' calculations on register data.

actual level and the level assuming changes in composition of educational groups are the only factor. It is obvious that LFP also increases for most education groups.

As shown in table 3.1, there are quite big differences by gender and educational level in how much the LFP has been increasing between 1995 and 2012. For men, the highest increase is found among individuals with vocational or short further education. The increase is small for those with a long theoretical education where the initial level was fairly high. For women, the

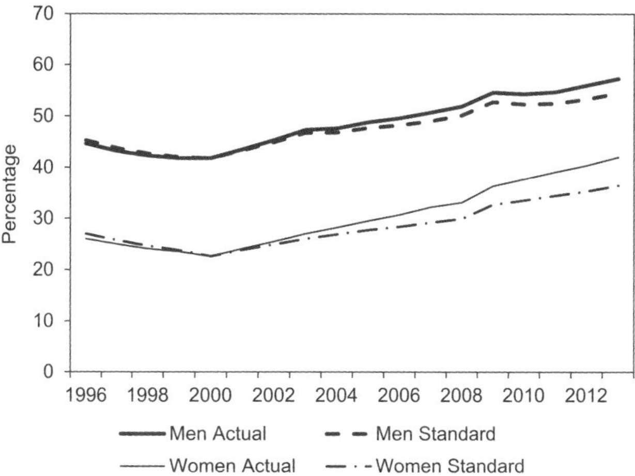

Fig. 3.11   LFP rates for men and women aged 60–64: Actual level and standardized for changes in education, 1995–2012 (1999 = 100)

Source: Authors' calculations on data from Statistics Denmark.

Table 3.1   **Change in LFP rates, percentage points, by educational groups in Denmark, 1995–2012**

	Men	Women
No postcompulsory education	6.9	7.7
Vocational + short further education	13.6	11.6
Medium-duration further education	3.4	13.4
Long theoretical education	2.9	5.9

Source: Authors' calculations on data from Statistics Denmark.

increase—as expected—is higher or nearly the same as men, with the highest increase found for women with a medium-duration further education.

Health problems are a common reason for early retirement. Here we focus on indicators for health among older individuals before and during the turnaround. While a multitude of register-based data are available on diagnoses, treatments, and prescription medicine on an individual basis, unfortunately, a long-run consistent general health indicator is not available. Instead, we rely on mortality as a crude indicator along with more incomplete evidence on self-assessed health. In figure 3.12, we show mortality at age 60 for men and women from 1980 to 2014. With a focus on the turnaround in LFP, the profile in male mortality shows a slightly steeper decline from the beginning of the 1990s that seems—so far—to end at the same time as the onset of the Great Recession. It is evident that the gap in mortality between men and women becomes smaller during the period. In

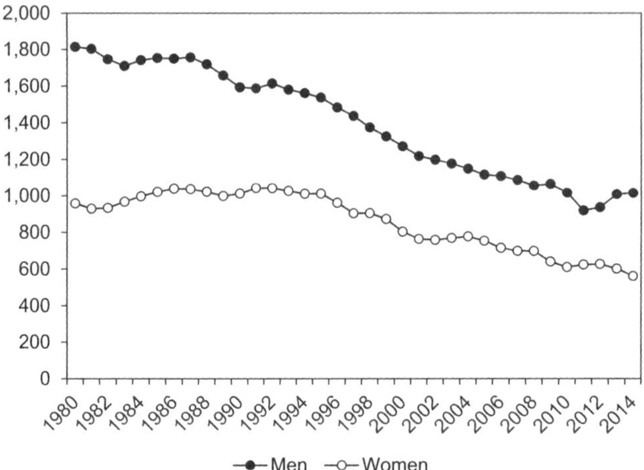

Fig. 3.12   Mortality at age 60, men and women, 1980–2014
Source: Authors' calculations on data from Statistics Denmark.

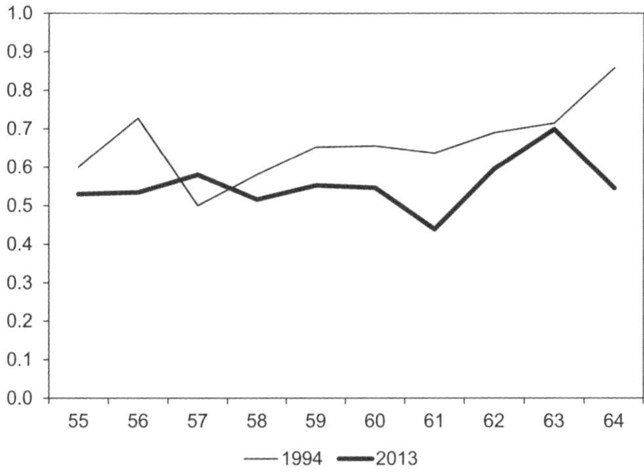

Fig. 3.13   Share of respondents with self-assessed health of fair–poor. National Institute of Public Health surveys, 1994 and 2013

relation to the turnaround in LFP, female mortality at 60 is stationary until the mid-1990s. After that, a steep decline occurs along with a steep increase in female LFP.

The National Institute of Public Health has conducted surveys for the years 1994 and 2013 with a question about self-assessed health with the same response categories as in the US Health and Retirement Study and in SHARE. In figure 3.13, we show the share of male respondents aged 55–64 in the two years who report their health to be in the category of fair to poor. With one

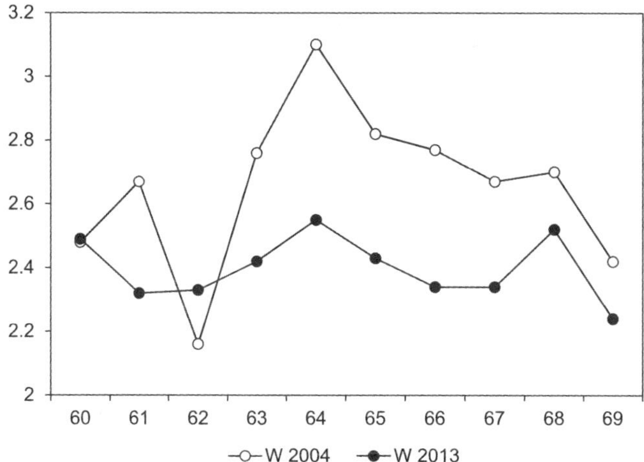

Fig. 3.14   Mean self-assessed health, women aged 60–69, share wave 1 (2004) and share wave 5 (2013)

Source: Authors' calculations.

exception, we find health on average to be reported as better in 2013 than in 1994—that is, we see a self-reported improvement occurring over the same interval of time as the increase in LFP for the age group 55–64.

A final indicator is found using data in SHARE from wave 1 (2004) and wave 5 (2013), exactly spanning the years of increase in LFP. We have calculated the mean value of the variable measuring self-assessed health, for men and women at every age between 60 and 69 in the two waves. The variable is defined as in the US Health and Retirement Study, with the outcome "excellent" set at one and "poor" set at five. For men, we find no difference in self-assessed health between 2004 and 2013. For women, on the other hand, we find, as shown in figure 3.14, a clear improvement between 2004 and 2013 corresponding with the steep increase in LFP.

The combined impact from education and self-assessed health is estimated in cross-section setting in table 3.2 using data from SHARE wave 5 collected in 2013. The upper panel presents the marginal effects in a probit estimation of LFP separately for men and women aged 60–64 and 65–69, respectively. In the upper panel of table 3.2, age and education are entered as continuous variables in years, assuming implicitly the same impact from one more year. Age, as expected, is found significantly negative in all cases, more so for individuals 60–64 years old than in the older group where everybody is above the age of eligibility for OAP. Years of education is found significant for men aged 60–64 and women aged 65–69. Finally, as expected, self-assessed health is found significant in all cases, most particularly for those 60–64 years old.

The lower panel in table 3.2 presents results from entering age as dummy variables, excluding ages 64 and 69. Education is in the same way changed to

Table 3.2   **Marginal effects in probit estimations of LFP, men and women, 60–64 and 65–69 years old (share W5, 2013)**

	60–64 years old		65–69 years old	
	Men	Women	Men	Women
Age	–0.086***	–0.102***	–0.044***	–0.029***
	(–12.46)	(–15.16)	(–6.52)	(–6.09)
Yedu	0.010***	0.002	0.003	0.004***
	(4.41)	(0.69)	(1.44)	(2.87)
Self-assessed health	–0.104***	–0.122***	–0.039***	–0.031***
	(–10.61)	(–14.18)	(–4.40)	(–4.91)
Pseudo R^2	0.1172	0.1374	0.034	0.0761
Age dummies:				
60	0.333***	0.377***	–	–
	(10.62)	(11.97)		
61	0.363***	0.238***	–	–
	(11.42)	(7.46)		
62	0.246***	0.294***	–	–
	6.60)	8.90)		
63	0.176***	0.013	–	–
	(5.49)	(0.39)		
64	–	–	–	–
65	–	–	0.194***	0.123***
			(6.49)	(5.41)
66	–	–	0.067***	0.063***
			(2.03)	(2.71)
67	–	–	0.060**	0.033
			(1.94)	(1.33)
68	–	–	0.038	0.047**
			(1.10)	(1.96)
Low education	–0.055***	–0.002	–0.003	0.037***
	(–2.04)	(–0.07)	(–0.12)	(2.45)
High education	0.064***	0.067***	0.044**	0.093***
	(2.34)	(2.63)	(1.89)	(5.96)
Self-assessed health	–0.101***	–0.120***	–0.037***	–0.031***
	(–10.36)	(–13.93)	(–4.14)	(–5.01)
Pseudo R^2	0.1259	0.1544	0.040	0.103
Number of observations	1,570	1,786	1,765	1,816

Note: Unemployment insurance is not possible at ages older than 64. For the 65–69 age group, the estimations are relevant for employment, not the broader concept of LFP.

a categorical variable, low education indicating up to 9 years of education, high education indicating more than 14 years, and the excluded category of "intermediate" education covering 10–14 years of schooling. Age has a clearly nonlinear effect. For both age groups, the youngest have higher LFP probabilities than those with the reference age. Regarding the categorical variables for education, having a high education implies a significantly

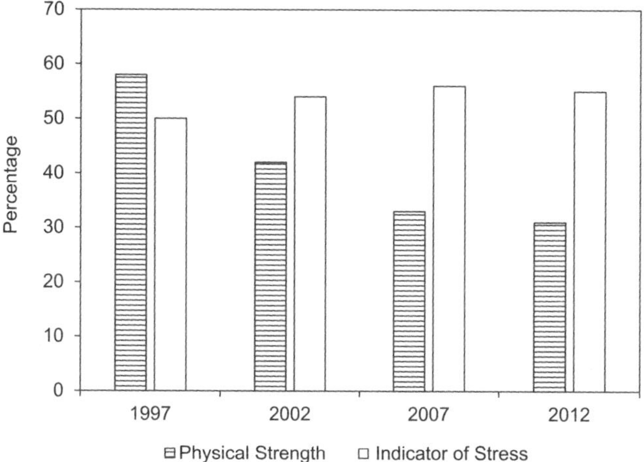

Fig. 3.15   Share of 57-year-old respondents who report that their job demands physical strength and share reporting stress and pressure on the job
Source: Authors' calculations from the Danish longitudinal survey of aging.

higher probability in all cases. For men aged 60–64, having a low education implies a significantly lower probability of LFP than in the excluded intermediate group. For women aged 65–69, we find the opposite pattern—that is, a higher probability of working for both those with low education and those with high education.

OECD (2013) points to another factor—changes in the nature of jobs— that might have made it more possible to continue working at higher ages. A challenge in this area is the lack of a long consistent series with indications primarily of whether jobs are demanding regarding physical strength. In the Danish longitudinal survey of aging, 57-year-old respondents still working were asked every 5 years from 1997 to 2012 whether their job demanded physical strength. As shown in figure 3.15, the share reporting this fell to nearly half the initial level over 15 years. At the same time, however, a nearly constant share of about half the respondents finds that their job is stressful, as characterized by "high demand for speed in performing work functions and tight schedules."

In a number of surveys, the National Research Center for the Working Environment has investigated different aspects of the physical demands in jobs. The question "How physically demanding do you usually find your current job?" is included in a survey for 2010 and 2012. The response categories are 0–10, with 10 as the most demanding. For those two years, the surveys find the results shown in table 3.3, organized by age and gender.

In spite of the difference in time between surveys being only two years, jobs are considered less physically demanding in all age groups. Earlier studies from the National Research Center for the Working Environment do

Table 3.3   **Self-assessed physically demanding character of jobs**

	Men		Women	
Age	2012	2014	2012	2014
18–24	5.30	5.09	4.80	4.40
25–34	3.77	3.45	3.41	3.29
35–44	3.57	3.15	3.14	2.88
45–54	3.79	3.33	3.28	2.90
55–64	3.45	3.18	3.31	2.98
Total	3.81	3.44	3.41	3.11

Source: National Research Center for the Working Environment, http://www.arbejdsmiljofor skning.dk/da/arbejdsmiljoedata/arbejdsmiljoe-og-helbred-20.

not contain one specific question like the 2010 and 2012 surveys but instead a range of different questions about the nature of physical challenges or problems in the current job. Between surveys in 2000 and 2005, there is a significant reduction of the physical demands in two out of five indicators, with insignificant change in the remaining three indicators. Between the surveys in 2005 and 2010, seven indicators became significantly lower while two increased. Overall, the results from the National Research Center for the Working Environment confirm, with a broader survey base than the one used in figure 3.15, that the physical demands in jobs have changed in a way that facilitates continued work at higher ages.

Figures 3.3 and 3.4 document that the increasing LFP among 60–64-year-olds represents an increase in employment and not unemployment. As a consequence, the demand side has accommodated the increasing employment of older workers at the same time that employment has gone down for younger age groups since 2008. It is not easy, however, to find any explicit indicator for the demand side. We summarize here one indicator capturing sectoral changes over recent years and two other imperfect proxies for the mean annual hours and the overall hourly wage by both age groups and gender.

First, figure 3.16 shows the big changes occurring in total employment and in the public-sector employment share over the last 20 years. Very dramatic changes are seen both in the years up to and in those following the onset of the Great Recession.

In relation to the turnaround, the composition of sectors by age and gender differs quite a lot, which might have consequences in this respect, especially among women aged 60–64. This is illustrated further in table 3.4.

It appears in table 3.4 that the sectoral shifts—at least for the period considered—contribute in explaining the turnaround, especially the increase in LFP among women aged 60–64. It reinforces an initial state where public-sector employees are older on average and the share of women is higher than in the private sector.

Fig. 3.16   Total employment and public-sector employment share, 1995–2015
Source: Authors' calculations on data from Statistics Denmark.

Table 3.4   **Change in employment in percentage points, 2008–2014, by sector, age, and gender**

	Public sector	Private sector
All wage and salary earners	–2.0	–5.4
All, 60–64 years old	+16.6	–4.6
Women, 60–64 years old	+23.5	–1.9

Source: Authors' calculations on data from Statistics Denmark.

Finally, two short and somewhat incomplete series based on microdata seem to support that the demand side has been important in accommodating the turnaround. First, figure 3.17 shows the mean actual number of hours worked for men and women in the labor market "core" 40–49 and 60–64 age groups. It seems evident that the turnaround is not in any significant way related to an adaptation to fewer hours worked by older workers.

Next, figure 3.18 shows overall mean hourly earnings for the same four groups as in figure 3.17. Here too the tentative conclusion is that the turnaround is not explained in any significant way by a wage adaptation by older workers.

3.4   Concluding Remarks

Since the beginning of the Great Recession in 2008, there has been only a little growth in production in Denmark. On this background, it is even more interesting that the employment rate has been growing among people

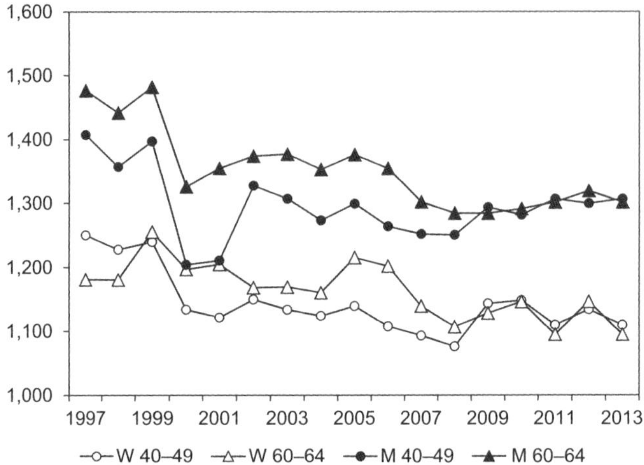

Fig. 3.17   Actual hours worked, 1997–2013, by age and gender
Source: Authors' calculations on register data.

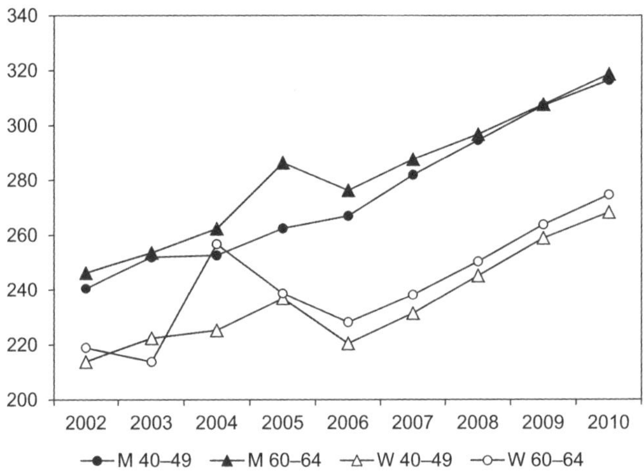

Fig. 3.18   Mean annual hourly earnings (DKK), 2002–2010, by age and gender
Source: Authors' calculations on register data.

60 and older and, in accordance with the macroeconomic profile, decreasing in younger age groups.

Actually, this turnaround in LFP in older age groups began already at the turn of the century, after decades with falling LFP for men and a stationary level for women in the 60 and older group. A number of factors have been discussed above as possible explanations for this remarkable trend reversal. First, policy reforms have been enacted in the years 1999–2012, both in relation to early retirement benefitsand to old-age social security pension. Reforms in this area are, however, phased in over a long period of time. Only the first of the policy changes seems to show up when looking at cohort profiles in LFP.

Next, education is expected to explain part of the development along with improved health, for which a number of indicators were present, all pointing to improvement. While both factors, also in a cross-section estimation of microdata, correlate with increasing LFP, they both have fairly smooth profiles over time without any break around the time of the turnaround. However, a shift-share analysis shows that LFP increases at the time of the turnaround in each educational group. For education and health indicators, we find bigger improvements for women than men corresponding with the steeper relative increase in LFP among women.

The specific nature of jobs is another factor that has been changing over time. A number of indicators point to an average reduction in the prevalence of physically demanding jobs, facilitating continued work at older ages. Finally, sectoral shifts may have had an impact at least in the most recent years. The Great Recession shifted employment somewhat toward the public sector, where average age and the share of female employees are higher than in the private sector.

A final question is whether the increase in LFP at higher ages can be expected to continue. A number of explanatory factors are expected to develop in a way that would further facilitate continued work. At the same time, globalization and rapid structural changes in many areas might be factors that would go against the effect from the reduced physical demands of jobs. A final factor is the demand side, which, so far, has accommodated the increase in labor supply in the 60 and older group.

References

Amilon, A., and T. H. Nielsen. 2010. "How Does the Option to Defer Pension Payments Affect the Labour Supply of Older Workers in Denmark?" In *Working at Old Age: Emerging Theories and Empirical Perspectives on Ageing and Work*, 190–209. Thessaloniki: CEDEFOP.

Larsen, M., H. B. Bach, and L. S. Ellerbæk. 2011. *55–70-åriges forbliven på arbejds-markedet. Adfærd, forventninger, aftaler og kendskab til regler* [55–70-year-olds' staying in the labour market. Behaviour, expectations, agreements and knowledge of rules]. Vol. 11, no. 13. Copenhagen: SFI—The Danish National Centre for Social Research.

Larsen, M., and L. S. Ellerbæk. 2012. *Evaluering af Jobplanen: Nuværende og kommende pensionisters kendskab til og betydning af reglerne for at arbejde* [Evaluation of the job plan: Current and future pensioners' knowledge of rules for working and importance of these rules]. Vol. 12, no. 14. Copenhagen: SFI—The Danish National Centre for Social Research.

Larsen, M., and P. J. Pedersen. 2015. "Labor Force Activity after 60: Recent Trends in the Scandinavian Countries with Germany as a Benchmark." IZA Discussion Paper No. 9393, IZA, Bonn, Germany.

———. 2016. "Hvorfor ramte krisen ikke de ældres beskæftigelse I OECD-landene?" [Why did the crises not hit the employment among the elderly in the OECD-countries?]. *Samfundsøkonomen* 2 (June): 49–55.

Ministry of Education. 1998. *Uddannelsessystemet it al gennem 150 år* [The education system in numbers over 150 years]. Copenhagen, Denmark: Ministry of Education.

OECD. 2013. "All in It Together? The Experience of Different Labour Market Groups following the Crisis." *OECD Employment Outlook 2013.* Paris: OECD.

———. 2015. *Ageing and Employment Policies: Denmark 2015; Working Better with Age.* Paris: OECD.

Explaining the Reversal in the Trend of Older Workers' Employment Rates
The Case of France

Didier Blanchet, Antoine Bozio, Corinne Prost,
and Muriel Roger

4.1 Introduction

Declining labor force participation (LFP) of older workers has been a topic of concern in many developed countries during the 1980s and 1990s, including Europe. The European Council fixed in 2001 the so-called Stockholm objective of reincreasing the employment rate of workers aged 55–64 and older to 50 percent in 2010. In 2010, a new target has been settled for 2020: reaching a global employment rate of 75 percent for the whole 20–64 age group, with a large part of this global target to be reached by increasing the employment rate of older workers. Designing policies to reach such goals requires identifying what had been the causes of the decline. A large amount of literature has been devoted to this question. Gruber and Wise (1999, 2004), among others, have related the decrease in older workers' labor market participation to the increase in pension benefit generosity or to the lack of financial incentives to postpone retirement. Empirical research has also focused on the substitution effects between the several pathways to retirement that are available before the normal retirement age (NRA; e.g., Coile, Milligan, and Wise 2016).

Yet a significant upturn in LFP rates has been observed in several developed countries since the beginning of the 2000s, which raises a new issue:

Didier Blanchet belongs to the French National Statistical Institute (INSEE).

Antoine Bozio is associate professor at the École des Hautes Études en Sciences Sociales (School of Advanced Studies in the Social Sciences) (EHESS) and an associate researcher at the Paris School of Economics (PSE).

Corinne Prost is deputy head of the Directorate for Research, Studies and Statistics (DARES) of the French Ministry of Labour.

Muriel Roger is professor of economics at CES Université Paris 1 Panthéon-Sorbonne.

For acknowledgments, sources of research support, and disclosure of the authors' material financial relationships, if any, please see https://www.nber.org/chapters/c14044.ack.

assessing what have been the main contributors to this increase. France is no exception to that. After having reached a very low point at the turn of the century, employment and the LFP rates of French older workers have started moving upward. They have now done so continuously for more than 10 years. This process is expected to go on during the next decades, contributing to the long-run stabilization of French pension expenditures (European Commission 2015; Conseil d'Orientation des Retraites 2015).[1] This reversal is generally presented as a direct consequence of successive pension reforms that, since 1993, have progressively changed requirements for full pension benefits. There is little doubt that these reforms have played a significant role. But their contribution deserves closer examination. For instance, Roger and Walraët (2008) have shown that there is an asymmetry in the impact of pension reforms on older workers' employment: an increase in generosity decreases their employment rate, but the reverse process can be more complex. Moreover, Coile and Levine (2010, 2011) show that the recent crisis has reshaped the approach to the question of older workers' retirement paths. They find that the effect of the crisis on retirement decisions among the least skilled workers, who generally have less-continuous careers than more skilled ones, is mainly due to its impact on the labor market. Older job seekers, with no income and dwindling employment prospects, antici-pate the date on which they will start drawing their pension. Older work-ers' employment also depends on workers' and firms' behaviors before the NRA, both of which are affected by changes in early retirement programs and unemployment insurance. Moreover, some independent socioeconomic factors could have led to increasing labor force attachment even without the help of reforms. These factors deserve exploration as well.

Disentangling the roles of these different explanations is the purpose of the present chapter. Several methods can be used to pursue this objective. In the following, we document the general situation in France over the recent period, exploring in a descriptive way the standard factors inventoried in the economic literature for explaining older workers' employment (Coile 2015). We will also rely on a dynamic microsimulation model (Blanchet et al. 2010) that has been developed and used at the French INSEE since the mid-1990s and whose main purpose is the analysis of pension policies. It is a powerful tool to simulate future changes in retirement behavior linked with changes in pension rules. But it can also be used in a retrospective way, providing counterfactual microsimulations of what retirement behavior would have been in the absence of reforms enacted since 1993. It can thus provide a detailed assessment of how legislation changed past behavior.

Section 4.2 will start by recalling the main aggregate figures for changes in LFP and employment rates over the long period. Section 4.3 will focus on

---

1. Currently representing 14 percent of the GDP, they are planned to remain more or less at this level until the middle of the century despite a context of rapid aging.

general socioeconomic factors. Section 4.4 will present the main legislative or institutional changes that have taken place and theorize which are candidates for explaining the reversal of these rates. Section 4.5 will then try to assess their roles. One first subsection will use available statistics to provide a simple accounting assessment of relative contributions of reduced access to early exit routes and delayed normal retirement. The second subsection will focus on the role of this latter factor using microsimulation. Our short conclusive section will insist on possible interactions between these factors and discuss some more prospective issues.

4.2 The Trend Reversal of Older Workers' Employment Rate

Figures 4.1 and 4.2 display LFP and employment rates for French men and women, derived from the Enquêtes Emploi (French Labour Force Surveys [LFSs]) for three age groups: 55–59, 60–64, and 65–69. They are completed by figure 4.3, which provides the unemployment rate, aggregated over the larger 55–64 age group, compared with the one observed for the whole 15–64 age bracket. The focus in this chapter will be on explaining trends since the early 1990s, but most of our graphs will provide a longer view, generally going back to the mid-1970s.

4.2.1 Men

Let us first concentrate on men. In 1975, LFP had already started to decline in France for male workers older than age 60. The NRA was still equal to 65, but various possibilities for earlier exits had been introduced—

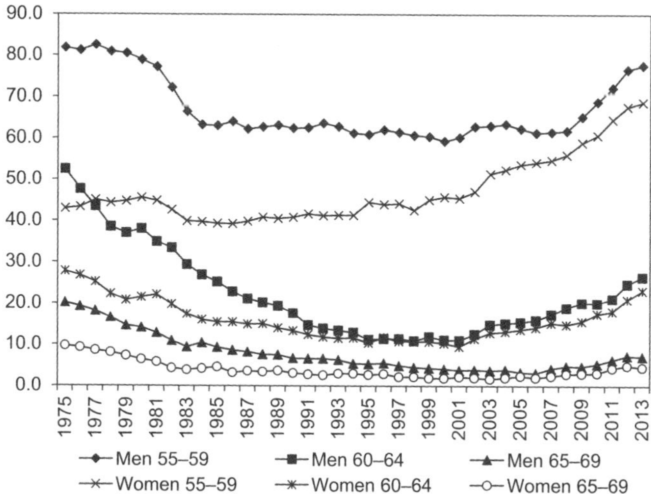

Fig. 4.1   LFP rates between ages 55 and 69 by gender and five-year age groups
Source: French LFS, INSEE.

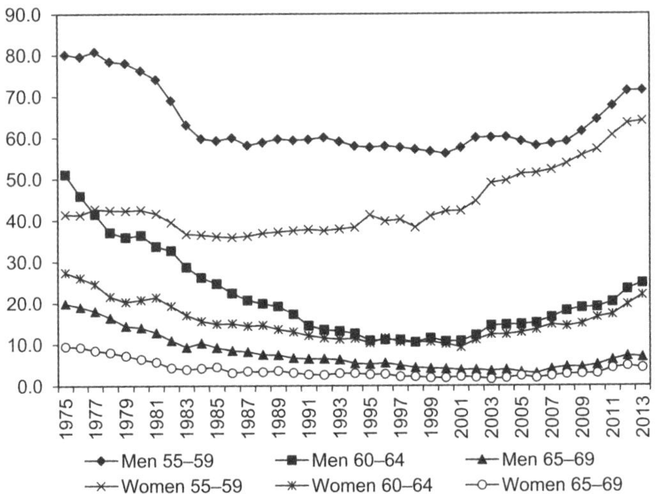

Fig. 4.2   Employment rates between ages 55 and 69 by gender and five-year age groups
Source: French LFS, INSEE.

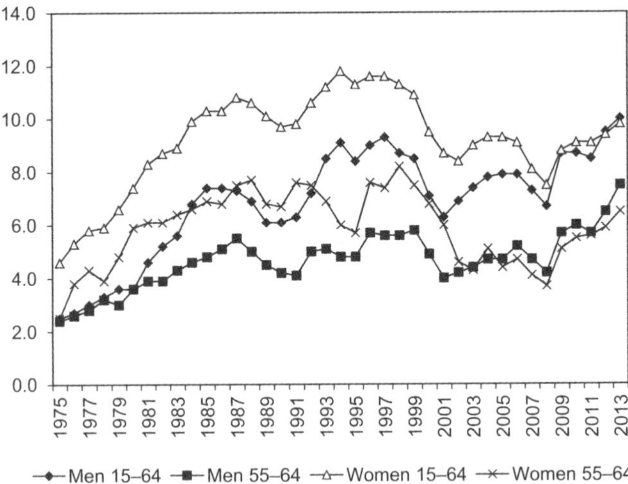

Fig. 4.3   Unemployment rates by gender, 55–64 age group and total population
Source: French LFS, INSEE.

in particular, early retirement schemes for some specific categories of workers in the 60–64 age bracket. As a consequence, about half of men aged 60–64 were already outside the labor market, and the LFP was only 20 percent for men aged 65–69 in 1975. Employment rates were very close to LFP rates, implying very low levels of unemployment: the unemployment rate was only 2 percent in the 55–64 age group, but very low rates prevailed as well for male workers of all ages.

In stark contrast with the already low LFP rates for those older than 60, both the LFP and employment rates in the 55–59 age group still stood at high levels, comparable to those of other Organisation for Economic Co-operation and Development (OECD) countries. This situation changed dramatically at the beginning of the 1980s. While LFP and employment rates for those older than 60 kept declining progressively and did so until the mid-1990s, the same rates for the 55–59 age group went through a short episode of strong decline: both rates lost about 20 percentage points between the late 1970s and the mid-1980s.

Continuing with the case of men, the contrast between progressive changes in the 60–64 age group and more sudden shifts in the 55–59 age group is also observed over the more recent period. After having smoothly reached their minimum values of about 10 percent in the mid-1990s, LFP and employment rates in the 60–64 age group have started reincreasing during the first half of the 2000s and did so in a progressive way that mirrored their previous progressive decline, resulting in a global V-shaped profile over the whole period. In 2014, the LFP rate for men aged 60–64 was back to 27 percent, and their employment rate was back to 23 percent—rates last observed in the early 1980s. The gap between LFP and employment rates is now larger than it was in 1975 due to larger unemployment rates. Even if they remain below average figures for the whole population, unemployment rates for older workers have significantly increased over the period—in particular after the 2008 financial crisis. But it is worth noticing that the recent increase in LFP has not just resulted in transforming pensioners into job seekers as could have been feared ex ante: there has also been a significant increase in the number of men older than age 60 who are actually working.

For the 55–59 age group, the recovery has been more concentrated in time, leading to a profile that is more U shaped than V shaped, with a particularly large time amplitude for the low part of the *U*. The low values reached around 1985 remained almost the same over the following 20–25 years and then had a period of rapid reincrease symmetrical to the 1980–85 episode. Current LFP rates are now back to their pre-1980 values. The movement is a little less pronounced for employment rates, due again to the increase of older workers' unemployment that has taken place in between, but however significant, these employment rates have regained about half of the 20 points they had lost between 1975 and 1985.

4.2.2 Women

On women's side, similar evolutions are under way but are partly hidden by increasing labor market involvement by successive cohorts of women all over their life cycles. LFSs and census data can be combined to provide a very long view of this labor market attachment, measured by LFP rates in

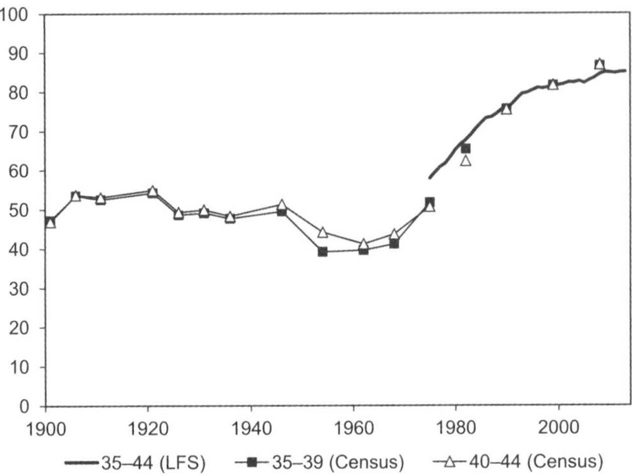

Fig. 4.4   LFP of women aged 35–44 by cohort
Source: Meron and Maruani (2012).

the middle of active lives, between 35 and 44 (Meron and Maruani 2012). Figure 4.4 shows no significant trend all over the first half of the last century, with only a local drop between 1946 and 1954 censuses due to a change in the way of recording activity for women in the agricultural sector. It is at the end of the 1960s that their LFP rate entered a phase of sustained growth, which brought it close to 80 percent at the end of the century. Cohorts concerned by this period of rapid increase are those born from 1930 to 1960—precisely those who started entering retirement ages during the 1990s, pushing up women's LFP and employment rates around the age of 60 all over the recent period.

For the 60–64 age group, this cohort effect is not sufficient to produce a series that qualitatively differs from the male ones. We get the same V-shaped profile as for men, the difference being only the lower levels in 1975: LFP and employment rates of 28 percent and 27 percent, a little more than one-half of those for men in the same period. The profiles for men and women have become progressively closer during the phase of decline until the second half of the 1990s, and both profiles now move upward very close to each other.

The same story can be told for LFP and employment rates in the 65–69 age group, but the situation is very different for the 55–59 age group. Here the cohort effect almost completely offsets the declining branch of the *U*. This is due to the fact that this declining branch has been intrinsically less pronounced for women because of their underrepresentation in industrial sectors where early retirement policies have been used the most intensively during this period. Due to the same cohort effect, entry into the phase of increasing LFP and employment rates in this 55–59 age group occurred ear-

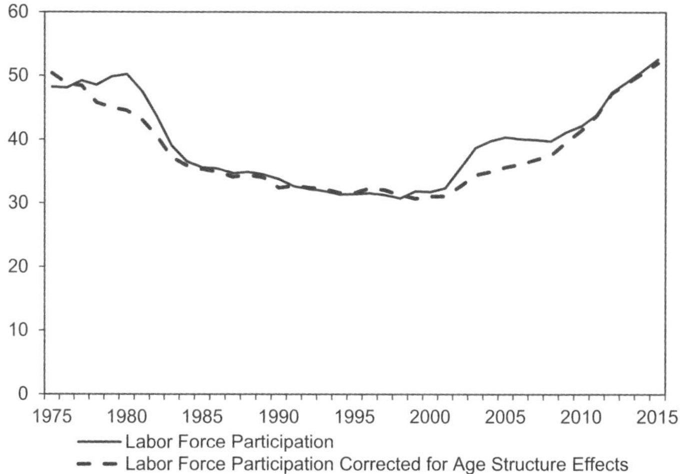

Fig. 4.5   LFP rate for the 55–64 age group, men and women, standard and corrected for age structure effects
Source: French LFS, INSEE, and DARES for the corrected series.

lier than it did for men, as soon as 1990, and the magnitude of the increase has been much more pronounced. Both rates have gained about 30 points between 1990 and now.

4.2.3   Control for Demographic Structure Effects

Combining men and women, figure 4.5 provides a more global vision of trends for the whole 55–64 age group in two versions: one based on standard LFP rates—that is, the total number of active people in the labor force divided by the total size of the age group—and one controlling for demographic structure effects within this age group. This control is necessary to correct for historical accidents that have affected the French age pyramid. In particular, the transition through the 55–64 age group of the very small cohorts born between 1915 and 1919—due to low birth rates during WWI—led to a temporary twist in the internal age structure of this age group that lasted from 1970 to 1985: one first phase with lower numbers than usual in the more active 55–59 age group, then a phase where this underrepresentation moved to the older, less active 60–64 group before returning to status quo.

A similar phenomenon occurred in 2000 with the arrival at age 55 of the first large cohorts born after 1945. It temporarily increased the global LFP beyond its normal trajectory, a gap that took 10 years to correct itself. The alternative LFP rate that corrects for these perturbations is more informative of real behaviors and confirms the general message, albeit with different timing. About half of the men and women in the 55–64 age group were working or seeking employment in 1975; this proportion progressively dropped down to about 30 percent during the 1990s and is now back to 50 percent, even if this target has been reached a little later than requested in the 2010 Lisbon agenda.

The question now is to sort out which factors have contributed the most significantly to this increase.

4.3   Could General Socioeconomic Factors Explain the Reversal?

Even without reforms, several factors could have contributed to the recent increase in the global LFP of the 55–64 group. Increasing women's attachment to the labor market is one of these, and it has already been exposed in the previous section. It will have to be kept in mind in subsequent analysis.[2] Other commonly cited factors are better health, higher education levels, or changes in labor market conditions. We successively explore the evolutions of these factors over the past decades to assess their potential contributions to explaining the U- or V-shaped profiles of the LFP and employment rates.

4.3.1   Health Changes

Health status is one factor that affects retirement decisions. Standard models of retirement behavior explain retirement decisions by the interaction between financial incentives and a small set of preference parameters, including the so-called preference for leisure: health status is an implicit component of this latter parameter, and an increasing body of literature tries to make its role more explicit. Survey data provide very rich sets of objective and subjective health indicators that can be used for assessing this role at the micro level (e.g., Behaghel, Blanchet, and Roger 2016). This contribution of health is more difficult to assess from a historical macro perspective due to the lack of homogenous aggregate time series: diagnosis and perception of health problems evolve over time and questionnaires are not always homogenous across successive surveys. All this hinders long-term comparability.

One solution to this comparability problem is to use mortality data as a proxy for morbidity. The hypothesis that mortality changes are a good proxy for morbidity changes is, of course, highly debatable: survival probabilities may increase without any significant improvement in health status.

2. It may also have had some spillover effects on men's retirement behavior, if we assume that the labor market position of one's spouse plays a role in retirement decisions (Schirle 2008). This chapter does not attempt to quantify this spillover effect, however. In the French case, Sédillot and Walraët (2002) showed that women's decisions in the labor market are indeed influenced by their spouse's status but that men are less sensitive to the situation of their wives as far as retirement decisions are concerned, suggesting that the contribution of this factor would have been, at best, minor.

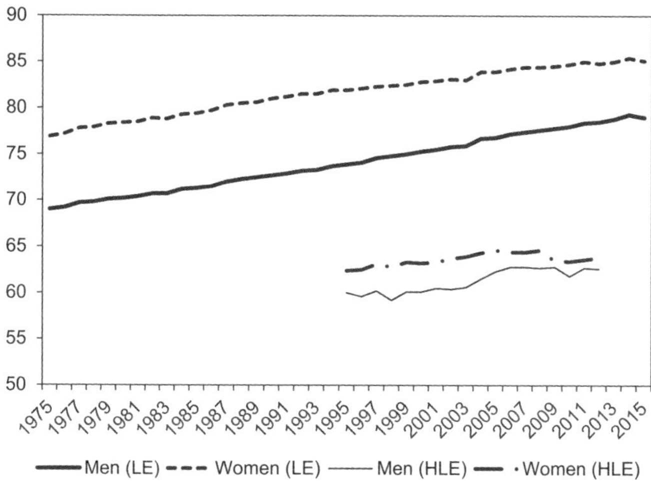

Fig. 4.6   Life expectancy and healthy life expectancy at birth
Source: INSEE.

But mortality series have the advantage of being homogenous by nature and easily available. Moreover, mortality can be in itself a direct determinant of retirement behavior: it is very likely that preference for early retirement is influenced by expected mortality, as people who anticipate higher mortality risks may be more likely to retire earlier if they want to spend a sufficient number of years as retirees. Lower expected mortality may conversely push retirement age upward, especially if people anticipate their consumption needs over increasingly long retirement periods.

Yet changes in life expectancy (LE) do not appear to be a plausible candidate for explaining the U-turn in observed retirement behavior. It is all over the last decades that LE has considerably increased in France: LE at birth went up from 69 years for men and 76.9 years for women in 1975 to 79 and 85.1 years, respectively, in 2015 with no acceleration over the recent years (figure 4.6).

The message is the same if we look at an indicator that corrects global LE for changes in health status. This indicator of healthy life expectancy (HLE) is a more recent concept available only for the last two decades. For this second indicator, curves are flatter, but the message is otherwise the same as with general LE, as the indicator shows no upward inflection in the 2000s that could account for increasing LFP rates over the same period. The small change that has been observed around 2009 has rather gone in the opposite direction. This message is also reinforced by Blanchet et al. (2016), who describe long-run evolutions of health in France using an indicator of self-assessed health (SAH) over the last 20 years. As for HLE, they do not observe any improvement in the SAH over the period.[3] Hence it is difficult to credit health changes for the reversal of the LFP trend from the mid-1990s.

4.3.2   Labor Market Conditions

Skills and wage levels are another set of socioeconomic factors that could account for the recent reversal. As for health, they can impact the supply side of the labor market. Higher skills are generally associated with jobs with richer contents, larger individual control, and fewer physical demands. These nonmonetary incentives to remain in the labor force are reinforced by the fact that these jobs also benefit from higher wage levels. In pension systems where replacement rates are generally decreasing with wage levels, this provides an additional motivation to later retirement.

But the same factors also act on the demand side of the labor market. Here it is the gap between wages or labor costs and productivity that potentially matters, productivity being dependent on skills. Wage levels and labor costs of older workers have indeed been a long-lasting concern in the economic literature. Aubert and Crépon (2003) underline the relevance of labor demand when trying to understand the participation rate of people aged older than 50. Among others, older workers' wages may be too high relative to their productivity if wages remain stable even in the case of skill obsolescence. This can induce unemployment or even exits from the labor market if employment prospects are too bad. France is one of the countries where this issue can be of particular importance due to a strong apparent wage premium for older workers.

As far as skills are concerned, figure 4.7 shows the shares of blue-collar workers among employed men and women aged 55–64. A local U-turn is observed for men in the mid-2000s, and it is relatively simultaneous with the one observed in LFP rates. But the relationship, if any, is hard to interpret, as it mixes causality in both directions. Exogenous changes in the global share of blue-collar workers may have induced higher or lower rates of exits from the labor force from one period to the next. But changes in exit rates have also shaped the composition of the employed population by skills. Facilitation of early exits has often benefited more than proportionately the blue-collar workers, reducing their share in global employment. Access to these early exit routes has been substantially reduced over the recent period, as will be shown in more details later, and may have led to a higher retention of blue-collar workers in old-age employment.

Similar problems of interpretation arise when interpreting wage data. Figure 4.8 displays the ratio between the average wage of full-time workers in the 51–60 age group to the same average wage in the entire population of

---

3. The lack of clear improvement in self-assessed health over time raises the issue of potential declaration biases. Whatever the reason for the flat trend, we can't use this information to document the reversal in LFP.

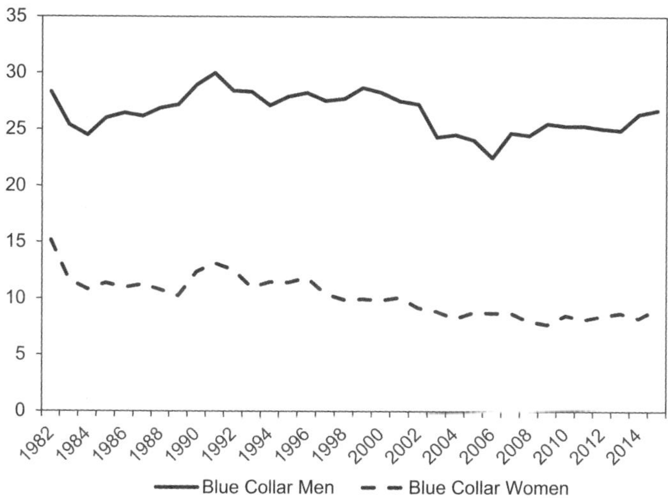

Fig. 4.7   Share of people aged 55–64 in blue-collar jobs
Source: French LFS, INSEE.

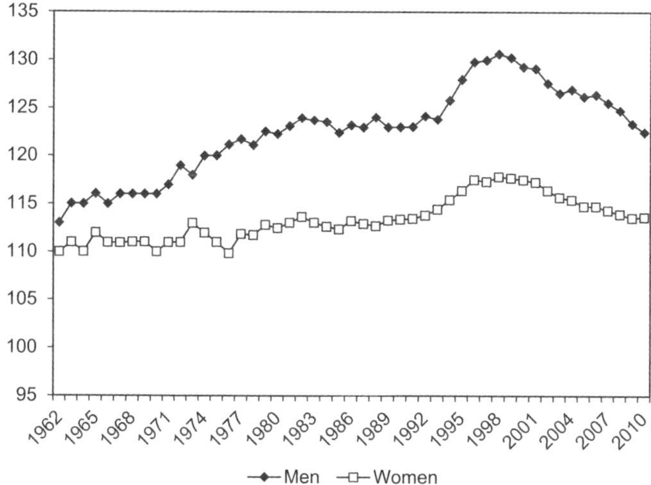

Fig. 4.8   A wage premium for older workers
Source: Annual Declaration of Social Data, INSEE.

full-time workers. Until 2000, this graph confirms the existence of a strong
and increasing apparent wage premium for older workers that reached a high
point at the end of the 1990s followed by a period of substantial decline. The
phenomenon is particularly important for men but has also been observed
for women. Here it is both the timing and the amplitude of the evolutions
that may appear consistent with a causal lecture running from wage rates to

LFP: an increasing wage premium would have been a handicap to increasing LFP rates until 2000, and wage moderation for senior workers after 2000 would have helped restimulate demand for these workers. However, the circularity problem reappears. Wages are observed only for the share of the older population that is actually at work. Declining LFP rates until the end of the 1990s have increased mean wages observed for senior workers because the less-skilled populations have been the most intensively affected by the phenomenon. The apparent wage premium would have been still higher if we had extended the age bracket above the age of 60: in the 60 and older age group, it is almost exclusively highly skilled white-collar workers who were still in the labor force when the LFP reached the low point of 10 percent shown on figure 4.2. The reversal of this wage premium can be a consequence as well as a cause of the reversal of LFP rates that followed this low point.[4]

Some previous studies also tend to relativize the idea that wage levels for French senior workers are a major causal factor explaining their low employment rates. In particular, following Hellerstein, Neumark, and Troske (1999) and Crépon, Deniau, and Perez-Duarte (2003), Aubert and Crépon (2003) have tested the equality between wage and productivity for older workers in France during a part of the period we analyze (firms are observed from 1994 to 2000). These authors estimate a profile of productivity that increases until age 40 and then remains stable. The age-productivity profile is similar to the age-labor cost profile, which means that the hypothesis that the lower employability of older workers can be explained by a significant wage-productivity gap seems rejected, at least before age 55. After this age, a slight productivity decrease occurs, but this decrease is not statistically significant. For older workers still employed, the wage-productivity gap does not seem to be a concern. Yet the full interpretation of the wage-employment nexus for older workers remains an open issue: one cannot rule out that nonemployed older workers are not employed because of the gap that exists between their reservation wage and their productivity level.

4.3.3   Education

What if we look at education levels? This cannot settle the debate about the contribution of the wage-productivity gap to low employment rates, but a separate look at education levels is interesting on its own. This variable has the advantage of being observable for the whole population, not only for people who are still employed. And its role is of particular importance in a context of rapid technological change. Following Aubert, Caroli, and

---

4. The additional bump from 1996 to 2006 might also have resulted from the same kind of demographic effect that was observed in figure 4.5 for LFP rates: the arrival of the first baby boom cohorts at age 50 in 1996 may have temporarily pushed up average wages for the whole age group.

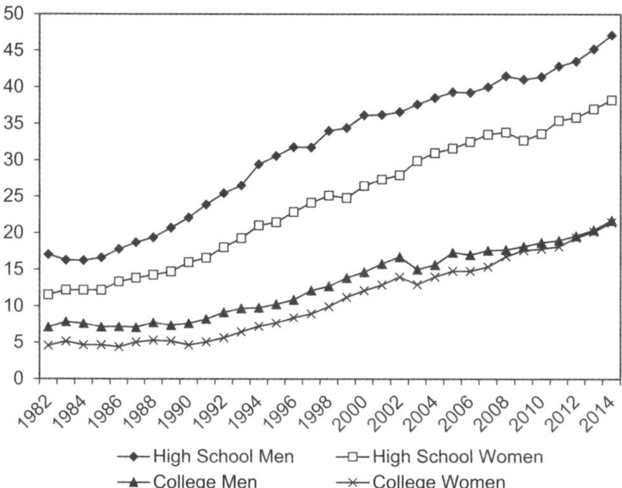

Fig. 4.9   Share of people aged 55–64 with high school or college degrees
Source: French LFS, INSEE.

Roger (2006), a large amount of literature shows the existence of an anti-age bias associated with IT and innovative workplace practices. In a context of rapid technological changes, this bias probably contributed to the low level of employment of older workers. An issue raised by these results has to do with the transitory or permanent nature of this phenomenon. The implication for older workers' employment rates is very different depending on whether the bias is limited to the time needed by older workers to learn about the new environment or whether it is a long-term consequence of the lower education levels of the older cohorts. In the latter case, an increase in education level at younger ages induces higher employment rates around 40 years later. In the case of the US, Blau and Goodstein (2010) and Banerjee and Blau (2016) show that changes in the educational composition of the older male population contributed to the increase of the older workers employment rates.

In France, the compulsory schooling age increased from 13 to 14 in 1936 and from 14 to 16 in 1959. We observe thus an increasingly educated population over the recent period (see figure 4.9). The increase in the education level is a good candidate to explain the increase in the employment level of older workers—and not only because it allows easier adaptations to technological or organizational innovations or because such workers face less adverse work conditions. Another direct mechanism is that access to a full-rate pension depends on the number of years of contribution; hence a more-educated workforce faces more incentives to retire later. This will be incorporated in the microsimulation model used in the last section. But what education is likely to explain is only a regular trend, not the U-turn that has been observed in the early 2000s. Explaining such a U-turn requires looking at other exogenous factors for which similar U-turns have occurred over this time period. This is the case for general pension rules that have been reformed several times over this period and also for rules governing other ways to leave the labor market before the minimum retirement age of 60.

4.4   Institutional Changes

We document in this section the numerous reforms that have affected pension arrangements in France and other schemes like early retirement or unemployment benefits.

4.4.1   Pension Reforms

The French pension system is relatively complex, and we do not pretend here to provide a systematic overview (more details were provided in previous volumes; see Blanchet and Pelé 1999).

Until the 1980s, all pension reforms in France aimed at increasing benefit levels and favoring early retirement. The last significant reform of this kind was implemented in 1983, with the so-called lowering of the retirement age to 60. The reform, in reality, did not change the French early retirement age (ERA), which was already equal to 60 before the reform; what it did was offer higher benefit levels at this age under the additional condition of having reached 37.5 years of contribution. Given that most male workers were fulfilling this condition (but not all female workers), it essentially offered full-rate benefits at this ERA.

Then, starting in the 1990s, the French pension system underwent a series of new reforms going in the opposite direction by reducing benefits or increasing ages at benefit claiming. The major reforms took place in 1993, 2003, 2010, and 2014.

The 1993 reform affected incentives to retire for private-sector workers in two ways. The first instrument has been the reduction of pension levels at the full rate: instead of being computed on the 10 best years of one's career, the average of past earnings used for the benefit formula has been progressively computed on a longer period—up to 25 years for people born 1948 or after. This change has been coupled with the application of a less-generous revalorization rule for these past earnings, replacing the reevaluation according to past wage growth with a reevaluation based on past inflation only. The second instrument has been a strengthening of the conditions required to get the full pension: it has been progressively increased from 37.5 to 40 years by one-quarter each year from cohort 1933 to cohort 1943.

The 2003 reform extended the 1993 reform in several directions. The first one has been toward public-sector employees. For them, the condition for a full-rate pension had remained at its pre-1993 value of 37.5 years of contribution, and they only incurred a small penalty for retiring before reaching that contribution period, the penalty automatically resulting from the proportionality between the pension level and the number of years of contribution. As a first step, the 2003 reform changed this length-of-career condition for these public-sector employees, raising it to 40 years, and it introduced a penalty of −5 percent per missing year of contribution. The penalty applying to private-sector employees was symmetrically aligned on this new value of 5 percent, as its initial level of 10 percent was much stronger than required for actuarial neutrality. The condition for obtaining the full rate was then made more stringent for both categories of workers: starting in 2008, the contribution period has been increased from 40 to 41.5 years, and the reform introduced a mechanism linking further increases of this parameter to changes in LE. Symmetrically to the move toward actuarial and homogenous penalization of early exits, the reform also introduced a new bonus for years of postponement beyond the full rate, initially equal to 3 percent and then further increased to 5 percent per year of postponement. Last and opposite to the general trend toward later retirement, the reform opened new possibilities for early retirement through the pension scheme itself (and not through separate early retirement schemes), under the label of "long career rules." However, this was limited to a very targeted population: workers who had started working (and contributing) very early, at ages 14, 15, or 16. They were offered the possibility to retire with the full rate as soon as age 56, 57, or 58, depending on additional conditions on contribution length.

This 2003 reform had, however, still ignored some specific categories of public-sector employees, those of large public firms benefiting from "special schemes" (railways, public transportation, and gas and electricity). These schemes were aligned on common rules in 2007 (contribution length, penalty for early retirement, etc.) even if pay compensation had to be offered to soothe opposition to this change.

The 2010 reform then affected all categories of workers from the public and private sectors. It consisted of an increase in the ERA and the "unconditional" full-rate age (UFRA), which gives access to a full-rate pension no matter the length of the contribution rate, by two years each. Put in other words, it shifted the age bracket within which people are expected to choose their retirement age from 60–65 to 62–67. For public-sector workers who still benefited from different reference ages (e.g., policemen, prison officers, or nurses), the increase was similar, with the ERA shifted from 55 to 57 and the UFRA from 60 to 62. At the same time, mandatory retirement rules—allowing employers to mandate that employees retire as soon as they reached the full rate—were relaxed and postponed to the age of 70.

In 2014, a last pension reform was introduced, which strengthened again the condition for full-rate benefits, and increased the contribution period from 41.5 years to 43 years. At the same time, "long career rules" were extended to include workers who started to work before age 20.

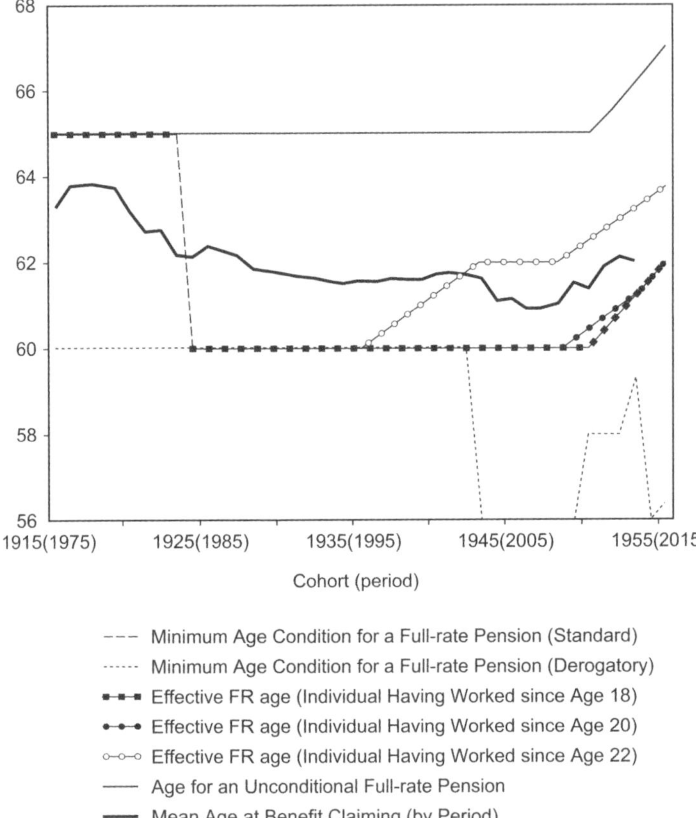

Fig. 4.10   Age indicators summarizing retirement rules in the general regime

All of this shows that it is very difficult to summarize retirement-age policies with a simple indicator. We rather propose several of them in figure 4.10:

- six indicators computed by cohort
  - the minimum age requested to get a full-rate pension, excluding derogatory situations
  - the same age, including all derogatory possibilities and possibilities offered by "carrières longues," corresponding to an extreme version of the notion of ERA
  - the effective full-rate age (FRA) for three illustrative ages at entry in the labor market (18, 20, or 22), assuming continuous careers afterward
  - the UFRA—that is, the one that applies to people with short careers

- one indicator computed by period, the effective age at benefit claiming that is assumed to be a good proxy of the age at which people reach the full rate in practice

Each of these indicators brings its piece of information, yet none of them is fully sufficient to offer a satisfactory picture of how retirement conditions have evolved over the period.

Using the age at which the unconditional full rate is attained gives an obviously distorted image of what retirement conditions have been or are: this age has never been below 65 and has started to increase recently and is now equal to 67; it is relevant only for people with short careers—mostly women—and not really representative of the real possibilities offered to the majority of the population.

More adequate is the age at which a full-rate pension starts being possible, excluding derogations. This age declined from 65 to 60 in 1984 and has recently increased to 62 after the 2010 reform. It therefore captures the kind of U shape we want to explain. It does so, however, in an overly simplistic way.

- It first ignores the fact that a full-rate pension was already offered unconditionally to some categories of workers before 1984. Of course, we can choose to incorporate these possibilities, but this leads to the extreme version of the ERA that is still less adequate: this indicator displays no change at all in 1984. Pushed to the limit of also introducing the very derogatory "carrières longues," it leads to the message that the 2003 reform has lowered the ERA, which is indeed true but only for a very small fraction of the population.
- Second and more important, this indicator ignores the contribution of changes in the career-length condition, which plays a central role in the French system and has been the instrument successively privileged by the 1993, 2003, and 2014 reforms.

What we need is an indicator that incorporates the impact of these latter reforms. This is the case with the FRA, which, in the French case, may seem the more in line with the notion of a NRA, but the problem is that this age is not a single age common to all individuals: it is highly dependent on individual characteristics, as shown by the three examples of people having started their working lives at 18, 20, or 22. Using effective ages at benefit claiming is one possible way to summarize this variability, the last one that is explored on the graph. It displays the expected reincrease at the end of the period. But this indicator is not fully satisfactory either, as it is more an indicator of how people reacted to age conditions rather than a pure indicator of how these age conditions did change. Moreover, being an average age over the flow of benefit claimers, it may send short-time messages that are difficult to interpret. Such is the case here concerning the decline observed just after the 2003 reform. This decline offers a distorted image of how the "carrières longues" system has impacted behavior. A temporary over-representation of early exits in yearly flows mechanically occurred just after the introduction of the system, pushing downward the average age of these years' claimers. This bias has been exacerbated if the reform simultaneously had the strongest postponement effects among people who already used to retire late. In this case, these people have found themselves temporarily underrepresented in the current flow of benefit claimers, still increasing the short-term downward bias of the indicator.

4.4.2   Other Schemes: Early Retirement Schemes, Unemployment, Disability

We must add possibilities offered by other routes of exit from the labor force to this variety of age indicators applying to normal pensions: (a) early retirement schemes (préretraites), or state-sponsored schemes offering transitory benefits before access to normal retirement; (b) unemployment insurance; and (c) the invalidity/disability route, which is relatively marginal in the French case.

Early retirement schemes appeared in France in 1963 with the ASFNE (Allocation spéciale du Fond National pour l'Emploi) for workers older than 60. This program had a replacement rate of 80 to 90 percent of the previous wage. In the 1970s, a new early retirement program was settled by the UNEDIC (the Unemployment Insurance) to provide early retirement benefits (garantie de ressources, or GR) on a large scale. The GR, initially limited to layoffs in 1972, was extended in 1977 to people who voluntarily left their job (Garantie de ressources démission, or GRD). It was targeted at the 60–65 age group. The replacement rate was 70 percent of the previous gross wage, thus higher than a full-rate pension. In the beginning of the 1980s, early retirement programs were extended to wage earners older than 55 with a change in the ASFNE rules and the creation of the CSPRD (Contrat de Solidarité préretraite démission), a scheme that offered a replacement rate of 70 percent to wage earners with more than 10 years of contribution who had resigned. In the meantime, the NRA had been decreased to 60 in 1983. With this decrease, early retirement schemes were expected to play no more than a marginal role. The GRD was gradually suppressed and the ASFNE benefits reduced. This scheme was restricted to the wage earners older than 57 in 1994 and definitively suppressed in 2011. Alternative early retirement programs with much narrower targets were created in the 1990s to replace the previous schemes. The Allocation de remplacement pour l'emploi (ARPE) and Congé de fin d'activité (CFA) schemes created in the mid-1990s were targeted to wage earners older than 58. Employers using the programs had to replace early retirees with younger workers under age

26. The ARPE and the CFA were suppressed in 2003. They were replaced in early 2000 by the Cessation d'activité de certains travailleurs salariés (CATS) and the Cessation anticipée d'activité des travailleurs de l'amiante (CAATA), which were even more focused. The CATS scheme is targeted to workers who had especially difficult working conditions (at least 15 years on an assembly line or with night work). The CAATA scheme targets workers exposed to asbestos.

With the reduction of early retirement schemes, the main new evolution favoring early exits during the 20 years after the mid-1980s has been the expansion of the unemployment insurance route. This essentially took place through the creation of the DRE (Dispense de recherche d'emploi), which was introduced in 1984. In the 1990s, DRE became numerically more important than early retirees. The system exempts unemployed people from an active job search past a certain age—55 at its creation. There were many changes, mostly decreases, in the eligibility age between 1984 and 2009 before a gradual increase to 60 in 2011. The DRE program was terminated in 2012 without changing unemployment benefits for older workers. The DRE did not give additional unemployment benefits. Yet there always were specific rules that give longer benefit entitlements to older unemployed people. One of these rules is that under certain conditions, older unemployed people are entitled to constant benefits until they become entitled to a full-rate pension. Special solidarity programs for unemployed people older than 50 also exist, but they are less generous.

Use of disability benefits in France is quantitatively limited (Behaghel et al. 2012). The French pattern of early transitions out of employment is basically explained by the low age of "normal" retirement and the importance of transitions through unemployment insurance and early retirement schemes before access to normal retirement. The progressive shift of the minimum retirement age from 60 to 62 and the parallel shift from 65 to 67 for the age at which a full-rate pension can be obtained, whatever the length of one's career, may change this situation. Several paths to disability have been open in France since the 1970s without many changes in the legislation except those regarding the level of disability required to be eligible. The main features of the system are the following: Before 60, the *pension d'invalidité* is for individuals with a disability rate over two-thirds. After 60, people may be eligible either if they are already benefiting from invalidity insurance before that age (retraite pour ex-invalides) or if they are declared incapable of work at that age, even if they were not previously benefiting from invalidity benefits (retraite pour inaptitude). They are eligible to the *pension d'inaptitude* for a disability rate over one half. Since 2010, a third path is open for people with difficult work conditions during their career (retraite pour penibilité). These people are treated as full-rate pensioners even if they do not fulfill conditions for the full rate as soon as they turn 60.

4.5   Can Reforms Explain the Trend Reversal? Two Approaches

Qualitatively, all the reforms described in the previous section are good candidates for explaining the V- or U-turns of employment and the LFP rates in the 55–64 age group. A quantitative assessment of their contribution is more difficult, however. The main difficulty in relating LFP of older workers to institutional changes comes from the fact that reforms have happened at the same time in all schemes (pension, unemployment insurance, and early retirement schemes), with numerous changes sometimes affecting different age groups or following formulas that are relatively complex, such as those stemming from the interaction between age and career-length conditions. We will consider two complementary ways to tackle these difficulties.

The first one will be purely descriptive, based on a count of the number of people in the different statuses at each period. In order to clarify the discussion, this will be done looking at the 55–59 and the 60–64 age groups separately. This approach will cover both regular retirement and other exit routes. The limit is that it does not fully identify how far these changes are the pure results of reforms or of other factors. The second one will be more analytical, based on counterfactual simulations of no-reform or partial-reform scenarios, but it will be limited to the case of regular retirement.

4.5.1   First Approach: Counting Numbers in the Various Statuses

For the 60–64 age group, we have documented a continuous drop in LFP from the early 1970s to the mid-1990s. These changes have been partly the result of the shift of the NRA from 65 to 60 that took place in 1983. To be precise, it is not a general access to full-pension entitlements at age 60 that has been introduced at this time—this access has been allowed only to people reaching age 60 with a total of at least 37.5 years of contributions to social security. Yet this condition was not really binding for cohorts that had started working on the average much before the age of 20: at that time, it indeed corresponded to a de facto move of men's NRA to 60.

Figures 4.1 and 4.2 have shown that this did not translate in a fully concurrent shift of LFP rates. No significant break occurred. LFP and employment rates had started to decline well before, due to the fact that many possibilities to leave before 65 were already available before 1984. Early retirement schemes for the 60–64 age group had started to develop as soon as 1965 in France and derogations to the 65 rule already existed within the normal pension system itself.

Figure 4.11 presents the share of the population in the main regular pension schemes of the private sector (régime general and CNAV) or in one of the multiple nonregular early retirement schemes, including special schemes from the unemployment insurance. Panel A shows these trends for the 60–64 age group. One can see very clearly how the 1983 reform substituted and amplified a trend led by the increase in early retirement schemes. This trend

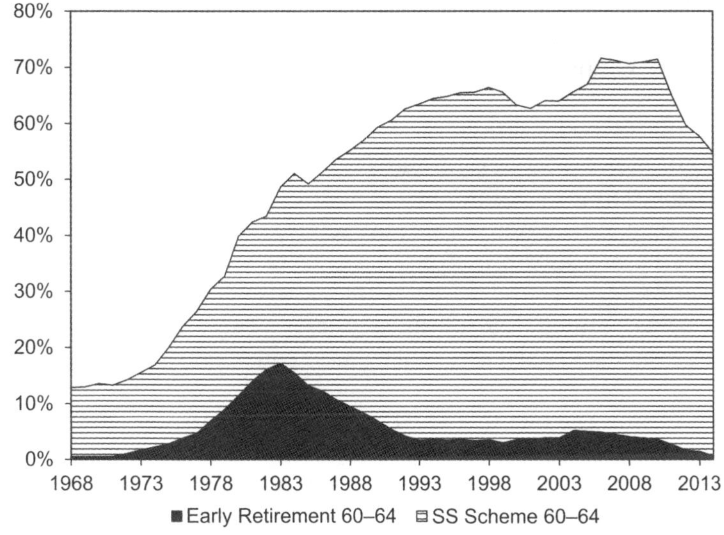

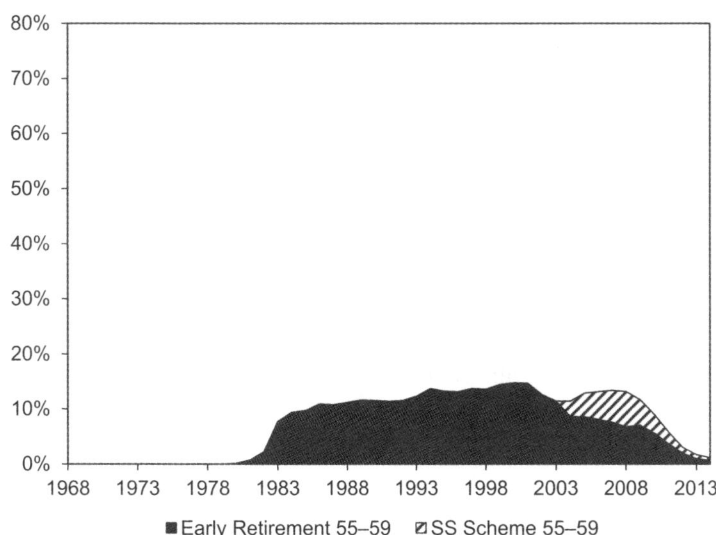

Fig. 4.11 Share of the population in retirement (private sector) or early retirement schemes

Sources: DARES for early retirement schemes, CNAV for main social security scheme, INSEE for population by age.

matches therefore the decline in LFP relatively well until 1994. The reversal in the trend, which can be documented from the early 2000s, is harder to spot, and it occurs mostly at the very end of the period with the 2010 reform, where the LFP changes and the numbers in retirement do match more clearly.[5]

For the 55–59 age group, the LFP dropped quickly between 1980 and 1984 but increased quickly from 2008 onward. This pattern is also more pronounced for men than women. Pundits often credit pension reforms for this reversal in LFP, sometimes putting forward the distance to retirement effect—that is, a "horizon effect" according to which all labor market transitions prior normal retirement move in line with the age of access to normal retirement (Hairault, Langot, and Sopraseuth 2006). Figure 4.11 shows that the LFP changes match very well with the end of early retirement schemes, once both unemployment insurance and social security schemes are taken into account. The fact that early retirement policies were more than proportionately targeted toward declining industrial sectors with lower rates of female workers helps explain why these schemes do match more closely the change in trends for male LFP.

4.5.2 Changes in Regular Retirement Behavior: A Microsimulation Approach

Descriptive information on how the split of the population between employment, retirement, early retirement, or unemployment has changed is sufficient to show that changes in early exit routes and normal retirement have both played significant roles in explaining the upward move of employment rates, with a prominent role for the first factor in the 55–59 age group and for the second one in the 60–64 age group.

We shall now focus on normal retirement and this latter group. In this case, we have the possibility of going further into the details of how the reforms produced the effects that have been observed, at least if we accept the idea that French retirement behavior remains strongly driven by changes in rules allowing access to a full-rate pension. There is, of course, some dispersion in behavior around this reference retirement age. It is even likely that this dispersion has increased, as the 2003 reform explicitly chose to encourage freedom of choice around this reference age through reduced financial penalties for anticipated exits and the introduction of quasi-actuarial bonuses for postponed departures. Yet this age remains both a social norm and the age at which a majority of people claim pension benefits. Exploring how reforms have changed the age at which people reach this full rate provides a good proxy for how they have increased effective retirement ages.

The only difficulty of this evaluation is that the age of access to this full

---

5. Figure 4.10 concerns only the private sector, but the 2003 reform also affected public-sector workers.

rate is highly dependent on individual characteristics. We need to know the number of years that the person has effectively contributed to any of the existing pension regimes when reaching age 60—hence a full knowledge of his or her employment biography. We also need information on some other characteristics that lead to add-on factors of the number of years effectively contributed: years covered by unemployment insurance are added to years of effective work, and in the case of women, having raised children also entitles them to additional pseudoyears of contribution.

Assessing the interaction between these individual factors and pension legislation can be done using a microsimulation model. Several pension models of this kind now exist in France, applying to either the whole population or some regime-specific population. The one we shall use here, the model Destinie, is of the first kind. It started being developed at the French INSEE in the early 1990s to provide simulations of how the 1993 reform was likely to impact retirement behavior in the short or long run—more specifically, the effect of progressively increasing the number of years for getting a full-rate pension from 37.5 to 40. This clearly called for a model that could predict the full distribution of the number of years of contribution reached at 60 for cohorts that would be affected by the reform, a task that is obviously easier to be performed by a dynamic microsimulation of careers at the individual level than by more aggregate models.

The version of the model that we use here (Destinie 2) was developed during the 2000s. As with any dynamic microsimulation model, it starts with an individual data set for its base year, the dynamic microsimulation basically consisting of "aging" this individual data set year after year by randomly drawing individual events that affect its members. This initial database is taken from the 2009 French wealth survey (enquête Patrimoine). Initial retirement status in this data set is known, and a standard microsimulation model would take this initial status as a given, limiting itself to generating new entries to retirement. This usual way of working would forbid simulating consequences of reforms that took place before 2009. But one characteristic of the model is that it ignores the information on pension status that is known from the survey; this status is instead reimputed based on pension entitlements derived from past careers observed in the sample. The reason for this reimputation is primarily technical: by using the same pension simulators for projecting pensions and reconstructing initial pension status and pension levels, the model avoids flow-stock discontinuities that would artificially bias its behavior at the beginning of the projection period. Here this feature will be used for another purpose. Since they are reimputed, initial situations can be set under counterfactual retrospective rules differing from actual rules. It is in that way that one can rewrite the recent history neutralizing part or the whole of legislative changes that have taken place since 1990.

The exercise is, of course, not without its limits. The model does not allow

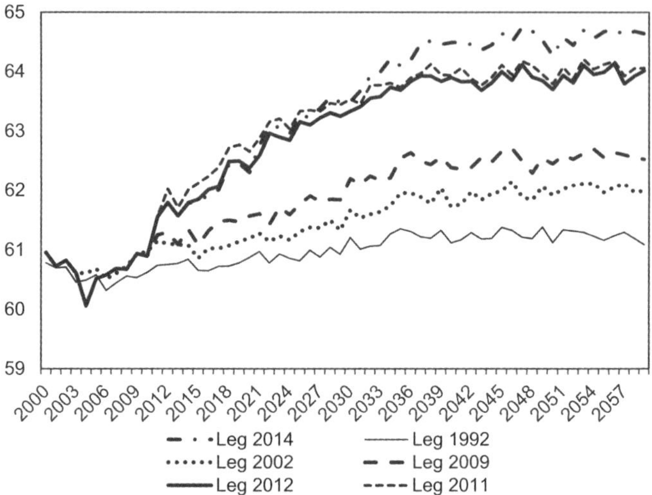

Fig. 4.12   Contributions of successive reforms to ages at benefit claiming
Source: Destinie 2 microsimulation model, INSEE.

reconstructing counterfactual behavior very far away in the past. The reason is that the reconstitution is affected by a bias that becomes increasingly important as time goes by. Some of the people who retire in the early 2000s die before the end of the decade. They are not observed in the initial database that is used by the model, and these people are more likely to be less-skilled people whose retirement ages were lower. This leads us to stop the backward reconstitution to 2000 just before the upturn we wished to reproduce. And the indicator produced is not the full counterfactual LFP rates for either the 55–59 or 60–64 age groups, as this would have also requested a reconstitution of past counterfactual labor-market behavior before normal retirement, which is not allowed by the current structure of the model. What we provide is less ambitious; it is just an evaluation of the mean age of yearly reconstructed flows of new retirees. This reconstitution is nevertheless informative. Results are given in figure 4.12.

First, even without reforms, changes in the composition of the population would have already accounted for a slight increase in retirement ages. This corresponds to the "leg 1992" line on the graph that shows what would have been observed if the 1992 rules had been maintained forever. What this scenario measures is essentially the impact of higher education levels from one cohort to the next. It would have contributed to an increase by a little less than one half year between 2004 and today and still another half year in projection until the final horizon of 2060. What matters here is the interaction with the initial condition of totalizing 37.5 years of contribution for getting the full rate. An increasing share of the population would have fallen short of this condition at the age of 60 and would have had to wait a few more quarters or years before retiring, even without reforms.

The impacts of the 1993 and 2003 reforms are shown by moving to the "leg 2002" and "leg 2009" lines—that is, the counterfactual scenarios simulated under rules that prevailed, respectively, just before the 2003 and 2010 reforms. These two 1993 and 2003 reforms did not change the minimum retirement age, left equal to 60; they changed only the conditions on the number of years of contributions, raised to 40 years for people born in 1943, in the case of the 1993 reform, and increased further to 41.5 years in the case of the 2003 reform. In 2016, both reforms had added about 0.4 year to the average age at benefit claiming, or 0.8 year on the whole. The impact does not limit to this. The interaction with increasing education levels generates a trend that goes on until the mid-2030s, where the global gain is of a little more than one year. While significant, the impact remains very progressive.

The consequences of the 2010 reform are very different: by raising the minimum age from 60 to 62 within only a few years and with only limited derogations, the reform has an immediate and strong impact on ages at benefit claiming, measured by the gap between the "leg 2011" and the "leg 2009" lines—nearly as much as the two previous reforms over the first five years of implementation.

Further legislative changes have been more limited. First, decisions made in 2012 aimed at moderating rather than amplifying the consequences of the 2010 reform. Like the 1993 and 2003 reforms, the last reform, implemented in 2014, affected the condition on the length of the contribution period, raised to 43 years for the 1970 cohort. The impact should not be negligible in the long run, adding still one half year to the long-run level and bringing it very close to 65 years, but by construction, the impact of this reform has been negligible at this stage.

One interesting complement to such simulations would be the confrontation with observed behaviors and, more specifically, with empirical studies treating whole or part of these past reforms as natural quasi experiments. Empirical evaluations of this kind have been performed by Bozio (2011) for the 1993 reform and by Baraton, Beffy, and Fougère (2011) for the consequences of the 2003 reform on a specific category of public-sector employees: teachers in secondary schooling. Both studies confirm a tendency of retirement behaviors to move in accordance with changes in age at access to the full rate. But applying standard ex post evaluation techniques to these reforms is difficult because of their progressivity and the fact that they have affected only limited numbers of selected individuals. The 2010 reform offers a framework that is much more convenient for the application of these techniques, since it created a strong discontinuity in retirement rules for quasi-adjacent cohorts. Some explorations of this new reform have been performed (Dubois and Koubi 2017; Rabaté and Rochut 2017). They also confirm the impacts of this reform close to the ones that we have micro-simulated. They also show that, though part of the impact has consisted of larger numbers of people moving to unemployment, another significant part has consisted in effective employment.

4.6   Conclusion

France has recently experienced a clear reversal in the trend of older workers' LFP and employment rates. After decades of continuous decline in the 1970s and 1980s, both rates have started to increase in the late 1990s and are now back to levels unseen since the early 1980s. Structural factors like better health, an increase in female LFP, or higher education levels may have played in the background but are unlikely to explain this reversal. The most likely explanations come from the many institutional reforms implemented since the 1990s; reduced access to early retirement schemes and pension reforms aiming to incentivize workers to delay their retirement have had a marked effect on the increased employment levels of older workers.

While the role of these reforms cannot be disputed, assessing their exact contributions is, however, a more difficult task. Ex post econometric techniques are an interesting possibility that we have briefly touched on at the end of this chapter; they are precisely designed to isolate pure causal impacts, all other factors being held constant. But their limit is that they can generally do no more than showing short-run local impacts for only some components of the reforms—those for which it is possible to isolate comparable and unaffected control groups. The retrospective counterfactual type of simulation that we proposed is better suited for a more global view of what the reforms produced. Such an approach, however, requires some structural behavioral assumptions whose realism may raise problems. The one we have retained here had the advantage of being simple and relatively realistic—retirement at the full rate—but other assumptions could have been made (Bachelet, Beffy, and Blanchet 2011).

Whichever empirical strategy is retained, the idea of separate contributions by the different reforms appears less straightforward than it may have seemed. Reforms interact with each other, and their global effect is not the simple addition of their specific effects taken separately. For instance, the pure role of a reform, such as the 2010 one that raised the minimum age, depends on how far previous reforms had already gone in pushing upward retirement ages above the initial minimum: the more people leaving after 60 due to prereform incentives, the lower the estimated impact of shifting the minimum to 62. Interactions are also at play with early retirement schemes or specific rules in unemployment insurance, and this interaction may work in several directions. Being forced to postpone retirement may induce a parallel shift in all forms of labor market transition before the NRA, according to the "horizon effect" hypothesis. But it can also push more people into these alternative routes. And reforms of these alternative routes may in turn affect normal retirement behavior: decisions to retire are dependent on what the last years of people's career have been. Interactions exist at last with general background socioeconomic factors, even if, because of their quasi-linear changes, we have argued that these factors are unable to directly account for the trend reversal that occurred during the 2000s.

Such analytical difficulties are all the more present when we move to prospective issues rather than just trying to explain recent changes. The trend toward higher LFP now seems well established, but for how long and how far will it go? The answer to this question depends on how all these factors will interact with each other. And it also depends on how long the simple model of retirement behavior that has been privileged here will remain relevant. It is under the "full-rate" assumption that we are led to predict an average age of retirement between 64 and 65 in 2040.

Whether this behavioral assumption will remain credible over the next decades is an open question. There are strong framing effects that are associated with this full rate: it is still perceived as the age at which it is considered socially "normal" to retire, and it will probably remain so for part of the population. But reforms have also explicitly aimed at eroding the strength of this social reference. First, there is the fact that incentives/penalties for retiring later or earlier than this age are now close to actuarial neutrality, implying that this age is no more "the" age at which it is financially the most rewarding to retire. Second, the NRA is no longer a pivotal age for employers on the demand side of the labor market. Until 2003, the importance of the FRA not only stemmed from the fact that it was the one providing the highest return on contributions from a supply side point of view; it was also due to the fact that it corresponded to the normal termination of the labor contract—that is, the possibility of a separation without the need of a layoff. This is no longer the case nowadays, and empirical evidence also shows that it has had a partial contribution to behavioral changes in the post-2003 period (Rabaté 2017). On top of all this, the liberalization of rules controlling the combination of work with the perception of pension benefits also made the role of this FRA increasingly fuzzy.

References

Aubert, P., E. Caroli, and M. Roger. 2006. "New Technologies, Organisation and Age: Firm-Level Evidence." *Economic Journal* 116 (509): 73–93.

Aubert, P., and B. Crépon. 2003. "La productivité des salariés âgés: Une tentative d'estimation." *Economie et Statistique* 368:95–119.

Bachelet, M., M. Beffy, and D. Blanchet. 2011. "Projeter l'impact des réformes des retraites sur l'activité des 55 ans et plus: Une comparaison de trois modèles." *Economie et Statistique* 441–42:123–43.

Banerjee, S., and D. Blau. 2016. "Employment Trends by Age in the United States: Why Are Older Workers Different?" *Journal of Human Resources* 51 (1): 163–99.

Baraton, M., M. Beffy, and D. Fougère. 2011. "Une évaluation de l'effet de la réforme de 2003 sur les départs en retraite: Le cas des enseignants du second degré public." *Economie et Statistique* 441–42:55–78.

Behaghel, L., D. Blanchet, T. Debrand, and M. Roger. 2012. "Disability and Social Security Reforms: The French Case." In *Social Security Programs and Retirement around the World: Historical Trends in Mortality and Health, Employment, and Disability Insurance Participation and Reforms*, edited by David A. Wise, 301–26. Chicago: University of Chicago Press.

Behaghel, L., D. Blanchet, and M. Roger. 2016. "Retirement, Early Retirement and Disability: Explaining Labor Force Participation after 55 in France." In *Social Security Programs and Retirement around the World: Disability Insurance Programs and Retirement*, edited by D. A. Wise, 251–84. Chicago: University of Chicago Press.

Blanchet, D., S. Buffeteau, E. Crenner, and S. Le Minez. 2010. "The New Destinie 2 Microsimulation Model: Main Characteristics and Illustrative Results." INSEE Working Paper No. G2010/13, INSEE, Paris, France.

Blanchet, D., E. Caroli, C. Prost, and M. Roger. 2016. "Health Capacity to Work at Older Ages in France." In *Social Security Programs and Retirement around the World: The Capacity to Work at Older Ages*, edited by D. A. Wise, 111–48. Chicago: University of Chicago Press.

Blanchet, D., and L.-P. Pelé. 1999. "Social Security and Retirement in France." In *Social Security and Retirement around the World*, edited by J. Gruber and D. A. Wise, 101–33. Chicago: University of Chicago Press.

Blau, D., and R. Goodstein. 2010. "Can Social Security Explain Trends in Labor Force Participation of Older Men in the United States?" *Journal of Human Resources* 45 (2): 328–63.

Bozio, A. 2011. "La réforme des retraites de 1993: L'impact de l'augmentation de la durée d'assurance." *Economie et Statistique* 441–42:39–53.

Coile, C. 2015. "Economic Determinants of Workers' Retirement Decisions." *Journal of Economic Surveys* 29 (4): 830–53.

Coile, C., and P. Levine. 2010. "Recessions, Reeling Markets and Retiree Well-Being." NBER Working Paper No. 16066, National Bureau of Economic Research, Cambridge, MA.

———. 2011. "The Market Crash and Mass Layoff: How the Current Economic Crisis May Affect Retirement." *B. E. Journal of Economic Analysis and Policy* 11 (1): article 22.

Coile, C., K. Milligan, D. A. Wise. 2016. "Introduction." In *Social Security Programs and Retirement around the World: Disability Insurance Programs and Retirement*, edited by D. A. Wise, 1–44. Chicago: University of Chicago Press.

Conseil d'Orientation des Retraites [Pensions Advisory Committee]. 2015. "Evolutions et perspectives des retraites en France: Rapport annuel du COR." Annual report. Paris, France.

Crépon B., N. Deniau, and S. Perez-Duarte. 2003. "Productivité et salaire des travailleurs âgés." *Revue française d'économie* 18 (1): 157–85.

Dubois, Y., and M. Koubi. 2017. "La réforme des retraites en 2010: Quel impact sur l'activité des séniors?" *Economie et Prévision* 211–12:61–90.

European Commission. 2015. "The 2015 Ageing Report: Economic and Budgetary Projections for the 28 EU Member States (2013–2060)." European Economy, 3/2015, Brussels, Belgium.

Gruber, J., and D. A. Wise, eds. 1999. *Social Security and Retirement around the World*. Chicago: University of Chicago Press.

———. 2004. *Social Security Programs and Retirement around the World: Micro-Estimation*. Chicago: University of Chicago Press.

Hairault, J. O., F. Langot, and T. Sopraseuth. 2006. "Les effets à rebours de l'âge de la retraite sur le taux d'emploi des seniors." *Economie et Statistique* 397:51–63.

Hellerstein J., D. Neumark, and K. Troske. 1999. "Wages, Productivity, and Worker Characteristics: Evidence from Plant-Level Production Functions and Wage Equations." *Journal of Labor Economics* 17:409–46.

Meron, M., and M. Maruani. 2012. "Un siècle de travail des femmes en France: 1901–2011." La Découverte: Paris, France.

Rabaté, S. 2017. "Can I Stay or Should I Go? Mandatory Retirement and Labor Force Participation of Older Workers." PSE Working Paper No. 2017–19, Paris-Jourdan Sciences Economiques, Paris, France.

Rabaté, S., and J. Rochut. 2017. "Employment and Substitution Effects of Raising the Statutory Eligibility Age in France." PSE Working Paper No. 2017–46, Paris-Jourdan Sciences Economiques, Paris, France.

Roger, M., and E. Walraët. 2008. "The Implications of Social Security for the Well-Being of the Elderly: The Case of France." INSEE Working Paper No. G2008/11, INSEE, Paris, France.

Schirle, T. 2008. "Why Have the Labor Force Participation Rates of Older Men Increased since the Mid-1990s?" *Journal of Labor Economics* 26 (4): 549–94.

Sédillot, B., and E. Walraët. 2002. "La cessation d'activité au sein des couples: Y-a-t-il interdépendance des choix?" *Economie et Statistique* 357–58:79–98.

5

Old-Age Labor Force Participation in Germany
What Explains the Trend Reversal among Older Men and the Steady Increase among Women?

Axel Börsch-Supan and Irene Ferrari

5.1 Introduction

A common finding among most industrialized countries is the increase in older men's labor force participation (LFP) since around the late 1990s, which is a stunning reversal from the long declining trend that began in the early 1970s. There are many factors that have been mentioned in the literature and may help explain this U-shaped pattern. In previous books of this series, it has been extensively shown, through descriptive evidence, case studies, and formal microeconometric analyses, how changes in public pension and disability insurance laws affect the retirement behavior of German workers (see Börsch-Supan and Schnabel 1999; Börsch-Supan et al. 2004; Börsch-Supan, Coppola, and Reil-Held 2012). Improved health and longevity are two other factors that have been analyzed in this series and that seem natural candidates contributing to LFP decisions of older workers (see Börsch-Supan and Jürges 2012; Jürges and Börsch-Supan 2017). Among other factors that have been suggested in the literature, the most cited are increased educational attainment, the shift toward less physically demanding jobs, couples' joint retirement decisions, and labor demand factors like increasing real wages and decreasing unemployment. Given that the population is projected to continue aging in the future,[1]

Axel Börsch-Supan is director of the Munich Center for the Economics of Aging (MEA) at the Max Planck Institute for Social Law and Social Policy (MPISOC), a professor of the economics of aging at the Technical University of Munich, and a research associate of the National Bureau of Economic Research.

Irene Ferrari is a postdoctoral researcher at the MEA at MPISOC.

For acknowledgments, sources of research support, and disclosure of the authors' material financial relationships, if any, please see https://www.nber.org/chapters/c14045.ack.

1. A study by the German Federal Statistical Office reports that in 2060 every third person (34 percent) will be at least 65 years old and the number of 70-year-olds will be twice the number of newborn children (see Statistisches Bundesamt 2009).

it is important to study the role of each factor in order to understand whether the current rising trend in LFP will continue, thus reducing the negative consequences of aging on fiscal sustainability, or whether it is going to slow down.

In this chapter, we will try to give an overall assessment of the relative contribution of these factors. We will first provide graphical evidence of the trends of variables that may be relevant, with the aim of investigating the presence or absence of common patterns between these factors and the LFP. Then, through a decomposition analysis, we will provide an empirical estimate of the contribution of some of these factors to the overall evolution of LFP. This allows us to picture what the LFP trend would have looked like if the distribution of any selected individual characteristic had not changed through time. In the analysis, we will also underline the differences in LFP trends between men and women, trying to shed light on the factors that might have contributed to these differences.

Given the evidence presented in this work and the results of the previous books in this series, we believe that, at least as it regards Germany, much of the change in the trend of older men's LFP registered in the mid-1990s may be explained by changes in public pension regulations and in particular by the phasing in of actuarial adjustments for early retirement. In fact, even if many of the variables studied may have contributed to the overall level of LFP, their trends do not show the U-shaped pattern observed for LFP. Regarding women, things look very different. The LFP trend of older women has in fact been continuously rising, as has that of younger women. The secular change of women's role in society seems thus to be the main driver of LFP in this case.

5.2   The Trend toward Later Retirement

Figure 5.1 shows that LFP in Germany for men of retirement age (≥ 55) follows a trend similar to that reported by other industrialized countries. This trend is characterized by a first phase in which LFP was constantly decreasing, followed by a reversal in the trend in the mid-1990s and a strong increase in LFP since then, which persists up to the present. Figure 5.2 shows the LFP of women for the same age categories. In this case, rather than a trend reversal, we observe a rather constant increase for the 55–59 age group and a reversal for the 60–64 age group that is much milder than the one characterizing men of the same age.

Figures 5.1 and 5.2 are based on the aggregate data provided by the Organisation for Economic Co-operation and Development (OECD).[2] Roughly the same patterns are visible in the microdata that the German

2. Data set: LFS—Sex and Age Indicators, "Welcome to OECD.Stat," OECD.Stat, https://stats.oecd.org/.

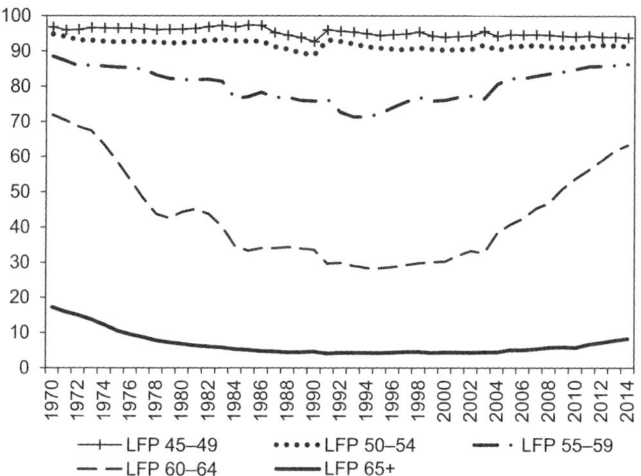

Fig. 5.1   LFP by age group, men (OECD)
Source: OECD.

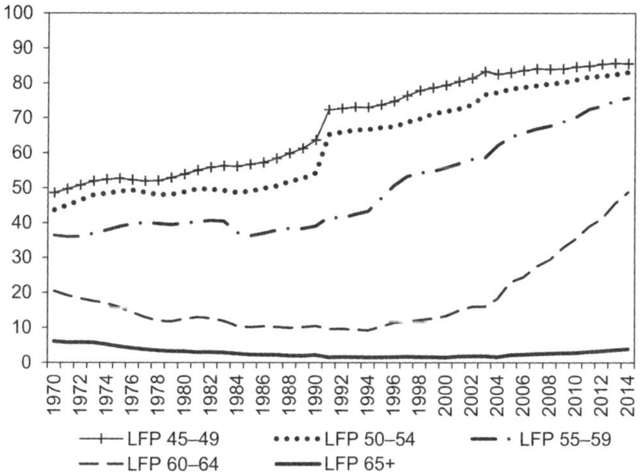

Fig. 5.2   LFP by age group, women (OECD)
Source: OECD.

Socio-economic Panel (GSOEP)[3] provides, which we will use for the detailed analysis in the sequel of this chapter (see figure 5.3). While the GSOEP survey started only in 1984, the trends for different age categories after

3. The GSOEP is a longitudinal data set resembling the Panel Study of Income Dynamics (PSID) in the United States. Our analysis drew on data from 30 waves of the GSOEP (version 30, 2015, DOI: 10.5684/soep.v30), spanning the period from 1984 to 2013.

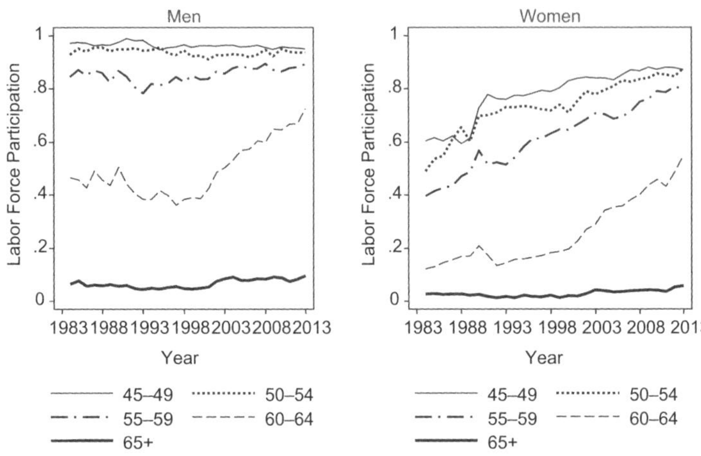

Fig. 5.3   LFP rate by age and gender, 1984–2013
Source: GSOEP.

that date resemble those obtained using OECD official data and reported in figure 5.1.

One may wonder whether the increasing trend in LFP after the age of 55 is only due to cohort effects affecting LFP at younger ages. For men, this does not seem the case: as figure 5.1 shows, LFP at ages 45–54 is not characterized by an increasing trend but was actually slightly decreasing.[4] For women, however, the LFP pattern at younger ages looks very different from that of men (figure 5.2). LFP of women aged 45–54 has been steadily increasing since the 1970s, and this may certainly explain at least part of the LFP increase at older ages.

This argument can be more clearly appreciated by looking at figure 5.4, which displays age-participation profiles by selected cohort groups using the GSOEP data. LFP of men remains basically constant for all birth cohorts considered up until age 55, and then it starts to diverge after this age. LFP of women, on the contrary, is clearly higher the younger the cohort considered at all ages.

Figure 5.5 presents the percentage of men and women at ages 50–80 in the labor force for the selected years. Also, from this perspective, we notice very close patterns for men up until around the age of 55. LFP at older ages is higher now than in 1994, but it was higher in 1984 than in 1994, confirming the trend reversal observed in OECD data. After age 67, however, the LFP has barely changed since 2004 and is now at the same level it was in 1984. Again, the picture looks very different for women. In this case, there has

---

4. The break in the series between 1990 and 1991 is due to the reunification of Germany. From 1991 onward, data are for unified Germany. See OECD (2019).

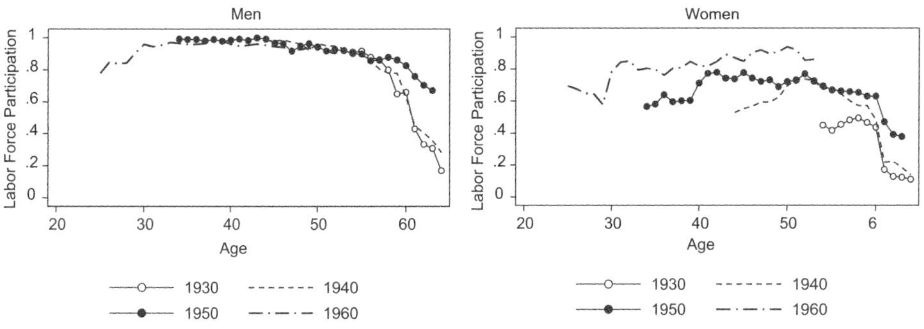

Fig. 5.4   LFP by cohort and gender
Source: GSOEP.

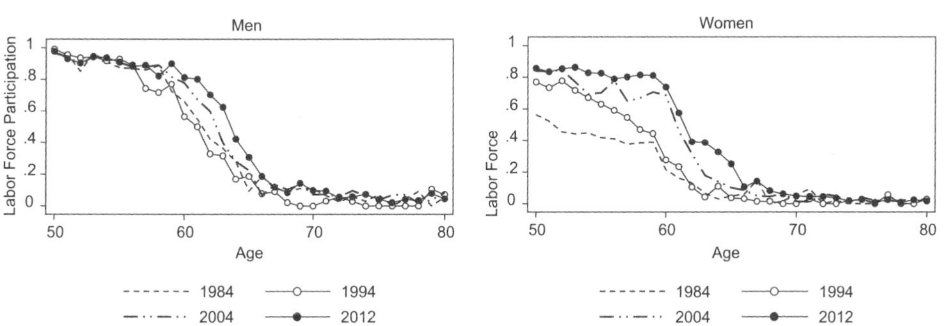

Fig. 5.5   LFP rates in different years, ages 50–80
Source: GSOEP.

been a clear increase in LFP at younger ages that is, however, slowing down decade after decade. From the second panel of figure 5.5, it is also evident that this increase in LFP is shifted to older ages in the subsequent years. Also for women, after the age of 66, barely any difference can be noticed in age-participation throughout the years. Figure 5.6, finally, shows that the LFP of older women is now very close to that for men.

5.3   Public Pensions in Germany

In this section, we will briefly describe the evolution of the public pension system in Germany, and we will show how this can be related to the trends in the LFP. The German pension system covers 85 percent of the German workforce, most of them working in the private sector. The remaining workforce is composed of civil servants, who are covered by a separate and more generous pension system, and the self-employed, who are mandatory participants in occupation-specific pension funds, voluntary participants

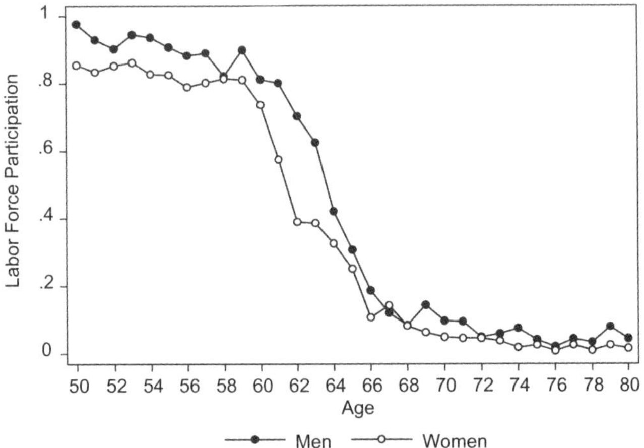

Fig. 5.6   LFP of men and women in 2012, ages 50–80
Source: GSOEP.

of the public pension system, self-insured, or a combination thereof. As explained in our previous works (see Börsch-Supan, Coppola, and Reil-Held 2012, 2014, 2016), the pay-as-you-go system was introduced in Germany in 1957, and since the beginning, it distinguished between old-age pensions and disability pensions. Eligibility for an old-age pension is conditional on reaching the respective early retirement age, which has varied greatly over time and across workers, while the normal retirement age was 65 for men until recently. In addition, eligibility is conditioned on a minimum number of contribution years, which varies by retirement pathway. Eligibility for a disability pension is instead conditional on being partly or fully unable to work and on a small minimum number of contribution years, independent of age. However, the difference in practice between the two is not so clear-cut, as both require five years of contributions and the record-based assessment of inability to work may be prone to leniency (see Börsch-Supan, Coppola, and Reil-Held 2012). These characteristics of the pension system are reflected in figures 5.7 and 5.8, which show the proportions of workers retiring with each possible pathway. In the 1960s, more than half of both men and women were retiring due to disability.

Besides these two major pathways, there are a number of variants of old-age pensions that generally allow lower retirement ages under certain circumstances. Already since 1957, an old-age pension for women and an old-age pension for the unemployed existed that could be drawn at 60 if certain (stricter) contribution requirements were met. Since unemployment was at a historic low in the 1960s and early 1970s (see figures 5.22 and 5.23), retirement via unemployment accounted for a tiny percent of all retirement entries (see figures 5.7 and 5.8). A sizable percent of women was instead retiring early through the old-age pensions for women.

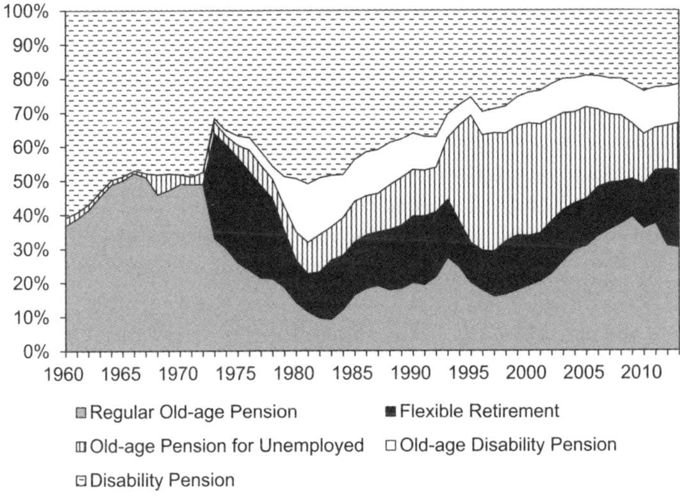

Fig. 5.7   Pathways to retirement, men
Source: Deutsche Rentenversicherung.

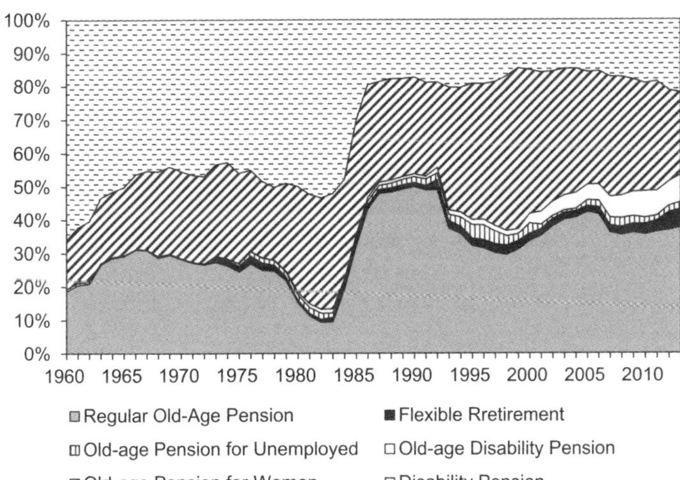

Fig. 5.8   Pathways to retirement, women
Source: Deutsche Rentenversicherung.

Despite these early retirement possibilities, the 1960s were the least generous period in terms of public pension eligibility (Börsch-Supan et al. 2015),
and this is reflected in the average retirement ages. Right before the 1972
reform, the average old-age pension retirement ages for men and women
were 65.1 and 62.7, respectively. In the case of disability pensions, the average retirement age was 57.8 among men and 59.8 among women. As can
be seen in figure 5.1, the LFP of men at the beginning of the 1970s was at

its highest level in the period considered: almost 90 percent for the 55–59 age category and 72 percent for the 60–64 age category. The same picture for women looks somehow different because, as we argued in the previous section, the LFP increase of older women is mainly due to cohort effects, which in turn reflect secular changes in the role of women in the labor market. Despite this, also in the case of women, it is possible to notice that LFP did not increase (for the 55–59 age category) and even decreased (for those older than 60) since the beginning of the 1970s without steadily recovering before the mid-1990s.

In 1972, in fact, a new phase began, characterized by increasing the generosity of the pension system. The 1972 reform basically provided new pathways to early retirement: long-term insured individuals could draw old-age pension benefits already at age 63, conditional on at least 35 contribution years without any actuarial adjustment to the retirement age. Besides, it introduced a special old-age pension for disabled workers that could be drawn at age 62 (later at 60) with less stringent health requirements than the disability pension. Figures 5.7 and 5.8 show how flexible retirement for long-term insured people contributed to the sudden decrease in regular old-age pensions and partly substituted for the disability pathway. Between 1984 and 1987, the creation of a "bridge to retirement" further increased the incentives to retire early. More generous unemployment benefits were introduced for older workers, which caused a dramatic increase in the unemployment rate for this category of workers (see figures 5.22 and 5.23) and substituted for disability pensions.

As a consequence, in 1982, the average retirement age dropped down to 62.3 and 61.5 years for men and women, respectively. As these new options partly substituted the disability pathway, the average age of disability retirement started to decrease as well. At the same time, the LFP dropped to the minimum of 28.4 percent in 1995 for the 60–64 age category and 71.3 percent in 1994 for the 55–59 age category.

In 1984, the eligibility requirements for the regular retirement age were reduced from 15 to 5 contribution years, while at the same time eligibility requirements for disability pensions were made less generous. This can again be visualized in figures 5.7 and 5.8, which show (especially for women) an increase in the share of regular old-age pensions and a contemporaneous decrease in disability pensions in the years 1984–92.

Due to the threat of demographic change and the risk of the pension system becoming unsustainable, since 1992 a sequence of reforms have been enacted that overall cut back on the generosity of the pension system. In 1992, benefits were anchored to net rather than gross wages, and adjustments to the chosen retirement age were introduced gradually between 1998 and 2006. These adjustments, still in place, are not actuarial but amount to 3.6 percent for each year of earlier retirement. In 2001, the generosity of the benefits was further reduced by the "Riester factor." At the same

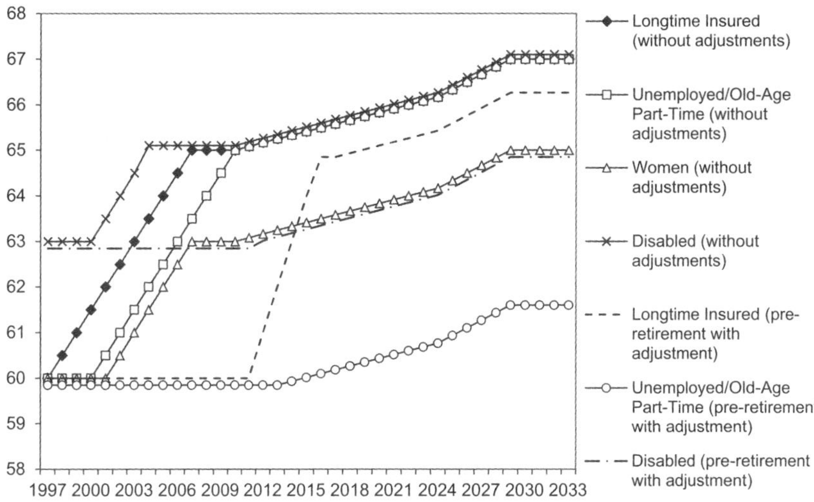

Fig. 5.9   Pension eligibility ages with and without actuarial adjustments

time, private "Riester pensions," a form of IRAs, were introduced to offset these benefit cuts in the public system (Börsch-Supan, Coppola, and Reil-Held 2012). Further relevant changes were decided in 2004, when the pension benefit indexation formula was modified to account for demographic developments (the "sustainability factor")[5] and the retirement age for the unemployed was raised to 63; a reduction in the proportion of individuals retiring through this pathway can in fact be seen in figure 5.7 after 2004. In 2007, the normal retirement age was gradually increased from 65 to 67 (to be phased in between 2012 and 2029), and retirement ages for other old-age pension pathways were increased as well.

Figure 5.9 depicts the increase in eligibility ages for the various pathways, with and without deductions. This figure shows that the age increases were mostly effective since 1998, suggesting a possible causal effect on actual retirement ages and on LFP. Figures 5.10 and 5.11 show that the average retirement age for old-age pensions has increased by two years since 1998 for both men and women. Besides, as noticed above, the LFP of workers older than 55 has experienced an increasing trend since the mid-1990s, and the strongest effect can be observed in the 60–64 age category.

As our most recent work in this international comparison project noticed (Jürges and Börsch-Supan 2017), it is unclear whether this positive trend will continue in the future since this will depend on future changes of the public pension rules. On the one hand, the increase of the eligibility age from 65 to 67 should contribute to maintaining the trend, and it is likely it will also

5. See Börsch-Supan and Wilke (2006).

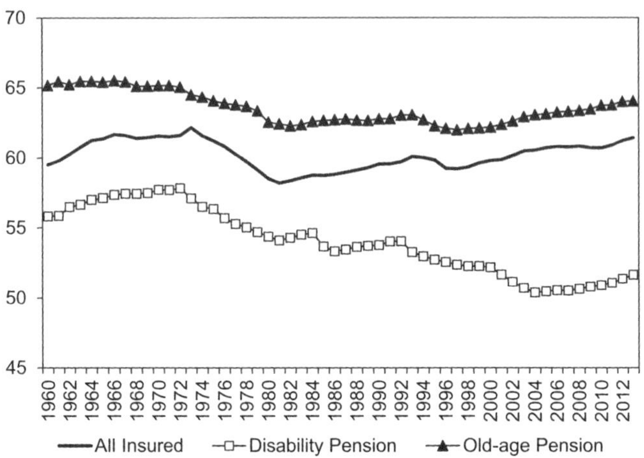

Fig. 5.10   Average retirement age, men
Source: Deutsche Rentenversicherung.

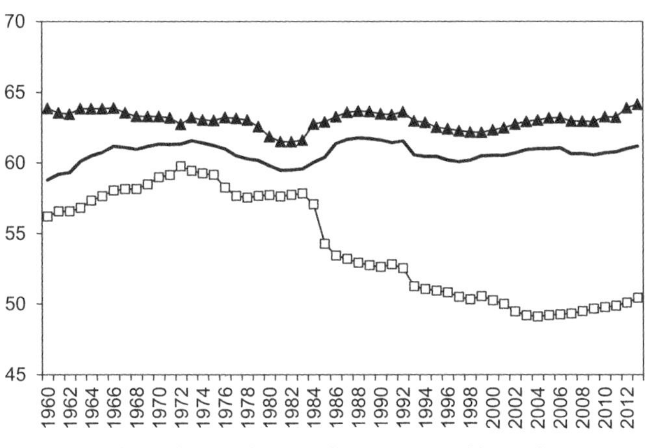

Fig. 5.11   Average retirement age, women
Source: Deutsche Rentenversicherung.

boost LFP in the 65–69 age group. On the other hand, in 2014, an early
retirement option at age 63 without actuarial adjustment was reintroduced
for those with 45 contribution years, which could partially offset the effect of
previous efforts toward more sustainability. In addition, current attempts to
make retirement more "flexible"—but without increasing the benefit adjustments to retirement age to an actuarial level—may backfire and precipitate
earlier retirement (Börsch-Supan et al. 2015).

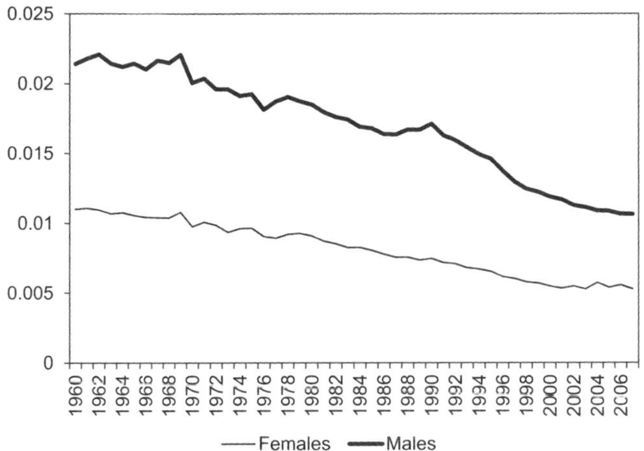

Fig. 5.12   Cohort mortality rates at age 60
Source: Human Mortality Database.

5.4   Historical Trends of LFP Determinants

5.4.1   Health

Health improvement and increased longevity seem natural candidates that could help explain the LFP of older workers, and for this reason, health and disabilities have been extensively studied in previous works of this series. Here we will concentrate in particular on common trends, if any, in the evolution of health and the LFP.

As a first step, we will document trends in mortality. The implicit assumption here is that a declining mortality reflects health improvements at earlier ages also, which, in turn, should predict higher ability to work. Figure 5.12 shows cohort mortality rates at age 60 by gender since 1960. It depicts a clear downward trend: during the last five decades, the mortality rate has halved for both men and women. However, the mortality of men was around two times that of women in 1960, so longevity of men is getting closer to that of women.

Figures 5.13 and 5.14 show one-year mortality rates for men and women in 1960, 1985, and 2010. Mortality rates are on a logarithmic scale, so the linear increase depicted actually represents an exponential increase in mortality rates by age. These figures tell us that mortality rates of women are lower than mortality rates of men at all ages and that mortality rates have sizably decreased since 1960, without showing signs of deceleration. Actually, for men the increase in longevity in the last 25 years has been higher than for women. A man in 1960 had a 5 percent probability of dying within

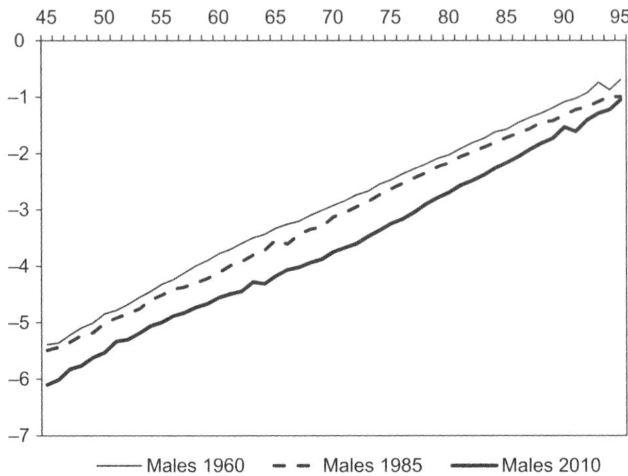

Fig. 5.13   One-year mortality rate (log scale) by age, men (1960, 1985, and 2010)
Source: Human Mortality Database.

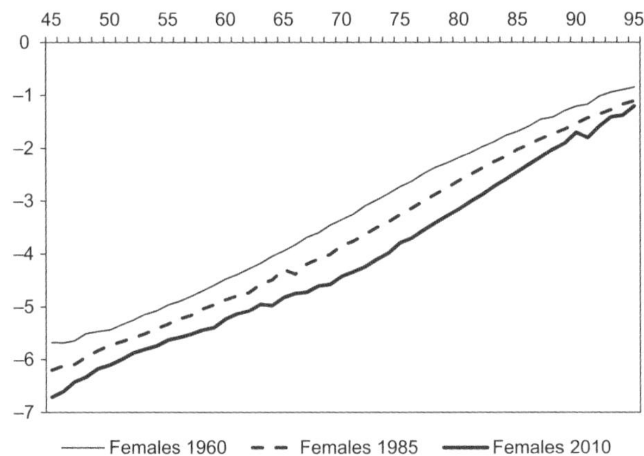

Fig. 5.14   One-year mortality rate (log scale) by age, women (1960, 1985, and 2010)
Source: Human Mortality Database.

the next year at age 69, while the same probability was reachcd at age 71 in 1985 and at age 77 in 2010. The respective ages for women are 73, 77, and 81.

Figures 5.15 and 5.16 depict the relative improvements in longevity by age for men and women, expressed as the ratio of mortality rates between 1985 and 1960 and between 2010 and 1985 (thus smaller numbers indicate larger improvements). These figures clearly show that the increase in longevity of men between 1985 and 2010 was two times larger than between 1960 and 1985, while for women the increase was constant. The relative gain between

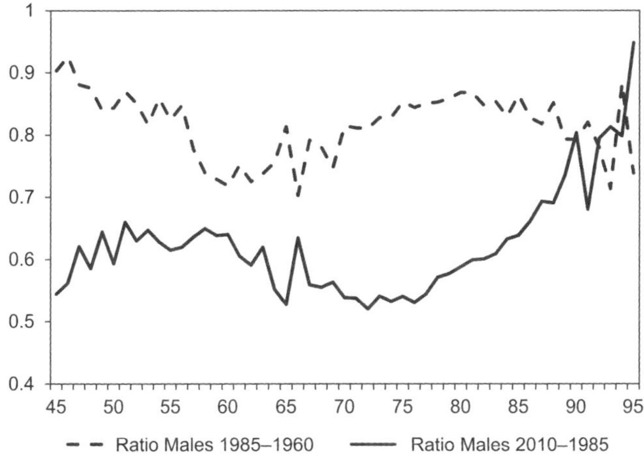

Fig. 5.15   Ratio of one-year mortality rates, men
Source: Human Mortality Database.

Fig. 5.16   Ratio of one-year mortality rates, women
Source: Human Mortality Database.

1985 and 2010 is thus higher for men than for women. The biggest relative gain in longevity for men was registered between ages 55–70 in the period 1960–85 and at later ages (65–80) in the period 1985–2010. For women, on the contrary, the biggest relative improvements have been around the same ages (65–80).

These findings are interesting when put in relation to LFP trends. Before the mid-1980s, when the relative longevity improvements of men were particularly strong for ages at risk of retirement, the LFP of this same age group

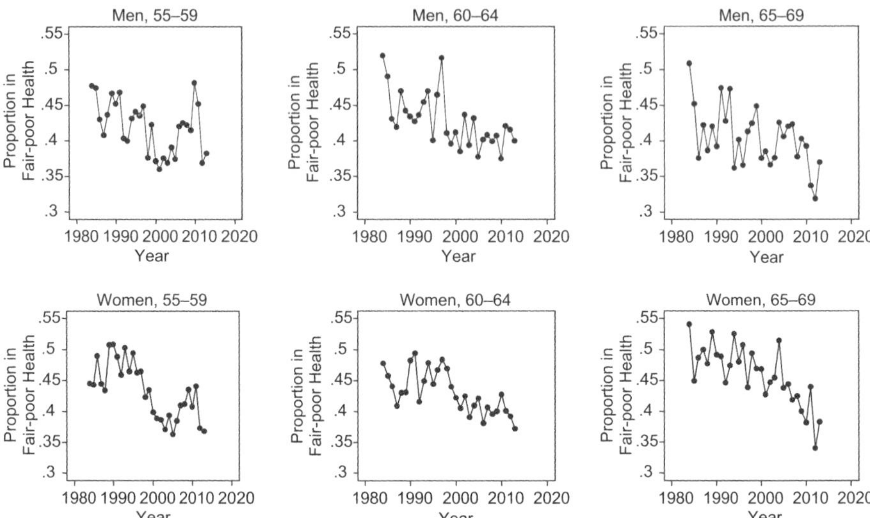

Fig. 5.17   Health dissatisfaction by sex and age group, 1984–2013
Source: GSOEP.

was in a decreasing trajectory. When the trend reversed, it did so especially for the 60–64 age group while remaining pretty stable for those older than 65, despite the fact that longevity was rising especially in this group. Regarding women, the biggest relative improvements have mainly affected women older than 65; however, this is the only age group among women where LFP has remained pretty stable throughout the years.

As longevity improvements are not a perfect measure of health, we conclude this subsection by showing some evidence on self-assessed health in Germany from GSOEP. We argue, however, that self-assessed health may not be a good measure of secular trends in health either. If individuals evaluate their health using a contemporaneous average healthy individual as a reference, it is possible that no trend at all is captured by self-assessed health, even if objective average health has actually improved through time.

GSOEP has collected data on satisfaction with health annually since the first wave in 1984. Health satisfaction is measured on a 0–10 scale, and we define "fair-poor health" as satisfaction below or equal to 5. Data on self-rated health are instead available only since 1992. In this case, "fair-poor" is defined as rating one's health as bad, poor, or satisfactory. Trends for these two variables are presented in figures 5.17 and 5.18, separately by gender and age group. First of all, it is clear that data are pretty volatile, another reason they should be interpreted with caution. In general, however, a downward trend in fair-poor health is present for both variables and in all categories considered. The trend is decreasing faster in the category of individuals

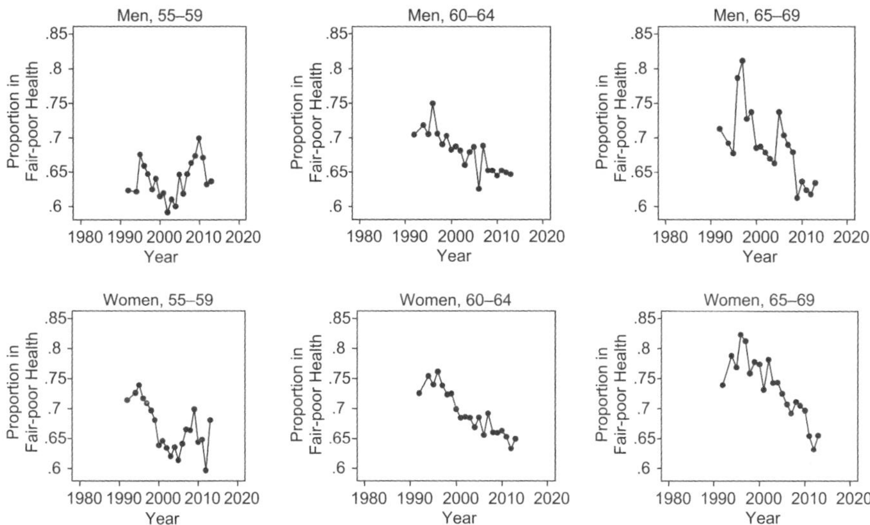

Fig. 5.18   Self-rated health by sex and age group, 1984–2013
Source: GSOEP.

older than 65. In this respect, the trends are compatible with the secular increase in life expectancy illustrated above.

In conclusion, although it is certainly plausible for health to be an important determinant of the level of LFP, it seems unlikely that it may have been the cause of the sudden trend reversal registered in the 1990s.

5.4.2   Education

Educational attainment is another crucial determinant of LFP, and increases in education can be expected to increase the ability, the willingness, and the opportunities to work at older ages. First of all, those with higher education start their career later and may thus need to work at older ages in order to reach certain eligibility requirements or benefit levels. Besides, education may be seen as an investment—better-educated workers are generally also paid more—which provides incentives to remain employed. Those with higher education are also less likely to become unemployed or discouraged. Finally, there is likely a positive relation between education and health at older ages and a negative relation between education and being employed in physically demanding jobs. In fact, those with a college degree are much more likely to be in the labor force at older ages: in the 2013 GSOEP sample, around 40 percent of men and 43 percent of women older than 55 holding a postsecondary diploma were in the labor force. The respective numbers for those without a high school diploma were 28 percent and 16 percent.

Figures 5.19 and 5.20 show the trends in upper secondary (high school)

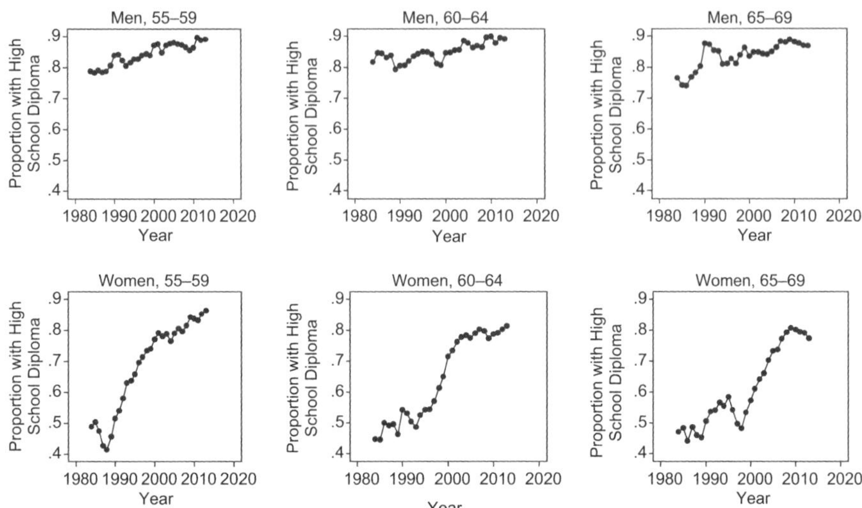

Fig. 5.19   Percentage with high school diploma by age group and gender, 1984–2013

Source: GSOEP.

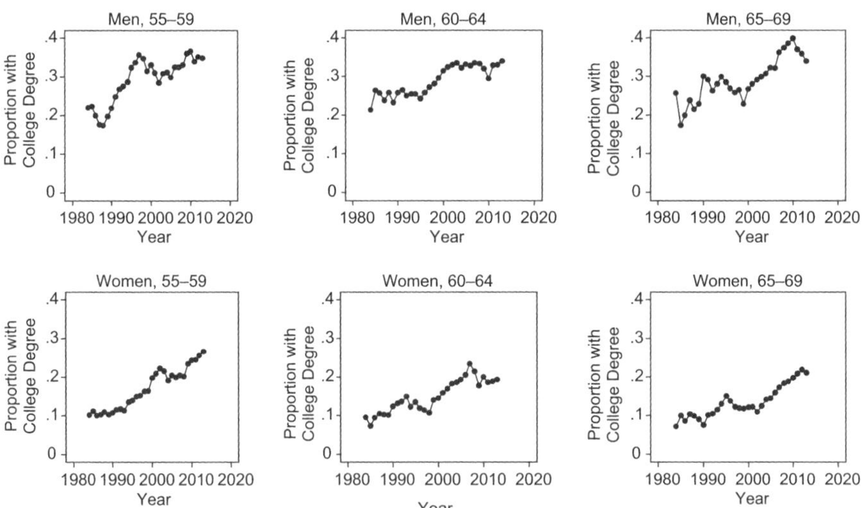

Fig. 5.20   Percentage with college degree by age group and gender, 1984–2013

Source: GSOEP.

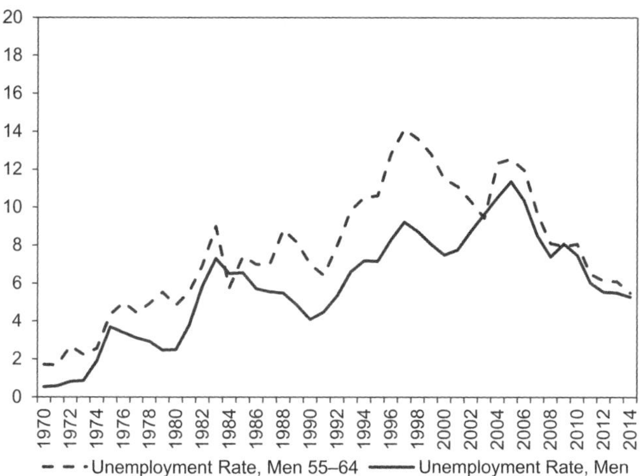

Fig. 5.21   Unemployment rate of men, 1970–2014
Source: OECD.

and postsecondary (college) attainment by gender and age group. A few interesting facts can be observed. First of all, for both genders and in all age groups, the proportion of individuals with high school or college has been increasing. The trend of women with a high school education is increasing much faster than for men, so much that the gender gap has almost disappeared in the younger cohort (55–59). The increase in college attainment is similar to that of men, but the gender gap is still present in all the cohorts considered.

Regarding men, the steepest increase is registered for college attainment. It is interesting to notice, however, that the educational gap among different cohorts is closing. In fact, even among prime-age men (40–44 years, which we do not show in the graphs), slightly more than one-third of individuals nowadays hold a college degree. It is thus likely that future gains in educational attainment will slow down. As increasing educational attainment has most likely played an important part in the LFP increase of older men, it is also possible that education will not be a crucial determinant of LFP trends in the future.

5.4.3   Labor Market Factors: Occupation, Real Wages, and Unemployment

Labor demand factors may be important drivers of older individuals' LFP as well, but they are often overlooked in the literature. In this section, we will in particular discuss the trends in the composition of employment, real wages, and unemployment.

Figures 5.21 and 5.22 show the trend in unemployment for men and women, separately for all workers and for older workers only. These graphs

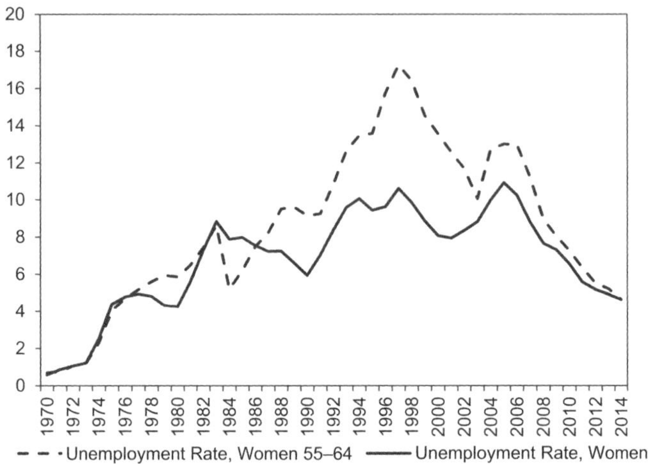

Fig. 5.22   Unemployment rate of women, 1970–2014
Source: OECD.

are remarkable because they track a set of important events in economic history. The first two peaks, around 1975 and 1983, may be explained by the two oil crises of 1973 and 1979. After that, instead of going back to precrisis levels, unemployment remained high, showing a pattern characterized by a hysteresis problem. It hit a high in 2005 and finally started decreasing after that date, probably caused by the incisive "Agenda 2010" labor market reforms in Germany.

If we look at the unemployment of older workers, we can recognize at least a few instances where unemployment of older workers diverges from general unemployment, likely due to new public pension and labor market regulations that affected only these workers (see Börsch-Supan and Schnabel [2010]). Specifically, during the 1980s, the two lines go in opposite directions and even cross. While unemployment in the population was decreasing, unemployment of older workers was increasing due to the "bridge to retirement" we discussed in section 5.3: more generous unemployment benefits induced more and more workers to use unemployment insurance as an early retirement pathway. This created a wedge in the unemployment of older and younger workers that started to decrease only after 1997, when actuarial adjustments for early retirement started to phase in. It thus seems that the unemployment of older workers in Germany has been indirectly affecting the LFP of older workers through the effect of public pension and labor market regulations rather than itself serving as a cause of early labor market exit.

Another factor to analyze is real wages growth. This is interesting also in light of the increase in education that we illustrated in the previous sub-

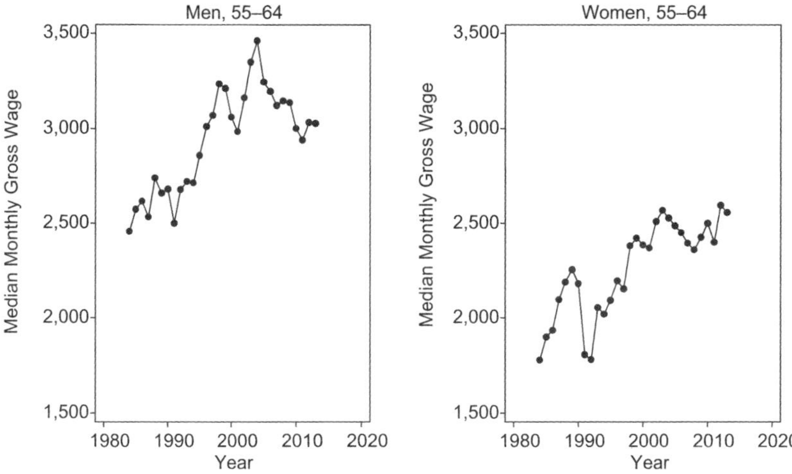

Fig. 5.23   Median gross monthly wages by gender (2010 euro), 1984–2013
Source: GSOEP.

section: as the workforce becomes more educated and thus more productive, we should expect to see this reflected in higher compensations, in both absolute terms and relative to younger workers, for whom increases in education are not as fast as for older cohorts anymore (see Burtless 2013). GSOEP has been asking respondents how much they earned from their work the previous month (both gross and net of taxes and social contributions to public pensions, unemployment, and health insurance) since 1984. Gross and net yearly income are only available from 1990 and 2000, respectively, so here we will only show monthly earnings, expressed in the 2010 euro.

In figure 5.23, we show the evolution of median gross wages for older workers by gender. We only include full-time workers to take into account the fact that older workers may disproportionately hold part-time jobs. Gross wages have been clearly increasing for both men and women, even if growth seems to have slowed down and even reversed, especially for men, during the 2000s. This trend, however, characterizes wages of all workers in Germany, as documented in Brenke (2009). The author shows that net real wages in Germany have hardly risen—and even declined between 2004 and 2008—not due to higher taxes or social security contributions but due to very slow wage growth.

This slow growth has happened despite the increase in workers' educational attainments and the shift toward more-qualified jobs. The latter is documented in figure 5.24, where we show the distribution of occupations by gender in the first and last available years of GSOEP. Professions that require higher qualifications have been growing in importance at the expense of professions based on manual labor or simple nonmanual activities. This

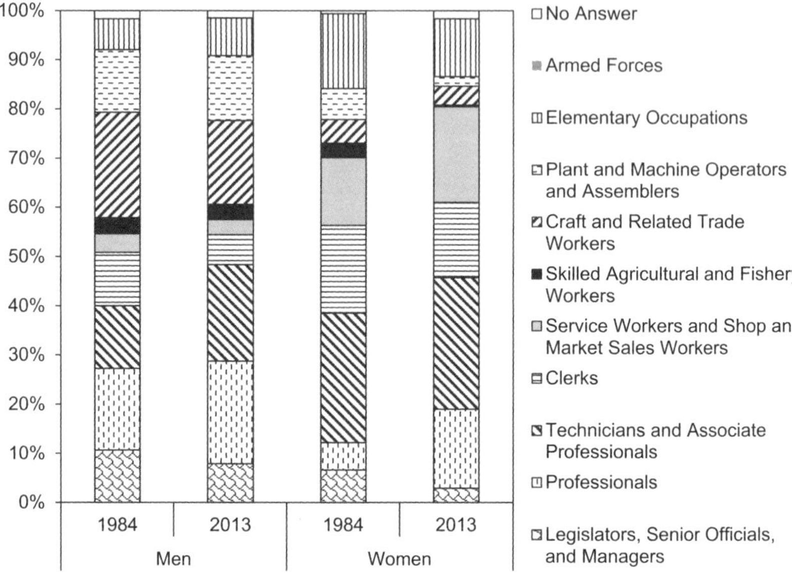

Fig. 5.24   Distribution of occupations by gender, 1984 and 2013
Source: GSOEP.

shift toward less physically demanding jobs[6] may itself contribute to explaining later retirement.

Despite the slowing of wage growth, we still expect the relative educational gain of older workers to be reflected in higher compensations relative to younger workers. Thus in figure 5.25, we show the median monthly wage of workers aged 55–69 as a percent of the median wage of prime-age workers (25–54). In fact, median wages of older workers tended to increase in the period considered relative to those of younger workers.[7] In the 1980s, wages were relatively higher for prime-age workers, but in the early and late 1990s, for both men and women, the situation reversed.

5.4.4   Spouse's LFP

Another argument that has been put forward in the retirement literature is that a spouse's LFP might be important for individuals' retirement decisions. There are two main potential explanations for why this might be true, which operate in opposite directions (see Schirle 2008). First of all, the extra family income earned by a working spouse allows the other

---

6. Cognitive aging, on the other hand, may represent a problem, especially for those with higher education.

7. As noticed by Burtless (2013), wages are only observed for workers. As low earners tend to leave the workforce earlier than high earners, observed median wages are higher than potential wages of all older individuals.

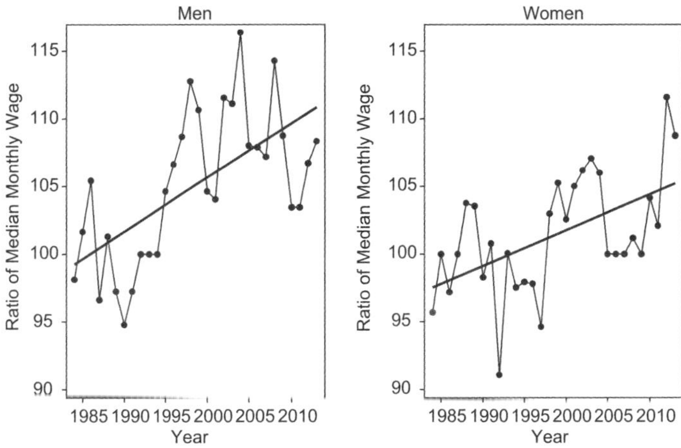

Fig. 5.25   Median monthly wages at ages 55–69 as a percentage of median monthly wages at ages 25–54
Source: GSOEP.

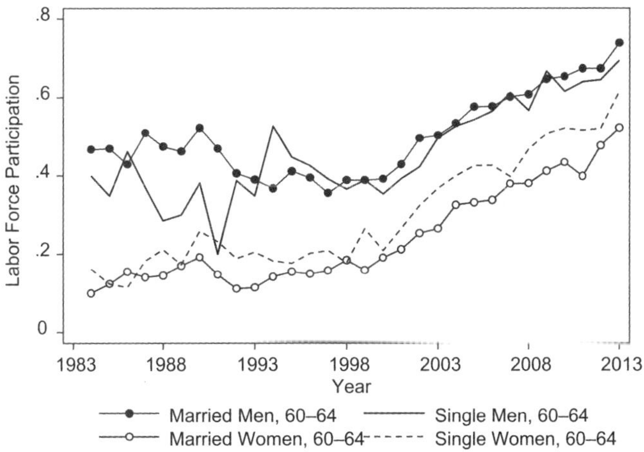

Fig. 5.26   LFP of individuals aged 60–64 by gender and marital status
Source: GSOEP.

spouse to enjoy more leisure (income effect), thus reducing his or her probability of being in the labor force. Second, if couples have a preference for shared leisure time, we can expect a joint retirement decision, which means a higher probability of being in the labor force as long as the spouse is in the labor force too.

To shed some light on this issue, we show in figure 5.26 the LFP trends of men and women aged 60–64 by marital status. We can notice that the U shape that we documented above for men seems to be driven by married man, as before the 2000s, the trend for single men looks quite different and somehow erratic. After the actuarial adjustments started to phase in, however, the trends for single and married men look very similar, increasing the suspicion that public pension rules may have had a crucial role in shaping the trend. Nevertheless, the strong increase in LFP of married women and the similar trends in LFP for married men and women may suggest that men in particular could have responded to the increase of their wives' LFP by postponing their exit from the labor market.

5.5   Decomposition Analysis

In this section, we propose a decomposition analysis of LFP in order to assess how much of the changes in LFP can be attributed to the three main factors presented above: education, health, and spouse's LFP. The original decomposition method was proposed by Oaxaca (1973) and Blinder (1973), and it consisted of decomposing changes (e.g., through time) or differences (e.g., between groups) in the mean of an outcome variable in both a component that reflects differences in the distribution of (observed and unobserved) characteristics and a component that reflects different returns to (observable and unobservable) characteristics. Since then, the literature on decomposition has expanded considerably; the main development consisted of going beyond the mean by extending the decomposition to other distributional parameters.

An important distinction exists between "aggregate" and "detailed" decompositions. In the former, the overall difference in outcomes between two groups is only divided into its two components: the "explained" one (attributable to differences in characteristics) and the "unexplained" one (attributable to different returns to characteristics). The "detailed" decomposition, which we employ in our analysis, allows us instead to look at the contribution to the overall difference of each individual covariate. Specifically, the detailed decomposition can apportion the explained and the unexplained effects into components attributable to each explanatory variable (see Fortin, Lemieux, and Firpo 2011).

In the following, we will adopt the decomposition strategy used by Schirle (2008): this is similar to the method developed by DiNardo, Fortin, and Lemieux (1996) but extended to the case of a binary outcome variable such as LFP. As we will consider many variables in our decomposition, the analytical description of the method is simplified by using a set of only two generic variables. Very broadly, this semiparametric method consists of fixing a baseline year ($s = 1984$, in our case) and creating for any subsequent year t counterfactuals of the participation rate, assuming each factor remained as in year s. If we repeat this exercise for every year up until 2013, we can get an estimate of how the evolution of LFP would have been over this entire period if the distribution of certain factors had remained constant after 1984.

The creation of the counterfactual is based on a reweighting function that captures the differences in the distribution of a certain explanatory variable between two periods. The decomposition proceeds by sequentially adjusting for each factor, introducing one covariate on top of those for which adjustments have already been made. One well-known shortcoming of this approach is that the result depends on the order in which the variables are introduced. For this reason, we will check the robustness of our result by reversing the order of decomposition.

The decomposition starts by defining the probability to participate in the labor force L in t, which may be written as

$$P_t(L = 1) = \sum\sum P_t(L = 1, X_1 = x_1, X_2 = x_2)$$
$$= \sum\sum P_t(L = 1 | X_1 = x_1, X_2 = x_2) \times P_t(X_1 = x_1 | X_2 = x_2)$$
$$\times P_t(X_2 = x_2),$$

where X_1 and X_2 represent two generic explanatory factors we are interested in and the summation is over the support of X_1 and X_2. In the first stage of the decomposition, we want to create a counterfactual probability representing what the participation decision would have been in t, had the distribution of X_1 stayed the same as in s:

$$P_{C1t}(L = 1) = \sum\sum P_t(L = 1 | X_1 = x_1, X_2 = x_2) \times P_s(X_1 = x_1 | X_2 = x_2),$$
$$\times P_t(X_2 = x_2) = \sum\sum P_t(L = 1 | X_1 = x_1, X_2 = x_2)$$
$$\times \psi_{X^1 | X^2} P_t(X_1 = x_1 | X_2 = x_2) \times P_t(X_2 = x_2)$$

where $\psi_{X^1 | X^2}$ is a reweighting function that, using Bayes's rule, can be rewritten as

$$\psi_{X_1 | X_2} = \frac{P(X_1 = x_1 | X_2 = x_2, T = s)}{P(X_1 = x_1 | X_2 = x_2, T = t)}$$
$$= \frac{P(T = s | X_1 = x_1, X_2 = x_2)/P(T = s | X_2 = x_2)}{P(T = t | X_1 = x_1, X_2 = x_2)/P(T = t | X_2 = x_2)}.$$

This transformation reduces a high-dimensional object into a one-dimensional object that can be estimated by pooling observation of year t and s and running a probit model[8] where the dependent variable indicates whether the observation belongs to year t or to year s.

---

8. The DiNardo et al. (1996) method is indeed "semiparametric," because of the parametric reweighting approach.

Similarly, we will then obtain a second counterfactual that also accounts for changes through time in X_2. Notice that this time the counterfactual tells what the participation decision would have been in t if the distribution of X_2 and X_1 had stayed the same as in s:

$$P_{C2t}(L = 1) = \sum\sum P_t(L = 1 | X_1 = x_1, X_2 = x_2)$$
$$\times \psi_{X_1|X_2} P_t(X_1 = x_1 | X_2 = x_2) \times \psi_{X_2} P_t(X_2 = x_2),$$

where the new reweighting function

$$\psi_{X_2} = \frac{P(X_2 = x_2 | T = s)}{P(X_2 = x_2 | T = t)} = \frac{P(T = s | X_2 = x_2)/P(T = s)}{P(T = t | X_2 = x_2)/P(T = t)}$$

can again be estimated as indicated above.[9]

The illustrated procedure can, of course, be extended to any number of explanatory variables. Here we concentrate on the factors that, in light of previous discussion, we deem important for explaining LFP in Germany: education, health, and spouse's LFP. The decomposition will be repeated for each $t \in [1985, 2013]$, keeping $s = 1984$ as the baseline year. As a first step, we need to estimate a pooled probit model of LFP, using GSOEP data from 1984 to 2013.[10] The model includes year and age dummies, education dummies, indicators for marital status, spouse's employment status, fair-poor health, and a quadratic in experience. We estimate this model using sample weights, separately for men and women. The reweighting functions include similar controls, and after having estimated their predicted values, they are multiplied by the original sample weights in order to obtain the counterfactual participation rates.

Figure 5.27 shows the counterfactual LFP of men in the 55–64 age group for the period 1984–2013. The graph shows that the effect of education, health, and spouse's labor force status seems to have increased up until the end of the 1990s and remained more stable after that date. If those characteristics had not changed after 1984, LFP in 2000 would have been around 5 percent lower than what was observed. The effect on health alone does not seem to be substantial, while the remaining wedge seems to be similarly driven by increases in education and in spouse's LFP. What is striking, how-

---

9. Notice that in the case of a binary variable, the reweighting function is

$$\psi_{X_2} = \frac{P(X_2 = x_2 | T = s)}{P(X_2 = x_2 | T = t)} = \begin{cases} \dfrac{P_s(X_2 = 1)}{P_t(X_2 = 1)} & \text{if } X_2 = 1 \\[2ex] \dfrac{P_s(X_2 = 0)}{P_t(X_2 = 0)} & \text{if } X_2 = 0. \end{cases}$$

10. By running a pooled model, we are implicitly assuming that the parameters describing the LFP decision do not vary through time. This assumption could be relaxed by running separate regressions for each year.

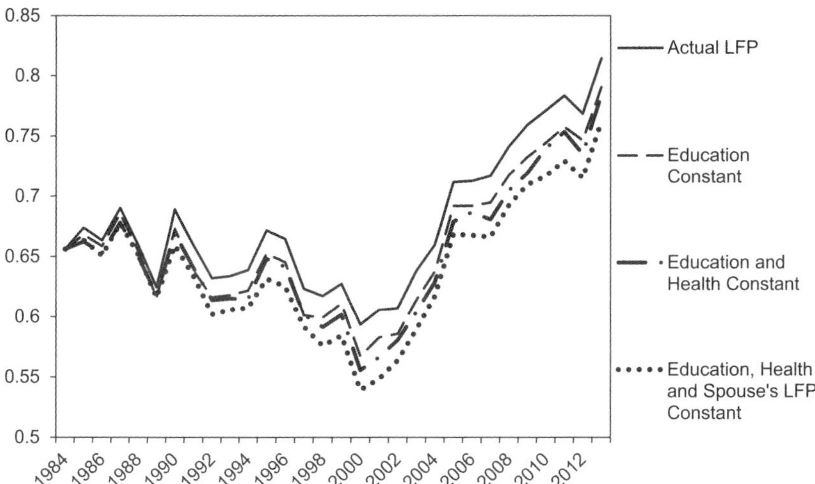

Fig. 5.27   Counterfactual LFP of men aged 55–64, 1984–2013
Source: GSOEP.

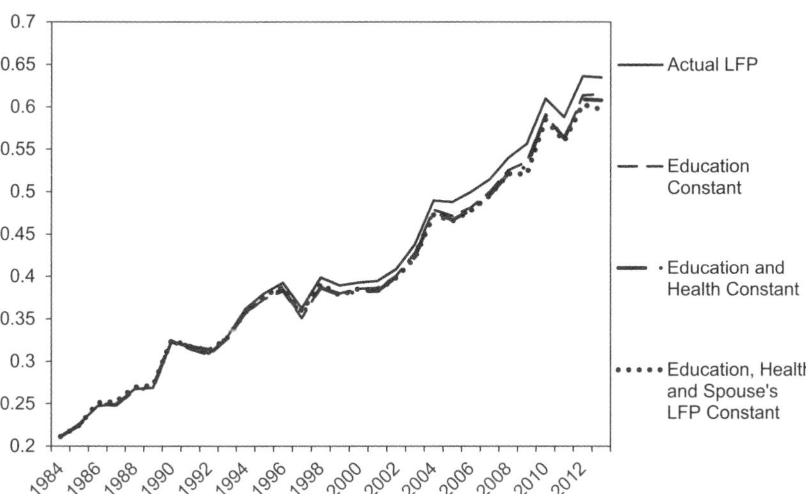

Fig. 5.28   Counterfactual LFP of women aged 55–64, 1984–2013
Source: GSOEP.

ever, is that these variables do not explain at all the fast increase in LFP registered after 2000: the difference between actual and counterfactual LFP in 2013 is still around 5 percent, as in 2000.

The picture for women looks even less suggestive for the hypothesis that education, health, or spouse's employment are the main drivers of their strongly increasing LFP. This can be seen from figure 5.28. In this case, the

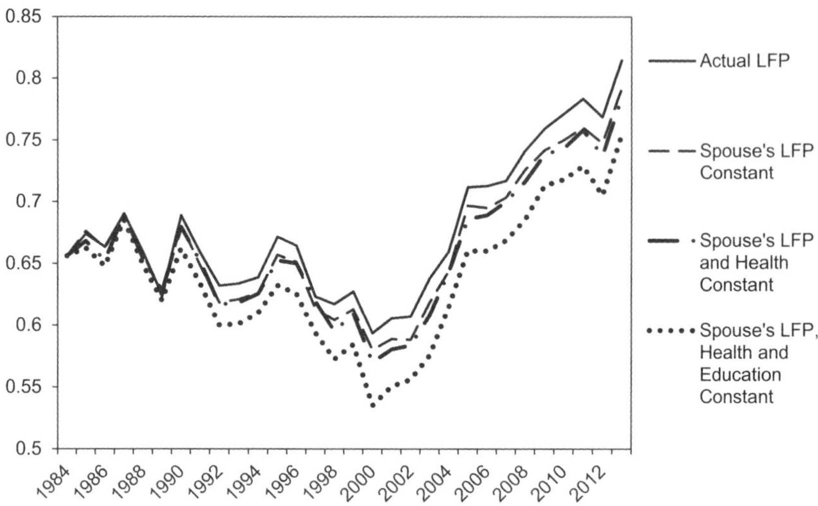

Fig. 5.29   Counterfactual LFP of men aged 55–64 (reverse order), 1984–2013
Source: GSOEP.

three factors seem to explain very little of the fast and constant increase in women's LFP. Besides, up until the end of the 1990s, basically no effect is visible. After that date, education drives the wedge between actual and counterfactual LFP. However, the effect of education seems smaller than expected in light of the steep increase in the education of women illustrated above.

These negative findings are robust against reversing the order of the explanatory variables. The path dependency is basically an omitted variables problem (see Fortin, Lemieux, and Firpo 2011), originated by the sequential introduction of covariates in the decomposition, so diverging results should be expected unless the effect of our factors of interest is uncorrelated with the excluded covariates. In order to check the robustness of the counterfactual analysis to the problem of path dependence, we also perform a reverse-order decomposition.

As shown in figures 5.29 and 5.30, for both men and women, the reverse decomposition has the effect of slightly increasing the overall gap between actual and counterfactual trends. Particularly, the effect attributed to education seems to become bigger. However, these small differences do not change our previous conclusions.

5.6   Conclusions

The LFP of older men in Germany experienced a remarkable reversal around the late 1990s. After a long declining trend that began in the early 1970s, the LFP for older men has strongly increased again. This increase has lasted until the present. In contrast, the LFP of older women in Germany has not experienced such a U-shaped pattern but has steadily increased since

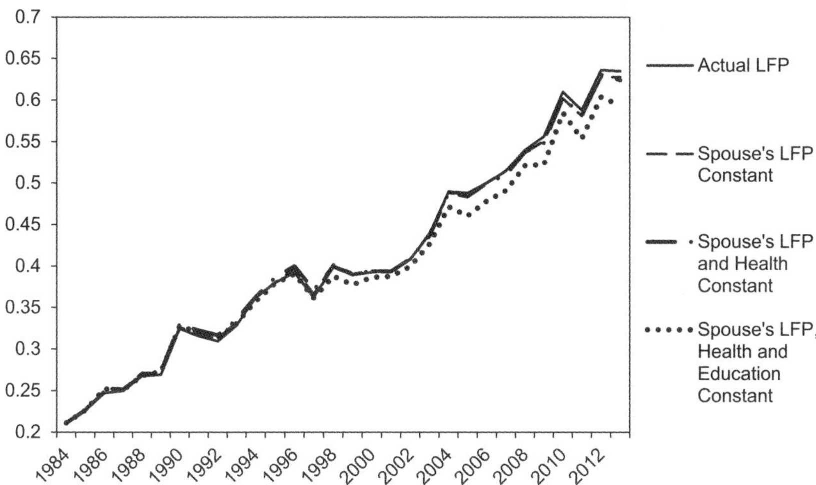

Fig. 5.30   Counterfactual LFP of women aged 55–64 (reverse order), 1984–2013
Source: GSOEP.

the 1970s. This chapter documents these trends and some potential drivers that have been mentioned in the literature and then uses a decomposition analysis to find out whether the three most prominent drivers—education, health, and spouse's employment—explain these trends.

Our answer is no. Regarding men's LFP, all three variables have a significant influence, but they do not explain the U-shaped reversal. Future work will therefore focus on the role of public pension rules in explaining the trend reversal among older men's LFP.

Regarding women's LFP, the three variables do not even have an economically substantive effect. Whether public pension rules play a role is unclear. Most probably, the secular change of women's role in society is the main driver of the steadily increasing LFP among German women.

Appendix

Data Sources

All data refer to former West Germany before 1991 and to reunited Germany afterward:

- For mortality data, see the Human Mortality Database (www.mortality .org).
- For LFP (where indicated) and unemployment rates, see the OECD stat site (https://stats.oecd.org/).
- For the average retirement age and retirement pathways, see the For-

schungsportal der Deutschen Rentenversicherung (http://forschung
.deutsche-rentenversicherung.de/).
- For all other data, see the GSOEP's various waves (www.diw.de/GSOEP
/en).

References

Blinder, A. S. 1973. "Wage Discrimination: Reduced Form and Structural Estimates." *Journal of Human Resources* 8 (4): 436–55.
Börsch-Supan, A., T. Bucher-Koenen, S. Kluth, M. Haupt, and N. Goll. 2015. "Vor-
und Nachteile höherer Flexibilität als Instrument zur Erhöhung der Beschäfti-
gung Älterer." MEA Discussion Paper 06-2015, Munich, Germany.
Börsch-Supan, A. H., M. Coppola, and A. Reil-Held. 2012. "Riester Pensions in
Germany: Design, Dynamics, Targeting Success and Crowding-in." NBER Work-
ing Paper No. 18014, National Bureau of Economic Research, Cambridge, MA.
Börsch-Supan, A., and H. Jürges. 2012. "Disability, Pension Reform, and Early
Retirement in Germany." In *Social Security Programs and Retirement around the
World: Historical Trends in Mortality and Health, Employment, and Disability
Insurance Participation and Reforms*, edited by David A. Wise, 277–300. Chicago:
University of Chicago Press.
Börsch-Supan, A., and R. Schnabel. 1999. "Social Security and Retirement in Ger-
many." In *Social Security and Retirement around the World*, edited by Jonathan
Gruber and David A. Wise, 135–80. Chicago: University of Chicago Press.
———. 2010. "Early Retirement and Employment of the Young in Germany." In
*Social Security Programs and Retirement around the World: The Relationship to
Youth Employment*, edited by Jonathan Gruber and David A. Wise, 147–66. Chi-
cago: University of Chicago Press.
Börsch-Supan, A., R. Schnabel, S. Kohnz, and G. Mastrobuoni. 2004. "Micro-
modeling of Retirement Decisions in Germany." In *Social Security Programs and
Retirement around the World: Micro-Estimation*, edited by Jonathan Gruber and
David A. Wise, 285–344. Chicago: University of Chicago Press.
Börsch-Supan, A. H., and C. B. Wilke. 2006. "The German Public Pension System:
How It Will Become an NDC System Look-Alike." In *Pension Reform: Issues
and Prospects for Non-Financial Defined Contribution (NDC) Schemes*, edited by
R. Holzmann and E. Palmer, 573–610. Washington, DC: World Bank.
Brenke, K. 2009. "Real Wages in Germany: Numerous Years of Decline." *German
Institute for Economic Research Weekly Report* 28 (5): 193–202. http://www.diw.de
/documents/publikationen/73/diw_01.c.342371.de/diw_wr_2009-28.pdf.
Burtless, G. 2013. "Can Educational Attainment Explain the Rise in Labor Force
Participation at Older Ages?" Center for Retirement Research, Boston College,
Issue Brief No. 13-13.
DiNardo, John, Nicole M. Fortin, and Thomas Lemieux. 1996. "Labor Market Insti-
tutions and the Distribution of Wages, 1973–1992: A Semiparametric Approach."
Econometrica 64 (5): 1001–44.
Fortin, N., T. Lemieux, and S. Firpo. 2011. "Decomposition Methods in Econom-
ics." *Handbook of Labor Economics* 4:1–102.
Jürges, H., L. Thiel, and A. Börsch-Supan. 2017. "Healthy, Happy, and Idle: Estimat-
ing the Health Capacity to Work at Older Ages in Germany." In *Social Security*

Programs and Retirement around the World: The Capacity to Work at Older Ages, edited by David A. Wise, 149–80. Chicago: University of Chicago Press.

Jürges, H., L. Thiel, T. Bucher-Koenen, J. Rausch, M. Schuth, and A. Börsch-Supan. 2016. "Health, Financial Incentives, and Early Retirement: Micro-simulation Evidence for Germany." In *Social Security Programs and Retirement around the World: Disability Insurance Programs and Retirement*, edited by David A. Wise, 285–330. Chicago: University of Chicago Press.

Oaxaca, Ronald. 1973. "Male-Female Wage Differentials in Urban Labor Markets." *International Economic Review* 14 (3): 693–709.

OECD. 2019. "Labour Force Statistics in OECD Countries: Sources, Coverage and Definitions." Labour Force Surveys. http://www.oecd.org/els/emp/LFSNOTES _SOURCES.pdf. Last updated January 2019.

Schirle, T. 2008. "Why Have the Labor Force Participation Rates of Older Men Increased since the Mid-1990s?" *Journal of Labor Economics* 26 (4): 549–94.

Statistisches Bundesamt. 2009. "Germany's Population by 2060—Results of the 12th Coordinated Population Projection." Federal Statistical Office. https://www .destatis.de/EN/Publications/Specialized/Population/GermanyPopulation2060 .pdf?__blob=publicationFile.

6

Employment at Older Ages
Evidence from Italy

Agar Brugiavini, Giacomo Pasini, and Guglielmo Weber

6.1 Introduction

The aim of this chapter is to explore and try to explain the increases in older Italian men's (and women's) labor force participation (LFP) and employment over the past 20 years. This is a general pattern common to most developed countries around the world, and many factors may have contributed to the recent increases in LFP and employment. These include changes in social security and disability insurance incentives, improving health and longevity, increasing education, a shift toward less physically demanding jobs, and rising female LFP (combined with the desire for joint retirement among couples).

Changes in the Italian social security system were prompted by the combination of high public debt and remarkably fast population aging. Population aging in Italy poses important challenges to the public pension system for three reasons. First, Italian public debt is particularly high (over 130 percent of GDP), and this is a particular concern given the low growth experienced in recent years. Second, Italy has a low fertility rate, around 1.4 (its population is aging from below). Third, Italians' life expectancy is among the

Agar Brugiavini is professor of economics at Ca' Foscari University of Venice.

Giacomo Pasini is professor of econometrics at Ca' Foscari University of Venice and a research fellow of Network for Studies on Pensions, Aging and Retirement (Netspar).

Guglielmo Weber is professor of econometrics at the University of Padua.

This chapter is part of the National Bureau of Economic Research's International Social Security (ISS) project, which is supported by the National Institute on Aging (grant P01 AG012810). The authors are indebted to Raluca Elena Buia for excellent research assistance. We also thank the members of the other country teams in the ISS project for comments that helped shape this chapter. For acknowledgments, sources of research support, and disclosure of the authors' material financial relationships, if any, please see https://www.nber.org/chapters /c14046.ack.

highest in the world and is rising (its population is aging from above). Given that the public pension system is fundamentally a pay-as-you-go system, this combination calls for a substantial increase in LFP at all ages (see Brugiavini and Peracchi 2012). Part of this increase may be obtained by encouraging female LFP (which is still relatively low in Italy compared to the US, the UK, or northern Europe), and part may be achieved by drawing in foreign workers (who compensate for aging from below). But aging from above calls for longer working lives—and the very low average effective retirement ages experienced in Italy until two decades ago suggest there could be major gains to be achieved by moving in this direction.

In light of the above, it is not surprising that the public debate has focused on how to increase the labor supply of workers in the 50–65 age group both by changing the incentives to retire and by introducing tighter conditions to be eligible for a public pension. Pension reforms have been implemented over the last three decades (starting in 1992), including a radical reform that was introduced in 2011 to ensure sustainability of public debt and postponed retirement age—by a wide margin for some—without offering an easy transition out of the labor force. In particular, a relatively large number of workers who had agreed on a separation from a firm on the expectation of shortly retiring on a public pension faced the prospect of long-term unemployment.

The chapter is organized as follows: we first provide some brief background on trends in LFP in Italy (section 6.2). In section 6.3, we briefly describe the Italian pension system and the recent reforms and perform a graphical analysis of the impact of various factors on the trends in the employment rate (ER) and the LFP. Section 6.4 presents an assessment of the effects of the variation in eligibility, education, and health improvements on the ER and the LFP by means of a simple linear regression. Section 6.5 concludes.

6.2   Data Sources and Description of the Italian Labor Market

In our analysis, we use data from various sources, as the information necessary to provide a complete description of the Italian labor market and pension system for the relevant years is not available in a single database. In order to guarantee comparability with the other countries presented in this study, we use the Organisation for Economic Co-operation and Development (OECD) as the primary source. In addition, we also make use of the following sources: (1) Italian National Institute of Statistics (ISTAT) for information on the labor market and education attainments, (2) the National Institute of Social Security (INPS) for information on eligibility requirements for the various pathways to retirement, (3) the Bank of Italy Survey of Household Income and Wealth (SHIW) for detailed information on education achievements by age groups, (4) the Human Mortality Database (HMD) data for mortality rates, and (5) Eurostat as a general source.

In particular, it should be noted that as far as the information on edu-

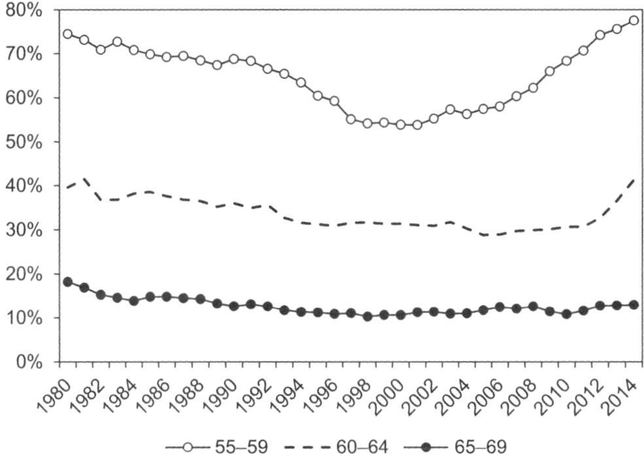

Fig. 6.1   LFP, men
Source: OECD and MARSS (ISTAT), see note a in the appendix.

cational levels is concerned, OECD and Eurostat provide the distribution
of educational attainments only for the wide 55–64 age group. Hence we
had to resort to the Bank of Italy SHIW in order to obtain information on
educational levels presented with a finer distribution by age (see appendix
to this chapter).

In order to provide a comprehensive view of the labor force trends prevailing in Italy, it is important to consider a sufficiently long time span: it is
well known that many important changes took place during the 1970s and
1980s regarding the educational system, the welfare system, and the industrial structure of the country. For comparability with the other chapters of
this book, we take for later years the data on LFP and ERs from the OECD
statistics. However, the OECD database does not go back far enough in
time—for earlier years, we gather the relevant information from the MARSS
database provided by ISTAT. As both data sets are based on the Labour
Force Survey (LFS), linking the two series is straightforward and does not
lead to arbitrary mixtures of different sources.[1]

LFP and ERs for older workers followed very similar patterns in the last
35 years, as is documented in figures 6.1 and 6.2 for men and figures 6.4 and
6.5 for women for three different age groups (55–59, 60–64, and 65–69).
While LFP and ER track each other closely for each age group, there are
clear gender and age differences.

Both LFP and ER series of men aged 55–59 have a U-shaped pattern: they
declined almost steadily from 1980 until 1997, remained around 55 percent
until the beginning of this century, and then started to rise. We see from
figure 6.1 that the LFP reached the same level in 2012 as in 1980 and con-

---

1. Comparing the two time series for the overlapping period, the result is almost identical.

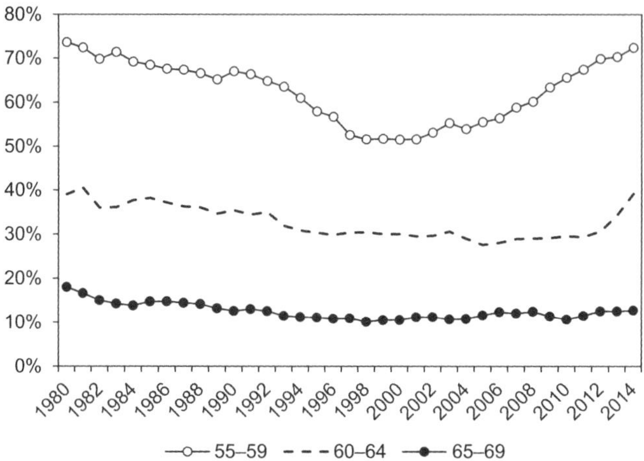

Fig. 6.2   Employment rates (ER), men
Source: OECD and MARSS (ISTAT), see note a in the appendix.

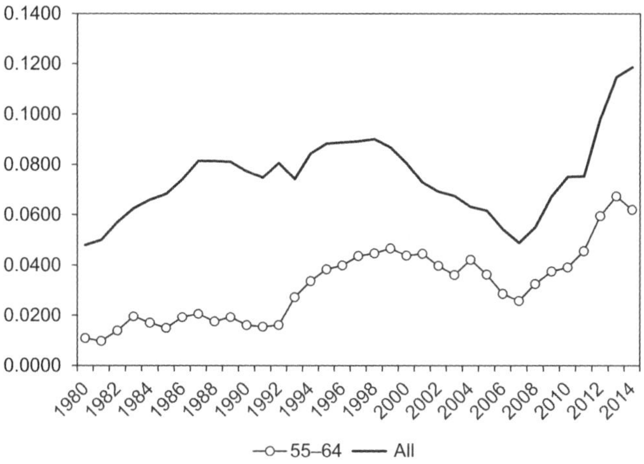

Fig. 6.3   Unemployment rates, men
Source: OECD and MARSS (ISTAT), see note d in the appendix.

tinued to increase thereafter; figure 6.2 shows that the ER also rose in recent years from its 1998 trough (52 percent) to 74 percent in 2014, but it has not yet reached its peak level of 1980 (76 percent). The discrepancy between the two series may be due to the widespread failure of older workers to find jobs in the midst of the Great Recession in the absence of specific welfare measures: until 2011, older workers who left their job automatically qualified for an early retirement pension, but this was no longer possible after the 2011 reform came into effect. This is somewhat confirmed by the trends of unemployment rates presented in figure 6.3; the unemployment rate of men

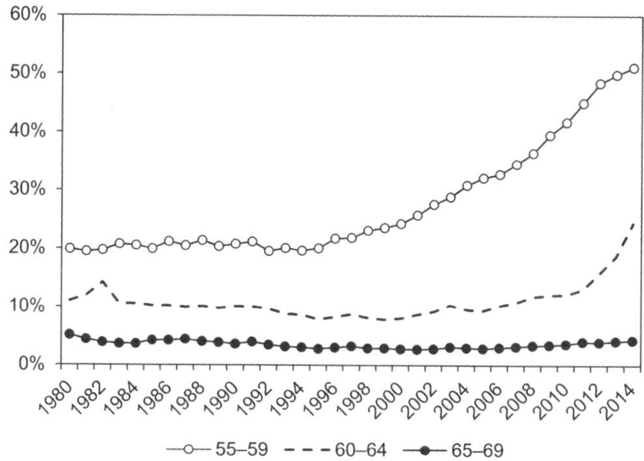

Fig. 6.4   LFP, women
Source: OECD and MARSS (ISTAT), see note a in the appendix.

in the 55–64 age group shows a steep growth in the last years of the sample period, in line with the general unemployment rate. Only in 2013, when youth unemployment was remarkably high in Italy, did the unemployment rate for older individuals exhibit a minor reversal.

Both LFP and ER series for the 60–64 age group decline slowly from values around 40 percent in 1980 to 28–29 percent in 2005. Then the trend flattens until 2011, when they start rising quickly, each increasing by 10 percentage points in three years and continuing to values comparable to the early 1980s.

The early downward trend is also noticeable for the older age group (65–69): LFP and ER were around 20 percent in 1980 and fell to 11 percent in 2011. In the next two years, they went up, albeit only by 2 percent.

The pattern of LFP and ER for women (figures 6.4 and 6.5) is markedly different and reflects the spectacular increase in labor market participation experienced by women all over the world in the second half of the 20th century, even though most of the increase takes place after the mid-1990s.

The LFP and ER of women aged 55–59 were both equal to 20 percent in 1980 and remained almost unchanged until the mid-1990s. From 1996 onward, both LFP and ER started increasing at a fast pace, reaching values above 45 percent in 2011. In the next three years, LFP and ER continued to increase, but their growth rate declined.

Regarding the 60–64 age band, only a small minority of women were involved in working activities until 2011: LFP and ER hovered around 10–12 percent from 1980 to 2011. As we saw for men, 2011 was a crucial year for women as well. Starting in 2012, the LFP and ER start to increase dramatically, reaching 24 percent in 2014. As for the oldest age group (women

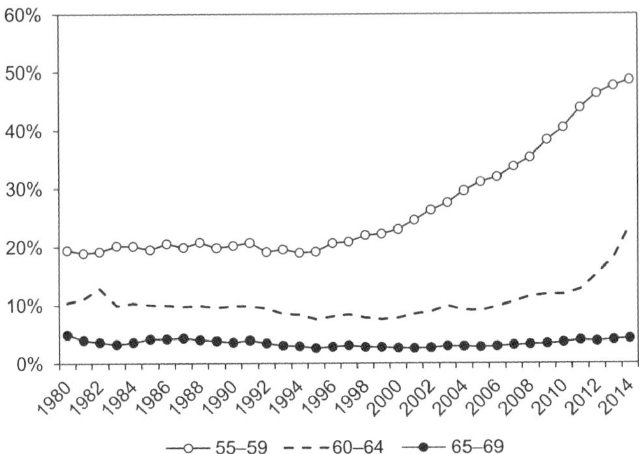

Fig. 6.5   ER, women
Source: OECD and MARSS (ISTAT), see note a in the appendix.

Fig. 6.6   Unemployment rates, women
Source: OECD and MARSS (ISTAT), see note a in the appendix.

aged 65–69), we see that less than 5 percent participate in the labor force throughout the period, with no relevant upward or downward trends. The unemployment rate for women aged 55–64 is relatively stable, as shown in figure 6.6.

The steady increase in education levels for both men and women, the progressive tightening of public pension eligibility criteria with the 1990s pension reforms, and the stark operation of the 2011 reform all contribute to explaining these patterns. To see how these factors interplay, we now focus on men's LFP.

6.3   Explaining the Pattern of the ER for Men: Education, Pension Reforms, and Longevity

In this section, we briefly review the basic rules of the Italian pension system that are relevant for the observed trends in the ER and the LFP rate of men in the 55–69 age group. Brugiavini and Peracchi (2016) provide a more detailed overview of the institutional details of the Italian pension system.

Italian men could retire in the public pension system through two distinct paths: an old-age pension or an early retirement (seniority) pension. Eligibility criteria for both were based on the number of years of contribution and an age limit. In the early years (until 1993), old-age pensions could be collected as early as 60 for men (55 for women), and early retirement pensions (EAR) were granted irrespective of age to retirees who had provided at least 35 years of contribution (or even less for particular groups of workers) to the system. Pensions benefits were earnings related and quite generous: a worker with a seniority of 40 years would collect a pension replacing 80 percent of his or her final salary. Also, the EAR benefits would not attract any actuarial penalty even for very young retirees in their 50s.

The reforms of the 1990s increased the retirement age and reduced benefits with the introduction of actuarially fair penalties and incentives. Two important reforms took place in 1992 and 1995, but the 1995 reform was more radical, changing both the eligibility rules and the calculation of old-age and early retirement benefits based on a notional defined-contribution (NDC) system. However, these changes were characterized by a long transitional phase and a "grandfathering" approach, protecting the older cohorts of workers, which made them effective with a considerable delay. Under the new system, the eligibility age for an old-age pension was increased gradually by one year of age every two years starting in 1994 until reaching age 65 for men and age 60 for women in 2000. The number of years of contribution required for an old-age pension was also increased gradually by one year every two years starting in 1993 until reaching 20 years of contributions in 2001. The transitional phase will be completed in 2032, when all retirees should retire under the NDC system; in the interim phase, benefits are computed as a weighted average of the pension benefit resulting from the old regime and the new regime (pro rata basis). As for the EAR, a worker could take early retirement in the year 1996 if aged 52, and if he or she had accumulated 35 years of contribution, the age limit increased in such way that in 2002, a worker would qualify at 57 years of age with 35 years of contribution. It is worth pointing out that the access to the EAR was also possible, independently of age, under the requirement in 1995 that a minimum contributive period of 35 years was satisfied. This requirement for the EAR increased over the sample period, reaching 40 years of contributions in 2008 (see tables 6.A.1 and 6.A.2 in the appendix).

In 2011, the Italian government enacted an important reform that changed the calculation of benefits in a radical way by implementing a more rapid

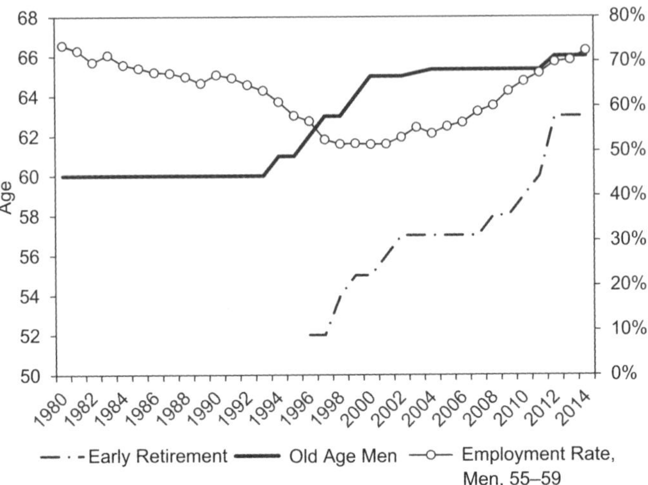

Fig. 6.7   Eligibility ages and employment rate for younger males aged 55–59

convergence to the NDC system. Furthermore, eligibility for an old-age pension became much tighter: in 2018, there would be no difference between men and women, and by 2050, the age requirement would become 69 years and 9 months for all types of workers. Under the new regime, which is currently in place, retirees can still access the EAR option, but a marked increase in the number of years of contributions needed for eligibility exists: 46 years for men and 45 for women by 2050. In the light of the patterns observed in our chapter, it is also relevant to point out that for those workers whose retirement benefits are computed entirely with the defined benefit method (the older cohorts), a penalty applies if the worker retires at an age younger than 62.

Figure 6.7 shows how the male EAR of individuals aged 55–59 varied over time between 1980 and 2014 (as already shown in figure 6.1) and how the old-age pension and early retirement eligibility ages evolved as a result of the various pension reforms described above.

We see that the old-age pension age gradually rose from 60 to 65, while the early retirement minimum age came into force in 1996 and quickly rose from 52 years of age (for those with at least 35 years of contributions) to 58 by 2010 and then jumped to 63 after the 2011 reform. The ER in the 55–59 age band kept falling until 1997 (in fact, many workers retired as soon as possible in the early 1990s in response to the public debate on the need to reform the pension system) but then rose steadily until 2014. It seems likely that the increase in ER over the last two decades was at least partly driven by the pension reforms. But other factors may have been at play, such as the increasingly higher proportions of high school and college graduates in that age group.

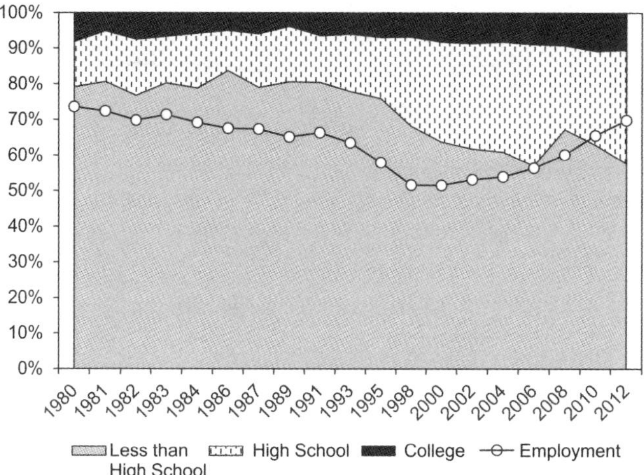

Fig. 6.8   Percentages of men with a high school or college degree and ER for men aged 55–59

Source: Eurostat and SHIW (see note d in the appendix).

Figure 6.8 displays the changing education mix of the male labor force aged 55–59. The key features to notice are the following: before 1995, 80 percent of men aged 55–59 (and even more women) had left school at 14 or younger. If their employers had paid pension contributions throughout their career, they could exit employment early (until 1993, with 35 years of contributions irrespective of age)—typically in their early 50s. The fraction of high school and college graduates in this age group started rising in the mid-1990s. By 2005, between 40 and 50 percent of men had left school at 19 or older, so they would not reach the minimum number of years of pension contributions (by then, 37) before age 57, if not later.

Those who attain a higher level of education enter the labor force at an older age and are induced by the seniority-based early retirement eligibility rules to keep working longer—and this also may contribute to explaining the rising ER of older workers in the last few years. It is also likely that higher-educated people are less keen to retire as soon as possible, as the types of jobs they have are less physically demanding and more rewarding, as we know from the effort-reward literature (Siegrist et al. 2006; Dal Bianco, Trevisan, and Weber 2015). Last but not least, the public pension system provides a higher incentive to stay at work the steeper the earnings age profile, which is typically associated with jobs performed by better-educated individuals.

The analysis of this particular age group of men suggests that the interaction of tighter early retirement eligibility rules and the increase in the fraction of high school graduates helps explain the sudden increase in LFP and ER for the 55–59 age group starting from the late 1990s. We leave a more formal investigation of the relative role played by each factor to section 6.6.

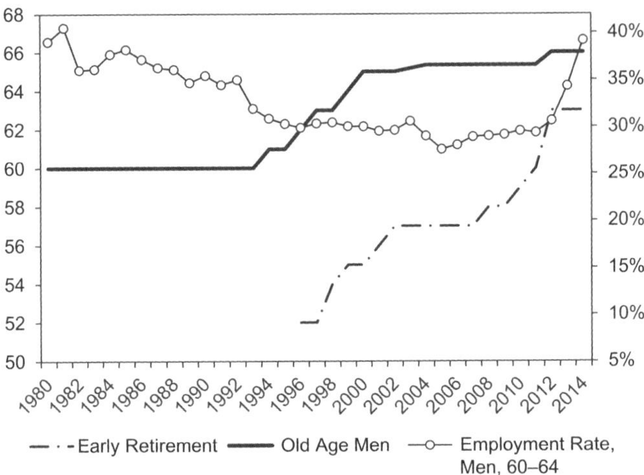

Fig. 6.9   Eligibility ages and employment rate for males aged 60–64

Fig. 6.10   Eligibility ages and employment rate for men and women aged 60–64

Figure 6.9 displays the ER of men for the 60–64 age group against time as well as the pension eligibility ages. We see that there was a downward trend in employment until 2005, which was followed by a slow but steady increase until 2011. As from 2012, the curve is steeply ascending: the ER increased from 30 to 40 percent in three years' time.

Figure 6.10 adds the ER for women of the same age group to this picture: the ER was roughly 10 percent until 2005, then slowly rose to 14 percent in 2011 and suddenly jumped to 23 percent in the last three years.

The slight increase of ERs between 2005 and 2011 is likely affected by a number of factors, including the tighter eligibility rules for early retirement

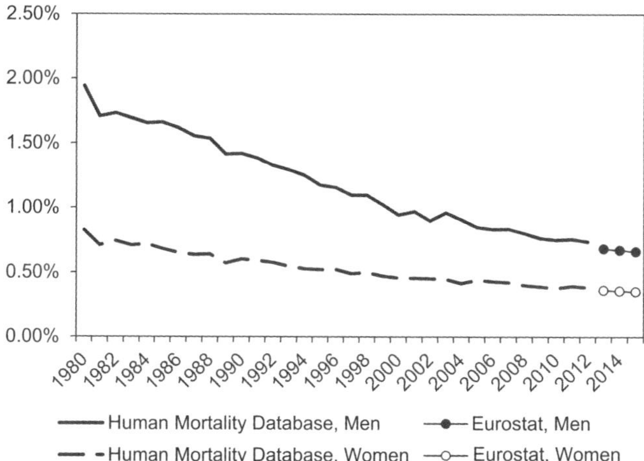

Fig. 6.11   Mortality rate at age 60, men and women
Source: 1980–2012, Human Mortality Database; 2013–2015, EUROSTAT Europop2013 population projections, main scenario (see note b in the appendix).

that came into force as a result of the implementation of the 1995 reform. The sudden increase from 2012 onward is instead most likely entirely attributable to the more radical and far-reaching 2011 reform (effective as of January 2012).

Finally, figure 6.11 displays mortality rates for Italian men and women aged 60, which falls steadily throughout the 1980–2014 period. This is reflected in rising life expectancies for all three age groups considered above. Given that longevity improvements should in principle be accompanied by better health, one may be tempted to conclude that the recent increases in LFP and ER can be attributed to better health. However, the improvements in longevity started well before 1995 and for a long time coincided with the decline in male LFP that we saw in figure 6.1. It is therefore unlikely that health improvements can explain the U-shaped time profiles in LFP and ER that we observe over the 1980–2014 period for men aged 55–59.

6.4   An Econometric Toy Model

The graphical analysis of the previous sections is, by its very nature, univariate—it considers one factor at the time. Also, each age group is treated in isolation. But these factors can be analyzed in a unified framework and age groups can be treated together if one is willing to specify a parametric model.

In this section, we propose a very simple linear model that allows the three factors at play—pension eligibility age, education, and health—to exert their joint influence on each variable of interest—the ER or the LFP indicator. Given that the dependent variable is expressed as a ratio and takes values between 0 and 1, the explanatory variables are expressed in similar terms.

Table 6.1   **Estimates for men, 1994–2014**

Variable	Employment rate	LFP rate
Δ eligibility	8.295**	8.820**
	(3.085)	(3.246)
Percentage of high school and college	1.830***	1.942***
	(0.261)	(0.274)
Δ life expectancy	–2.218	–2.315
	(2.492)	2.622
_cons	–0.232*	–0.253**
	(0.090)	(0.094)
Observations	63	63
R^2	0.461	0.465

We specify the following estimable equation:

$$y_{it} = a_0 + a_1 \Delta elig_t + a_2 HS_{it} + a_3 \Delta life_{it} + u_{it}, \; i = 1 \ldots 3; \; t = 1994 \ldots 2014,$$

where the dependent variable, y_{it}, is either the ER or the LFP rate of the i-th age group in year t. In the sequel, we pool the three age groups (55–59, 60–64, and 65–69) together, but we keep males and females distinct—that is, we estimate separate equations by gender.

The explanatory variables are the following:

$\Delta elig_t$ is the rate of change in the eligibility age—that is, the change in eligibility age between year $t - 1$ and t, divided by the eligibility age at time $t - 1$.

HS_{it} is the proportion of individuals with high school or more education of age group i at time t.

$\Delta life_{it}$ is the rate of change in life expectancy for age group i between year $t - 1$ and t.

Finally, u_{it} is an error term that we assume is not correlated with the explanatory variables.

We estimate the model over the second half of the sample period because eligibility age starts changing as a result of the mid-1990s pension reforms. It does not vary over the earlier part of the sample period (1980–93) when the only criterion that qualified a person for a pension was his or her job seniority (years of contributions). We introduce only one eligibility age (the old-age or normal pension age) in the model because the pension reforms raised both old-age pension and early retirement eligibility ages (and the former started rising earlier), so the two are therefore almost collinear.

Table 6.1 shows the estimates for the ER and the LFP for men. The two sets of estimates are sufficiently close that we can focus our comments on the ER equation. We estimate a significant, positive effect of eligibility age on the ER for these age groups. Given that the explanatory variable (which does not vary across groups by construction) has a sample average of 0.0069,

Table 6.2   **Estimates for women, 1994–2014**

Variable	Employment rate	LFP rate
Δ eligibility	1.765	1.89
	(1.142)	(1.195)
Percentage of high school and college	1.296***	1.345***
	(0.135)	(0.14)
Δ life expectancy	0.322	0.365
	(1.239)	(1.294)
_cons	–0.141***	–0.146***
	(0.035)	(0.036)
Observations	63	63
R^2	0.616	0.612

the contribution of this factor to the ER increase during the sample period is roughly 0.057—that is, 5.7 percent. The effect of higher education is also positive and highly significant, whereas the increase in life expectancy has a counterintuitive negative sign, but the parameter estimate is not statistically significant.

Table 6.2 reports a similar set of estimates for women—we now focus on the LFP, because this is a more interesting indicator for women, but stress that the signs and significance of coefficients are roughly the same across panels. Not surprisingly, in the light of the upward trend in female LFP, the effect of the pension reforms is smaller and insignificant. The only driving force we find is the change in the educational mix: the secular increase in the proportion of women with a high school degree or additional education has a strong positive and significant effect on their LFP. Finally, the improvement in life expectancy has a positive effect, but the coefficient is insignificantly different from zero.

6.5   Conclusion

In this chapter, we have documented recent trends in employment and the LFP among the Italian "young" old (ages 55–69). We have seen that LFP is particularly low and stable among the 65–69 age group but that major changes occurred over time for the younger groups.

A striking feature of the Italian labor market is the low but fast-rising female LFP. This is partly attributable to increased education and may help explain past and future changes in male participation and employment at older ages if men take into account the LFP of their spouses. This is an interesting topic for future research but is beyond the scope of our analysis.

Male LFP between ages 55–59 has changed dramatically over the years: after a steady fall in the 1980s and early 1990s, there was an impressive increase, leading to higher participation in very recent years compared to the early 1980s. This generates a U-shaped time profile of the ER for this age group. The 1990s were also the years when major public pension reforms were introduced in Italy. But other potential determinants of the LFP decisions were also changing over time: mortality was decreasing and the proportion of highly educated individuals was rising.

The ER of the older age group (60–64) was much more stable until very recently, when the more radical pension reform of 2011 pushed men to stay in the labor force until age 62 at least.

We have estimated a simple econometric model to assess the relative importance of all these factors on LFP and employment. We have found that the rise in both LFP and ER among men after 1995 is largely explained by two main factors: the increase in the eligibility age for public pension and the improved educational mix of the workforce. Improved health (approximated by decreased mortality) does not appear to have played a role, even though more specific health indicators may be needed before a firm conclusion can be drawn on this.

Appendix

Table 6.A.1   **Eligibility requirements for early retirement**

| | | Private employee | |
| | | Years of contributions only | |
Year	Age + years of contribution	Men	Women
1980	Any age + 35	35	35
. . .	. . .	. . .	. . .
1994	Any age + 35	35	35
1995	Any age + 35	35	35
1996	52+35	36	36
1997	52+35	36	36
1998	54+35	36	36
1999	55+35	37	37
2000	55+35	37	37
2001	56+35	37	37
2002	57+35	37	37
2003	57+35	37	37
2004	57+35	38	38
2005	57+35	38	38
2006	57+35	39	39
2007	57+35	39	39
2008	58+35	40	40
2009	58+35	40	40
2010	59+36	40	40
2011	60+36	40	40
2012	63+20	42 years and 1 month	41 years and 1 month
2013	63+20	42 years and 5 months	41 years and 5 month
2014	63+20	42 years and 6 months	41 years and 6 month

Table 6.A.2   **Eligibility requirements for old-age retirement**

	Defined benefit			Notionally defined contribution		
Year	Men	Women	Years of contribution	Men	Women	Years of contribution
1980	60	55	15	—	—	—
. . .	. . .	. . .	. . .	—	—	—
1992	60	55	15	—	—	—
1993	60	55	16	—	—	—
1994	61	56	16	—	—	—
1995	61	56	17	—	—	—
1996	62	57	17	57	57	5
1997	63	58	18	57	57	5
1998	63	58	18	57	57	5
1999	64	59	19	57	57	5
2000	65	60	19	57	57	5
2001	65	60	20	57	57	5
2002	65	60	20	57	57	5
2003	65	60	20	57	57	5
2004	65	60	20	57	57	5
2005	65	60	20	57	57	5
2006	65	60	20	57	57	5
2007	65	60	20	57	57	5
2008	65	60	20	65	60	5
2009	65	60	20	65	60	5
2010	65	60	20	65	60	5
2011	65	60	20	65	60	5
2012	66	62	20	66	62	20
2013	66	62	20	66	62	20
2014	66	63	20	66	63	20

Legend for the Italian Data

a. The series LFP_5559_M, LFP_5559_W, EMP_5559_M, and EMP_5559_W; LFP_6569_M, LFP_6569_W, EMP_6569_M, and EMP_6569_W; LFP_6064_M, LFP_6064_W, EMP_6064_M, and EMP_6064_W are drawn from the OECD data. They start in the year 1983 and are not available in the previous years; data for 1980–82 come from MARSS data (ISTAT).

b. The series MORT_60_M and MORT_60_W come from the HMD up to 2009; for the years 2010–13, the source is Eurostat. Information for 2014 is missing for both sources, and we produced an interpolation based on the available data. Also, life expectancy by age groups used in the regression comes from this source.

c. The source for the data in HS_5564_M, HS_5564_W, and COLL_55_64 is Eurostat starting with 1992. From 1989 to 1992, data are from SHIW weighted series with missing years when no survey took place. Before 1986, data are from historical archive SHIW surveys, and only age class is given.

Information is weighted. The SHIW survey started in 1977 and collects information on the income, savings, economic, and financial behavior of Italian households. Since 1989, the survey has been conducted every two years. In order to obtain complete series for the distribution of educational levels by age groups, we imputed the missing intermediate values by linear interpolation.

   d. UE_55_64_M, and UE_55_64_W, or the unemployment rates for the men and women in the age group 55–64, come from OECD starting with 1993. Although they were available from the OECD data, we substituted the data between 1980 and 1992 with MARSS data (Italian LFS) due to unexplained inconsistencies in OECD data between the series before 1992 and after 1993 (which lead to a significant peak in the data in 1993). MARSS data do not present this pattern, have the same source as OECD data (the Italian LFS), and are very similar to the OECD data for the years after 1993.

References

Brugiavini, A., G. Pasini, and G. Weber. 2017. "Health Capacity to Work at Older Ages: Evidence from Italy." In *Social Security Programs and Retirement around the World: The Capacity to Work at Older Ages*, edited by David A. Wise, 181–218. Chicago: University of Chicago Press.

Brugiavini, A., and F. Peracchi. 2012. "Health Status, Welfare Programs Participation and Labour Force Activity in Italy." In *Social Security Programs and Retirement around the World: Historical Trends in Mortality and Health, Employment, and Disability Insurance Participation and Reforms*, edited by David A. Wise, 175–215. Chicago: University of Chicago Press.

———. 2016. "Health Status, Disability Insurance, and Incentives to Exit the Labor Force in Italy: Evidence from SHARE." In *Social Security Programs and Retirement around the World: Disability Insurance Programs and Retirement*, edited by David A. Wise, 411–54. Chicago: University of Chicago Press.

Dal Bianco Chiara, Elisabetta Trevisan, and Guglielmo Weber. 2015. "'I Want to Break Free': The Role of Working Conditions on Retirement Expectations and Decisions." *European Journal of Ageing* 12:17–28.

Siegrist, Johannes, Morten Wahrendorf, Olaf von dem Knesebeck, Hendrik Jürges, and Axel Börsch-Supan. 2006. "Quality of Work, Well-Being, and Intended Early Retirement of Older Employees: Baseline Results from the SHARE Study." *European Journal of Public Health* 17 (1): 162–68.

Labor Force Participation of the Elderly in Japan

Takashi Oshio, Emiko Usui, and Satoshi Shimizutani

7.1 Introduction

An aging population has an adverse impact on the fiscal positions of social security programs and long-term growth potential, and encouraging labor force participation (LFP) is needed to mitigate demographic pressures. Moreover, social security benefits have been reducing the elderly's incentives to work (Gruber and Wise 1999). As such, previous studies have demonstrated that social security programs' enhanced generosity has been reducing the elderly labor supply despite general improvement in their health condition (Usui, Shimizutani, and Oshio 2016; Wise 2017). At the same time, the transition from work to retirement has become more complicated and diversified among the elderly via disability and unemployment insurance programs, as well as core public pension schemes (Wise 2012, 2016).

An association between social security benefits and elderly work/retirement decisions has been observed in Japan, although the elderly LFP rate is much higher than in other advanced countries (Yashiro and Oshio 1999). Additionally, the elderly LFP had been on a downward trend since the 1960s and was amplified by a long-term decline in the proportion of self-employed workers and farmers. Furthermore, compared to other countries,

Takashi Oshio is a professor at the Institute of Economic Research at Hitotsubashi University.

Emiko Usui is an associate professor at the Institute of Economic Research at Hitotsubashi University.

Satoshi Shimizutani is a senior research fellow at Ricoh Institute of Sustainability and Business.

For acknowledgments, sources of research support, and disclosure of the authors' material financial relationships, if any, please see https://www.nber.org/chapters/c14047.ack.

disability insurance programs play a limited role in the transition from work to retirement (Shimizutani, Oshio, and Fujii 2015).

However, in the last two decades, there has been a remarkable change in the elderly labor market in Japan. The elderly LFP and, more specifically, employment rates have been on an uptrend after a stabilizing period in the early 2000s. Several factors have contributed to these trends, including changes in incentives related to social security and disability insurance programs, improved health and longevity, increased educational attainment, a shift toward less physically demanding jobs, and rising female LFP (combined with the desire for joint retirement among couples). Their relative importance is likely to differ substantially across countries, and some of them may be less relevant to Japan.

In this study, we overview the recent trend of the elderly LFP in Japan and discuss what factors have contributed to its rebound. We focus on employment, considering that the unemployment rate among the elderly has been relatively low and stable in Japan. Our findings highlight the role played by changes to public social security programs as key determinants of the variation in the elderly's long-term employment trend.

The remainder of the chapter is organized as follows: section 7.2 provides an overview of recent trends in elderly employment, with specific reference to social security programs; section 7.3 discusses factors that could have contributed to the recent increases in elderly employment; section 7.4 focuses on social security incentives and their impact on the long-term evolution of elderly employment based on the results of Oshio, Oishi, and Shimizutani (2011); and section 7.5 concludes the chapter.

7.2   Recent Trends in Elderly Employment and Social Security Programs

7.2.1   Employment Patterns of Elderly Men

The overview of the elderly's recent employment trends uses aggregated data from Labour Force Surveys (LFSs) released by the Ministry of Internal Affairs and Communications. Figure 7.1 depicts recent fluctuations of male employment rates, dividing them into four age groups (55–59, 60–64, 65–69, and 65+). The data of those aged 65–69 are available only from 2002.

The employment rate of those aged 55–59 has been staying high at around 90 percent, despite cyclical fluctuations, because these ages are lower than the mandatory retirement and pensionable ages. Meanwhile, the employment rate of those aged 60–64 bottomed in the early 2000s but has been rising since. This age group has been dominating the dynamics of elderly employment, with the timing of the rebound after the late 1990s, as observed in other advanced countries. The employment rate of those aged 65–69 has also been on an uptrend since the mid-2000s, albeit more modestly than for the 60–64 age group. This movement presumably reflects the cohort effect:

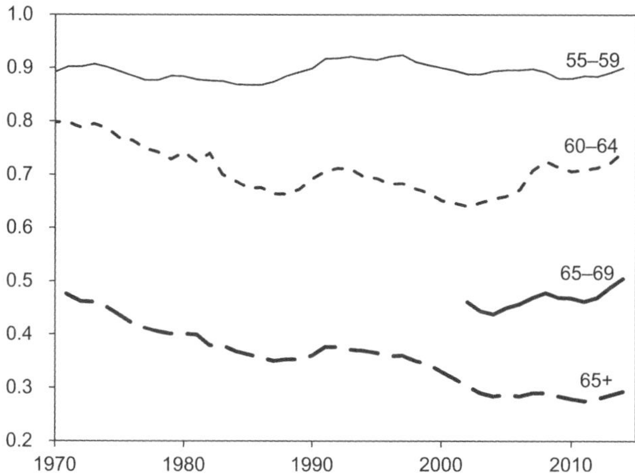

Fig. 7.1   Employment rate, males

those more active at age 60–64 are more inclined to stay in the workforce at age 65–69. Moreover, the employment rate of those aged 65 and older stopped declining in the mid-2000s, probably due to the increase of those aged 65–69.

Consequently, the employment of elderly males stabilized in the early 2000s and has been on an increasing trend since. This evolution has been largely led by those aged 60–64, an age group that is usually transitioning from work to retirement and thus is most likely to be affected by the overall economic conditions and social security programs. As younger age groups tend to be close to full employment and older ones are more likely to have retired, both have a limited impact on the changes in elderly employment.

Nonetheless, the turnaround of the 60–64 age group's LFP is not fully attributable to a change in macroeconomic conditions. Figure 7.2 compares the employment rate of this male age group with the national male unemployment rate (on a reverse scale). As seen in this figure, the elderly's employment rate had been moving with the nationwide unemployment rate until the late 1990s. However, in the early 2000s, the gap between two variables started to widen, deviating from their previous comovement. The elderly have been increasing their labor supply since then, despite the growth of nationwide unemployment due to the overall economic downturn. Additionally, this figure suggests that institutional changes affected the elderly's labor market in the early 2000s and that tighter national labor-market conditions around 1990 accounted for a delayed trough of elderly employment compared to other countries.

A plausible factor for the elderly employment rebound in the early 2000s was an increase in the eligibility age of the Employees' Pension Insurance (EPI), a public pension program for employees in the private sector. The

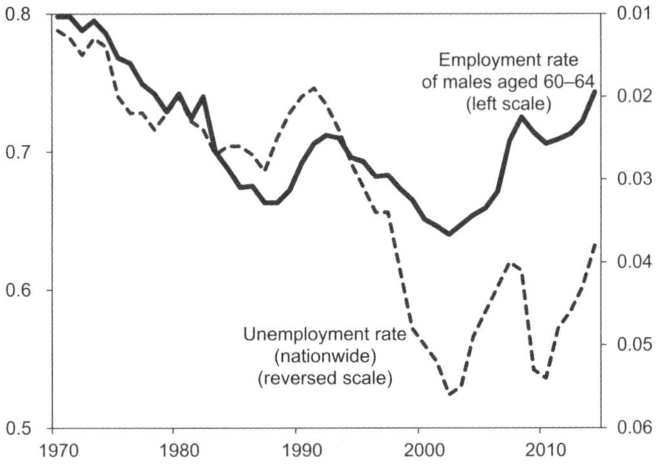

Fig. 7.2   Unemployment rate for males aged 60–64 and at the national level

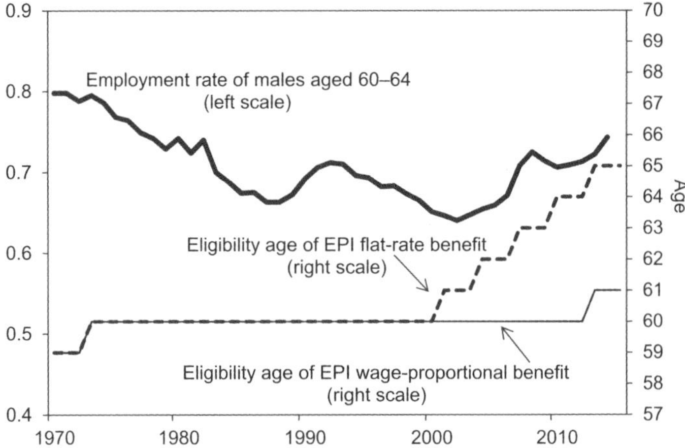

Fig. 7.3   Employment of males aged 60–64 and eligibility age for EPI benefits

EPI benefits consist of a flat-rate component (basic pension) and a wage-proportional one. The eligibility age for male EPI members was 60 for both components, but the flat-rate one was raised by one year every three years starting in 2001, increasing the age to 65 by 2013. The eligibility age of the wage-proportional benefit has been raised by one year every three years since 2013 and is scheduled to increase to 65 by 2025. Figure 7.3 compares the evolution of the eligibility age for EPI benefits and the employment rate of males aged 60–64 and shows that both an increase in the employment rate and the timing of its start were closely associated with an increase in the eligibility age for the flat-rate benefit from age 60.

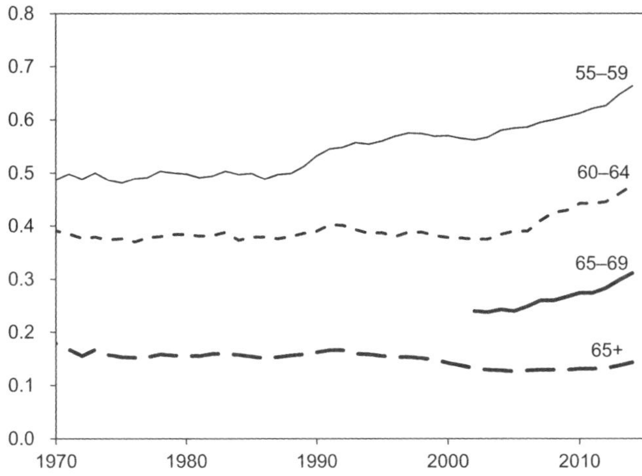

Fig. 7.4   Employment rate, females

Along with an increase in the eligibility age of EPI benefits, a series of policy measures to stimulate the elderly LFP were implemented. First, the Continuous Employment Benefits for the Elderly was introduced in 1995 to subsidize 15 percent of the preretirement wage for those aged 60–64 who kept working after mandatory retirement. Second, the disincentive effects of the *Zaishoku* pension benefits (i.e., income-tested EPI benefits for active employees) were reduced in 2005. Finally, the Law for the Stabilization of Employment of the Aged was enforced in 2000, 2004, and 2012 to recommended/required firms to keep employing workers until at least 65. These policy measures allowed EPI members to postpone retirement, resulting in an increase in the employment rate of the 60–64 age group since the early 2000s.

7.2.2   Employment Patterns of Elderly Women

The elderly female employment also has been increasing in recent years, although there are some differences from the case of males. As such, figure 7.4 depicts the female employment rate, dividing it into four age groups (55–59, 60–64, 65–69, and 65+). Unlike males, the rate of employment for the 55–59 age group started rising in the late 1980s, and after a short pause, it resumed rising. Meanwhile, the employment rate of the 60–64 age group remained almost constant, at a level slightly lower than 40 percent until the mid-2000s, and subsequently started rising abruptly somewhat later than the men's. The trend for the 65–69 and 65-and-older age groups are similar to those for men.

Additionally, the dynamics of female employment rates are closely related to increases in the eligibility age of EPI benefits. Figures 7.5a and 7.5b compare the evolutions of the EPI eligibility age with the employment rates of females aged 55–59 and 60–64, respectively. However, the EPI eligibility age

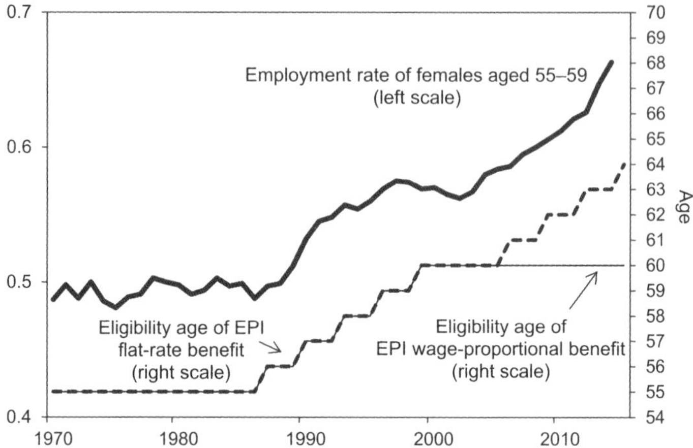

Fig. 7.5a   Employment of females aged 55–59 and eligibility age for EPI benefits

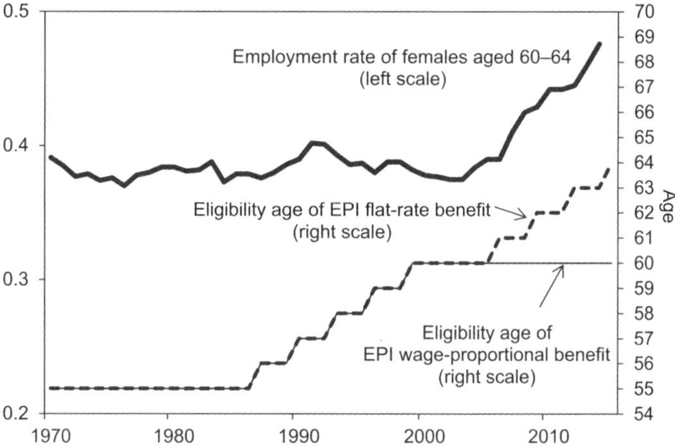

Fig. 7.5b Employment of females aged 60–64 and eligibility age for EPI benefits

differs between men and women. Unlike for males, the eligibility age for the flat-rate and wage-proportional benefits—both of which used to be set at 55, five years younger than for males—had been raised by one year every three years from 55 in 1987 to 60 in 1999. The eligibility age of the flat-rate benefit resumed rising in 2006, five years later than for males.

An increase in the employment of the female 55–59 age group during the late 1980s and 1990s (not observed for males) was consistent with the adjustments of the EPI eligibility age (figure 7.5a). For those aged 60–64, the employment rate started increasing in the mid-2000s, after a modest increase compared to the previous decades (figure 7.5b). This change was

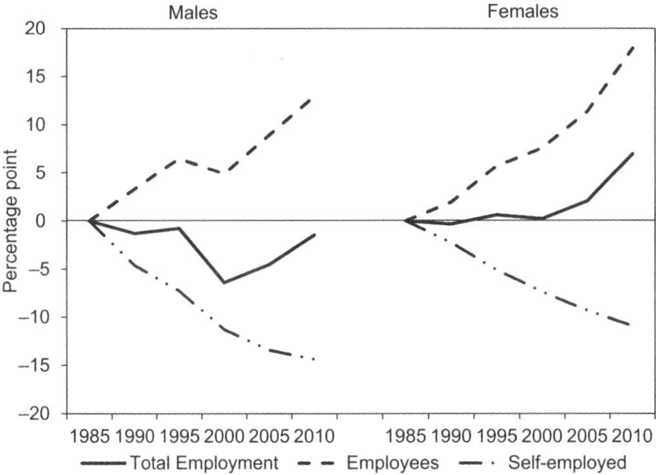

Fig. 7.6   **Decomposed changes in total employment for ages 60–64**

consistent with an increase in the eligibility age of the EPI flat-rate benefit starting in 2006, which has also encouraged those aged 55–59 to stay longer in the labor force, since the employment rate for those aged 55–59 resumed rising in the mid-2000s.

7.3   Determinants of Elderly Employment Increases

7.3.1   Employed and Self-Employed Workers

The previous section overviewed the recent increase in elderly employment, with specific reference to the increases in the eligibility age for EPI benefits. This section discusses other factors that may have favorably affected the elderly LFP, such as a decrease in self-employed workers, an increase in part-time workers, higher education, more jobs that require less physical exertion, and improving health conditions.

As such, we focus on different trends of employed and self-employed workers (including farmers). A reduction in self-employed workers has led to a long-term downtrend of elderly employment, meaning that the recent rebound was driven by an increase in employed workers. In addition, the work/retirement decisions of self-employed workers are not likely to have been affected, at least directly, by recent social security reforms, as they are covered by the National Pension Insurance (NPI), which has only the flat-rate benefit and a fixed eligibility age of 65 since 1960, although the amount of the benefit has changed.

To capture the different trends of employment between employed and self-employed workers, figure 7.6 decomposes workers aged 60–64 into these two groups and compares their contributions to changes in employment rate since 1985 for both males and females. The data are based on the population census released by the Ministry of Internal Affairs and Communications.

For males, we observe that the proportion of self-employed workers to the total population aged 60–64 declined steadily from 31.4 percent in 1985 to 17.1 percent in 2010 and contributed negatively to the overall employment rate of this age group. In addition, there are no changes in the curve for this group, which is consistent with no change in the eligibility age for NPI benefits. In contrast, the proportion of employed workers increased, with a short period of reduction in 1995–2000. An increasing number of employees aged 60–64, who used to retire, are now continuing to work. This increase has been offsetting a reduction in the proportion of self-employed workers, leading to a U-shaped rebound of the employment rate for this age group. The short period of reduction corresponds to a postboom reduction in the elderly labor demand.

We observe a similar development for females: an increase in employed workers has been offsetting a decrease in self-employed workers. However, unlike males, females' overall employment rate has not been falling since 1985, and the increase in employed workers has been smoother than for males, probably reflecting the lack of changes in the EPI eligibility age for this age group (until 2013).

7.3.2   Full- and Part-Time Employees

The previous subsection confirms that the recent increase in elderly employment accounted for an increase in employees rather than self-employed individuals. Subsequently, we divide employed workers into full- and part-time groups. Based on the data from the LFS, figure 7.7 compares the proportion of part-time workers among the total number of employees between the 55–64 and 65-and-older age groups for males and females.

For males aged 60–64, the proportion of part-time employees has remained low between 1990 and 2015, although it has been gradually rising. This suggests that an increase in employment for those aged 60–64 has reflected the postponed retirement of full-time employees who responded to the raised eligibility age of EPI benefits. For those aged 65 and older, the proportion of part-time employees has been increasing more, suggesting that those who have retired from their jobs and/or started to claim EPI benefits were inclined to stay in the labor force as part-time workers.

For females, the proportion of part-time employees has been much higher than for males for both age groups. The proportion has been increasing over recent decades for both 55–64 and 65-and-older age groups, indicating that the recent increase in elderly female employment has been concentrated on part-time work.

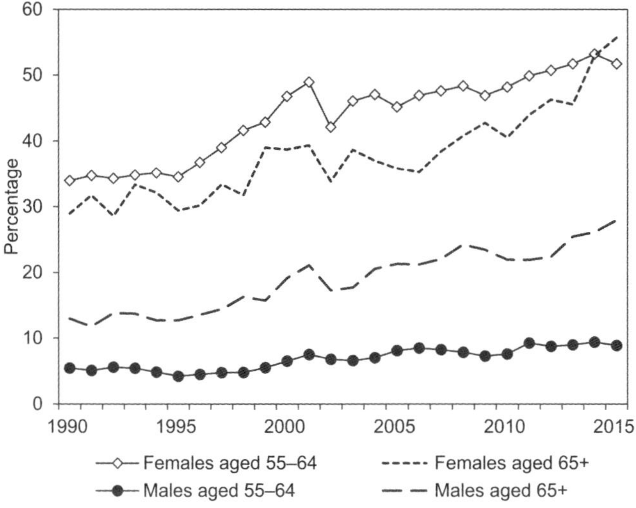

Fig. 7.7   Proportion of part-time workers

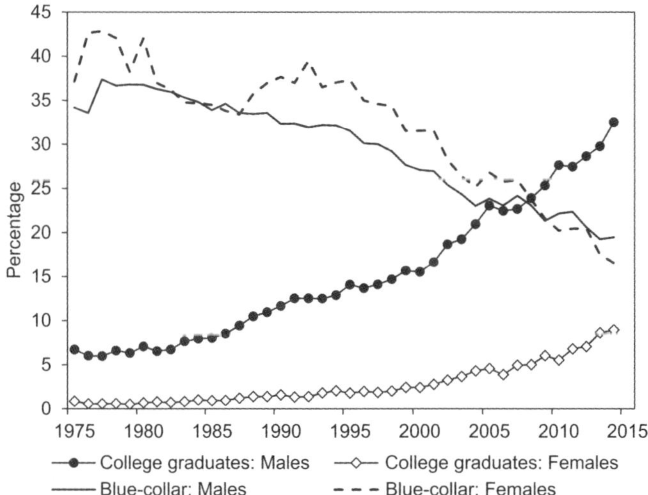

Fig. 7.8   Proportion of college graduates and blue-collar workers

7.3.3   Higher Education and Fewer Physical Constraints

There are two structural changes in the elderly labor market that have probably contributed to their employment in recent decades—that is, an increasing proportion of highly educated workers and a decreasing proportion of blue-collar workers (figure 7.8). Combined with the health conditions

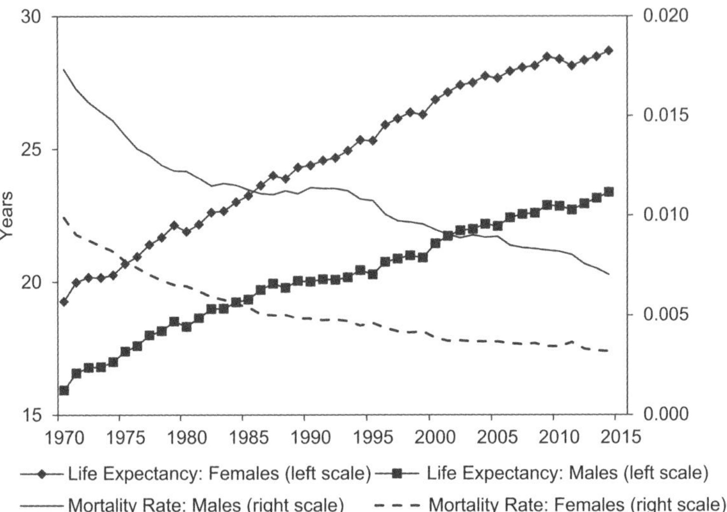

Fig. 7.9   Life expectancy and mortality rates at age 60

improvement, these two factors have allowed employees to stay longer in the labor force.

Moreover, the proportion of those who graduated from college or other higher education has been rising remarkably. According to the wage census of the Ministry of Health, Labour and Welfare, the proportion of college (including graduate school) employees aged 55–64 rose from 6.7 percent to 32.5 percent for males and from 0.9 percent to 9.0 percent for females between 1975 and 2014. Meanwhile, the proportion of blue-collar workers declined from 34.2 percent to 19.5 percent for males and from 37.1 percent to 16.6 percent for females during the same period, along with a shift from the manufacturing to the service sector.

7.3.4   Improving Health Conditions

Another important factor for elderly employment is the health and longevity improvement. To confirm this, we looked at two health variables— that is, life expectancy and mortality rates at age 60 over the last two decades (figure 7.9), based on the data from the life tables released by the Ministry of Health, Labour and Welfare. Life expectancy at age 60 has increased from 15.9 to 23.4 years for males and from 19.3 to 28.7 years for females between 1970 and 2014. Consistently, the mortality rate at age 60 has been declining from 0.0173 to 0.0070 for males and from 0.0099 to 0.0032 for females during the same period.

The two measures confirm substantial improvement in the elderly's health conditions, which would allow them to remain active and work longer. However, the elderly males have been reducing LFP over time in response to wider

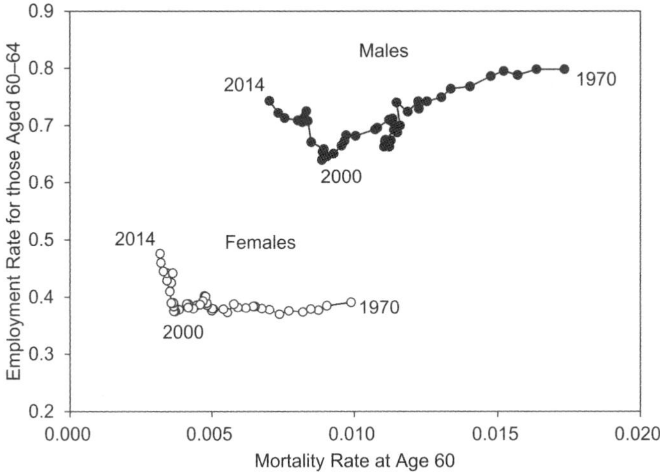

Fig. 7.10   **Mortality rate at age 60 and employment rate for ages 60–64**

coverage of social security programs and increasing benefits (Yashiro and Oshio 1999). Consequently, the employment rate of elderly males has been positively correlated with their mortality rate, with both variables declining simultaneously. This fact suggests that, first, improving health conditions have not led a rebound in elderly male employment, even if they may have prevented it from declining further. Second, substantial work capacity remains unutilized among elderly males, meaning that social security reforms can potentially enhance elderly employment (Usui, Shimizutani, and Oshio 2016).

However, the relationship between elderly employment and health has changed remarkably since the early 2000s and differs substantially between males and females. Figure 7.10 shows the combinations of the mortality rate at age 60 and the employment rate of those aged 60–64 for males and females between 1970 and 2014.

For males, both mortality and employment declined until around 2000, resulting in their positive correlation. Around 2000, the curve of their combinations turned up and to the left—that is, the employment rate rebounded, while the mortality rate continued to decline. A series of social security reforms and related policy measures—in particular, an increase in the eligibility age of EPI benefits—made the elderly males stay longer in the labor force, deviating from the previous negative correlation between health and employment. In other words, a series of policy reforms made it possible to realize the potential working capacity, which had been created by improved health conditions.

The observed relationship between health and employment changed remarkably in the mid-2000s for elderly females as well. Until then, the curve had been nearly flat, indicating that employment had been nearly constant, as observed in figures 7.4 and 7.6b, despite improved health conditions. In the mid-2000s, the curve turned up and left, which roughly corresponded to an increase in elderly female employment in response to a rise in the eligibility age for EPI benefits starting in 2006. As for males, social security reforms helped utilize the elderly's work capacity due to improved health and longevity.

7.4   Social Security Incentives and Elderly Employment

7.4.1   Social Security Incentives and Option Values

As discussed in the previous sections, an increase in the eligibility age for EPI benefits seems to have been closely related to the rebound of elderly employment. However, recent social security reforms, which have been launched almost every five years since 1954, have incorporated other measures as well. Notably, social security reforms from 1985 and after have been reducing the overall generosity of benefits—in particular, by reducing the benefit multiplier of wage-proportional benefits in contrast to the previous reforms that aimed to raise it. This section evaluates the impact of these reforms in terms of the option value (OV), as per Oshio, Oishi, and Shimizutani (2011).

The OV model assumes that an individual compares utility today with that at the optimal future retirement age and chooses the optimal retirement age as such. The indirect utility function over work and leisure of an individual aged t, $V_t(r)$, is expressed as

$$V_t(r) \equiv \sum_{s=a}^{r-1} p_{s|t} d^{s-t}(y_s)^g + \sum_{s=r}^{D} p_{s|t} d^{s-t}[kB_s(r)]^g, \quad 0 < g < 1, \ k \geq 1,$$

assuming that he or she will retire at age $r(\geq t)$. $B_s(r)$ is the benefit that an individual is expected to receive at age $s(\geq r)$, d is the cumulative discount rate, $p_{s|t}$ is the probability of being alive at age s (conditional on being alive at age t), D is the maximum age, y is the wage income while working, g is a parameter of risk aversion, and k is a parameter that accounts for the disutility of labor ($k \geq 1$). $B_s(r)$ usually tends to rise as r increases, reflecting a longer period of premium contributions, and is equal to 0 if s is below the eligibility age.

The optimal retirement age maximizes indirect utility—that is, the age at which the utility gain derived from the additional work wage increase begins to be outweighed by the utility loss from retirement income decrease. As such, OV is defined as the difference between indirect utility from retirement at optimal age r^* and indirect utility from retiring today and can be expressed as

$$OV_t(r) \equiv V_t(r^*) - V_t(r).$$

To compute OV, the values of k and g are required. Using data obtained from the LFS, we search for the combination of k and g that maximizes the good fit of the model, which regresses LFP on OV. We find that the combination of $k = 2.0$ and $g = 0.75$ and of $k = 3.0$ and $g = 0.75$ are most appropriate for males and females, respectively. Consequently, we adopt the typical person approach developed by Engelhardt and Gruber (2004)—that is, we apply the same earnings profile to all cohorts and construct incentive measures according to the available social security programs. Specifically, we use the 1935 birth cohort as a benchmark and assign its earnings profile to every subsequent cohort. Based on this earnings profile, we calculate OV under the existing annual social security program. Finally, we calculate its annual weighted average by gender.

In addition, we conduct counterhistorical simulations to estimate how social security reforms have affected the elderly's labor supply since 1985. We examine what OV would have looked like if the government had not implemented major social security reforms. For example, to estimate the impact of the 1985 and subsequent reforms, we construct all the parameters in the social security programs, including the benefit multiplier, premium rates, and eligibility ages fixed in 1984, and generate the paths OV would have taken since 1985 without any reform. In the same manner, we can construct the paths without reforms since the 1989 reform and roughly interpret the difference between these simulated paths as the impact of the 1985 reform. The experiments can be repeated to capture the impact of each reform.

7.4.2   Assessing the Changing Generosity of Social Security Programs

Figures 7.11a and 7.11b depict the estimated evolution of the weighted average of OV for those aged 55–69 to capture the changing overall generosity of social security programs for males and females, respectively. The U-shaped OV curves bottomed around 1995 for males and 1990 for females. This is consistent with social security programs starting to reduce generosity in the 1985 reform, considering a transition period.

A turnaround in the generosity, which is reflected in the U-shaped OV curves, led to a turnaround of elderly employment. As seen in figures 7.1 and 7.4, the tighter labor market conditions in the aftermath of the economic expansion of the late 1980s obscured the relationship between the OV and elderly employment. In addition, the rise in elderly employment rates was triggered by increases in the eligibility age for EPI benefits. However, a series of social security reforms starting in 1985 has been modulating the momentum of enhancing elderly work incentives by reducing the overall generosity of social security programs.

Figures 7.11a and 7.11b also present the results of these counterhistorical

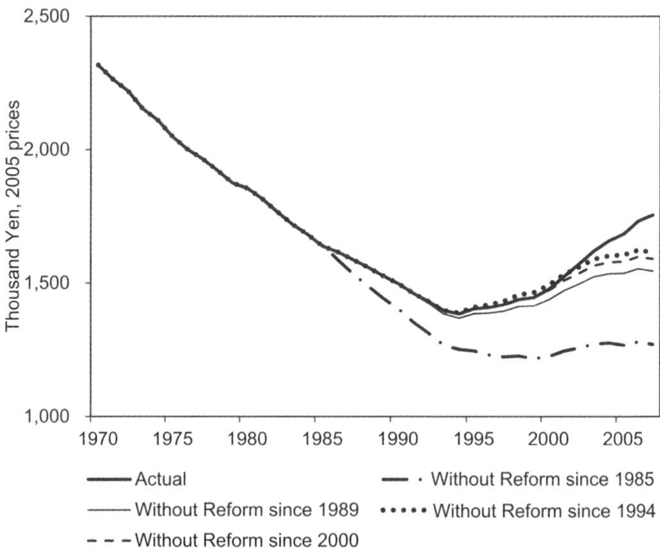

Fig. 7.11a   Impact of social security reforms on OV, males aged 55–69

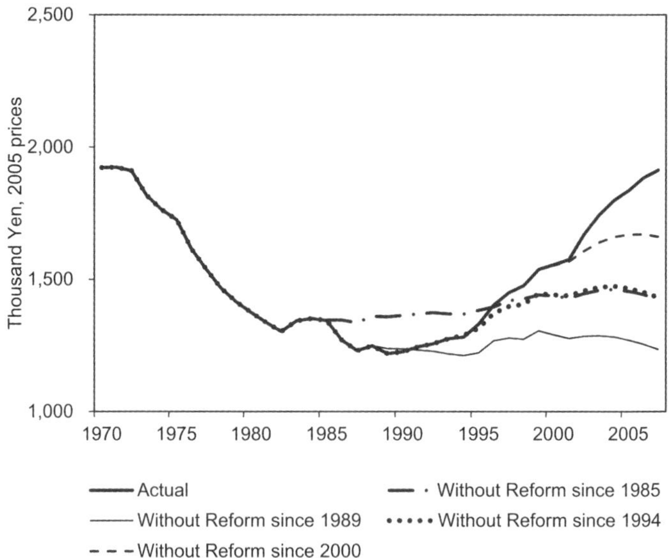

Fig. 7.11b   Impact of social security reforms on OV, females aged 55–69

simulations on OV to assess the impact of social security reforms since 1985. For males (figure 7.11a), the curve labeled "Without reform since 1985" depicts the path OV would have taken if the social security reform stopped just before the 1985 reform. In this case, OV for males would have declined further and would have leveled off in the late 1990s, as all the cohorts would have adopted the scheme that was applied just before the 1985 reform. The series of reforms since 1985 shifted the OV curve downward; however, the impact of the 1985 reform was larger than that of any other reform.

The impact of social security reforms is also observed in the case of females (figure 7.11b). The impact differs from that of males in that the 1985 reform raised the generosity of the programs for females until the mid-1990s, judging by the comparisons between the actual OV curve and the "Without reform since 1985" one. The 1985 reform called for a gradual increase in the eligibility age for females from 55 to 60, raising net benefits due to a prolonged period of premium contributions, which was much shorter than for males. Nevertheless, the figure confirms that the generosity of social security programs has been gradually decreasing since the late 1980s, similar to the case for males.

Oshio, Oishi, and Shimizutani (2011) estimated the impact of social security reforms on the elderly's LFP based on the counterhistorical simulations of OV. They reported that social security reforms since 1985 increased the labor force by 0.7–1.9 percent and 0.6–0.9 percent for men and women, respectively, per year between 1995 and 2007.

7.5 Concluding Remarks

As in most advanced countries, Japan has experienced increases in elderly LFP in recent years. In this study, we overviewed the recent trend of elderly employment and examined what factors have contributed to its rebound since the early 2000s. Improved health and longevity, increased education levels, and a shift toward less physically demanding jobs seem to have allowed the elderly to stay longer in the labor force.

However, the rebound and its timing in regard to elderly employment have been more closely linked to changes in social security incentives, especially the increases in the eligibility age for public pension benefits. The reduced generosity in social security programs since the mid-1980s has been a key driver of the recent increase in elderly employment, and a series of social security reforms have helped utilize the elderly's potential work capacity, owing to improving health conditions and other favorable factors for the elderly's LFP.

References

Engelhardt, G. V., and J. Gruber. 2004. "Social Security and the Evolution of Elderly Poverty." NBER Working Paper No. 10466, National Bureau of Economic Research, Cambridge, MA.

Gruber, J., and D. A. Wise, eds. 1999. *Social Security and Retirement around the World*. Chicago: University of Chicago Press.

Oshio, T., A. S. Oishi, and S. Shimizutani. 2011. "Social Security Reforms and Labor Force Participation of the Elderly in Japan." *Japanese Economic Review* 62 (2): 248–71.

Shimizutani, S., T. Oshio, and M. Fujii. 2015. "Option Value of Work, Health Status, and Retirement Decisions in Japan: Evidence from the Japanese Study on Aging and Retirement (JSTAR)." In *Social Security Programs and Retirement around the World: Disability Insurance Programs and Retirement*, edited by David A. Wise, 497–535. Chicago: University of Chicago Press.

Usui, E., S. Shimizutani, and T. Oshio. 2016. "Health Capacity to Work at Older Ages: Evidence from Japan." NBER Working Paper No. 21971, National Bureau of Economic Research, Cambridge, MA.

Wise, D. A., ed. 2012. *Social Security Programs and Retirement around the World: Historical Trends in Mortality and Health, Employment, and Disability Insurance Participation and Reforms*. Chicago: University of Chicago Press.

———. 2016. *Social Security Programs and Retirement around the World: Disability Insurance Programs and Retirement*. Chicago: University of Chicago Press.

———. 2017. *Social Security Programs and Retirement around the World: The Capacity to Work at Older Ages*. Chicago: University of Chicago Press.

Yashiro, N., and T. Oshio. 1999. "Social Security and Retirement in Japan." In *Social Security and Retirement around the World*, edited by J. Gruber and D. A. Wise, 239–67. Chicago: University of Chicago Press.

Why Are People Working Longer in the Netherlands?

Adriaan Kalwij, Arie Kapteyn, and Klaas de Vos

8.1 Introduction

Over the last two decades, social security programs and pension schemes around the world have been redesigned to create stronger incentives for continued work at older ages (Gruber and Wise 2004; Wise 2012, 2016). These reforms have, for a large part, been triggered by the rapidly declining labor force participation (LFP) of men at older ages since the 1970s while life expectancy continued to rise (figures 8.1 and 8.2). For the Netherlands, this increase in life expectancy has been just under two months per year on average since 1950. For women, since the end of the 1970s, LFP has risen at ages 55–59 but has notably dropped at ages 60–64 from over 11 percent in the mid-1970s to around 8 percent in the mid-1990s (figure 8.3). Apart from people living longer, a strong decline in fertility rates has amplified the aging of Dutch society. Completed fertility has dropped during the second half of the 20th century from around three children per woman during the mid-1950s to around 1.7 in 2014 (figure 8.4). Increased life expectancy and decreased fertility have initially caused the total dependency ratio—that is, the number of people younger than 20 and older than 64 as a percentage of the number of people aged 20–64—to decrease from 1971 onward, as there were relatively fewer children. Since the mid-1990s, however, the total dependency ratio has started rising again due to a continuing increase in the

Adriaan Kalwij is an associate professor at the Utrecht University School of Economics.

Arie Kapteyn is professor of economics, a director of the Center for Economic and Social Research at the University of Southern California, and a research associate of the National Bureau of Economic Research.

Klaas de Vos is a researcher in the quantitative analysis department at CentERdata.

For acknowledgments, sources of research support, and disclosure of the authors' material financial relationships, if any, please see https://www.nber.org/chapters/c14048.ack.

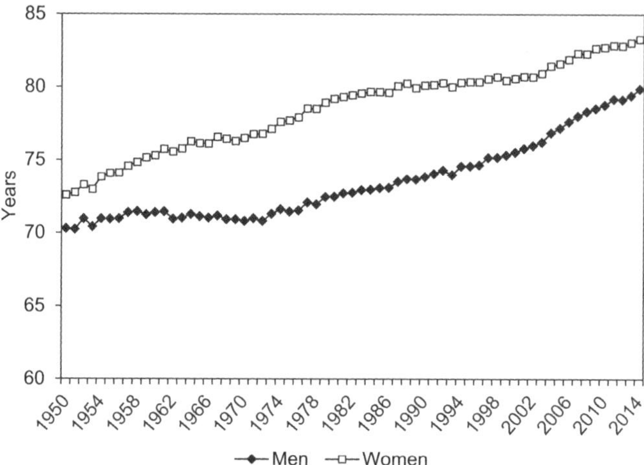

Fig. 8.1   Life expectancy at birth over the years 1950–2014
Source: Statistics Netherlands, http://statline.cbs.nl.

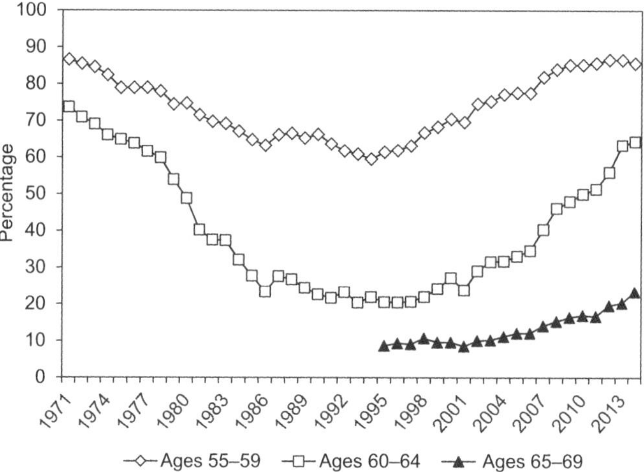

Fig. 8.2   Men's LFP by age for the period 1971–2014
Source: OECD, http://stats.oecd.org/.

share of the population aged 65 and over (figure 8.5). The aged dependency ratio—that is, the number of people older than 64 as a percentage of the number of people aged 20–64—has increased from about 19 percent in 1971 to 29 percent in 2014. The aging of Dutch society gained momentum after 2011 when the baby boom generation began to reach the normal retirement age of 65, and the aged dependency ratio is predicted to further increase to about 50 percent in 2050 (Statistics Netherlands 2018). The aging of the Dutch population has raised concerns about the burden on public finances,

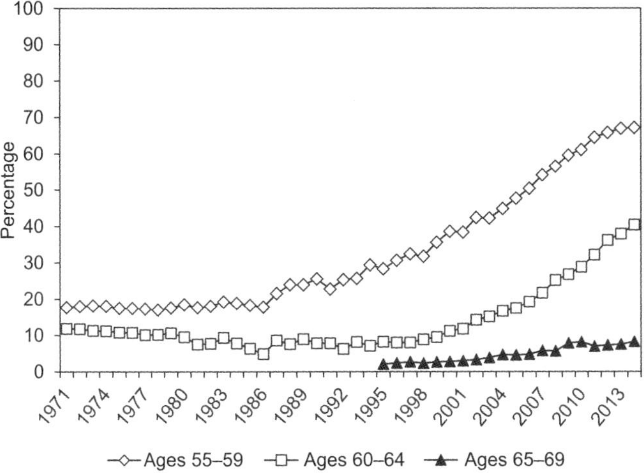

Fig. 8.3   Women's LFP by age for the period 1971–2014

Source: OECD, http://stats.oecd.org/.

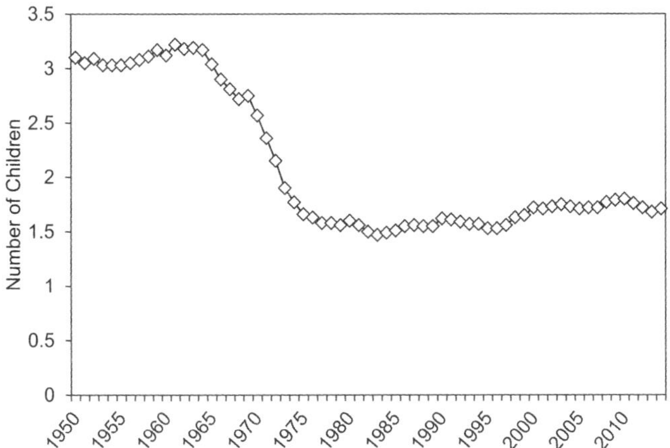

Fig. 8.4   Completed fertility*

Source: Statistics Netherlands, http://statline.cbs.nl.

* The predicted number of children for women born in the years 1950–2014, given the age-specific fertility rates in those years.

as it increases public expenditures on, for instance, long-term care and retirement pensions (OECD 2011; Van Ewijk et al. 2006).[1] One way to alleviate this burden is to increase the LFP at older ages, as it will increase tax revenues

---

1. Reforms aimed at a reduction of public health care expenditures, such as decreased coverage of health care and long-term care insurance, are unlikely to have impacted the LFP, and a discussion of these is beyond the scope of this chapter.

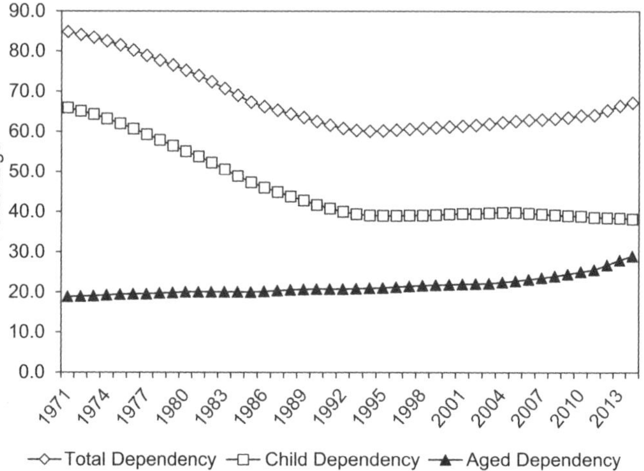

Fig. 8.5   Dependency ratios for the years 1971–2014*

Source: Statistics Netherlands (downloaded March 2, 2016; http://statline.cbs.nl).

* The total dependency ratio is defined as the number of people younger than 20 or older than 64 as a percentage of the number of people aged 20–64. The child dependency ratio is defined as the number of people younger than 20 as a percentage of the number of people aged 20–64. The aged dependency ratio is defined as the number of people older than 64 as a percentage of the number of people aged 20–64.

and, when stimulated by an increased normal retirement age, reduce public pension expenditures.

This chapter discusses explanations that have been suggested in the literature for the strong rise in men's LFP since the mid-1990s (figure 8.2). The reason for restricting our discussion to this period is that 1995 (or thereabouts) turns out to be a pivotal year for many countries, including the Netherlands, after which the LFP rates of older workers increased sharply after a long period of decline (see chapter 1).[2] Two important necessary conditions for an individual to keep working at older ages are being in good health and having the skills to remain attractive to employers. These conditions are discussed in sections 8.2 and 8.3, respectively. Next, section 8.4 discusses the role institutions may have played in the rise of the LFP rates of older workers. Section 8.5 discusses the overall findings, the restrictions of the underlying analyses, and implications for future labor market participation of older workers.

8.2   Health and LFP

Staying healthy is necessary to keep working at older ages. In this section, we take mortality and healthy life expectancy, as well as the percentage of

2. The roles that early retirement schemes and disability insurance have played in the declining men's LFP during the 1980s are discussed in Kapteyn and de Vos (1999) and Koning and Lindeboom (2015), respectively.

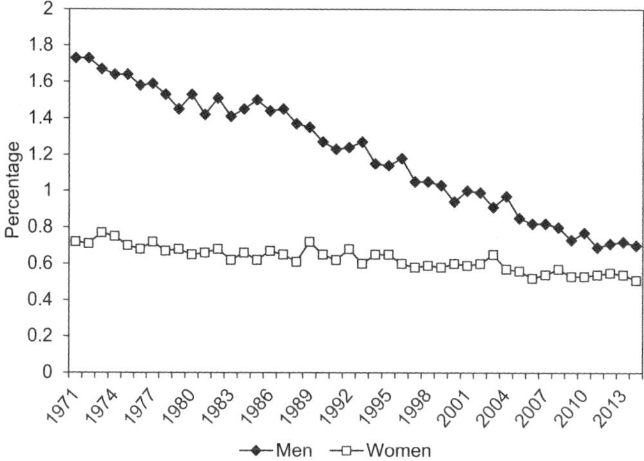

Fig. 8.6   Mortality rate at age 60 by year and gender
Source: Statistics Netherlands, http://statline.cbs.nl.

people receiving disability insurance (DI), as measures for the health of older workers.

8.2.1   Health and Mortality

When looking at mortality data, one can conclude that health at all ages has improved over long periods of time. Life expectancy at birth in the Netherlands has doubled from around 40 years in 1850 (the earliest records available) to currently around 80 years (Human Mortality Database 2018). Although initially reductions in infant mortality caused this increase, at older ages, health has improved significantly as well. The mortality rate at age 60 (men and women combined), for instance, has declined from around 3 percent in 1850 to 2.5 percent in 1900 and to 1.2 percent in 1950. Currently, it is about 0.6 percent. Figure 8.6 shows a stronger decline in men's than in women's mortality at age 60 in recent decades. These declines in mortality rates are a global phenomenon and can be attributed to (interrelated) factors such as a decline in infectious diseases, medical innovations, improved living standards, better nutrition, and public health and social policies (Cutler, Deaton, and Lleras-Muney 2006).

Increases in life expectancy are not always accompanied by an equal rise in the expected healthy life years. For this reason, Statistics Netherlands has computed healthy life expectancy—an adjustment of life expectancy for the actual health status of individuals.[3] A visual inspection of the trends

3. See statline.cbs.nl. Healthy life expectancy is defined as the number of years an individual of a particular age can expect to live in good health, assuming the current risks of death and bad health apply. Taken into account is if a person perceives him or herself to be in good health (self-assessed health), if he or she is without physical limitations (no long-term limitations in mobility, sight, and hearing) and without chronic diseases (heart condition and/or myocardial

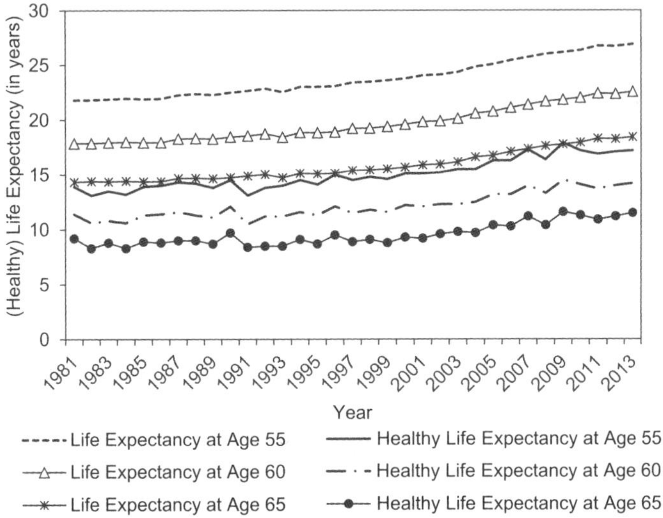

Fig. 8.7   Men's (healthy) life expectancy by year and age
Source: Statistics Netherlands, http://statline.cbs.nl.

in figures 8.7 and 8.8 of men's and women's life expectancy and healthy life expectancy at different ages suggests that life expectancy and healthy life expectancy are closely related. Using the numbers on which these figures are based, we find that, on average over the past 25 years, healthy life expectancy as a share of total life expectancy is about 0.60–0.63 for men and 0.55–0.59 for women. These shares reveal that while women live longer, they spend relatively more years in bad health than men. It is noteworthy that—for instance, at age 65—healthy life expectancies for men and women have converged. The difference was about two years in the early 1980s and is nowadays close to zero. Almost all the additional years of life expectancy that women aged 65 have gained since the early 1980s are spent in bad health, and as a result, the remaining healthy life expectancies at age 65 of men and women are nowadays about equal. This suggests a stronger improvement in men's health than in women's health at age 65.

8.2.2   Health and DI

The DI scheme in the Netherlands mandates social insurance for all workers against earnings loss due to adverse health events. In principle, therefore,

---

infarction, asthma, chronic bronchitis, pulmonary emphysema, or chronic nonspecific pulmonary disease, cancer, stroke, diabetes, serious or chronic gastrointestinal disorders, chronic arthritis [Bechterew's disease, chronic rheumatism, rheumatoid arthritis], serious or chronic backache [including slipped disk], degenerative arthritis in hips or knees, hypertension [high blood pressure], migraine or recurring serious fits of headache), and if the person is in good mental health (based on the Mental Health Inventory [MHI-5], determined by the balance of positive and negative feelings).

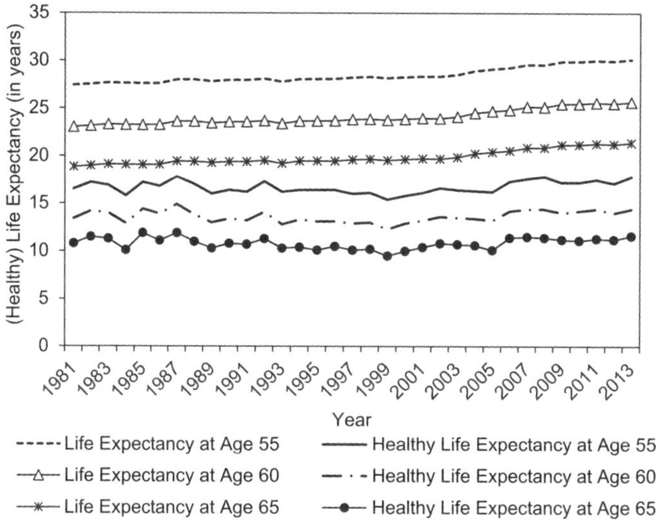

Fig. 8.8   Women's (healthy) life expectancy by year and age
Source: Statistics Netherlands, http://statline.cbs.nl.

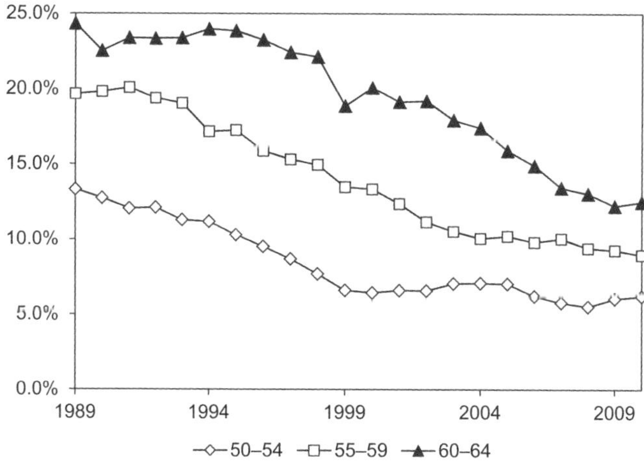

Fig. 8.9   Men's disability insurance rate by year and age
Source: Statistics Netherlands, Income Panel Study (IPO). DI rates are the percentage of people receiving DI.

the percentage of people receiving DI measures the health of older workers. Koning and Lindeboom (2015) show that there is a decline in DI recipients from about 1992 onward for the entire Dutch working population. Figure 8.9 shows that for older men, the percentages of people receiving DI have been steadily declining since 1989. Over the years 1989–93, this decline is most pronounced for men aged 50–54. A similar decline is observed for

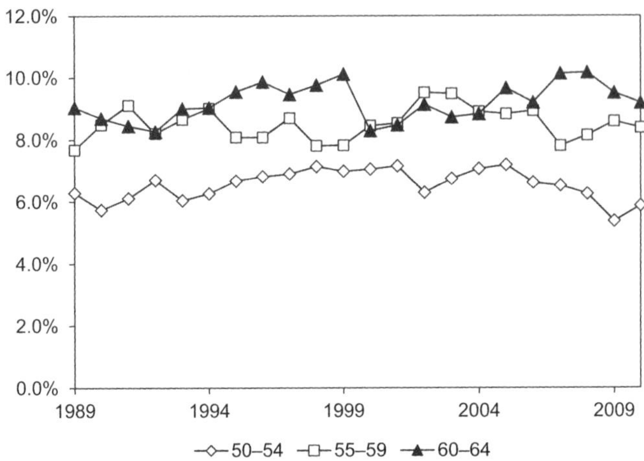

Fig. 8.10   Women's disability insurance rate by year and age

Source: Statistics Netherlands, IPO. DI rates are the percentage of people receiving DI.

these cohorts 5 years later over the years 1994–98 (at ages 55–59) and 10 years later over the years 1999–2003 (at ages 60–64). If the percentage of people receiving DI were to measure the health of older workers, it would suggest (in line with the observations based on mortality rates in section 8.2.1) that the younger cohorts are relatively healthier than the older cohorts (for a given age). Figure 8.10 shows that for women, the DI rates are relatively stable despite the strong increase in women's employment rates (figure 8.3), which may also suggest an improvement in the health of older female workers. DI rates are a function of not just health but also institutions governing flows into and out of the DI system. At least part of the observed changes is also affected by institutional changes, as will be argued below.

8.3   Skills

Part of the explanation for the rapidly declining LFP of older workers since the mid-1970s may be skill-biased technological change (SBTC; Autor and Katz 1999). SBTC has increased the demand for higher-educated workers at the expense of lower-educated workers. Many of the skills of lower-educated older workers have become obsolete and are no longer in demand. The occupations that demanded these skills often included manual and physically demanding tasks that have been replaced by capital intensive equipment such as machines. In addition, and especially since the 1990s, automation—that is, a shift to capital intensive equipment that makes use of computers—has taken over routine-based tasks that happen to be relatively more often performed by (older) workers with median levels of education

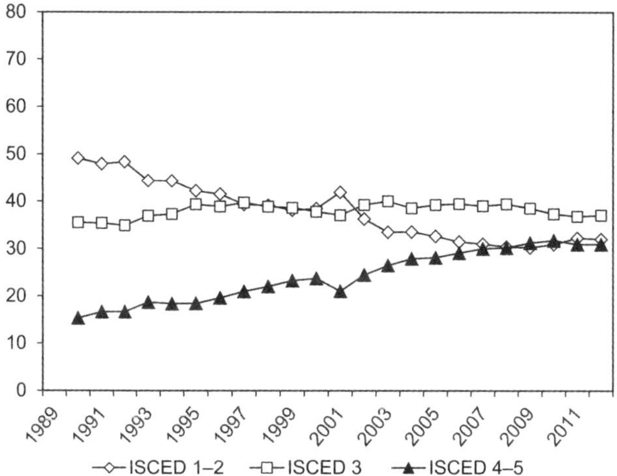

Fig. 8.11   Levels of education of men aged 55–65 by year
Source: Statistics Netherlands, LFS (Enquete Beroepsbevolking; EBB). ISCED: 1997 International Standard Classification of Education (ISCED).

(Autor and Dorn 2009; Goos, Manning, and Salomons 2014).[4] One of the explanations for the rapid rise in LFP from the mid-1990s may, therefore, be related to shifts in the composition of employers' demand toward non-routine occupations and high-skill workers. To investigate the plausibility of that explanation, we consider the change in the educational and occupational distributions among older workers.

Levels of education are defined according to the 1997 International Standard Classification of Education (ISCED; UNESCO 1997). ISCED 1–2 will be referred to as a low level of education, ISCED 3 as a medium level of education, and ISCED 4–5 as a high level of education. Figure 8.11 shows that the percentage of higher-educated men aged 55–64 has doubled over the 1989–2012 period. Over the same period, the percentage of lower-educated men aged 55–64 has decreased by almost 20 percentage points. These trends have resulted in a continuous increase in the level of education of older workers. Figure 8.12 shows similar trends for women in this age range, with even stronger increases in the percentage of higher- and median-educated women and a stronger decrease in the percentage of lower-educated women. While the levels of education for men are higher than for women, the figures show convergence, as women in the younger cohorts are closing this gap. In addition, Kalwij, Kapteyn, and de Vos (2016) find that the level of education is one of the important determinants of employment at older ages and that the exit rates from employment are largest for the lower educated. Taking these findings together suggests that the increased LFP rates of older work-

---

4. This is often referred to as routine-biased technological change (RBTC).

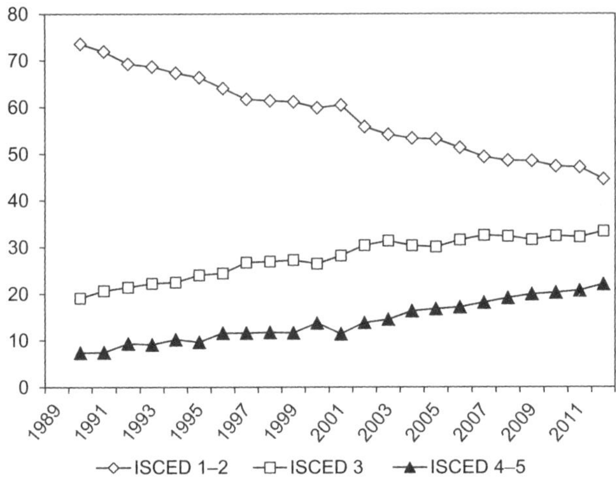

Fig. 8.12   Levels of education of women aged 55–65 by year

Source: Statistics Netherlands, LFS (Enquete Beroepsbevolking; EBB). ISCED: 1997 ISCED

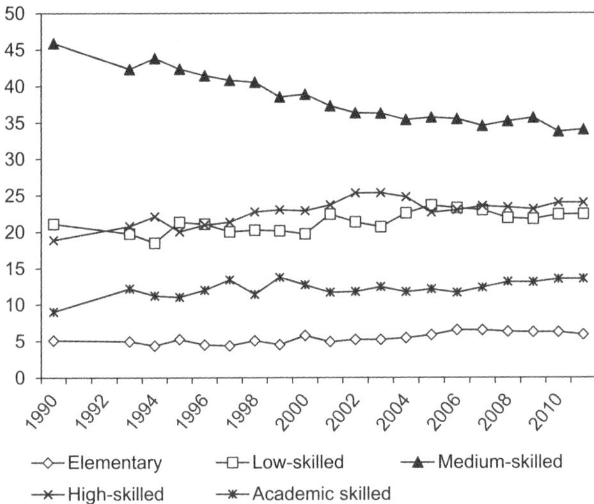

Fig. 8.13   Types of jobs (skill levels) by year for men aged 55–64

Source: Statistics Netherlands, LFS (Enquete Beroepsbevolking; EBB). Skills levels are defined based on the SBC 1992 classification (http://www.cbs.nl/nl-NL/menu/methoden/classificaties/overzicht/sbc/1992/default.htm).

ers can at least partly be explained by the increased levels of education of older workers, which made them more attractive to employers.

Figure 8.13 shows that in particular, median-skilled jobs have been disappearing for men, an 11 percentage point drop over the 1990–2011 period, while the high- and academic-skilled jobs have increased (together about a

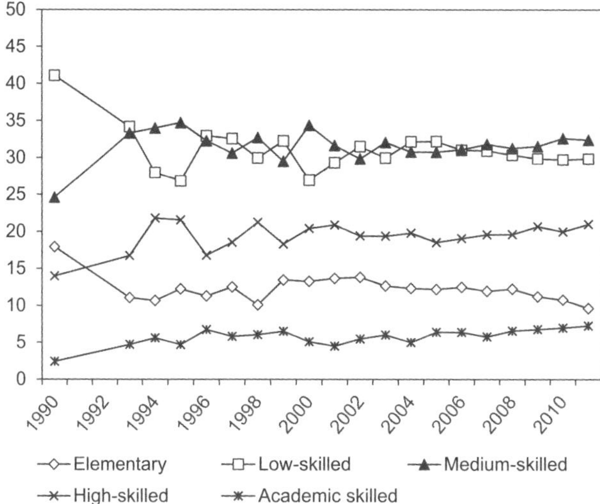

Fig. 8.14   Types of jobs (skill levels) by year for women aged 55–64

Source: Statistics Netherlands, LFS (Enquete Beroepsbevolking; EBB). Skills levels are defined based on the SBC 1992 classification (http://www.cbs.nl/nl-NL/menu/methoden/classificaties/overzicht/sbc/1992/default.htm).

10 percentage point increase). The percentages of low-skilled and elementary jobs remain relatively constant between 1990 and 2011. For women, figure 8.14 shows a slightly different picture. Although (relative) job growth for women has also been mainly in high- and academic-skilled jobs (together about a 12 percentage point increase), the percentage of median-skilled jobs has also increased by about 8 percentage points. At the same time, there have been very large drops in low-skilled jobs (11 percentage points) and elementary jobs (8 percentage points). The Dutch situation of a relative rise in medium-skilled jobs for women, as opposed to the relative drop for men, appears to be in contrast to the empirical evidence provided for the US that computerization of tasks reduces employment in routine task-intensive occupations for male and female workers (Autor, Dorn, and Hanson 2015).

To sum up, the shifts in the level of education and skill composition of older male workers (figures 8.11 and 8.13) are likely to have contributed to the rise of LFP rates among older men from the mid-1990s onward, as the entering cohorts more often had the skills demanded than the retiring cohorts.

8.4   Institutions and LFP

From the end of the 1970s onward, generous early retirement (ER) schemes were introduced. Early on, these were often called young-for-old programs. As this name suggests, the main idea was that if older workers left the workforce, younger people would take their places. The introduction of

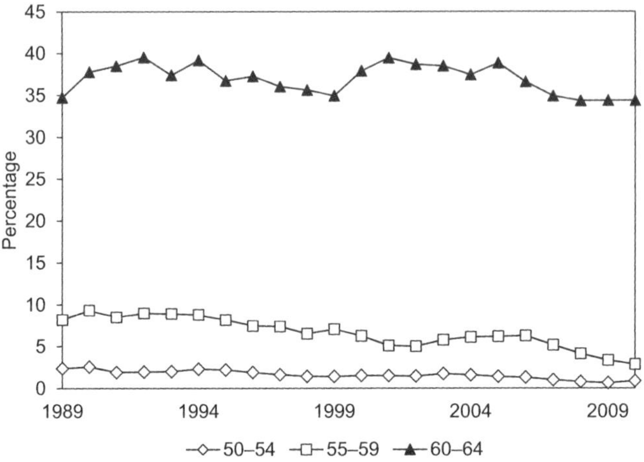

Fig. 8.15   Early retirement (ER) rates for men aged 50–64
Source: Statistics Netherlands, IPO. ER rates are the percentage of people receiving ER pensions.

these ER schemes was a policy reaction to very high youth unemployment and relatively unhealthy older male workers (section 8.2) who often had jobs that were becoming obsolete (section 8.3). This, together with the fact that the benefits were quite generous, made these schemes very attractive for both employees and employers. Net replacement rates were high, and the programs were mainly financed by the current workforce. As shown in figure 8.15, the ER option has been taken by over one-third of the people aged 60–64. ER rates have rapidly declined since the mid-1990s among people younger than 60, but ER rates among 60–64-year-old people remained high for many more years and started to decline after about 2006. As it turns out, empirical evidence suggests that the ER schemes did not create additional employment for the young (Kapteyn et al. 2010). One explanation for this is that, as mentioned earlier, many jobs that were left behind by early retirees involved obsolete tasks. Support for this explanation is given by Kalwij, Kapteyn, and de Vos (2010), who find that employment of the young and old are not substitutes and may even be complements. As described in the introduction, the popularity of the ER schemes has led to rapidly declining labor market participation rates of older workers from the late 1970s onward, reaching a historical low in the early 1990s (Kapteyn and de Vos 1999).

At the end of 1980s, Dutch policymakers' reactions to the historically low labor market participation rates of older workers, in combination with the aging of the Dutch population, involved a series of reforms implemented from the early 1990s onward, such as making ER benefits less generous and imposing stricter eligibility rules for DI and unemployment insurance (UI; see appendix). The necessity of the reforms has been amplified by a series of crises such as the dotcom crash in 2000–2001, the 2007–8 financial crisis, and housing market and euro crises in its aftermath, which have shown the financial vulnerability of the Dutch social security and pension system (e.g., Kalwij et al. 2015). The latter sequence of events created the momentum for increasing the normal retirement age in the Netherlands. The normal retirement age is the age at which people start receiving a public old-age pension. Up until 2012, the normal retirement age was 65. It will increase gradually to 66 in 2018 and 67 in 2021. After that, it will be further raised in line with increases in population life expectancy, up to age 70 and three months.

The LFP rates shown in figures 8.2 and 8.3 suggest that the reforms of the past two decades may have been successful, as these rates have strongly risen from the onset of the reforms in the mid-1990s. Men's LFP at ages 60–64 has tripled over this period from 20 percent in 1995 to over 60 percent in 2014. For men aged 55–59, the LFP has substantially increased from 61 percent in 1995 to 86 percent in 2014 (figure 8.2). Figure 8.3 shows, from the mid-1990s onward, similar trends for women as for men but at lower levels. Previous empirical studies of the impact of less-generous ER schemes also suggest that these reforms have contributed to the increase in the LFP of the 55–64 population from less than 30 percent in the mid-1990s to 45 percent in 2007 (Euwals, de Mooij, and van Vuuren 2009; Kapteyn and de Vos 1999; Van Oorschot 2007).

As shown by Burkhauser and Daly (2011), the number of DI beneficiaries per worker in the Netherlands, which for a long time was among the highest in the developing world, decreased below the comparable figure for the US, which suggests that DI reforms may also have had considerable impact. The findings of de Jong, Lindeboom, and van der Klaauw (2011) suggest that stricter screening of DI applications has reduced long-term sickness absenteeism and DI applications. In line with these latter results, Kalwij, de Vos, and Kapteyn (2016) show that the reduction over the last decades in the percentage of older workers who have exited the labor market through DI has mainly been achieved by restricting access to the DI scheme and is not due to a reduction in the generosity of disability benefits.

8.4.1 Pathways

One way in which adverse labor market effects of the DI and ER reforms could manifest themselves is that older workers who lose their jobs end up unemployed if stricter criteria make them no longer eligible for ER or DI. Figure 8.16, however, shows that men's employment rates have followed similar trends as the participation rates of figure 8.2, and unemployment rates had in fact decreased substantially to about 2 percent just before the dot-com crisis of 2001 (figure 8.17). Since then, unemployment rates have been rising, following the business cycle, among older workers to around 7 to 8 percent. Similar patterns are observed for women's employment and unemployment rates (figures 8.18 and 8.19).

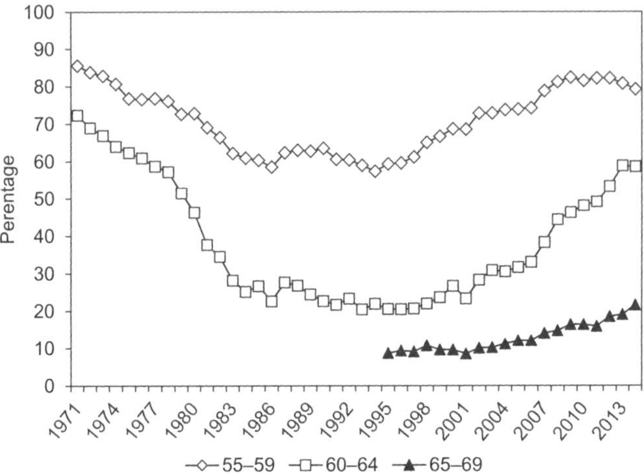

Fig. 8.16   Men's employment rate by year and age
Source: OECD, http://stats.oecd.org/.

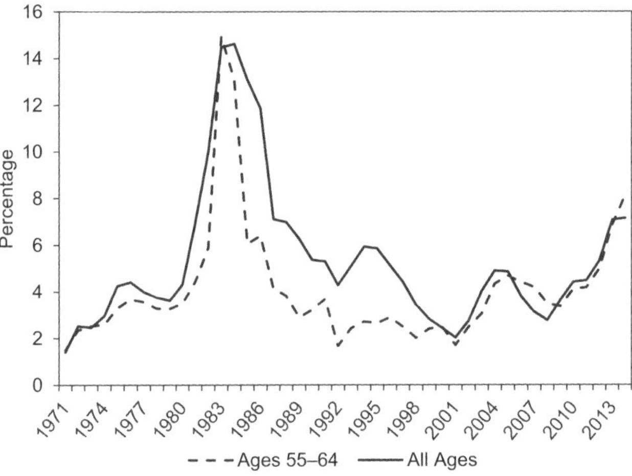

Fig. 8.17   Men's unemployment rate by year and age
Source: OECD, http://stats.oecd.org/.

Older workers are more likely to have job protection than young workers (as it is based on tenure) and to be relatively expensive and may have obsolete skills (section 8.3). These features, together with the fact that employers and employees bear little of the costs, made DI and ER schemes attractive pathways to retirement during the 1980s and 1990s. Koning and Lindeboom (2015) make a convincing case that the DI system provided incentives to use DI as an alternative for UI or ER. Figures 8.17 and 8.19 show that during

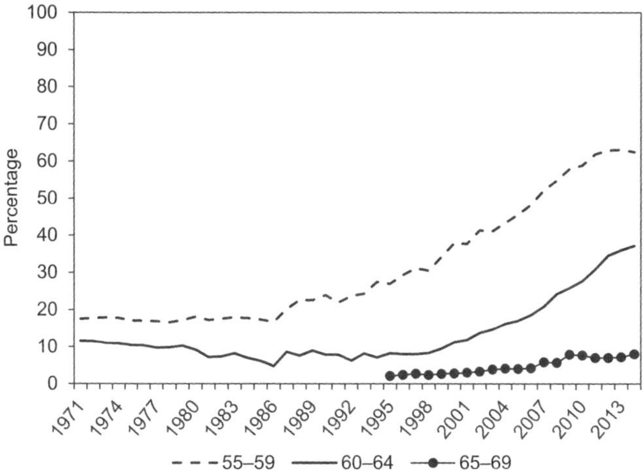

Fig. 8.18   Women's employment rate by year and age
Source: OECD, http://stats.oecd.org/.

Fig. 8.19   Women's unemployment rate by year and age
Source: OECD, http://stats.oecd.org/.

the 1980s and 1990s, the unemployment rates for older workers were relatively low compared to those for all workers, and this relative difference has gradually diminished since the mid-1990s, when stricter eligibility rules for ER and DI benefits were introduced. These observations suggest that as long as the eligibility criteria were lenient, ER and DI schemes were used to lay off redundant workers. Nevertheless, it appears that restricting the ER and DI pathways has not resulted in a substantially increased use of the UI

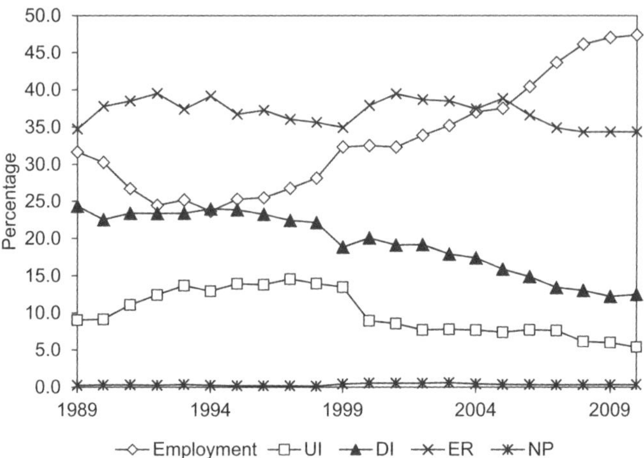

Fig. 8.20   Employment, UI, DI, ER, and nonparticipation rates of men aged 60–64 by year and age

Source: Statistics Netherlands, IPO. All rates are a percentage of people aged 60–64.

pathway. As discussed in the appendix, the various institutional reforms have affected a wide range of social security programs, including ER, DI, and UI. On balance this has limited the possibilities for substitution.

8.5   Discussion

The economic literature and some of the findings above suggest that the introduction of ER schemes at the end of the 1970s, together with lenient eligibility rules for DI and UI, resulted in a strong reduction in LFP among the older population in the two decades thereafter. Likewise, reforms of social security programs and pension schemes since the mid-1990s with the purpose of creating stronger incentives for continued work at older ages, such as stricter eligibility rules for ER, UI, and DI, have been quite effective in the Netherlands. Figure 8.20 shows that most of the increase in employment among men aged 60–64 has been accompanied by a decrease in UI and DI recipients, while ER rates remained high until recently. These policies have largely been designed in response to changes in economic circumstances, some of which we have highlighted in this chapter in sections 8.2 and 8.3.

Figures 8.2 and 8.3 suggest, however, that probably not all the LFP and employment changes are due to institutional changes. These figures show that participation rates above the normal retirement age of 65 have, from the mid-1990s onward, increased by 15 percentage points for men (almost tripling) and 6 percentage points for women (almost quadrupling) despite the fact that these groups have been less affected by the reforms of social security programs and pension schemes since the mid-1990s since they were mainly targeted at people younger than 65.

This may suggest that factors other than institutions, such as the health and skills of older workers (sections 8.2 and 8.3), may have played an important role in people working longer and the strong increases in LFP at all ages since the mid-1990s. Or, at a minimum, these other factors provided the necessary conditions for DI and ER reforms to achieve their goals. For instance, the improved health of older people may have facilitated the reforms over the last two decades, as it ensured the necessary extra work capacity (Kalwij, de Vos, and Kapteyn, 2016).[5] In this interpretation, the reforms provided people the incentives to keep on working, and their improved health and better skills made it possible for them to do so.

A final factor that has gained recent attention in the literature is the impact of the strong rise in women's employment at older ages, as shown in figure 8.18, on men's employment behavior. Men and women make joint retirement decisions, and an individual is more likely to continue working if his or her spouse works longer (Schirle 2008; Bloemen, Hochguertel, and Zweerink 2015). Hence more men are likely to continue working if their wives are working; the strong rise in women's LFP is likely to have had its own positive impact on men's LFP.

Looking toward the future, less generous pensions and a continuing increase in the normal retirement age are likely to contribute to further increases in LFP. Two concerns are often raised in the policy debate. First, keeping older people working longer may adversely affect the employment of the young. Especially in times of high youth unemployment, this argument is put forward. As we discussed above, however, the empirical evidence of Kalwij, Kapteyn, and de Vos (2010) and of references therein suggests this is not a reasonable concern. Empirical findings of previous studies do not support the hypothesis that the employment of the young and old are substitutes. In other words, encouraging later retirement is unlikely to have adverse effects on youth employment. A second concern is that there may be adverse effects of working longer on health. For instance, the relatively smaller decline in women's than men's mortality at age 60 (figure 8.6) is often attributed to the rise in smoking among women (Pampel 2002) and—possibly related to this in part—the increased LFP of women and corresponding work-related stress, which, in turn, has been shown to increase

5. Based on a combination of population mortality and survey data, additional work capacity in 2013 is estimated to be about 31 percentage points at ages 60–64, to increase to 53 percentage points at ages 65–69, and to reduce to about 44 percentage points at ages 70–74. At ages 55–59, additional work capacity is close to zero. These findings suggest that at ages 55–59, participation rates nowadays are as high as one can expect based on the health of this population, but health per se is not a restrictive factor for higher participation rates at older ages (Kalwij, Kapteyn, et al. 2016).

the risk of cardiovascular disease (Kivimäki et al. 2002; Kouvonen et al. 2005). Overall, the empirical evidence for the causal impact of work on health at older ages is mixed. Kalwij et al. (2013) and Neuman (2008) find that retirement has no adverse health effects; Charles (2004), Hemingway et al. (2003), and Coe and Zamarro (2011) find a positive effect on health; and Kuhn, Wuellrich, and Zweimueller (2010), Behncke (2012), and Dave, Rashad, and Spasojevic (2008) conclude that retirement may have a negative impact on health.

Appendix

Social Security System Reforms, 1995–2016

In table 8.A.1, we provide a comparison of the benefits for older workers and retirees available in 1995 and 2016. In table 8.A.2, we provide a timeline of the most important reforms to the system between both years. In the remainder of this appendix, we will discuss the main characteristics of the benefit system and the implemented reforms. A large part of this discussion is based on De Vos, Kapteyn, and Kalwij (2012).

State Pension

The Dutch benefit system is characterized by a clear distinction between benefits for persons younger than the state pension (SP) age and benefits for older persons. The latter receive the flat-rate SP. Until 2013, the SP age was 65, but in the aftermath of the credit crisis, the government used the opportunity to introduce a gradual increase of the SP age in order to ensure the future sustainability of the pay-as-you-go SP. The SP age will reach 66 in 2018 and 67 in 2021 and is to be linked to life expectancy thereafter. The flat-rate SP is supplemented when the spouse is younger than the SP age and has a low income. This supplement will be gradually abolished, starting in 2015.

Occupational Pensions

In many cases, the SP is supplemented by a (fully funded) occupational pension (OP), which ideally supplements the SP to 70 percent of previous earnings. Until the early 2000s, most OP rights were calculated on the basis of final earnings, but currently most pension rights are calculated on the basis of the average earnings during employment. Furthermore, until recently, most OPs were indexed on the basis of the wage index. However, following the credit crisis and the dramatic reduction of the market interest rates, most pension funds have had to suspend indexation or indeed lower the pensions in order to meet the legal solvability criteria (cf. Kalwij et al. 2015).

Table 8.A.1   **A comparison of state pension (SP), occupational pensions (PP), early retirement (ER), unemployment insurance (UI), and disability insurance (DI) between 1995 and 2016**

	1995	2016
SP	At age 65, a person receives flat-rate pension with a supplement for a younger spouse with low earnings.	At age 65.5 (to be increased to 67 in 2021 and follow life expectancy thereafter), a person receives a flat-rate pension; the supplement for younger spouse is being abolished.
PP	From the SP age, this usually supplements SP to at most 70 percent of final earnings, indexed with the wage index.	From the SP age, this usually supplements SP to at most 70 percent of average earnings; indexation suspended.
ER	From about 60 to SP age, a person receives up to 80 percent of final earnings with no actuarial adjustment.	Earlier retirement is still possible but has an actuarially adjusted pension.
UI	In case of job loss, a person receives 70 percent of final earnings (with cap) for at most 4.5 years, followed by 70 percent of minimum wage for at most 3.5 years up to SP age. No job search is required when he or she is older than 57.5 years.	In case of job loss, a person receives 70 percent of final earnings (with cap) for at most 38 months up to SP age. An active job search is required.
DI	In the first year, a person receives a sickness benefit of at least 70 percent of the last wage. Next, he or she receives a DI of at most 70 percent of last wage, the percentage depending on the loss of earnings capacity. Duration depends on age but lasts from age 59 until the SP age. Next, a lower benefit (often supplemented by private insurance) is received until SP age. There is relatively easy access to DI, but retesting has started.	The benefit is available up to the SP age. A person receives at least 70 percent of the last wage from the employer (up to a cap) for the first two years; reintegration programs during this time encourage the return to work. When the loss of earnings capacity is more than 80 percent and the probability of ever being able to work again is low, the benefit is 75 percent (up to a cap) until the SP age. In other cases (35–80 percent loss of earnings capacity), the benefit level falls after a period depending on age and/or length of previous employment. There is strict screening of reintegration attempts, disability, and loss of earnings capacity.

ER

For persons younger than the SP age, until recently, various pathways to retirement were available. ER was introduced in most sectors during the 1970s, mainly in reaction to rising unemployment (cf. Kapteyn et al. 2010), and at least until the end of the 1990s, in most cases it consisted of an offer too good to refuse, usually allowing retirement at age 60 or thereabouts. In particular, workers retiring later than the earliest possible ER date were not compensated by higher benefits or lower taxes, so they faced an implicit tax rate of more than 100 percent (cf. Kapteyn and de Vos 1999). Notably, ER was not the result of government policy but the outcome of negotiations

Table 8.A.2   **Timeline reforms to state pension (SP), early retirement (ER), occupational pension (PP), unemployment insurance (UI), and disability insurance (DI)**

	SP	ER/PP	UI	DI / (long-term) sickness insurance
1995			Eligibility revised, short-term benefit introduced	1994–1996: Retesting of younger DI recipients (<45) using stricter criteria
1996				Sickness benefit privatized; employer pays 70 percent of earnings (1 year)
1998				(i) Introduction of (limited) experience rating DI contributions employer. (ii) Public employees included in DI
2000–2005		Trend toward actuarially fairer flexible ER/PP age		
2001			Public employees included	
2002				Strict reintegration in case of sickness
2003			Abolition of continuation benefit	Experience rating for small employers abolished

2004		Trend toward PP based on average earnings rather than final earnings		(i) Sickness benefit period: two years (ii) Strict reevaluation DI recipients younger than 50
2006		ER: Fiscal friendly treatment of ER contributions repealed	Benefit period shortened; higher benefit first two months	Introduction of new DI: strict distinction between partially and fully, permanently disabled
2008				Experience rating DI abolished
2008–		PP: indexation often limited, trend toward DC benefits		
2013–	Gradual increase of the SP age from 65 to 66 in 2018 and to 67 in 2021, to be linked to life expectancy thereafter			
2015–	Supplement for a younger spouse abolished			
2016–			Further shortening benefit period	

Main sources: SP: http://www.svb.nl; DI, UI: Kroniek van de sociale verzekeringen, 2008, http://www.uwv.nl.

between trade unions and employers. However, the government facilitated ER by making ER contributions tax deductible.

The prospect of exploding costs once the large baby boom cohorts started to reach the ER age turned out to be sufficiently threatening for effective reforms to be put in place by the end of the 1990s. In most cases, a cost reduction as a result of reducing the effective ER entitlement was combined with the introduction of a more-or-less actuarially fair system. As a result, an employee could still opt for retiring early but with a reduced pension, or he or she could retire later with a higher pension. By 2006, the government dealt a final blow to the old ER systems by effectively terminating the tax exemption for ER contributions that would enable a retirement age lower than 65. Only systems offering a replacement rate of at most 70 percent at the pension age of 65 and actuarially fair reductions when an earlier pension age is chosen can still collect tax-exempt contributions.

UI

For workers approaching 60 who were not entitled to ER—for example, because of an insufficiently long employment history or because they worked at a firm that did not offer ER—and who could not plausibly be retired via DI, UI offered a third pathway to retirement before the SP age of 65. In most cases, it offered a replacement rate of 70 percent, and furthermore, until recently, it required no obligation to search for employment after the age of 57.5.

As of 2004, persons aged 57.5 or older receiving UI are no longer exempt from the requirement to seek work. In other words, they are no longer "automatically" receiving UI until age 65 but have to try to find work and, in theory, accept a job offer. Moreover, as of October 1, 2006, the maximum duration of UI is 38 months. After that period, all that is left is a means-tested entitlement to social assistance with a benefit equal to the net minimum wage. Starting in 2016, the maximum duration of UI will be further reduced. It will be limited to 24 months in 2019.

DI

Introduced in 1967, the Dutch DI (WAO, *Wet op de Arbeidsongeschiktheids-verzekering*) aimed to insure employees against loss of earnings as a result of a long-term inability to work due to illness or incapacity. If, after having been ill for a period of one year, the employee could not resume work, he or she would be entitled to an earnings-related DI benefit, which could last until the employee reached the statutory retirement age of 65.

Starting in the 1970s, the numbers of individuals on DI in the Netherlands showed a continuous increase until the 1990s. These numbers were much higher than expected when the new DI legislation was introduced and much higher than might be expected given the average health status of the population. In fact, in the mid-1970s when unemployment was rising dramatically, the route to DI was generally used by employers as a path of least resistance to shed superfluous employees. For the employee, DI was both more acceptable socially and more attractive than UI, in particular because the benefit could be received until age 65, when the old-age pension would kick in.

With the increase in the number of benefit recipients, expenditures on DI started to rise dramatically, and since the start of the 1980s, government policy has sought to reverse the trend of the ever-increasing DI expenditures by various reforms to limit access to DI, increase the number of persons exiting DI, and lower the average DI benefit.

When actions like lowering the replacement rate of DI from 80 to 70 percent and limiting access to the full DI to partially disabled and unemployed new entrants did not result in reversing the trend of ever-increasing numbers of DI recipients, the government introduced a series of measures in the early 1990s: the duration of the full DI benefit was limited for new entrants younger than 50, stricter disability criteria were introduced for entry into DI, and younger DI recipients were to be retested. Mainly because most employees took out private insurance to compensate for the shorter duration of the full DI benefit for younger persons, DI remained an attractive option. Aside from limiting the access and the generosity of the benefit, policies were also introduced to shift the costs to firms with high numbers of employees exiting to DI. First, the costs of sickness benefits were charged directly to the employer for two to six weeks (1994) and later on for a full year preceding the exit to DI. Second, in 1998, experience rating was introduced: for large firms in particular, the DI contributions were partly based on the DI record of the firm in question. A high exit rate into DI resulted in higher contributions.

All these reforms still did not succeed in substantially reducing the numbers of DI recipients, and by 2002, the feeling was that enough was enough and the time had come for a more radical approach. From 2002 on, during the year of sickness preceding exit to DI, the employer and employee became jointly responsible for taking sufficient action for reintegration into the workforce. Moreover, this sickness period could be extended if insufficient reintegration measures had been taken. Beginning in 2004, the exit to DI would only happen after two years of sickness, during which time the employer would pay the sickness benefits. In 2006, the new DI law (WIA, *Wet werk en inkomen naar arbeidsvermogen*) made a strict distinction between full and permanent disability and partial or temporary disability. Those falling within the former category received a generous 75 percent of their previous earnings until age 65 (IVA, *Inkomensvoorziening Volledig Arbeidsongeschikten*). The latter would receive a less generous benefit (WGA, *regeling Werkhervatting Gedeeltelijk Arbeidsongeschikten*) depending on the previous earnings, the number of weeks worked before, the current earnings (if any), and the percentage of previous earnings that the employee was deemed to be capable of earning. Furthermore, once again, a retest operation was set up for existing DI beneficiaries younger than 50 (whose DI remained unchanged).

References

Autor, D., and D. Dorn. 2009. "This Job Is 'Getting Old': Measuring Changes in Job Opportunities Using Occupational Age Structure." *American Economic Review Papers and Proceedings* 99 (2): 45–51.

Autor, D., D. Dorn, and G. Hanson. 2015. "Untangling Trade and Technology: Evidence from Local Labor Markets." *Economic Journal* 125 (584): 621–46.

Autor, D. H., and L. F. Katz. 1999. "Changes in the Wage Structure and Earnings Inequality." In *Handbook of Labor Economics*. Vol. 3A, edited by Orley Ashenfelter and David E. Card, 1463–555. Amsterdam: Elsevier.

Behncke, S. 2012. "Does Retirement Trigger Ill Health?" *Health Economics* 21:282–300.

Bloemen, H., S. Hochguertel, and J. Zweerink. 2015. "Joint Retirement of Couples: Evidence from a Natural Experiment." IZA Discussion Paper No. 8861, Institute for the Study of Labor (IZA), Bonn, Germany.

Burkhauser, R. V., and M. Daly. 2011. *The Declining Work and Welfare of People with Disabilities*. Washington, DC: American Enterprise Institute for Public Policy Research.

Charles, K. K. 2004. "Is Retirement Depressing? Labor Force Inactivity and Psychological Well-Being in Later Life." *Research in Labor Economics* 23:269–99.

Coe, N., and G. Zamarro. 2011. "Retirement Effects on Health in Europe." *Journal of Health Economics* 30 (1): 77–86.

Cutler, D., A. Deaton, and A. Lleras-Muney. 2006. "The Determinants of Mortality." *Journal of Economic Perspectives* 20 (3): 97–120.

Dave, D., I. Rashad, and J. Spasojevic. 2008. "The Effects of Retirement on Physical and Mental Health Outcomes." *Southern Economic Journal* 75:497–523.

de Jong, P., M. Lindeboom, and B. van der Klaauw. 2011. "Screening Disability Insurance Applications." *Journal of the European Economic Association* 9:106–29.

de Vos, K., A. Kapteyn, and A. Kalwij. 2012. "Disability Insurance and Labor Market Exit Routes of Older Workers in the Netherlands." In *Social Security and Retirement around the World: Historical Trends in Mortality and Health, Employment, and Disability Insurance Participation and Reforms*, edited by David A. Wise, 419–47. Chicago: University of Chicago Press.

Euwals, R., R. de Mooij, and D. van Vuuren. 2009. *Rethinking Retirement*. CPB Netherlands Bureau for Economic Policy Analysis.

Goos, M., A. Manning, and A. Salomons. 2014. "Explaining Job Polarization: Routine-Biased Technological Change and Offshoring." *American Economic Review* 104 (8): 2509–26.

Gruber, J., and D. A. Wise, eds. 2004. *Social Security Programs and Retirement around the World: Micro-Estimation*. Chicago: University of Chicago Press.

Hemingway, H., M. Marmot, P. Martikainen, G. Mein, and S. Stansfeld. 2003. "Is Retirement Good or Bad for Mental and Physical Health Functioning? Whitehall II Longitudinal Study of Civil Servants." *Journal of Epidemiology and Community Health* 57:46–9.

Human Mortality Database. 2018. http://www.mortality.org. Data retrieved on February 28, 2018.

Kalwij, A., R. Alessie, J. Gardner, and A. A. Ali. 2015. "Inflation Experiences of Retirees." *Netspar Industry Paper Series*, Design Paper 43, Network for Studies on Pensions, Aging and Retirement, Le Tilburg, Netherlands.

Kalwij, A., K. de Vos, and A. Kapteyn. 2016. "Health, Disability Insurance and Labor Force Exit of Older Workers in the Netherlands." In *Social Security Programs and Retirement Around the World: Disability Insurance Programs and Retirement*, edited by David A. Wise, 211–49. Chicago: University of Chicago Press.

Kalwij, A., A. Kapteyn, and K. de Vos. 2010. "Retirement of Older Workers and Employment of the Young." *De Economist* 158 (4): 341–59.

———. 2016. "Work Capacity at Older Ages in the Netherlands." NBER Working Paper No. 21976, National Bureau of Economic Research, Cambridge, MA.

Kalwij, A., M. Knoef, and R. Alessie. 2013. "Pathways to Retirement and Mortality Risk in the Netherlands." *European Journal of Population* 29 (2): 221–38.

Kapteyn, A., and K. de Vos. 1999. "Social Security and Retirement in the Netherlands." In *Social Security and Retirement around the World*, edited by Jonathan Gruber and David A. Wise, 269–303. Chicago: University of Chicago Press.

Kapteyn, A., K. de Vos, and A. Kalwij. 2010. "Early Retirement and Employment of the Young in the Netherlands." In *Social Security Programs and Retirement around the World: The Relationship to Youth Employment*, edited by Jonathan Gruber and David A. Wise, 243–59. Chicago: University of Chicago Press.

Kivimäki, M., P. Leino-Arjas, R. Luukkonen, H. Riihimäki, J. Vahtera, and J. Kirjonen. 2002. "Work Stress and Risk of Cardiovascular Mortality: Prospective Cohort Study of Industrial Employees." *British Medical Journal* 325 (7369): 857.

Koning, P. W. C., and M. Lindeboom. 2015. "The Rise and Fall of Disability Enrollment in the Netherlands." *Journal of Economic Perspectives* 29 (2): 151–72.

Kouvonen, A., M. Kivimäki, M. Virtanen, J. Pentti, and J. Vahtera. 2005. "Work Stress, Smoking Status, and Smoking Intensity: An Observational Study of 46,190 Employees." *Journal of Epidemiology and Community Health* 59:63–9.

Kuhn, A., J. P. Wuellrich, and J. Zweimueller. 2010. "Fatal Attraction? Access to Early Retirement and Mortality." IZA Discussion Paper No. 5160, IZA, Bonn, Germany.

Neuman, K. 2008. "Quit Your Job and Get Healthier? The Effect of Retirement on Health." *Journal of Labor Research* 29:177–201.

OECD. 2011. *Pensions at a Glance 2011: Retirement-Income Systems in OECD and G20 Countries*. Paris: OECD.

Pampel, F. C. 2002. "Cigarette Use and the Narrowing Sex Differential in Mortality." *Population and Development Review* 28 (1): 77–104.

Schirle, T. 2008. "Why Have the Labor Force Participation Rates of Older Men Increased since the Mid-1990s?" *Journal of Labor Economics* 26 (4): 549–94.

Statistics Netherlands. 2018. https://statline.cbs.nl/Statweb/. Data retrieved on February 28, 2018.

UNESCO. 1997. "International Standard Classification of Education: ISCED 1997." November. http://www.unesco.org/education/information/nfsunesco/doc/isced_1997.htm.

Van Ewijk, C., N. Draper, H. ter Rele, and E. Westerhout. 2006. "Aging and the Sustainability of Dutch Public Finances." CPB report no. 2001/1, CPB Netherlands Bureau for Economic Policy Analysis, The Hague, Netherlands.

Van Oorschot, W. 2007. "Narrowing Pathways to Early Retirement in the Netherlands." *Journal of Poverty and Justice* 15:247–55.

Wise, D. A., ed. 2012. *Social Security Programs and Retirement around the World: Historical Trends in Mortality and Health, Employment, and Disability Insurance Participation and Reforms*. Chicago: University of Chicago Press.

———. 2016. *Social Security Programs and Retirement around the World: The Capacity to Work at Older Ages*. Chicago: University of Chicago Press.

Trends in Labor Force Participation of Older Workers in Spain

Pilar García-Gómez, Sergi Jiménez-Martín, and Judit Vall Castelló

9.1 Introduction

The large increase in life expectancy and old-age dependency ratios urged a change in the trends of early retirement and lower work participation rates that were observed during the 1980s and early 1990s. Employment rates in many Organisation for Economic Co-operation and Development (OECD) countries reversed this trend and started to increase (following a U-shaped pattern) since the mid-1990s. In a majority of countries, this increase has been largest for men aged 60–64, but men aged 55–59 and 65–69 in most (though not all) countries have also experienced an increase in their participation rates. Labor force participation (LFP) and employment rates of women have also been increasing since the mid-1990s, although the previous trend was not negative, and in some countries, it was even positive. In Spain, mothers with low participation and education have been replaced in the labor market by more-educated high-participating daughters (Boldrín, Jiménez-Martín, and Peracchi 2001). In fact, the labor market participa-

Pilar García-Gómez is an associate professor at the Erasmus School of Economics at the Erasmus University Rotterdam.

Sergi Jiménez-Martín is professor of economics at Universitat Pompeu Fabra, an affiliated professor of the Barcelona Graduate School of Economics, and chair of Fedea-La Caixa Economía de la Salud y Hábitos de Vida.

Judit Vall Castelló is an assistant professor at the Department of Economics of Universitat de Barcelona and a research fellow at the Institute of Economics in Barcelona, the Institute for the Study of Labor (IZA), and Centre de Recerca en Economia i Salut—Universitat Pompeu Fabra.

We acknowledge financial help from project ECO2017-83668-R as well as from a RECERCAIXA grant. For acknowledgments, sources of research support, and disclosure of the authors' material financial relationships, if any, please see https://www.nber.org/chapters /c14049.ack.

tion of women has practically doubled in the last 35 years in Spain, from 28 percent in 1977 to 53 percent in 2014, converging but still not reaching LFP rates of men.

Many factors may have contributed to the recent increases in LFP and employment, including changes in the incentives from social security, other early retirement routes like disability insurance (DI) or unemployment insurance, improving health and longevity, increasing levels of education, a shift toward less physically demanding jobs, and the growth of female LFP (combined with the desire for joint retirement among couples).

There is a line of work (see García-Pérez, Jiménez-Martín, and Sánchez-Martín [2013] and the references therein) that emphasizes the importance of social security and employment regulations in determining the labor force behavior of older workers. Using administrative data, research finds that economic incentives have a strong impact on labor market decisions in Spain. Unemployment regulations are shown to be particularly influential for retirement behavior, along with the more traditional determinants linked to the pension system. In particular, the early retirement route (see also Gruber and Wise 1999 or Hairault, Langot, and Sopraseuth 2010) of unemployment insurance is particularly important in Spain. However, there were no substantial modifications to the system around 1995 to explain a change in the previous labor force trends of older workers.

One of the key factors behind the increase in employment trends could be the strong growth of the Spanish economy observed after the 1993–95 recession. Felgueroso and Jiménez-Martín (2009) show that the Spanish economy experienced a very strong job creation period between the mid-1990s and 2007, allowing the overall employment rate to increase by about 20 percentage points. This affected all population groups regardless of education and gender. The implications of such a period of prosperity were very important. Spain moved from the last position in the employment rate of the EU15 to the average level, overtaking Italy (7 percentage points), catching up with France (1 percentage point), and cutting the distance to countries like the UK, Germany, and Finland (4–6 percentage points).

Finally, another potential factor is human capital accumulation (Felgueroso and Jiménez-Martín 2009). Between 1996 and 2008, the reduction of the share of low-educated individuals in Spain at ages 40–59 has been about 20 percentage points (thereby reducing the overall differences with other EU15 countries). This may have strong implications for LFP and employment of older workers and also for the type of jobs they can do.

In this chapter, we explore, from a descriptive point of view and using a variety of data sources, the potential influence of these factors in explaining the employment trends over the last decades in Spain. Neither changes in the underlying social security rules nor changes in health conditions can explain the change in trends observed around 1995. However, we document three factors that are potential drivers of these observed changes: the overall

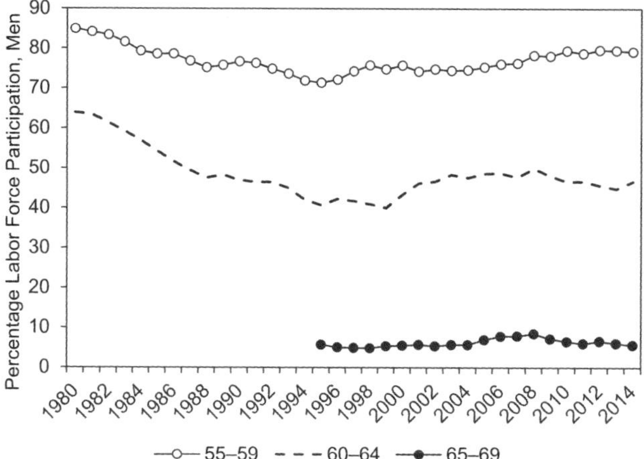

Fig. 9.1   LFP rates for older men in Spain, 1980–2014 (age groups 55–59, 60–64, and 65–69)
Source: Authors' calculation based on OECD data.

growth of the employment rate observed in the 1995–2007 period, differences across cohorts in the skill composition, and increases in the labor force attachment of wives.

The rest of the chapter is organized as follows. Section 9.2 reviews the main trends in LFP observed in the last 30 years, section 9.3 explores the potential factors behind these trends, and section 9.4 concludes.

9.2   Trends in LFP and Employment for Older Men in Spain

In this section, we present evidence on the evolution of LFP rates and employment rates for Spanish men aged 55–69. We divide older men into three age groups: those aged 55–59, those in the 60–64 age bracket, and those aged 65–69 (above the normal retirement age of 65 years old).

We first use data from the OECD statistics database to plot trends in the LFP from 1980 to 2014 for men in these three age groups. Figure 9.1 shows that, as expected, the LFP rates are highest for the youngest group and stay above 70 percent for the entire period. Their LFP rate was over 80 percent in the early 1980s, but this rate decreased smoothly until 1995, when it hit the lowest value over the period (70 percent), and then started increasing. The LFP trends for men aged 55–59 continuously increased until 2008, when the Great Recession hit Spain. The LFP of this age group has remained stable at around 80 percent thereafter.

The LFP rates of men aged 60–64 present a similar U shape between 1980 and 2008 with four particularities. First, the overall LFP levels are lower. Second, the drop between the start of the period, when LFP rates were above

60 percent, and the mid-1990s was larger. Third, trends did not immediately reverse after 1995, but the LFP rates of men aged 60–64 were stable at the lowest level of the period (40 percent) until 1999. Fourth, while LFP rates increased between 2000 and 2008, they stayed at 50 percent, 10 points below the rates at the start of the period. In addition, the LFP rates of men aged 60–64 slightly decreased during the Great Recession.

Last, for the oldest group of individuals aged 65–69, the OECD only has data from 1995 to 2014. We can see that the LFP rates of this group of individuals are very low and have remained below the 10 percent level. This is reasonable taking into account that the normal retirement age in Spain is set at 65. Although the levels are low, we can see a similar evolution of LFP rates for this older group of workers—increasing from 1995 to 2008, when the rate reached the highest level of the period (10 percent), and decreasing during the recent economic crisis.

In order to shed light on the evolution of the LFP rates of men aged 65–69 over the whole period, we use quarterly data from the Spanish Labour Force Survey (LFS; Encuesta de Población Activa, or EPA) for the 1977–2015 period.[1] The left panel of figure 9.2 shows that there was a sharp decrease in the LFP rates for this age group between the late 1970s, when more than 30 percent of men aged 65–69 were in the labor force, and the mid-1990s, when participation rates were slightly above 5 percent.

Figure 9.3 shows employment rates for the same age groups of men and the same time period using data from the OECD. First, we see that both the trends and the levels of employment of men above the normal retirement age (65–69) are the same as the LFP rates (see figure 9.3 and the right panel of figure 9.2). Therefore, men aged 65–69 in Spain only stay active in the labor force if they remain employed. Similarly, the evolution of employment rates is almost the same as the LFP rates for the group aged 60–64. We can see that their employment rates started particularly high in 1980 (60 percent) and decreased steadily until the mid-1990s when they were below 40 percent. From the late 1990s, the employment rates of men aged 60–64 increased mildly until the onset of the economic crisis in 2008, which reduced employment rates for men in this age group. Last, although employment rates of the youngest group (55–59) follow a similar trend as their LFP rates, they seem more affected by the business cycle. For example, while there is an overall decreasing trend between the early 1980s and mid-1990s, there

1. The EPA is a rotating quarterly survey carried out by the Spanish National Statistical Institute (*Instituto Nacional de Estadística*). The planned sample size consists of about 64,000 households with approximately 150,000 adult individuals. Although the survey has been conducted since 1964, publicly released cross-sectional files are available only from 1977. The 1977 questionnaire was modified in 1987 (when a set of retrospective questions were introduced), in the first quarter of 1992, in 1999, and in 2004. The EPA provides fairly detailed information on labor force status, education, and family background variables, but like most of the other European-style LFSs, no information on health is provided. The reference period for most questions is the week before the interview.

A Participation rate 65–69, Men

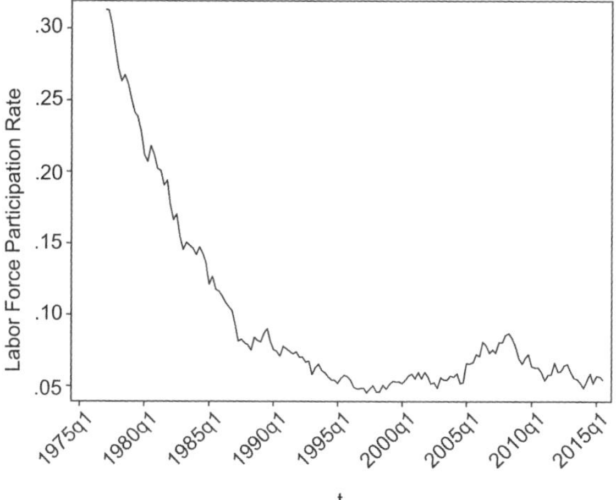

B Employment rate 65–69, Men

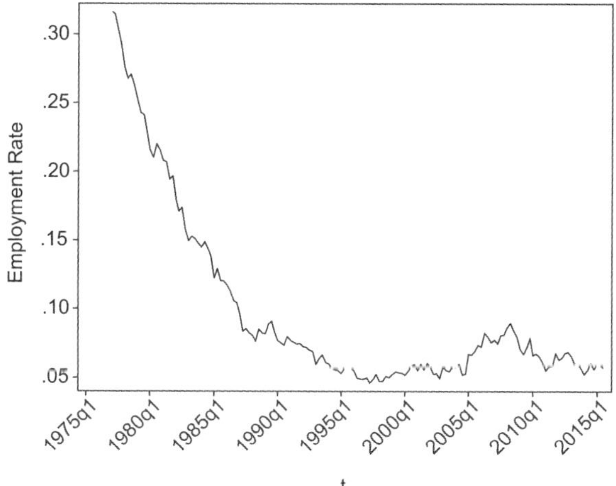

Fig. 9.2   LFP and employment rates for men aged 65–69 (1978–2015)
Source: Authors' calculation based on data from the Spanish LFS.

is a mild increase in employment rates around the late 1980s. Similarly, while the LFP rates of men aged 55–59 have remained stable after the onset of the Great Recession, we see that their employment rates have decreased from over 70 percent in 2007 to 60 percent in 2014.

Figure 9.4 plots the changes in the employment rates of older workers (aged 55–64) in OECD countries between 2004 and 2014 in order to place the Spanish case in an international perspective. The first thing to be noted is that employment rates have grown in almost all OECD countries (except

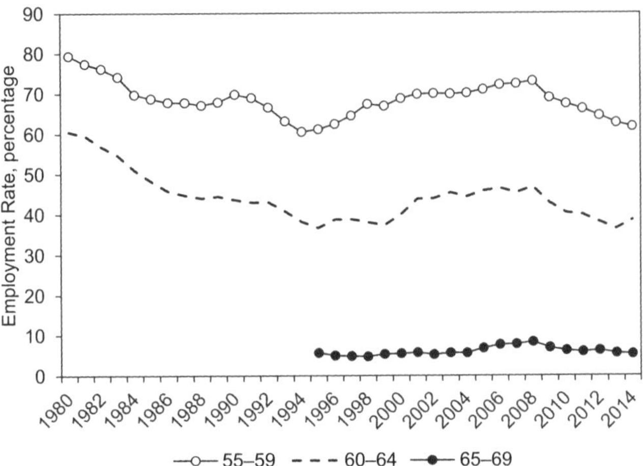

Fig. 9.3   Employment rates for older men in Spain, 1980–2014 (age groups 55–59, 60–64, and 65–69)

Source: Authors' calculation based on OECD data.

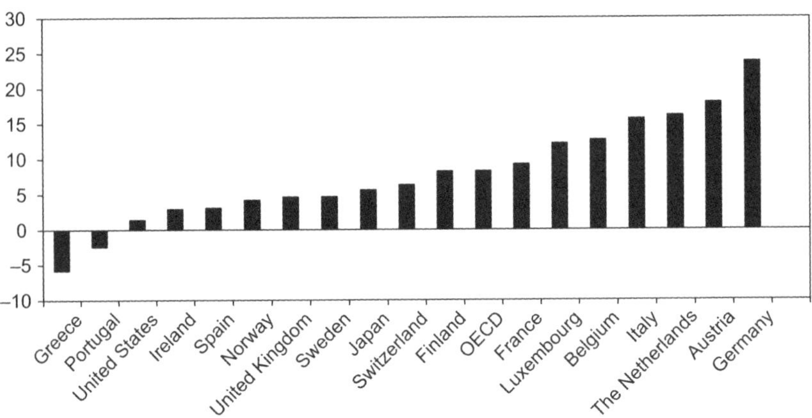

Fig. 9.4   Percentage point changes in employment rate of older workers in OECD countries, 2004–2014

Source: Authors' calculation based on OECD (2015) data.

Greece and Portugal) for individuals aged 55–64. We can also see that Spain is one of the countries where employment rates for this age group have increased the least (below 5 percent). In other European countries, like Germany, the Netherlands, or Italy, employment rates have increased by more than 15 percentage points. Furthermore, figure 9.5 also shows that in 2014, employment rates of workers aged 55–59, 60–64, and 65–69 in Spain were one of the lowest across the OECD.

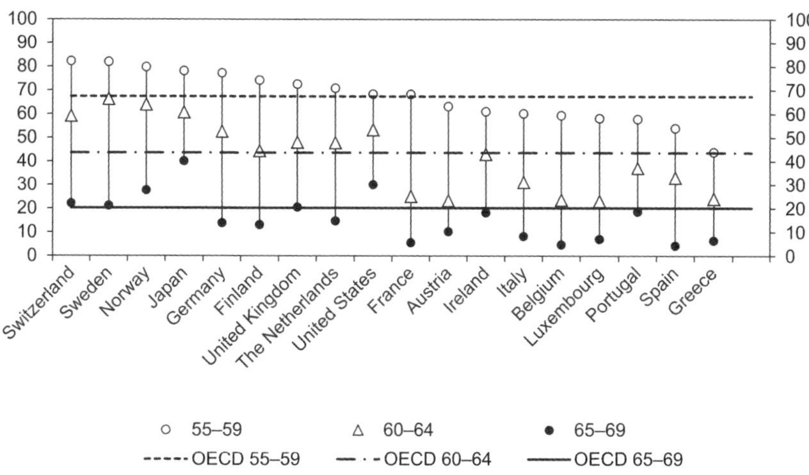

Fig. 9.5 Employment rates of workers aged 55–59, 60–64, and 65–69 in 2014 in OECD countries

Source: Authors' calculation based on OECD (2015) data.

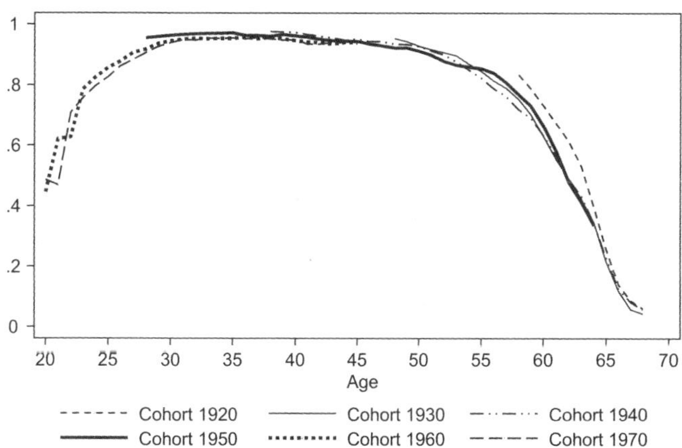

Fig. 9.6 LFP trends for different cohorts of men in Spain

Source: Authors' calculation based on data from the Spanish LFS.

Previous figures suggest that the increase in LFP and employment rates of the age group 60–64 occurred about five years after the increase in the younger age group (55–59). This suggests that changes in these trends may be driven by cohort effects. Therefore, we obtained LFP and employment rates over the working life for different cohorts using data from the Spanish LFS. In particular, figure 9.6 and figure 9.7 plot the LFP and employment profiles for ages 20–68 for the cohorts of Spanish men born in 1920, 1930, 1940, 1950, 1960, and 1970. We see that there are no main differences in LFP

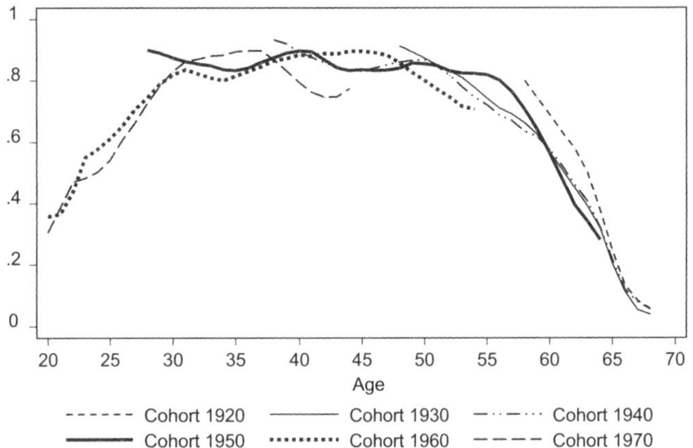

Fig. 9.7   Employment trends for different cohorts of men in Spain
Source: Authors' calculation based on data from the Spanish LFS.

and employment rates across cohorts for men aged 20–50 beyond possible business-cycle effects on employment. However, a few differences appear among older workers. The LFP and employment rates were higher at ages 57–68 for the oldest cohort of men (1920), while the differences between the other cohorts were smaller. However, it seems that the LFP rates of the cohort born in 1950 between ages 55 and 62 were slightly higher than the LFP rates of the cohorts born in 1940 and 1930. This was only partially translated into employment, as employment rates of this cohort suddenly decreased at the late 50s when they were affected by the economic crises in 2008, so employment rates of men in their early 60s in this cohort are even lower than the rates of the preceding two cohorts.

9.3   Why Have LFP Rates for Men in Spain Been Increasing since the Mid-1990s?

In this section, we provide some descriptive evidence to shed light on the possible drivers behind the trend reversal in the LFP rates for men in Spain observed in the mid-1990s. In particular, we explore the potential contributions of changes in financial incentives, health status, skill levels, labor market conditions, and women's LFP.

9.3.1   Changes in Social Security Benefits

The Spanish old-age pension system is a defined benefit pay-as-you-go system. There have been many reforms to the Spanish old-age pension system in the last 30 years (see table 9.1 for a summary and Boldrín, García-Gómez, and Jiménez-Martín [2010] and García-Gómez, Jiménez-Martín, and J. Vall Castelló [2012] for detailed expositions of the changes in the old-age pension system in Spain). Since the 1985 reform, there have been substantial parametric reforms in 1997, 2002, 2007, and 2011 and a nonparametric reform in 2013.[2]

9.3.1.1   The Old-Age Pension System after the 1985 Reform

The key ingredients of the Spanish pension system were set in the 1985 reform. Eligibility for the old-age pension benefits in Spain requires having contributed to the system for at least 15 years. The pension amount is calculated by multiplying a regulatory base by a percentage that depends on the age of the individual and the number of years he or she has contributed to the system. The pension amount is capped from below by the minimum pension, which is currently about the same level as the minimum wage (see Jiménez-Martín [2014] for details), and from above by the maximum benefit (between four and five times the minimum wage).

Under the 1985 regime, a worker could enter into the pension system at the normal retirement age of 65 (if he or she did not have any job with an affiliation with the social security system), and those who had first contributed to the system benefit in 1967 could early retire at 60. In order to compute the pension, the regulatory base was obtained by dividing by 112 the wages of the last 96 months before retiring, and the percentage applied to this regulatory base was the following:

$$\begin{cases} 0 & \text{if } n < 15 \\ 0.5 + 0.03(n - 15) & \text{if } 15 \le n \le 25 \\ 0.8 + 0.02(n - 25) & \text{if } 25 < n < 35 \\ 1 & \text{if } 35 \le n, \end{cases}$$

where n is the number of years of contributions to the system.

9.3.1.2   The 1997, 2002, and 2007 Reforms

In 1997, the number of contributory years used to compute the benefit base was progressively increased from 8 to 15 years,[3] and the formula to calculate the replacement rate was also made less generous. On the other hand, the 8 percent penalty applied to early retirees between the ages of 60 and 65 was reduced to 7 percent for individuals with at least 40 years of contributions at the time of early retirement.

In 2002, further changes in the old-age system were introduced. Before 2002, only individuals who had contributed to the system earlier than 1967

---

2. The 2013 reform cannot be classified as parametric because, by linking benefits to life expectancy, it changes—at least partially—the spirit of the system.

3. In 1997, the last 108 months were included, the last 120 months in 1998, the last 132 months in 1999, the last 144 months in 2000, the last 156 months in 2001, and the last 180 months from 2002 onward.

could benefit from early retirement at 60, while the rest had to wait until the normal retirement age of 65. In 2002, early retirement at age 61 was made available for the rest of the population. At the same time, there was an impulse in the partial and flexible retirement schemes to provide the possibility of combining income from work with old-age benefits and the introduction of incentives for individuals to retire after the legal retirement age of 65.[4] At the same time, the possibility to access early retirement at 61 was extended to some involuntary unemployed individuals—in particular, those registered in the employment office during the last six months with at least 30 years of contributions into the old-age system.

In 2007, the incentives to retire later than age 65 were further increased, providing an additional 3 percent, instead of the 2 percent introduced in 2002. In addition, two restrictions were added: first, the individual must have contributed for at least 2 out of the last 15 years to have access to the old-age pension system, and second, the proportional part related to the extra monthly salaries was now excluded from the computation of the number of contributed years. On the other hand, the 8 percent penalty applied to early retirees between the ages of 60 and 65 was reduced to 6–7.5 percent `for those individuals with at least 30 years of contributions, depending on the number of years contributed. In addition, the contributions for unemployed workers older than 52 were increased so they would receive a higher old-age pension when retiring.

Although these reforms have tried to increase the labor supply of older male workers, the existing evidence (see, for example, García-Pérez, Jiménez-Martín, and Sánchez-Martín [2013] and the references therein) does not show any clear link between these reforms and the increased labor supply of older male workers.

9.3.1.3   The 2011 Reform

The demographic and labor market developments during the first years of the Great Recession led the Spanish government (forced by the EU pressure to reduce the underlining future deficits) to introduce a reform to the pension system in 2011. In this reform, two crucial elements were changed: the extension of the number of years of contributions taken into account to compute the benefits and the increase in the normal retirement age (from 65 to 67, gradually).[5] This second change was extremely relevant for Spain because the normal retirement age had not been amended since the year it was first established in 1919. These two changes caused a cut in the generosity of the pension system. The first one reduced the replacement rate by about 10 to 20

---

4. An additional 2 percent per additional year of contribution beyond the age of 65 for workers with at least 35 years of contributions was on top of the 100 percent applied to the regulatory base.

5. The age was increased one month each year from 2013 to 2018 and by two months each year thereafter.

Table 9.1   **Main reforms of the pension system in Spain since 1985**

1985	• The minimum mandatory years of contribution increases from 8 to 15. • The number of contributive years used to compute the pension increases from 2 to 8. • Several early retirement schemes are introduced; partial retirement and special retirement are at age 64.
1997	• The number of contributive years used to compute the pension increases from 8 to 15 (progressively by 2001). • The formula to compute the benefits is made less generous. • The 8 percent penalty applied to early retirees between the ages of 60 and 65 is reduced to 7 percent for individuals with 40 or more contributory years.
2002	• Early retirement is available only from age 61. • Impulse partial retirement makes it possible to combine retirement with work. • Unemployed people aged 61 can retire if they have contributed for 30 years and are registered in employment offices for the previous 6 months. • Incentives to retire appear after age 65.
2007	• Fifteen "effective" contributory years are used to calculate the pension. • Reduction from 8 percent to 7.5 percent of the per-year penalty is applied to early retirees between 60 and 65 for individuals with 30 contributory years. • Incentives to stay employed after age 65 are broadened. • Increased contributions to the old-age pension system are made by the Social Security Administration for individuals receiving the special scheme of unemployment assistance for those aged 52 and older.
2011	• The number of contributive years used to compute the pension increases from 15 to 20. • The normal retirement age increases from 65 to 67. • Eligibility conditions for early retirement are modified.
2013	• A sustainability factor is introduced. • New scheme appears to make pension and work income compatible.

percent depending on the worker's characteristics and earnings history, and the second reduced the social security debt with those individuals planning to retire at the normal retirement age. The reform also changed (restricted) the eligibility conditions for early retirement, but the effects of these changes are less clear.[6] Finally, note that since the reform barely changed the eligibility conditions to access to the minimum pension, those workers expecting to receive the minimum pension (basically individuals with a low income and short contributive careers) are expected to be less affected by this reform (Jiménez-Martín 2014).

The case of Spain is not an isolated one, as most European countries have initiated or are about to initiate a process of pension reform (European Commission 2012). In the majority of cases, the reform involves the follow-

6. See Benítez-Silva, García-Pérez, and Jiménez-Martín (2013) for a description of other changes introduced by the 2011 reform.

ing three elements: (1) delaying the normal retirement age (but relaxing the requirement to make compatible work and pension income), (2) reducing the system's generosity, and (3) introducing a sustainability factor, which adds some uncertainty to the final benefit, thereby moving the respective system from a defined benefit to a defined contribution model.

The 2011 Spanish reform (law 27/2011), which included elements (1) and (3) above, should, in normal circumstances, have been sufficient to alleviate the medium-term financial pressure on the Spanish pension system. However, some studies consider the reform to be insufficient (Díaz-Giménez and Díaz-Saavedra 2017; Sánchez-Martín 2014, 2017) from a financial point of view.

9.3.1.4   The 2013 Reform and the Sustainability Factor

The importance of the 2013 reform lies in the introduction of an automatic link between the initial pension and the evolution of life expectancy: the sustainability factor (Conde-Ruiz and Gonzalez 2016). Therefore, it was an attempt by the government to ensure that its short- and long-term social security finances were under control. The pension system in Spain is a defined-benefit, pay-as-you-go scheme, so the pension does not fulfill any criteria of financial balance. Thus when the demographic variables (e.g., life expectancy) or economic variables (primarily, the relationship between the contributors and pensioners and their productivity) that impinge on the system deteriorate, the system becomes unbalanced. The sustainability factor, among other things, automatically adjusts the system when exposed to these demographic changes and thus can be seen as a mechanism that transforms a defined benefit scheme, such as that operated by Spain, to a defined contribution scheme.[7]

The sustainability factor has two key components: the intergenerational equity factor (IEF) and the pension revaluation index (PRI). The IEF aims to provide equal treatment to those who retire at the same age and with the same employment history but who have different life expectancies. This factor has not given rise to much controversy, since it seems reasonable that if pensioners are to receive the same total pension throughout their retirement, an individual with a greater life expectancy should receive a little less each year. The second factor fixes a budgetary constraint on the economic cycle, and as such, it is relatively flexible in the short term. However, the discretionary rule chosen by the government guarantees that even though social security revenues are insufficient to cover pension costs, pensions should increase each year by at least 0.25 percent and by no more than the annual change in the consumer price index + 0.25 percent.[8]

---

7. See, in this regard, http://www.fedeablogs.net/economia/?p=32680.

8. See Sánchez-Martín (2014, 2017) for a description of the functioning of the IEF and the PRI made by two members of the reform commission.

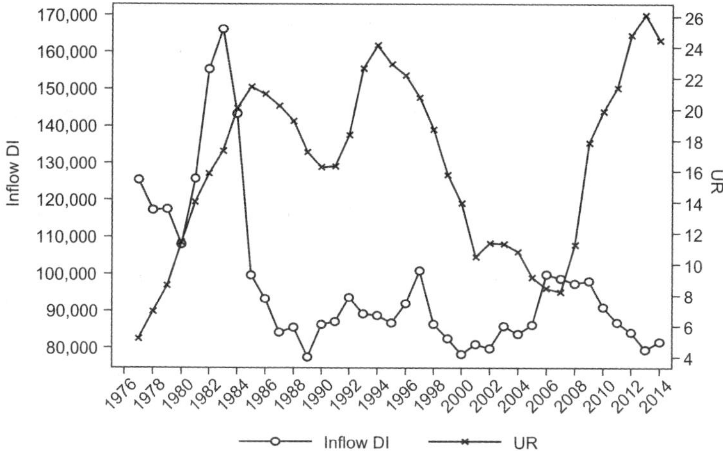

Fig. 9.8   New contributory disability benefits granted each year and unemployment rate (1977–2014)

Source: Authors' calculation using data from Spanish Social Security Administration for the inflow to disability insurance (DI) and data from the Spanish National Institute of Statistics for the unemployment rate (UR).

In summary, the 2011/2013 pension reforms, by reducing benefit expectations and also by including some incentive to work longer (partial benefit compatibility after the normal retirement age), are expected to incentivize the labor supply of older workers in Spain (see Sánchez-Martín 2014, 2017); however, it is still too early to fully detect their implications in the data.

9.3.1.5   Other Routes into Early Retirement

Another factor that may affect the labor market behavior of older workers is disability and unemployment insurance policies. Both the main characteristics of the disability system as well as its main reforms are extensively documented in García-Gómez, Jiménez-Martín, and J. Vall Castelló (2012).

Figure 9.8 shows the evolution of the number of new disability benefits granted each year (or inflow to DI) and the unemployment rate during the years 1976–2014 in Spain. In contrast to other industrialized countries, DI inflow in Spain does not show a continuous increase during the last decades (see OECD [2010] for OECD countries). As stated before, this low historical increase in the inflow could be a result of the stringency of the Spanish system (Jiménez-Martín, Juanmarti Mestres, and Vall Castelló 2018). More specifically, the government implemented a reform of the system in 1985 that increased the requirements to be granted a disability benefit. As clearly shown in figure 9.8, this reform seems to have immediately reduced the inflow to DI and kept it at a low level since then. However, around 1995, we do not detect any reduction in the inflow that can justify the strong increase in the employment rate of older workers thereafter.

Finally, between 1995 and 2011, there was a special unemployment scheme for those workers aged at least 52 (UB52+) who (a) are eligible for a retirement pension, except for their age and (b) have an income below 75 percent of the monthly minimum wage. In 2011, the program was restricted to workers aged at least 55 (UB55+).

The benefit can be collected until the person reaches retirement age—either early or normal. During this time, the individual collects UB52+ or UB55+, and until 2011, the system was assigning a fictitious contribution equal to 125 percent of the minimum wage. After the 2011 reform, the contribution varies with the length of the contributive career. The existing evidence (e.g., García-Pérez and Sánchez-Martín 2015) illustrates that UB52+ or UB55+ limits the job search of low-income workers, thereby reducing participation in the labor market.

9.3.2   Trends in Self-Assessed Health and Mortality

Another potential explanation of the increase in the LFP of Spanish men since the mid-1990s would be an improvement in health status that could allow older workers to remain longer in the labor market. We investigate the plausibility of this hypothesis by looking at trends in mortality using data from the Human Mortality Database and trends in self-reported health using data from a series of Spanish Health Surveys (*Encuesta Nacional de Salud*, ENS).[9]

Figure 9.9 plots mortality rates at age 60 for Spanish men and women from 1980 to 2012. We can see a steady decline in these mortality rates for both men and women. In addition, the decrease is slightly stronger for men, suggesting that the gender gap in mortality has narrowed over time. However, these trends do not necessarily translate to an improvement of health, as the international evidence is inconclusive regarding whether changes in mortality are translated to a compression or expansion of morbidity (Klijs, Mackenbach, and Nusselder 2009). For the Spanish case, it seems that these improvements in mortality rates at older ages have, at most, partially translated into improvements in self-assessed health. Figure 9.10 presents the percentage of men and women who declare themselves to be in fair or poor health at ages 55–64 in Spain. We see that even if mortality rates at age 60 have constantly decreased for both men and women in Spain since the early 1980s, only a minor improvement is found in self-assessed health status from 2006. In addition, García-Gómez, Jiménez-Martín, and J. Vall Castelló (2012) show that the percentage that reports having reduced their principal activity because of a health problem has increased over the same period together with the prevalence of hypertension, cholesterol, obesity,

---

9. ENS is a set of nationwide cross-sectional surveys that collect information on health, health care use, lifestyles, and socioeconomic characteristics of the Spanish population. We use data from the cross-section ENS in 1987, 1993, 1995, 1997, 2001, 2003, 2006, 2009, 2011, and 2014. Self-assessed health is defined as the percentage of individuals who rate their general health as fair or poor.

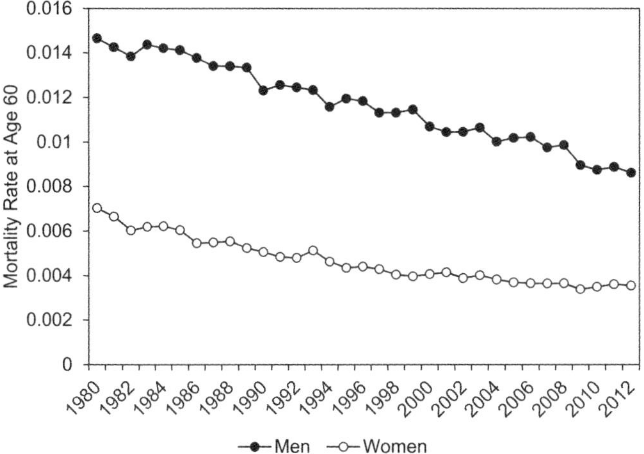

Fig. 9.9   Mortality rates at age 60 for men and women in Spain
Source: Authors' calculation based on data from the Human Mortality Database.

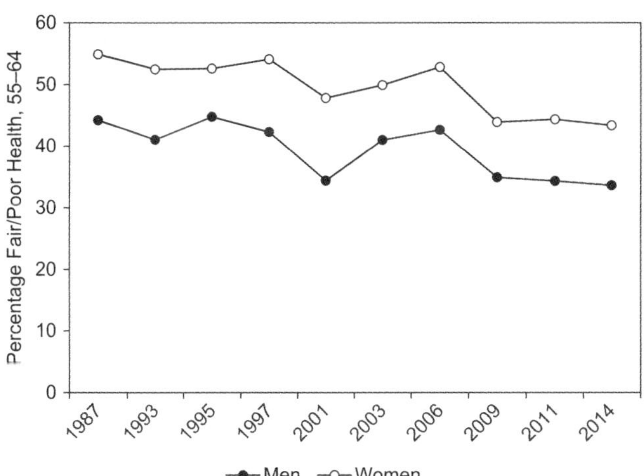

Fig. 9.10   Percentage of men/women in fair or poor health at ages 55–64 in Spain
Source: Authors' calculation based on data from the Spanish Health Survey.

and the number of hospitalizations due to mental problems in Spain for the same age groups over the same time period. Therefore, it seems unlikely that changes in the health of the population can explain changes in the LFP trends of older workers in Spain.

9.3.3   Trends in Human Capital

Another potential explanation of the increase in the LFP observed after the mid-1990s would be an increase in the skill level of Spanish men approaching the retirement age, which could lead to a stronger labor force

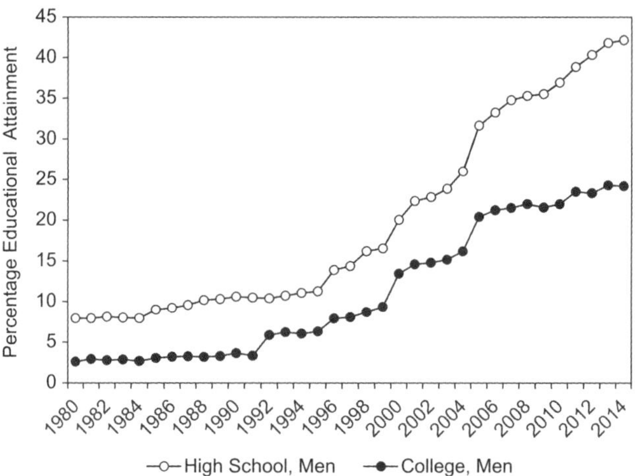

Fig. 9.11   Trends in educational attainment for men aged 55–64 in Spain, 1980–2014

Source: Authors' calculation based on data from the Spanish LFS.

attachment. Figure 9.11 plots the trend in educational attainment for men aged 55–64 in Spain from 1980 to 2014 using data from the Spanish LFS. We see a strong increase over time in both high school and college attainment for older Spanish men. While in 1980 only 8 percent of men aged 55–64 had completed a high school degree (and only 3 percent had a college education), in 2014, 41 percent of men aged 55–64 had a high school diploma, and 25 percent of them had a college degree. Moreover, their educational attainment increased slowly from 1980 until the mid-1990s but grew quite sharply from the mid-1990s until 2014. Therefore, we see that the shift in the trends in the LFP and employment rates coincides with the arrival of more educated cohorts.

A similar evolution can be observed for the percentage of Spanish men with a blue-collar job from 1980 to 2014 (see figure 9.12). We see that the percentage of men working in blue-collar occupations remained pretty stable—around 70 percent from 1980 to 1994. However, from 1995 on (and coinciding with the growth in educational attainment observed in figure 9.11), the percentage of Spanish men in blue-collar jobs started steadily to decrease from 70 percent to a level below 60 percent. Again, this confirms that changes in the skill level of older workers may be (at least partly) behind the trends in labor market participation and employment rates in Spain.

9.3.4   Business-Cycle Conditions

As previously discussed, business-cycle conditions may also be behind some of the trends in the LFP and employment rates. Figure 9.13 compares

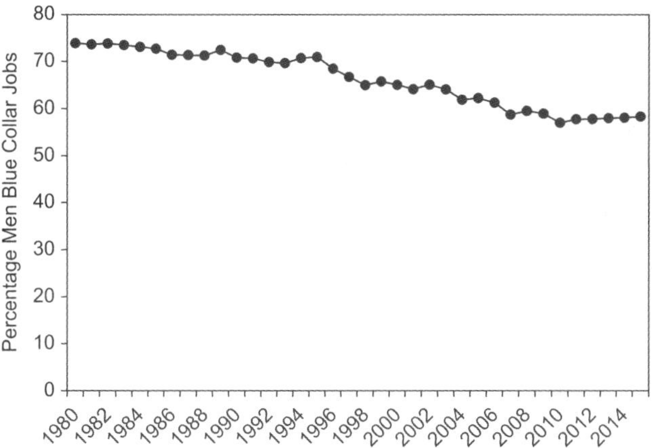

Fig. 9.12   Percentage of men workers aged 55–64 in blue-collar jobs in Spain, 1980–2014

Source: Authors' calculation based on data from the Spanish LFS.

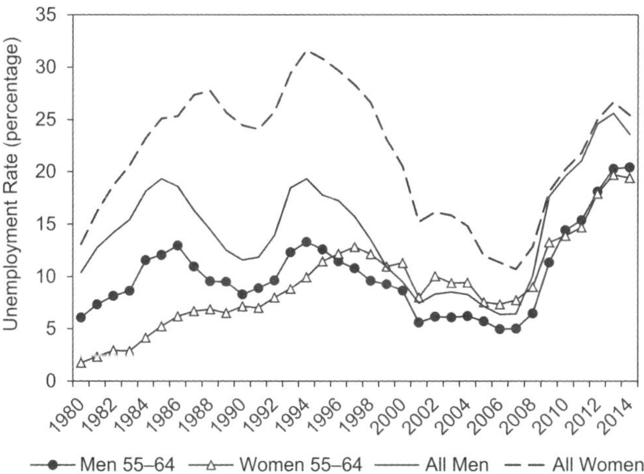

Fig. 9.13   Unemployment rate in Spain, all men / all women and those aged 55–64, 1980–2014

Source: Authors' calculation based on data from OECD.

trends in unemployment rates between 1980 and 2014 for men and women aged 55–64 and the overall working-age population using data from the OECD. First, we notice that unemployment rates for men move in parallel for both men of working age and men aged 55–64, although the levels for the older workers are always lower.[10] A similar picture, although at even higher

10. See Dolado et al. (2013) for an analysis of unemployment for young individuals in Spain.

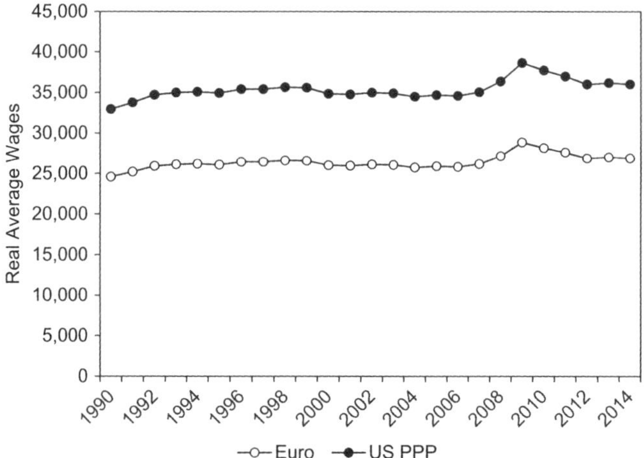

Fig. 9.14   Real average wages of Spanish workers, 1990–2014
Source: Authors' calculation based on data from OECD.

levels until the onset of the economic crises, is found for the unemployment rate of all women of working age. However, trends in unemployment rates of women aged 55–64 present a different pattern during the first half of the period. Their unemployment rate was below 5 percent in the early 1980s but continuously increased until reaching almost 15 percent in 1997. Since then, the trends move in parallel to the other age groups.

Thus by looking at figure 9.13, we can see that business-cycle conditions may have played an important role in explaining the increase in the LFP and employment rates of older men, since in the mid-1990s, unemployment rates strongly decreased for all age groups from this point onward (until the onset of the economic crisis in 2008) as a result of the strong improvement in the economic cycle in Spain.

Another potential explanation for the higher labor market attachment after the mid-1990s could be higher wages. However, there have been almost no changes in real wages in Spain over the last two decades (see figure 9.14). We see that real average wages only increased after the onset of the economic crises in 2008. However, this is due to a composition effect, as low-paid workers in temporary contracts were laid off first (Puente and Galán 2014).

9.3.5   Employment and the LFP of Spouses

Schirle (2008) estimates that between one-fourth and one half of the increase in older men's LFP in the United States, Canada, and the United Kingdom can be explained by the effect of their wife's participation decisions. Figures 9.15 and 9.16 plot LFP rates and employment rates for women aged 55–59, 60–64, and 65–69 over the 1980–2014 period using data from the OECD. We see that trends in employment (figure 9.16) follow the trends

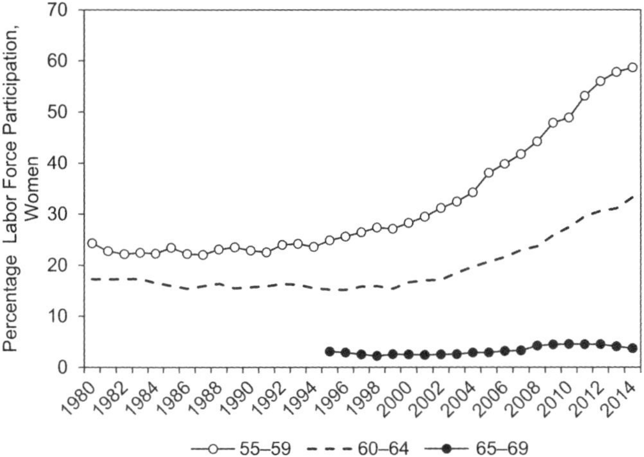

Fig. 9.15   LFP of Spanish older women, ages 55–59, 60–64, 65–69 in 1980–2014
Source: Authors' calculation based on OECD data.

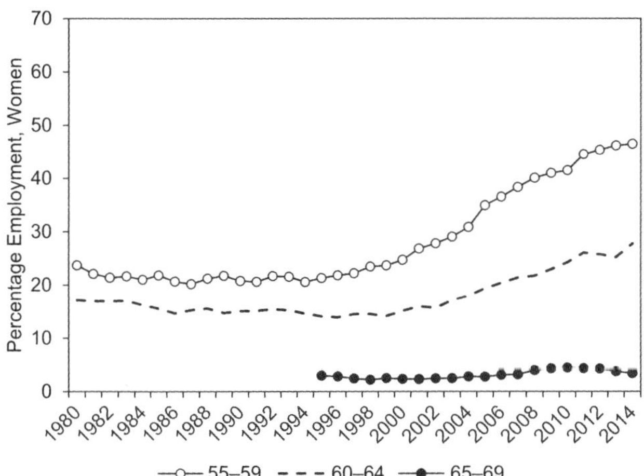

Fig. 9.16   Employment of Spanish older women, ages 55–59, 60–64, and 65–69 in 1980–2014
Source: Authors' calculation based on OECD data.

in LFP rates very closely (figure 9.15). Moreover, until the mid-1990s, the levels are similar, suggesting that almost all older women still active in the labor market were also employed. In addition, we see that participation rates remained flat at around 23 percent for women aged 55–59 and 16 percent for women aged 60–64 until the mid-1990s. Similar to the trends observed for men, we find that participation rates of women aged 55–59 started increasing first around 1995, followed by the rates of the older age group (60–64) about

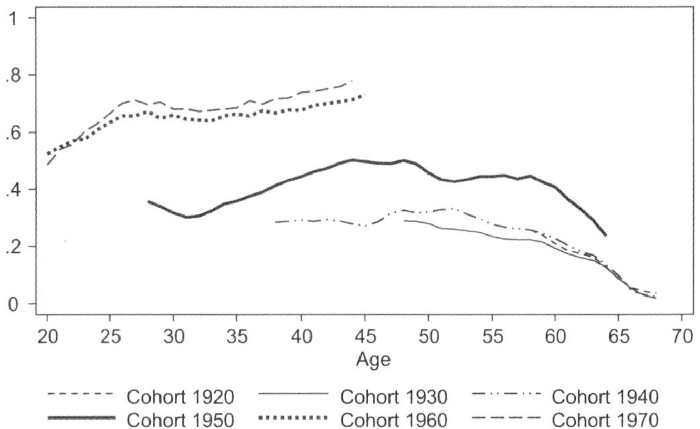

Fig. 9.17   LFP of Spanish women by cohort
Source: Authors' elaboration using data from the Spanish LFS.

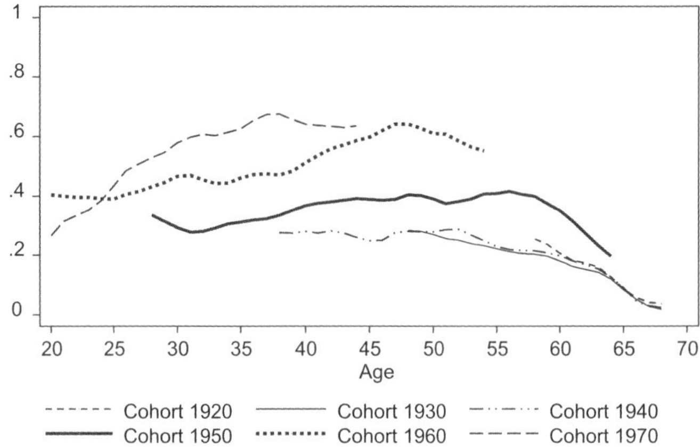

Fig. 9.18   Employment rates of Spanish women by cohort
Source: Authors' elaboration using data from the Spanish LFS.

five years later. At the end of the period, and despite the economic crises, almost 60 percent of women aged 55–59 were in the labor market, although only about 45 percent of them were employed. Last, we find that both the LFP and the employment rates of women aged 65–69 have remained low (between 2.5 percent ánd 4 percent) throughout the observation period. This is similar to the trends observed for men in this age group.

The five-year difference in the turning point in the trends suggests that cohort differences in labor market behavior may be relevant. Figures 9.17 and 9.18 plot the LFP and employment profiles for ages 20–68 for the cohorts of Spanish women born in 1920, 1930, 1940, 1950, 1960, and 1970

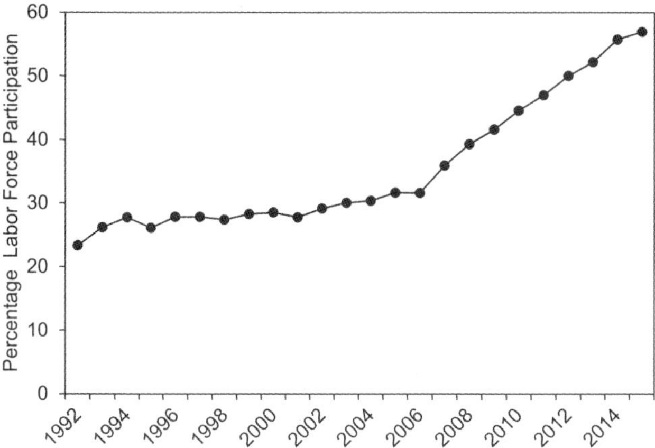

Fig. 9.19   20 years lagged LFP rate of Spanish women at ages 35–44
Source: Authors' elaboration using data from the Spanish LFS.

using data from the Spanish LFS. We see that there were no differences in the participation rates of women from the cohorts born in 1920, 1930, and 1940. However, we observe that the LFP rates of the subsequent cohort (born in 1950) were almost 20 percentage points higher, and a similar increase is observed between the cohort born in 1950 and the cohort born in 1960. Subsequent gains are smaller, and as a result, the LFP rate at younger ages of the last cohort (born in 1970) was still far below the rates observed among men.

The stronger attachment to the labor market of more recent cohorts of women can also be seen in figure 9.19. It plots the 20-years-lagged LFP rate of Spanish women at ages 35–44—that is, the LFP of women aged 55–64 when they were 20 years younger. We see that the LFP for the younger ages of the cohorts of women aged 55–64 has been steadily increasing since the early 1990s, and this increase has become steeper over the last decade.

Similar to the evidence shown for men, educational attainment of women aged 55–64 has been improving over the last few decades. In fact, in figures 9.10 and 9.20, we can see that these trends move almost in parallel, although the percentage with both high school and college have been always lower for women aged 55–64 compared to men aged 55–64.

All in all, these figures provide suggestive evidence that a stronger attachment of women to the labor market may be one of the drivers of the observed increase in labor market participation and the employment of older male workers. To the extent that the labor force attachment of future older women is expected to be higher based on the current participation at younger ages, one could expect further increases in the LFP of older men in the coming two decades.

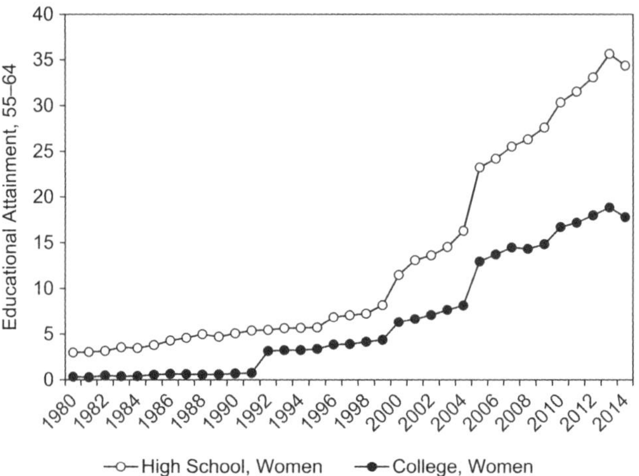

Fig. 9.20   Educational attainment of Spanish women aged 55–64, 1980–2014
Source: Authors' elaboration using data from the Spanish LFS.

9.4   Conclusions

Similar to other OECD countries, the LFP rates of older Spanish workers were falling until the mid-1990s, when there was a reversal in the trend. The LFP rates of older Spanish men have been increasing since then, although at a slower pace than other OECD countries.

We explore to what extent several factors can be behind these trends. First, we conclude that the (old-age) social security system (except perhaps for the disability component) has played a marginal (at most) role on this reversal, given the lack of major changes in social security benefits until the last set of reforms in 2011 and 2013. Future work should evaluate whether these last reforms have a substantial effect on the labor supply of older workers like one would expect given the fundamental changes in some of the main parameters of the old-age pension system. In addition, we cannot rule out that the set of reforms have introduced a higher uncertainty about future benefits over time. This increased uncertainty could have played a role.

Second, we also rule out that changes in the health status of the population are responsible for the reversal of this trend. Mortality rates at age 60 have been decreasing at a steady pace since the 1980s for both men and women in Spain. However, there is no change in this trend from the mid-1990s that could help explain the change in the LFP trends at that time. Similarly, data on self-assessed health shows a mild improvement in subjective health only from 2006.

We find that the overall increase in employment (due to the strong economic growth since 1995) is one of the factors that can explain the increase in LFP and employment rates of older Spanish men. Furthermore, differences across cohorts in both the skill composition and the labor attachment of wives are also potential drivers of these changes in the labor market outcomes of older men. We find that the share of males with high school or college degrees starts increasing at the same point in time as the employment and LFP trends reverse. Similarly, at this point in time, the percentage of older workers in blue-collar jobs starts decreasing.

Finally, we find strong cohort effects in female LFP and employment rates. In particular, the increase in the LFP, employment, and educational attainment of women in the same age group coincides with the reversal of the men's trend.

In this chapter, we have documented changes in LFP rates for older men in Spain since the 1980s. Although all the evidence presented is descriptive and we cannot estimate any causal relationship, we have pinpointed some potential factors that can explain (at least part) of the increase in the LFP rates of older men in Spain since the mid-1990s.

Further research needs to establish the causality of these relationships and the extent to which each of the factors discussed in this chapter is responsible for explaining the increase in older men's participation rates in Spain.

Appendix

Table 9.A.1 Spanish Social Security system

				Social Security system				
	Eligibility	Early and normal retirement ages	Benefit Formula	Actuarial adjustment	Earnings test	Reforms implemented since 1990	Disability insurance	Other key programs
Contributory pensions from 2002 to 2013	15 years of covered employment	—ERA: 61 or 63 —NRA: 65 and 3 months, currently on the from 65 to 67	Average of 15 last covered wages. Minimum pensions: Basic rate for age 65 with no spouse is 8,883 euros (varies with age and spouse)	—Benefits reduced by 6–8 percent per year before NRA —Benefits increased by 2–3 percent per year after NRA	50 percent of pension for those qualifying (full contributive career)	**1997** —Number of years contribution in formula increased from 8 to 15; less generous replacement rate; incentives to longer careers. **2002** —Early retirement only from age 61. —Impulse partial retirement; possible to combine it with work. **2007** —15 "effective" contributory years are used to calculate the pension. —Reduction from 8 percent to 7.5 percent of the per-year penalty applied to early retirees between 60 and 65 for individuals with 30 contributory years. —Broaden incentives to stay employed after age 65. **2011** —Years of contribution in benefit formula from 15 to 20. —NRA from 65 to 67. —Eligibility conditions for early retirement are modified. **2013** —Sustainability factor + new scheme for work/pension compatibility.	Medical screening leading to 33 percent increase in disability. Four levels of disability. Benefits is an average of the average covered wage of last eight (or two in case of accident) years.	Survival pension and dependent benefits
Not contributory old-age pensions	Means tested, insufficient contributions for the contributory regime	Age 65+	Fixed amount in 2015, 5,136.6 euros, 14 installments	NA	NA	None		

References

Benítez-Silva, H., J. I. García-Pérez, and S. Jiménez-Martín. 2013. "Evaluación de las consecuencias laborales de la reforma de 2011 y de reformas alternativas." *Revista Economía Española y Protección Social* 5:35–62.

Boldrín, M., P. García-Gómez, and S. Jiménez-Martín. 2010. "Social Security Incentives, Exit from the Workforce and Entry of the Young." In *Social Security Programs and Retirement around the World: The Relationship to Youth Employment*, edited by J. Gruber and D. A. Wise, 261–94. Chicago: University of Chicago Press.

Boldrín, M., S. Jiménez-Martín, and F. Peracchi. 2001. "Sistema de pensiones y mercado de trabajo en España." Madrid, Spain: Fundacion BBVA.

Conde-Ruiz, J. I., and C. I. Gonzalez. 2016. "From Bismarck to Beveridge: The Other Pension Reform in Spain." *SERIEs* 7 (4): 461–90.

Díaz-Giménez, J., and J. Díaz-Saavedra. 2017. "The Future of Spanish Pensions." *Journal of Pension Economics and Finance* 16 (2): 233–65.

Dolado, J. J., M. Jansen, F. Felgueroso, A. Fuentes, and A. Wölfl. 2013. "Youth Labour Market Performance in Spain and Its Determinants: A Micro-level Perspective." OECD Economics Department Working Paper 1039, OECD, Paris, France.

European Commission. 2012. "The 2012 Ageing Report: Economic and Budgetary Projections for the 27 EU Member States (2010–2060)." http://ec.europa.eu/economy_finance/publications/european_economy/2012/pdf/ee-2012-2_en.pdf.

Felgueroso, F., and S. Jiménez-Martín. 2009. "The 'New Growth Model': How and with Whom?" Working Paper 2009-39, Fedea, Madrid, Spain.

García-Gómez, P., S. Jiménez-Martín, and J. Vall Castelló. 2012. "Health, Disability, and Pathways into Retirement in Spain." In *Social Security Programs and Retirement around the World: Historical Trends in Mortality and Health, Employment, and Disability Insurance Participation and Reforms*, edited by D. A. Wise, 127–74. Chicago: University of Chicago Press.

García-Pérez, J. I., S. Jiménez-Martín, and A. R. Sánchez-Martín. 2013. "Retirement Incentives, Individual Heterogeneity and Labor Transitions of Employed and Unemployed Workers." *Labour Economics* 20 (C): 106–20.

García-Pérez, J. I., and A. R. Sánchez-Martín. 2015. "Fostering Job Search among Older Workers: The Case for Pension Reform." *IZA Journal of Labor Policy* 4:21. https://doi.org/10.1186/s40173-015-0045-6.

Gruber, J., and D. A. Wise, eds. 1999. *Social Security and Retirement around the World.* Chicago: University of Chicago Press.

Hairault, J. O., F. Langot, and T. Sopraseuth. 2010. "Distance to Retirement and Older Workers' Employment: The Case for Delaying the Retirement Age." *Journal of the European Economic Association* 8 (5): 1034–76.

Jiménez-Martín, S. 2014. "The Incentive Effects of Minimum Pensions." *IZA World of Labor* 84:1–10.

Jiménez-Martín, S., A. Juanmarti Mestres, and J. Vall Castelló. 2018. "Great Recession and Disability in Spain." *Empirical Economics* 56 (5): 1623–45. https://doi.org/10.1007/s00181-017-1396-1.

Klijs, B., J. Mackenbach, and W. Nusselder. 2009. "Compression of Morbidity: A Promising Approach to Alleviate the Societal Consequences of Population Aging." Netspar Discussion Paper No. 12/2009–058, Network for Studies on Pensions, Aging and Retirement, Le Tilburg, Netherlands.

OECD. 2010. *Sickness, Disability and Work: Breaking the Barriers: A Synthesis of Findings across OECD Countries.* Paris: OECD.

———. 2015. *Pensions at a Glance 2015.* Paris: OECD.

Puente, S., and S. Galán. 2014. "Analysis of Composition Effects on Wage Behaviour." *Banco de España Economic Bulletin*, February, 25–28.

Sánchez-Martín, A. R. 2014. "The Automatic Adjustment of Pension Expenditures in Spain: An Evaluation of the 2013 Pension Reform." Working Paper No. 1420, Banco de España, Madrid, Spain.

———. 2017. "Proyecciones financieras y de bienestar del sistema español de pensiones: Modelización en equilibrio general." Technical report EEE2017-03, Fedea, Madrid, Spain.

Schirle, T. 2008. "Why Have the Labor Force Participation Rates of Older Men Increased since the Mid-1990s?" *Journal of Labor Economics* 26 (4): 549–94.

The Recent Rise of Labor Force Participation of Older Workers in Sweden

Lisa Laun and Mårten Palme

10.1 Introduction

Between 1963 and 2000, the labor force participation (LFP) rate among males in the 60–64 age group in Sweden fell from around 85 to 55 percentage points (e.g., Palme and Svensson 1999). However, since then, the LFP has started to rise again and is now above 75 percent in the age group (e.g., Johansson, Laun, and Palme 2015). Although the long-term development for female LFP has been dominated by the great increase in the employment of married women, the recent development shows a similar pattern to that of men.

In this chapter, we analyze the background of the recent increase in the LFP of older workers in Sweden. We first look at how the population has changed with respect to characteristics known to be associated with the probability of being active in the labor market among older people. These characteristics are health, educational attainment, and the work environment, which the worker must meet if he or she decides to work. Finally, considering the pattern of joint retirement decision of couples, we look at the extent to which the increased LFP rate of married women could explain the increased probability of older men deciding to work longer.

Lisa Laun is a researcher at the Institute for Evaluation of Labour Market and Education Policy (IFAU).

Mårten Palme is professor of economics at Stockholm University.

This chapter is part of the National Bureau of Economic Research's International Social Security (ISS) project, which is supported by the National Institute on Aging (grant P01 AG012810). Lisa Laun gratefully acknowledges financial support from the Swedish Research Council for Health, Working Life and Welfare, FORTE (dnr 2013–0209). For acknowledgments, sources of research support, and disclosure of the authors' material financial relationships, if any, please see https://www.nber.org/chapters/c14050.ack.

In the second part of the chapter, we study the extent to which the recent institutional changes in the income security system and labor market regulations may have contributed to the development. First, we look briefly at the potential effects of the major reform of the old-age pension system in Sweden that was initiated in 1998. Second, we study the effects of the introduction of age-targeted income tax credits in 2007. Third, we summarize the experiences of the change in the mandatory retirement age in 2001. Finally, we study the potential effects of the more stringent rules for eligibility in Sweden's disability insurance (DI) program that were gradually implemented.

We do not attempt to identify any "causal effects" of any policy intervention. Our analysis is merely descriptive in the sense that we look at the coincidences of trends or long-term changes in society. Throughout, we have chosen to look at men and women separately. The reason for this choice, as will be apparent from our description in section 10.2, is that men and women experienced a very different development in their participation in the labor force in the most recent decades.

10.2 The Development of LFP and Employment of Older Workers in Sweden

Figure 10.1 shows the evolution of the LFP for the 55–59, 60–64, and 65–69 age groups for males and females, respectively. By comparing the graphs for males aged 60–64 with the corresponding one for those aged 55–59, it can be seen that the development follows the same pattern, although the development for the older age group is more dramatic: there is a marked trend toward a decreased LFP until the late 1990s in both age groups and then a reversed trend. In the 60–64 age group, there is a decrease from 85 percent in 1963 to about 57 percent in 2000 and then an increase to around 75 percent by the end of the period. The corresponding change in the 55–59 age group is from almost 95 percent to below 85 percent in 2000 and then a recovery to about 90 percent.

For the oldest age group, those aged 65–69, the graph shows a marked decrease in LFP until the late 1970s. This primarily reflects the gradual change in the mandatory and normal retirement ages from 67 to 65 on the Swedish labor market. The graph also shows a marked increase in LFP by the end of the period under study—from below 20 percent in 2000 to around 26 percent by the end of the period.

As is immediately apparent from the figures, the graphs for female LFP tell a very different story from the male ones. The development for females until the late 1980s is dominated by the trend toward increased LFP. After that, the development of the two gender groups has been remarkably parallel.

This development is highlighted in figure 10.2. In this figure, the graphs for

A   Labor Force Participation 1963–2016, Males

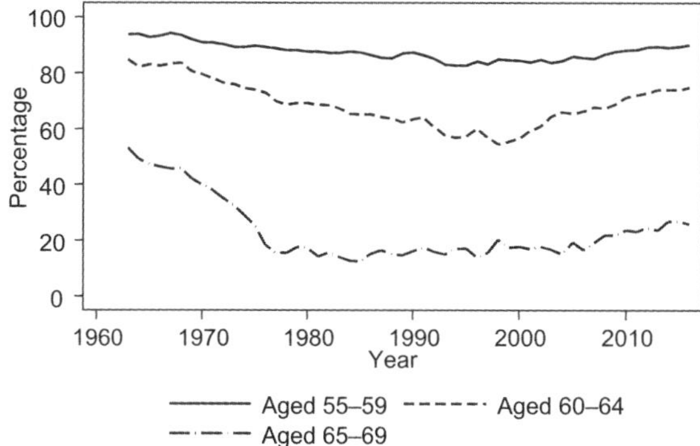

B   Labor Force Participation 1963–2016, Females

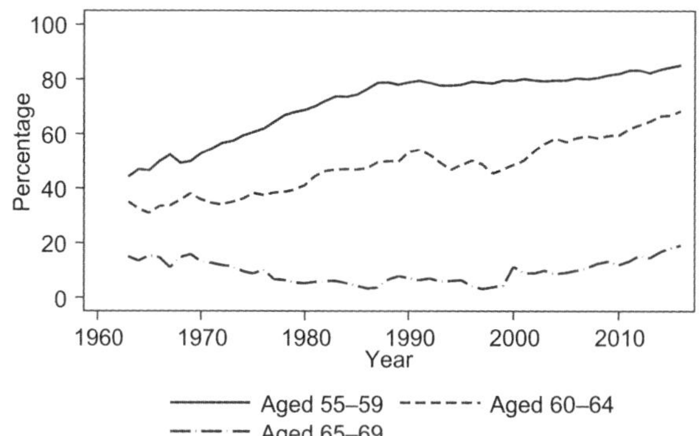

Fig. 10.1   Development of LFP rates in different age groups, males and females, 1963–2016

Source: Swedish LFS

the two gender groups in the same age group have been placed in the same diagram. It can be seen that the convergence between males and females happened five years later in the 60–64 age group compared to the 55–59 one, which is a pure cohort effect. This means that the increase in female LFP relative to the male LFP stopped around the cohort born in 1935. There is no tendency to further convergence in the LFP for cohorts born later.

Figure 10.3 shows the development of the employment rate for the same age groups as in figure 10.1 over the same period. It can be seen that this development follows a very similar pattern compared to the LFP rates. This means that the unemployment rate is not driving the long-term changes in employment. Figure 10.4 shows the development of unemployment rates separately. It can be seen that this development is closely connected

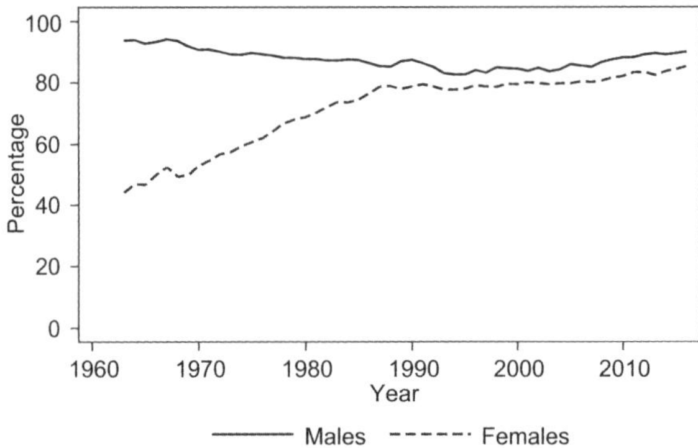

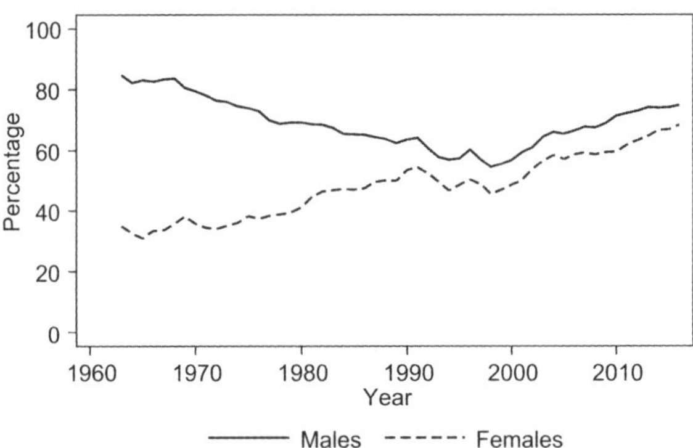

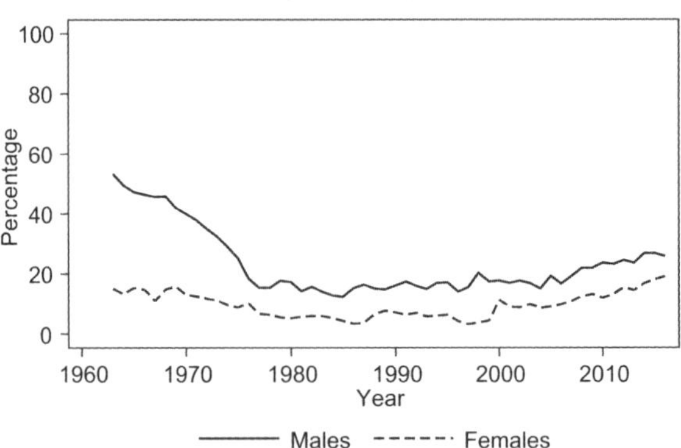

Fig. 10.2   Development of LFP rates for males compared to females in different age groups, 1963–2016

Source: Swedish LFS.

A Employment 1963–2016, Males

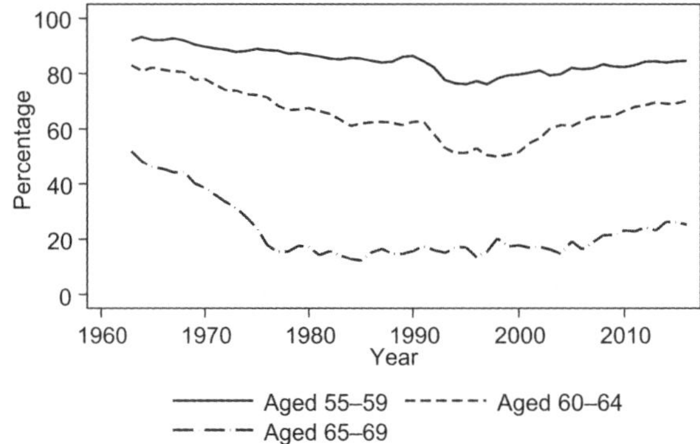

B Employment 1963–2016, Females

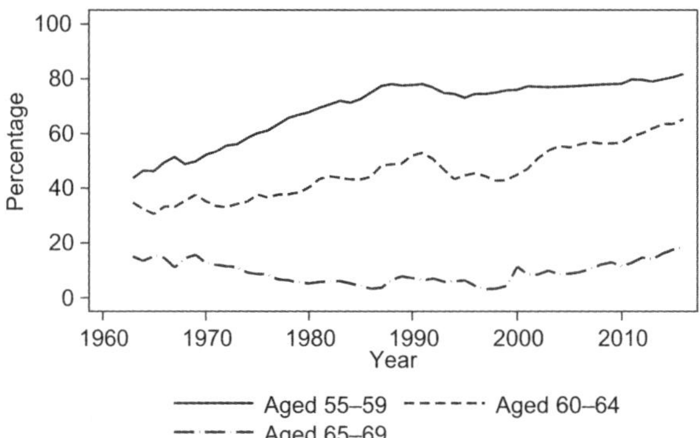

Fig. 10.3   The development of employment by age, males and females, 1963–2016
Source: Swedish LFS.

to the Swedish business cycle, with major recessions in the early 1980 and 1990s.

To sum up, there is a U-shaped development of the LFP of older men in Sweden over the observed period. Although there has been a strong trend toward a higher LFP in recent years, it should be noted that the average rates are still much lower than the ones observed in the early 1960s in all age groups under study. The diagrams where we placed the graphs for the development of male and female LFP in the same age groups together suggest that there is no increase in the relative female LFP after the cohort born in 1935. These graphs also suggest that the recent trend toward increased male LFP is driven by changes across birth cohorts rather than by period effects. This interpretation is further supported by the fact that business-cycle changes and fluctuations in the unemployment rate seem to have very limited effects on the LFP rates.

A Unemployment 1963–2016, Males

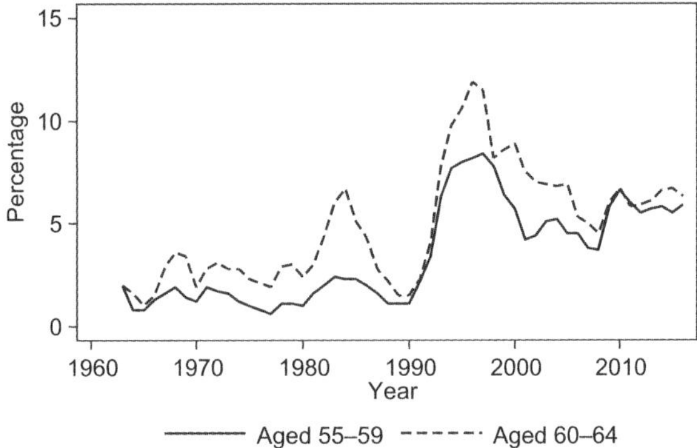

B Unemployment 1963–2016, Females

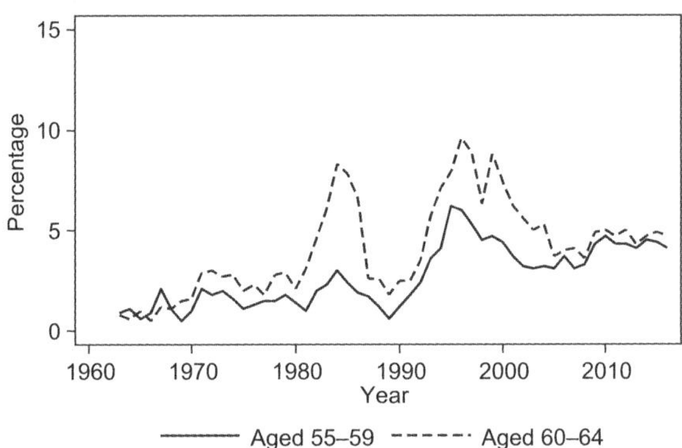

Fig. 10.4   The development of unemployment by age, males and females, 1963–2016
Source: Swedish LFS.

10.3   Changes in Characteristics of the Population Aged 55–59 and 60–64

10.3.1   Improved Health

A possible background to the higher LFP rates is that the population simply improved its health status, allowing people to work at older ages. A first problem when assessing the empirical relevance of the hypothesis is how to measure changes in population health. One way is to look at changes in mortality. Figure 10.5 shows the development of mortality rates between 1960 and 2015 in the 55–59 and 60–64 age groups and for males and females, respectively.

Figure 10.5 shows several interesting patterns in the development of mortality. While there is a steady improvement in survival for women in both age groups, the development shows little change for men between 1960 and

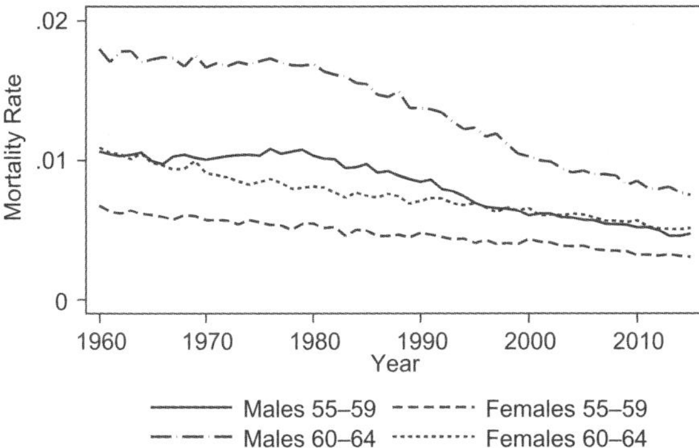

Fig. 10.5   Development of mortality rates, age groups 55–59 and 60–64, males and females, 1960–2015

Source: Swedish Cause of Death Register.

the mid-1980s. However, since then, there is a larger decrease in mortality for men than for women. The gender gap in mortality in the older age group has shrunk markedly in recent years. In the 35-year period since 1980, the mortality rate among men aged 60–64 has more than halved from about 1.7 percent to below 0.8 percent.

A limitation of using mortality to analyze the background to changes in LFP is its low validity: the marginal worker is probably different from the marginal survivor in the ages under study. It is conceivable that much of the improvement in survival rates in recent years is located in groups of people that are far from entering the labor force.

A complement to the mortality rates is to look at the development of self-assessed health measures. We use data on self-assessed health obtained from the six different waves of the Swedish Level of Living Survey (LNU). The LNU is a panel survey administrated by the Institute for Social Research at Stockholm University, where about 6,000 individuals aged 16–74 are interviewed about their health, work, social contacts, and economic conditions, as well as their participation in the society.[1]

Figure 10.6 shows the development of three different health indicators obtained from survey questions. The first one asks about the ability to walk up stairs, the second one about the ability to walk 100 meters, and finally, the third one about the ability to run 100 meters. Again, we look at the 55–59 and 60–64 age groups.

It is apparent from the upper panel of figure 10.6, showing the development for males and females together, that there is a steady improvement in

---

1. The sample size of 6,000 individuals implies that there are on average about 100 observations in each birth cohort. Since we split the sample by gender and use five-year age intervals, we get a sample size of around 250 observations in each cell we report.

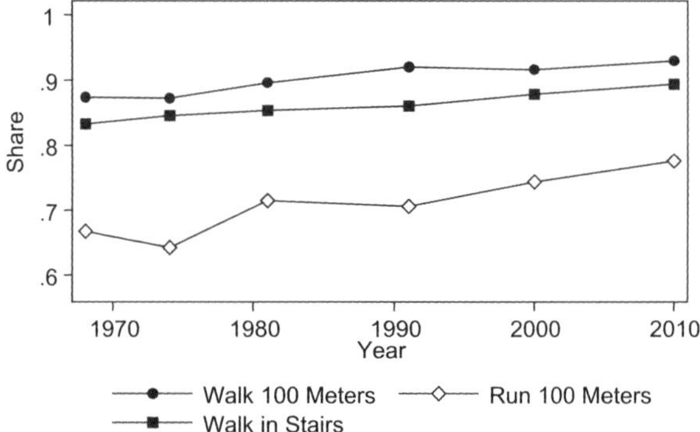

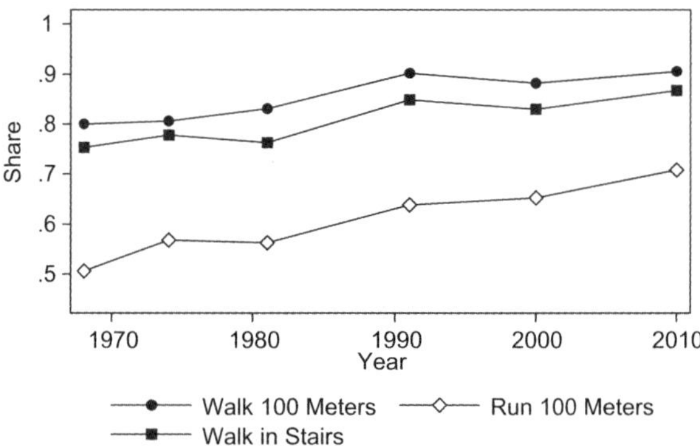

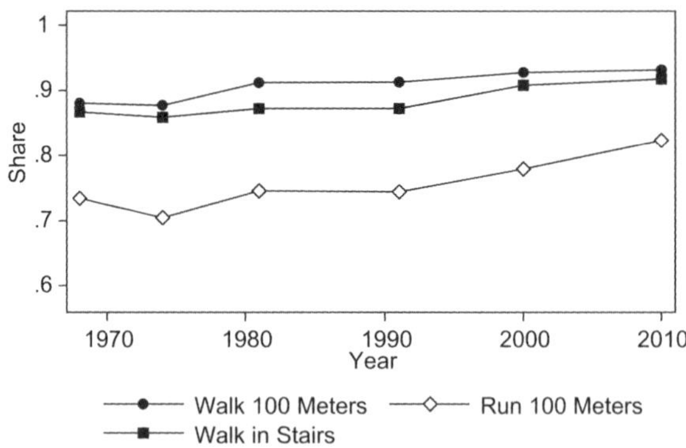

Fig. 10.6 Share that is "able to walk 100 meters," "able to run 100 meters," and "able to walk up stairs," age groups 55–59 and 60–64, males and females

Source: Authors' calculations from the 1968, 1974, 1981, 1991, 2000, and 2010 waves of the Swedish Level of Living Survey.

D Health indicators, Males aged 60–64

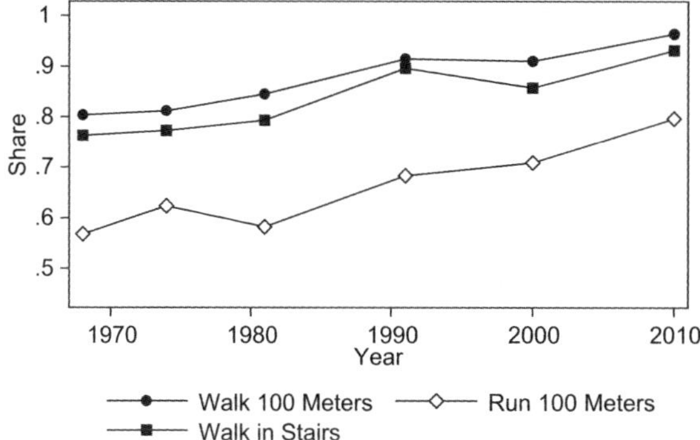

E Health indicators, Females aged 55–59

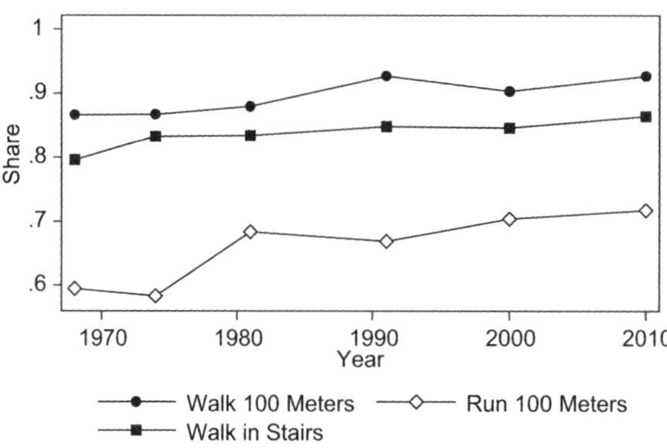

F Health indicators, Females aged 60–64

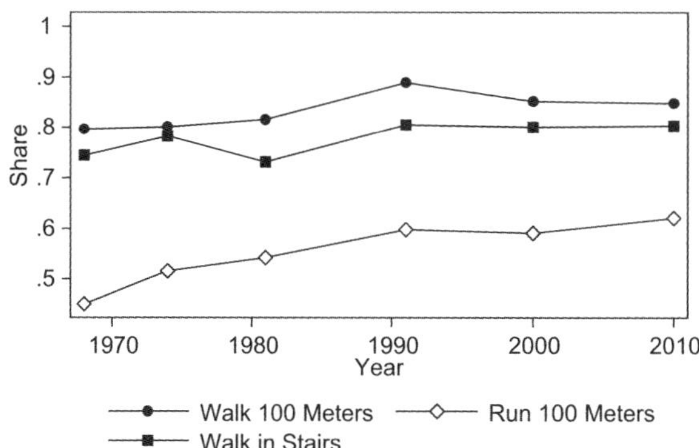

Fig. 10.6   **(cont.)**

all three measures and in both age groups over the observed period. The largest improvement is in the 60–64 age group. In this group, the share of individuals that claim they are able to run 100 meters has increased from 50 percent in 1968 to 70 percent in 2010.

In the lower two panels of figure 10.6, we show the development in the two age groups for males and females, separately. This division reveals that the development can, to a larger extent, be attributed to men. It can be seen that almost 80 percent of the men aged 60–64 claim that they are able to run 100 meters in 2010 compared to 62 percent for females. This gender gap was much smaller in 1968.

In the 1991, 2000, and 2010 waves of the LNU, there is a summary measure of the individuals' health status from the answer to the question on whether the respondent is in "good," "fair" or "poor" health. Figure 10.7 shows the development of the share reporting fair or poor health over the three surveys. In the upper panel, the development is shown for males and females together, divided in the 55–59 and 60–64 age groups, respectively. The lower panels show the development for males and females separately.

Figure 10.7 reveals that there is a substantial improvement in the health status measure over the almost 20-year period covered by the surveys. In the older age group, the share reporting fair or poor health decreases from almost 42 to about 32 percent. The lower panel shows that the improvement again primarily can be attributed to men. The largest change is in the older age group. Between 2000 and 2010, the share of those claiming to be in fair or poor health decreased from about 43 to less than 25 percent—a decrease of about 40 percent.

To sum up, we look at the development of three different types of measures for population health: mortality, self-assessed measures of physical ability, and self-assessed summary health measures. Interestingly, all these measures give a similar picture of the development: there is a continuous improvement in health, and it seems that there has been a somewhat accelerated improvement for older men in recent years. Improved health thus seems to be a prominent factor in explaining the rise in the LFP among the elderly. In fact, in a previous study (Johansson, Laun, and Palme 2015), we find that the recent increase in the LFP is smaller than the health improvement for older workers if we assume that workers with a particular health status could work as much as workers with the same health status worked in the past.

10.3.2   Changes in Educational Attainment

It is well known from previous studies that more-educated individuals retire later (e.g., Venti and Wise 2015). Our Swedish data shows that the difference in the employment rate between low-educated (compulsory schooling or vocational training as the highest level) and high-educated (secondary schooling or higher) workers is 11.8 percentage points in the 55–59 age group

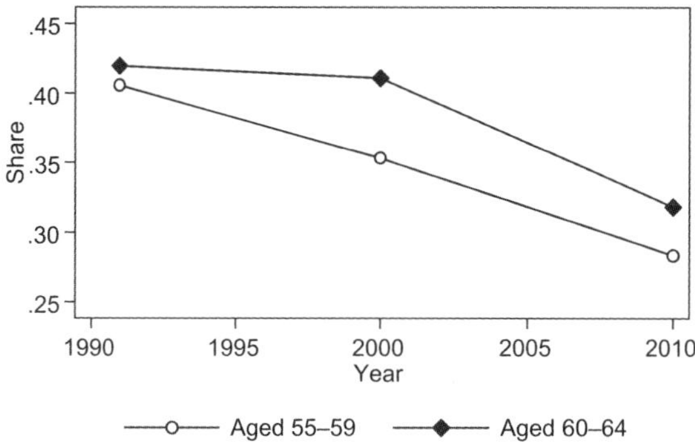

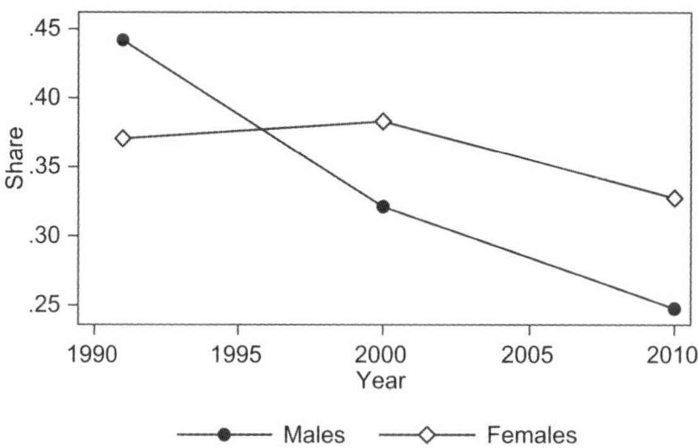

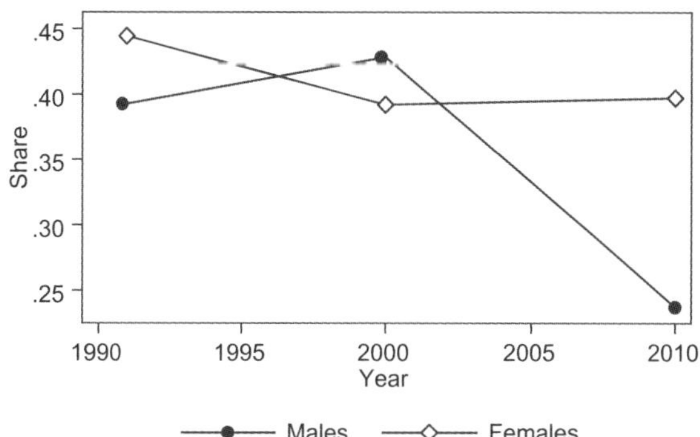

Fig. 10.7   Development of the share claiming they are in fair or poor health, age groups 55–59 and 60–64, males and females

Source: Authors' calculations from the 1991, 2000, and 2010 waves of the Swedish Level of Living Survey.

A   Share with a High School Degree Aged 55–64

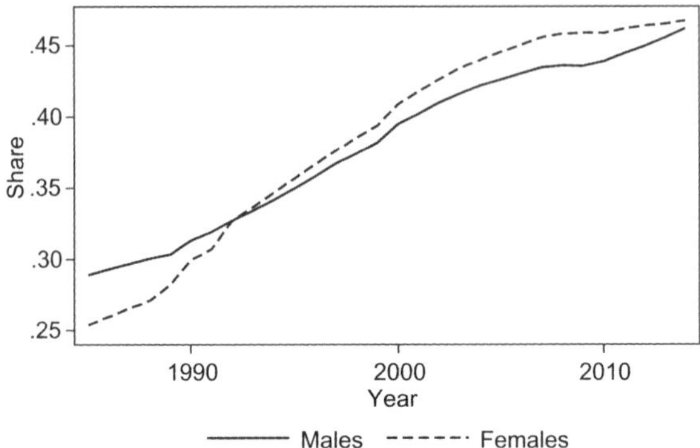

B   Share with a College Degree Aged 55–64

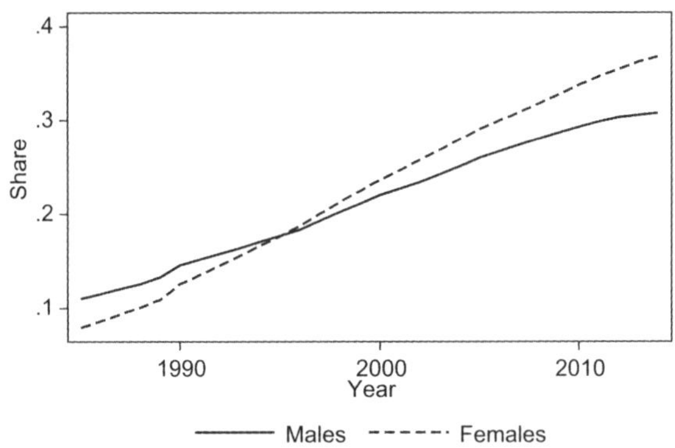

Fig. 10.8   Share of high school graduates in the 55–64 age group between 1985 and 2014, males and females; share of graduates from university/college in the 55–64 age group between 1985 and 2014, males and females
Source: Swedish Education Register.

(72.3 vs. 84.1 percent). The corresponding difference among 60–64-year-olds is even larger: 14.3 percentage points (56.3 vs. 70.6 percent).

A possible background to the increase in the LFP of older workers could therefore simply be that the cohort reaching older ages in recent years are more educated than previous ones and therefore retire later. Figure 10.8 shows the change in educational attainment for the 55–64 age group between 1985 and 2014. The left panel shows the share that has graduated from high school and the right panel shows the corresponding share of college graduates.

Figure 10.8 shows a great change in the educational attainment of the age group. The largest change is for women. During the period covered by figure 10.8, the educational qualifications of women surpassed those of males mea-

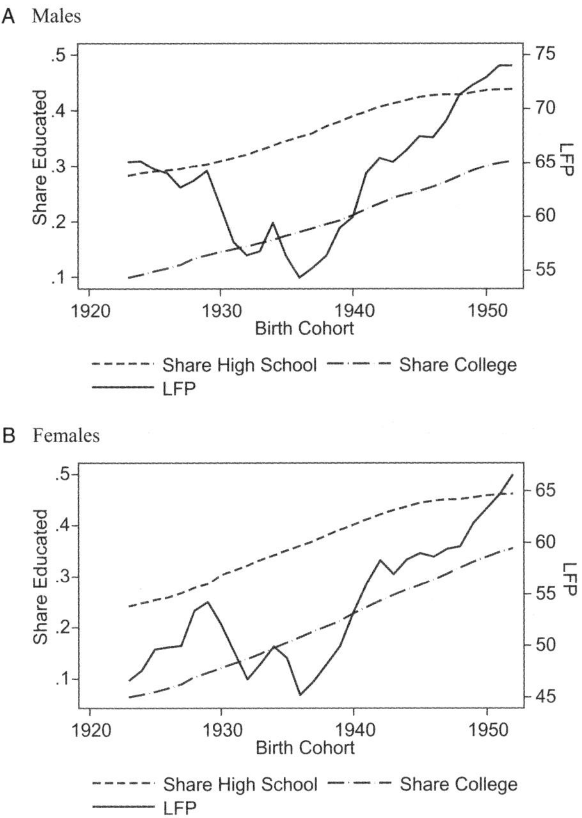

Fig. 10.9   Development of LFP by cohort of birth and share graduating from high school and college/university, respectively, in the 60–64 age group
Source: Swedish LFS and Swedish Education Register.

sured as the share graduating from both high school and college. Between 1990 and 2005, the share of women aged 55–64 with a high school degree increased from less than 30 percent to about 45 percent, and the share graduating from college increased from around 10 percent to about 30 percent.

In figure 10.9, we display the graphs showing the change in educational attainment along with those showing the evolution of the LFP in the 60–64 age group. Note that we have changed the age group for the education measures to the age group where most of the increased LFP took place. We have also changed the label of the x-axis to the year of birth of the midpoint of the age group under study—that is, age 62. The left panel shows the results for males and the right one for females.

The message in the graphs is somewhat mixed. On the one hand, one could argue that the educational attainment also increased across the birth

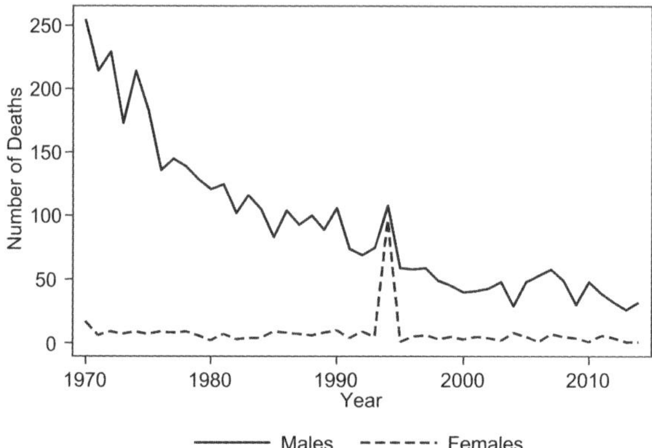

Fig. 10.10   **Number of deaths in work accidents between 1970 and 2014, males and females**
Source: Swedish Work Environment Authority.

cohorts born in the 1930s, when the LFP in the age group actually decreased, and that the LFP continued to increase for the cohorts born in the 1950s, although the increase in educational attainment markedly slowed down. On the other hand, the graphs show that when the educational attainment grew the most—in particular for higher education—for the cohorts born in the 1940s, the LFP started to increase.

10.3.3   Less-Demanding Jobs

It is well known that the jobs in postindustrial societies have become less physically demanding. This change could, of course, have contributed to the higher LFP rates in recent years. Let us therefore look into how the changes in the work environment match the changes in the LFP rates.

As for the measure of population health, there are different ways of measuring changes in the work environment. Figure 10.10 shows the number of deaths in work accidents between 1970 and 2014. The advantage of this measure is its high reliability, since all work accidents in Sweden have to be reported to the Swedish Work Environment Authority (Arbetsmiljöverket).[2] The validity of the measure could, on the other hand, be questioned, since fatal work accidents are quite rare events and only reflect a very limited aspect of the work environment.

Figure 10.10 reveals a very steady trend toward fewer deaths for males in work accidents between 1970 and 2000. After that, the annual number of deaths in work accidents seems to have stabilized on a level of about 50 deaths. For females, the number of deaths in work accidents has been very

---

2. Before 2001, this was called the National Board of Work Security (Arbetarskyddsstyrelsen).

low throughout the entire period, except for the spike in 1994 that can be attributed to the MS *Estonia* ship disaster.[3]

Comparing the changes in the number of deaths in work accidents with the trends in LFP rates in figure 10.1, it can be seen that the developments do not support the idea that changes in the work environment are a driving force behind the increase in employment among the elderly. During the major decrease in LFP among older men between 1970 and 2000, there was a large decrease in deaths in work accidents, and when there was no change in the number of deaths in work accidents after 2000, there was a marked increase in the LFP rates.

Figure 10.11 shows the evolution of three different measures of how the physical demands at workplaces have changed for the 55–59 and 60–64 age groups, respectively. The data source is the six different waves—obtained in 1968, 1974, 1981, 1991, 2000, and 2010—of the LNU. The three measures are self-reported assessments of the extent to which the work includes heavy lifting, if the respondent considers his or her work to be physically demanding, and if the job requires "daily sweating" to be performed. The left panels show the results for the 55–59 age group and the right ones the results for the 60–64 age group. The upper panels show the results for both genders and the two bottom ones for the males and females, respectively.

The results show that there is a substantial reduction in the physical demands of the jobs for both age groups during the period covered by the surveys if we use the measures "heavy lifting" and "daily sweating." Looking at the graphs with the two gender groups combined, it can be seen that both these measures decreased from around 40 percent in both age groups in 1968 to slightly above 10 percent in 2010. The graphs for the separate gender groups reveal that this development is primarily driven by the men. The third measure, the extent to which the respondent considers his or her job to be physically demanding, changes very modestly over the period.

The results shown in figure 10.11 do not support the hypothesis that lessened physical demands in the labor market are the driving force behind the increase in the LFP among the elderly. The results show that the largest decrease in the physical demands happened between 1968 and 1991 and can be attributed to the male workers. As we showed in figure 10.1, the LFP rates decreased radically during these years. When the LFP for men increased between 2000 and 2010, there appears to be little change in the physical requirements at the workplaces.

In addition to physical demands from work tasks, the psychological or

---

3. The MS *Estonia* was a cruise ferry that sank in the Baltic Sea in September 1994 and was one of the worst maritime disasters of the 20th century, with 852 lives lost. Among them was a large group of Swedish municipality employees. Since the trip was work related, the casualties were classified as work accidents.

A Males and Females Aged 55–59

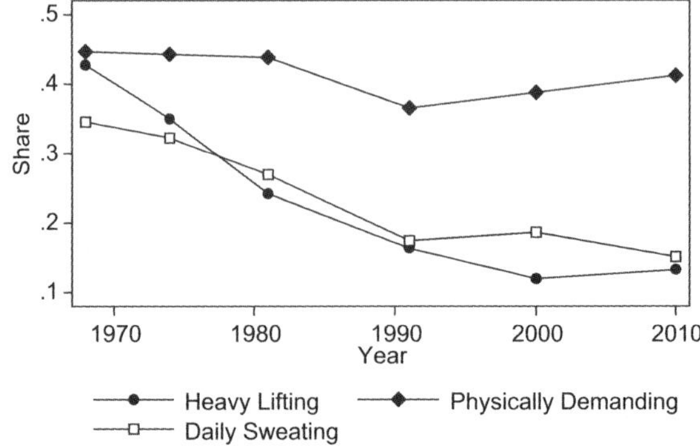

B Males and Females aged 60–64

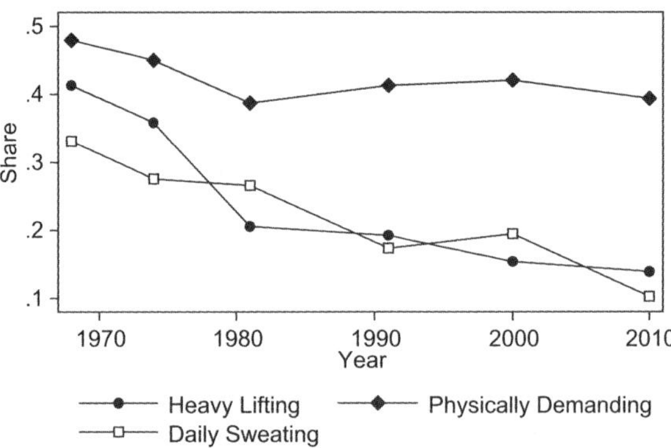

C Males Aged 55–59

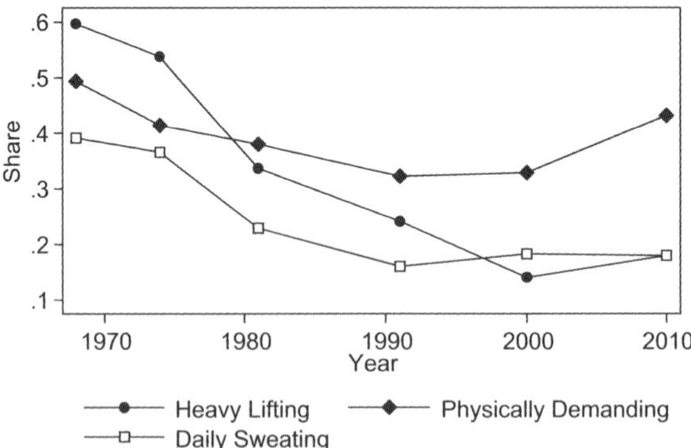

Fig. 10.11 Development of three self-assessed measures of the physical work environment in the 55–59 and 60–64 age groups: "Work includes heavy lifting," "work is considered to be physically demanding," "work requires daily sweating," males and females

Source: Authors' calculations from the 1968, 1974, 1981, 1991, 2000, and 2010 waves of the Swedish Level of Living Survey.

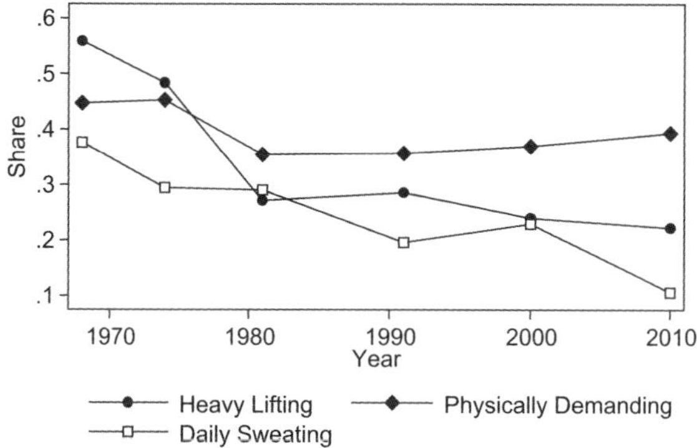

D   Males Aged 60–64

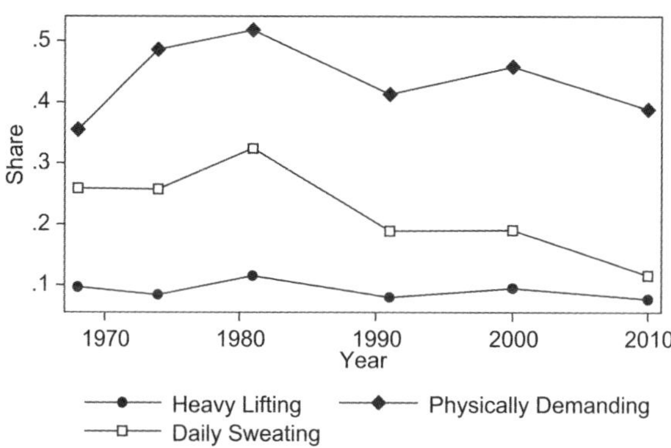

E   Females Aged 55–59

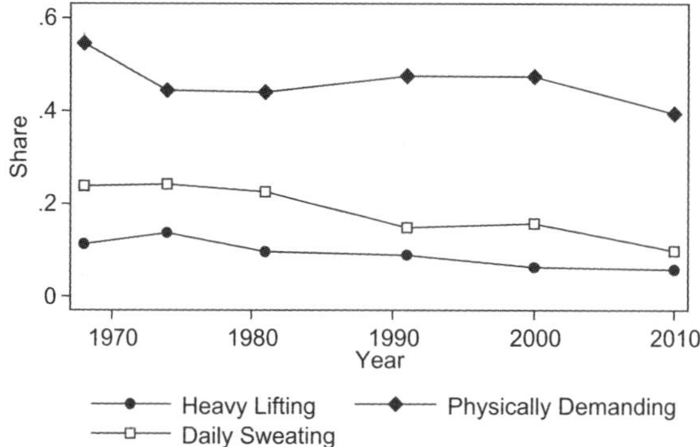

F   Females Aged 60–64

Fig. 10.11   **(cont.)**

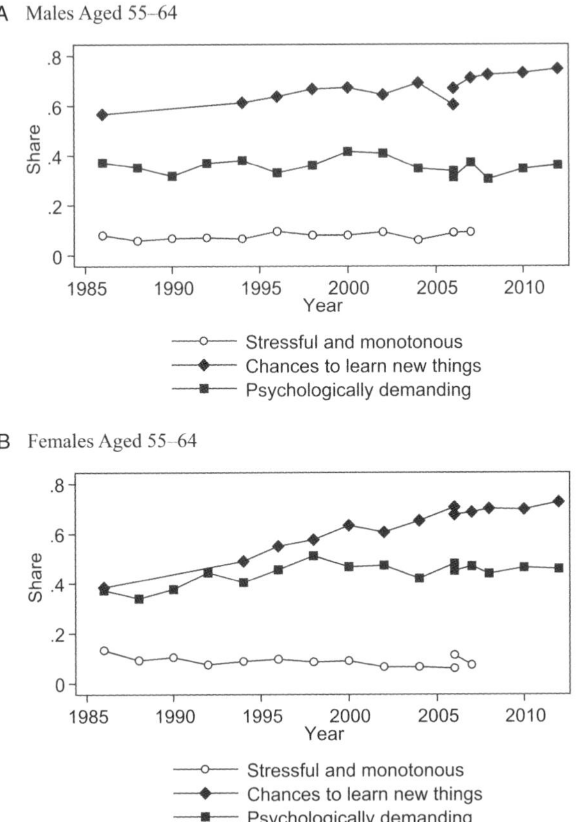

Fig. 10.12   The development of psychological and social work environmental indicators, males and females, 1986–2012

Source: Statistic Sweden ULF surveys 1986–2012.

social factors in the work environment may be important determinants for how long a person decides to stay in the labor force. Figure 10.12 shows the development of six different indicators for the psychosocial work environment of Swedish workplaces between 1986 and 2012 in the 55–64 age group. The left panels show the development for men and the right ones the corresponding developments for women. The upper panels show the share of workers who find their jobs "stressful and monotonous," who have chances "to learn new things" at work, and who find their jobs "psychologically demanding."

The lower panels show three different aspects of the extent to which the workers feel that they are in command of their own work situation—first, whether they can "plan their own work"; second, if they can "decide their work pace"; and third, if they can "influence their work schedule."

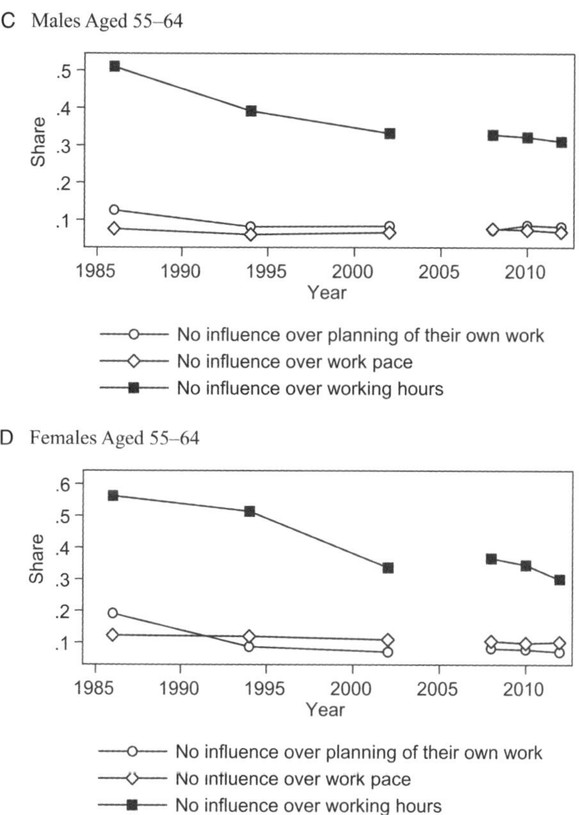

Fig. 10.12   (cont.)

Taken together, the graphs show very little change in any indicators except two. A larger share of the workers feel that they are able to learn new things at their workplace, and a lower share feels that they have no influence over their work schedule. The change of the first indicator is much larger for females—from 40 percent in 1986 to almost 75 percent in 2012. The corresponding change for males is from 60 to 75 percent. The change in work schedule flexibility is also larger for females, although the difference is much smaller.

10.3.4   Joint Decision-Making

As we documented in section 10.2, an important change in the composition of the Swedish labor market since the 1960s is the feminization of the labor force. This change has implied a major shift in the finances and labor supply incentives of most Swedish families, including the incentives to exit from the labor force. The wives' participation decision may have two counteracting effects on the husbands' decision to remain working. First,

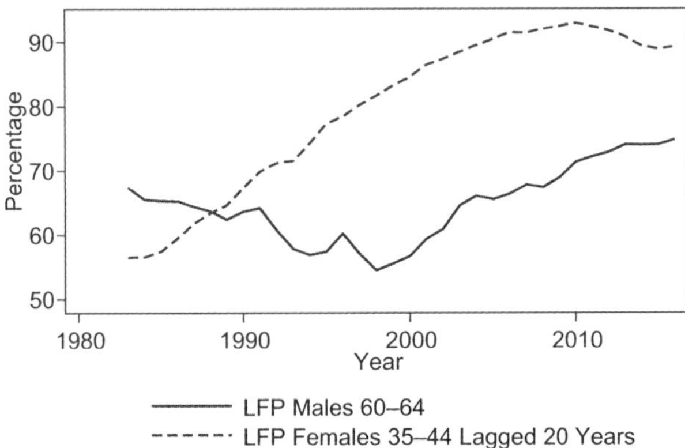

Fig. 10.13   LFP rates of Swedish men aged 60–64 along with LFP rates of females ages 35–44, lagged by 20 years between 1980 and 2016
Source: Swedish LFS.

since the household's disposable income will increase as a result of the wife's income, it will create an income effect toward exiting the labor force for the husband. Second, since leisure time after retirement may be enjoyed to a greater extent if the husband can spend the time with his wife, the wife's participation may decrease the husband's propensity to retire.

Several empirical studies have found evidence that the wife's retirement status significantly affects the husband's decision to leave the labor force (e.g., Gustman and Steinmeier 2000). Schirle (2008) finds that the increase in the male LFP rates since the mid-1990s in the United States, Canada, and the United Kingdom can be attributed to increased female participation in the workforce to a substantial degree. To investigate the extent to which this could also be the case in Sweden, we plot the LFP rates for females aged 35–44, lagged 20 years back in time along with the LFP rates for males in the 60–64 age group. The reason for using lagged LFP rates for the cohort of women married to the men under study rather than the current rates is to avoid the obvious endogeneity problem when correlating the series.

The result of this exercise is shown in figure 10.13. The figure shows that there is a joint positive trend in both series after the LFP rates among 60–64-year-old men started to increase in 2000. However, it also shows that there is an even stronger increase in female LFP corresponding to the long downturn in participation of older men between 1980 and 2000. We thus have to conclude that husbands' responses to increased female LFP do not seem to be a dominating factor behind the recent increase in the LFP of older men.

There are at least two possible explanations for why the increasing trend in female LFP did not seem to explain the delayed retirement of men in Sweden even though, according to the result obtained in Schirle (2008), this is the case in the United States, Canada, and the United Kingdom. First, the major expansion of female LFP happened more than a decade earlier in Sweden than in the countries included in Schirle's study. We are thus comparing different periods. Second, there may be differences in preferences in Swedish households compared to the countries studied by Schirle.

Two empirical studies on Swedish data support the second explanation. Selin (2017) investigates the husband's retirement responses to a change in the wife's retirement incentives and finds no significant effects despite strong direct effects on the wife's LFP. Laun (2017) too finds no significant retirement responses to spouses' prolonged work lives following the introduction of age-targeted tax credits in Sweden.

10.4 Recent Institutional Changes Affecting LFP of Older Workers

10.4.1 Swedish Pension Reform

A major pension reform was decided in the Swedish parliament in 1998. The primary aim of the reform was to make the pension system financially robust. Projections showed that the prereform defined benefit (DB) system required increased payroll taxes to be financially viable in an environment of an aging population. An additional aim was to strengthen the relationship between the contribution made to the system and the benefits received—that is, the actuarial fairness of the system—which affects the economic incentives for labor supply.

There were the three main elements of the reform:

1. As opposed to the old supplementary, income-related DB national pension plan (ATP), the new pension scheme is a so-called notional defined contribution (NDC) plan. The payroll tax devoted to the public old-age pension system is fixed to 18.5 percent of the individuals' annual wage sum in the new system.[4] Of these, 16 percent is devoted to a pay-as-you-go system based on so-called notional accounts and the rest—that is, 2.5 percent—is devoted to a fully funded scheme.

2. The sizes of the individual benefits from the new pay-as-you-go scheme are proportional to the contributions made throughout the insured individual's life cycle. In the prereform scheme, they are proportional to the earnings received during the individual's best 15 years in the labor market and with reductions if he or she contributed fewer than 30 years to the scheme. There was also an actuarial reduction of 0.5 percent for each month the pension

---

4. Due to a 7 percent tax deduction, the effective rate is actually $18.5 \times (1 - 0.07) = 17.21$ percent.

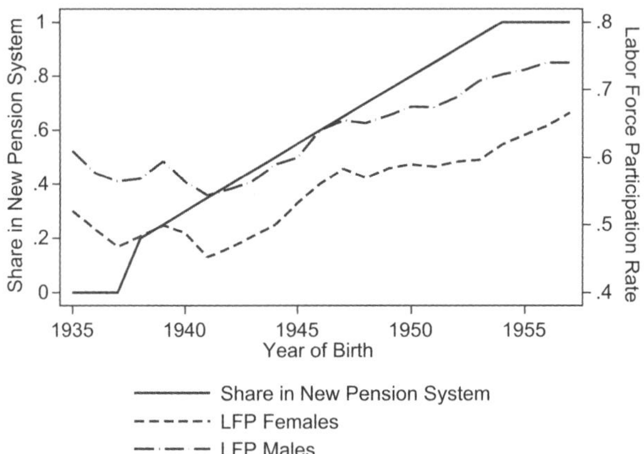

Fig. 10.14   Implementation of the new Swedish old-age pension scheme and LFP rates in the 60–64 age group by cohort of birth, males and females
Source: Swedish LFS.

was claimed before the 65th birthday and a 0.7 percent increase for each month the pension was delayed after that age. There is no earnings test in any of the two pension systems.

3. A fully funded pension program was introduced. For this part, the insured individual is able to choose between a large number of private fund managers or remain in the default fund, managed by the public authorities.

The new pension system was implemented gradually by year of birth. The first cohort to be covered by the postreform system consisted of those born in 1938. They are covered by 20 percent in the postreform system and by 80 percent in the prereform one. For every subsequent birth cohort, the share of coverage from the new system is increased by 5 percent until those born in 1954, who are covered to 100 percent by the postreform system.

Figure 10.14 shows the share to which each birth cohort is assigned in the new pension system along with graphs for the LFP rates in the 60–64 age group. The birth cohort corresponding to a particular year of the LFP is calculated at the midpoint of the age group at age 62. It can be seen that there indeed is a striking resemblance between the implementation of the new public pension system across cohorts and the LFP rate in the age group under study. The increase in the LFP starts with the cohorts born in the early 1940s and continues until those born in the mid-1950s. This applies to both men and women.

Our next step in investigating the credibility of the hypothesis that the pension reform contributed to the pattern of delayed retirement is to take a closer look at how incentives to remain in the labor force changed as a result of the reform and how that may have affected the retirement behavior for the period. Laun and Wallenius (2015) posed a related research question. They use a dynamic programming model calibrated on aggregate data for retirement behavior in the Swedish labor market and predict how the postreform pension system would change retirement behavior when fully implemented. Their results suggest that the pension reform would have a very strong effect on retirement behavior: retirement is predicted to be delayed by 2.5 years on average in the workforce.

The retirement age, when the worker exits the labor market, does not need to be the same as the age when he or she starts to claim pension benefits. A fundamental difference between the new and the old pension system is that pension wealth in the new system is linked to when the worker stops paying contributions to the system. In the old system, the actuarial adjustment is linked to when the person starts to claim benefits. This means that there will be no actuarial adjustments if a worker retires at age 62 but starts to collect his or her pension benefits at age 65.[5]

This means that there are different economic incentives for the timing of a labor market exit and for the timing to start to claim benefits. Laun and Wallenius (2015) look at the decision to exit the labor market and stop contributing to the pension scheme, conditional on the date when the worker starts to claim benefits. This procedure assumes that the workers are not credit constrained in their retirement decision, in the sense that they have to start to claim benefits at the same time as they retire. Under this assumption, the pension reform has a strong effect on the incentives to stay in the labor force.

To compare the economic incentives to stay at the labor market in the pre- and postreform pension systems, we first confine ourselves to the timing of claiming benefits. Figure 10.15 shows the results from a calculation of two incentive measures for a median income earner in the cohort born 1930. The first one, shown in the left panel, is the replacement level, calculated as the share of the pension income of median earnings the year before retirement. The second one, shown in the right panel, is the benefit accrual rate, calculated as the change in the social security wealth from delaying retirement one year. The dark lines with circles show the outcomes for the prereform system, and the lighter lines with squares show the ones for the postreform pension scheme.

The results show that the replacement level is somewhat lower in the new system. As a result of the different indexing in the two systems, this difference is to some extent dependent on the assumption about growth and inflation rates made in the simulations. We have assumed a growth rate of 1.6 percent and use real measures for the calculations. The results for the accrual rates show no great differences between the two systems. This confirms the conclusions of Palme and Svensson (1999) that the prereform system was not far from actuarially fair.

---

5. The actuarial adjustment in the new system is determined by an annuity divisor, which is a function of life expectancy at the date when the person starts to claim benefits.

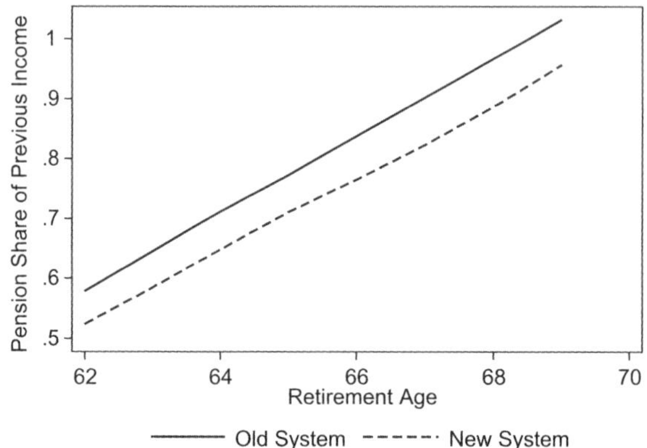

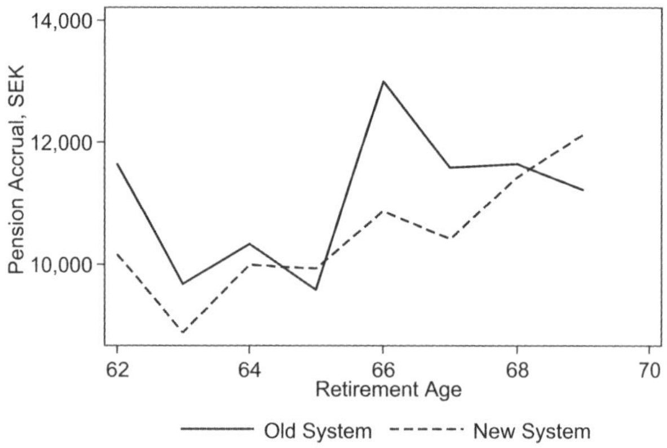

Fig. 10.15   Two incentive measures for a median income earner born in 1930 by retirement age for pre- and postreform old-age pension system, respectively
Source: Authors' calculations for a median income earner born in 1930.

Figure 10.16 shows the average age of pension withdrawal across the birth cohorts born between 1935 and 1944 for males and females, respectively. Three graphs are displayed in each panel: One corresponds to those who finance their exit from the labor market with income security programs other than old-age pensions—namely, through DI, unemployment insurance (UI), or sick pay insurance programs. One corresponds to those who receive an old-age payment from a public, occupational, or private pension after they leave the labor force. The third includes the whole population—that is, the two groups combined.

Figure 10.16 shows that very little has happened across the included

A Pension Withdrawal Age, Males

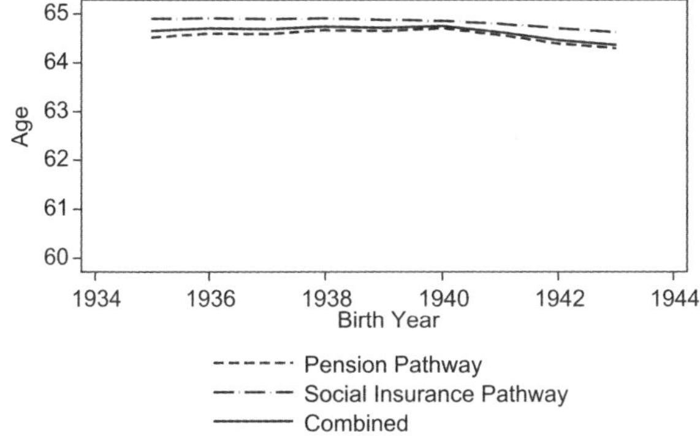

B Pension Withdrawal Age, Females

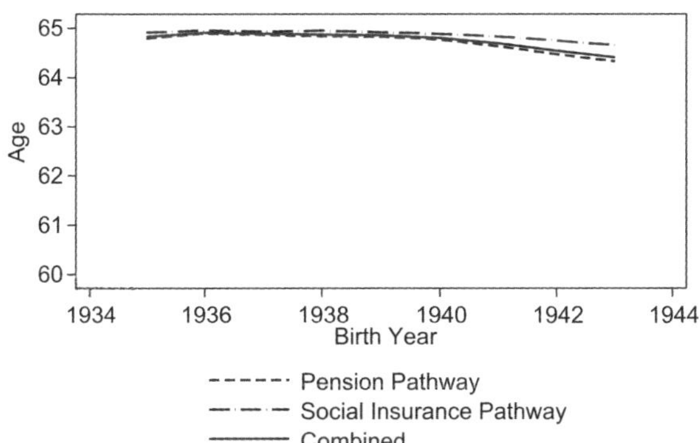

Fig. 10.16   Average age of old-age pension withdrawal by pathway of exit from the labor market, cohorts born 1935–1944, males and females, respectively

Source: Authors' calculations from the LOUISE database.

cohorts, among both males and females. There is almost no change between the 1935 birth cohort and the one born in 1940. There is, however, a slight decrease of about 0.2 years in the average claiming age between those born in 1940 and those born in 1944 in all groups and for both males and females. These small changes in claiming behavior are consistent with the small changes in incentives to delay claiming that we documented in figure 10.15.

We proceed by studying how retirement behavior has changed. The upper panel of figure 10.17 shows how the average retirement age has changed across cohorts for males and females separately. The retirement age is defined as the age during the last observed year with earnings above one price base amount, followed by at least two years with earnings below one price base amount. There are three graphs in each panel: one showing the retirement age for the entire population and two for the old-age and social insurance pathways separately.

A   Retirement Age, Males

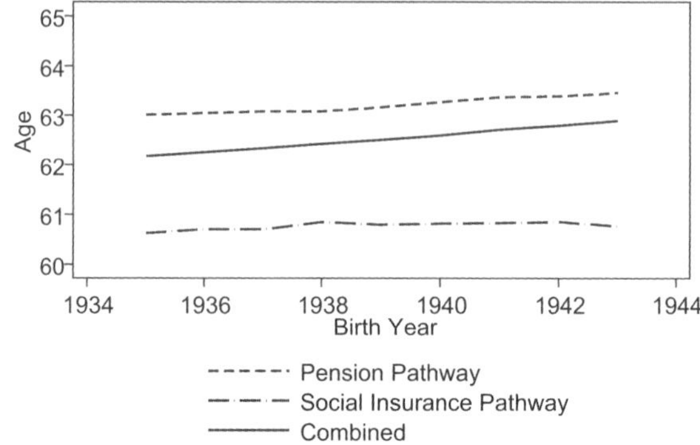

B   Retirement Age, Females

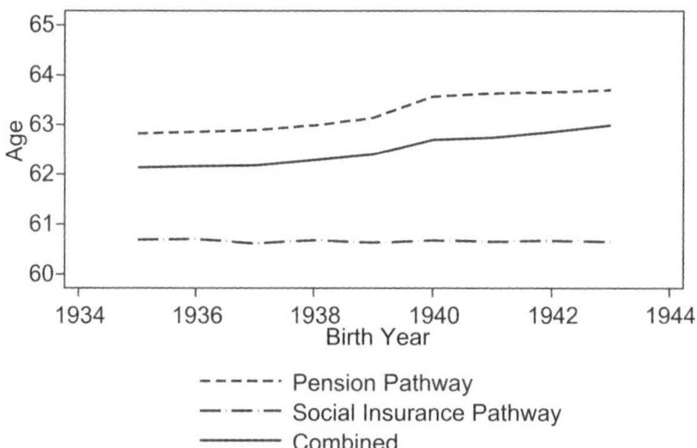

Fig. 10.17   Upper panels: Average retirement age by year of birth. Lower panels: Share exiting the labor force by the pathway of retirement and year of birth, males and females

Source: Authors' calculations from the LOUISE database.

The figure reveals an interesting pattern. First, for both men and women, the average retirement age has increased by almost a year from the first to the last cohort. For the social insurance path, there has been no change. For the group using the old-age pension pathway, it is indeed a change toward delayed retirement, but the change is smaller than for the overall population. For men, the change in this group is about half of the change in the entire population.

This result suggests that there has been a compositional change to a smaller share using the social insurance pathway. This change is documented in the lower panel of figure 10.17. As expected, the change is largest for the male subgroup, where there is a 15 percentage point decrease in the share leaving the labor force through the social insurance pathway—from 35 percent in the 1935 cohort to about 20 percent in the 1943 cohort.

C   Share by Pathway, Males

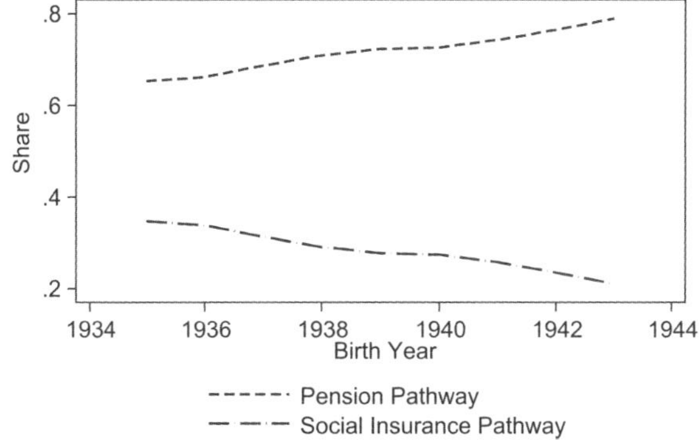

D   Share by Pathway, Females

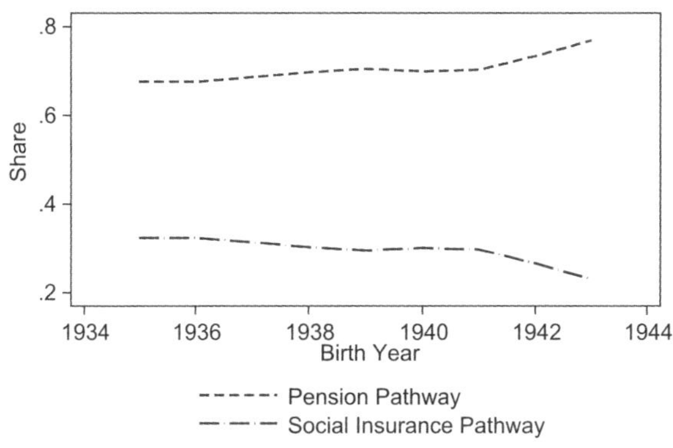

Fig. 10.17   (cont.)

One way to assess the extent to which the overall delayed retirement can be attributed to either a larger share using the old-age pension pathway out of the labor force or the delayed retirement of those using this pathway is to calculate the average retirement age by using the probabilities of the two pathways for the 1935 birth cohort and the average retirement ages for the 1943 cohort. This exercise tells us that about 55 percent of the overall change in the average retirement age for males over the period can be attributed to the change in the relative importance of the two pathways. The corresponding number for the female population is 33 percent—that is, about one-third.

The delayed retirement across cohorts for those who use the old-age pension pathway to leave the labor force is consistent with the idea that the stronger incentives to stay in the labor force in the new pension scheme actually affected behavior. However, it is important to stress that there is also a compositional change across cohorts toward a larger share of individuals in the pension pathway with inferior health, who would have been eligible for

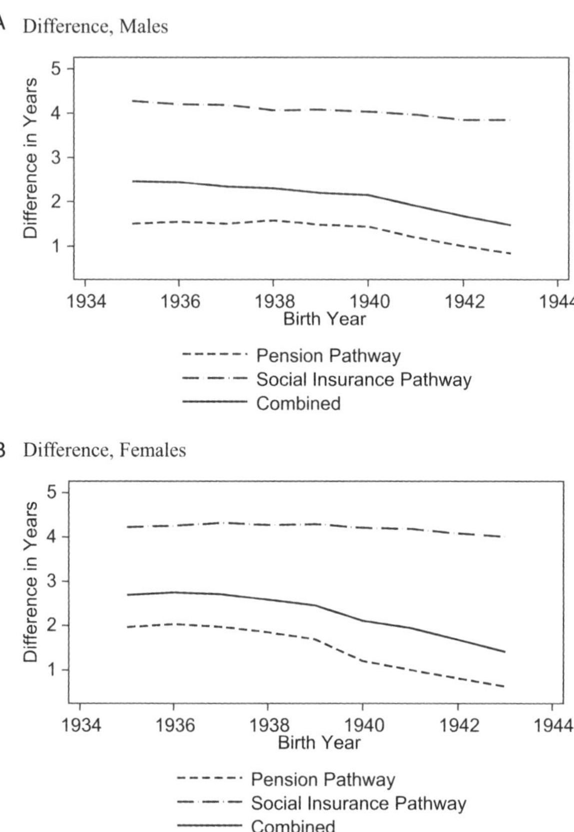

Fig. 10.18   Difference between average age of exit from the labor market and average age of claiming of old-age pension benefits, cohorts born 1935–1943, males and females

Source: Authors' calculations from the LOUISE database.

DI with the more lenient screening of the older cohorts. This compositional change is counteracted by a general improvement in population health.

A necessary condition for the postreform system to generate very different incentives for retirement is that the workers have access to a nonactuarially fair program to cover the time gap between when he or she retires and when the person starts to claim benefits. Johansson, Laun, and Palme (2017) suggest that this was actually the case for some groups in the labor market—in particular, white-collar workers in the private sector. In addition to that, there could also be individual agreements between the employer and the worker on severance payments, which also affect the incentives to retire.

A requirement for this to be empirically relevant is a larger discrepancy on average between the date the individuals start to claim their pension benefit and when they actually retire in the older cohorts, with a stronger attachment to the prereform public pension system. Figure 10.18 examines

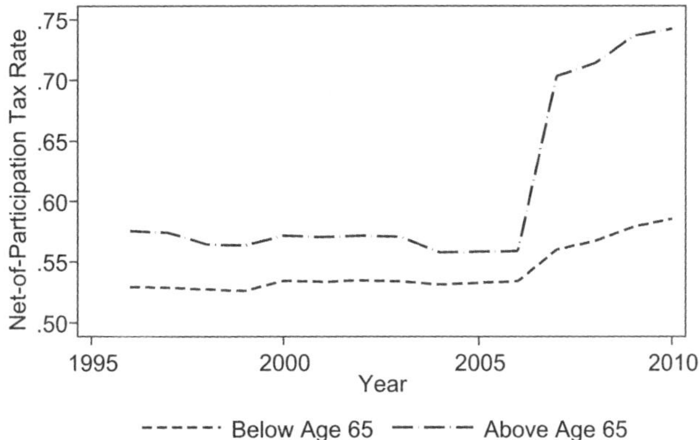

Fig. 10.19   Changes in the net of the participation tax rate for a median income earner below and above age 65, 1996–2010
Source: Authors' calculations from the LOUISE database.

if this is the case. The graphs show this gap for the three groups considered in figures 10.16 and 10.17. The results show that the difference has indeed decreased for the group that exits through the old-age pension pathway. The change is largest for females, which concurs with the result that the largest change in retirement behavior was among females.

10.4.2   Tax Reform in 2007

An earned income tax credit reform was introduced in Sweden in 2007 by the newly elected center-right government. The purpose was to encourage an increased labor supply, in particular among low-income earners. Unlike in most other countries, the Swedish earned income tax credit was not phased out at higher earnings. Importantly, the size of the tax credit was larger for workers who were older than age 65 at the beginning of the tax year. The earned income tax credit applies to earnings but not to income from public pension or public transfers. The tax credit is a function of earned income, the basic deduction, and the municipality income tax rate. An additional element of the 2007 reform was that the payroll tax rate was reduced from 26.37 percent to 10.21 percent for workers older than age 65 at the beginning of the tax year. The purpose was to stimulate the demand for older workers.

Figure 10.19 shows how the net of the participation tax rate for workers younger and older than age 65 has changed during 1996–2010 for a median-income earner. The figure takes the municipal and state income tax, the basic deduction, the earned income tax credit, and the payroll tax rate into account. The net of the participation tax rate shows the net earnings as a fraction of the total wage cost to the employer. The reforms in 2007 substantially increased the net of the participation tax rate of workers older than age 65. The introduction of the earned income tax credit also slightly increased the net gain from working for workers younger than age 65, although not to the same extent.

Laun (2017) analyzes the combined effects of the earned income tax credit and the payroll tax reduction for workers older than age 65 and finds that the tax credits increased employment at the extensive margin among workers just above age 65. The participation elasticity was estimated to be 0.22, amounting to an increase in the LFP of about 5 percent. Even if the effect of the age-targeted tax credits is significant, it is relatively small. However, the tax credits have probably contributed to ease up the strong norms about retiring on the 65th birthday.

For workers younger than age 65, there is no evidence that the smaller change in the tax burden due to the introduction of the EITC in 2007 has impacted the retirement decision of these ages. For these age groups, the increase in the LFP began long before the age-targeted tax credits came into place. The tax credits can probably primarily explain the increased LFP for individuals older than age 65.

10.4.3   Changes in Mandatory Retirement Ages

Almost all the labor market in Sweden is covered by central agreements between trade unions and employers' confederations. In most cases, these agreements include retirement ages for the workers. Before 2001, most agreements had a stipulated retirement at the 65th birthday. This was also supported in the labor market legislation. Workers older than age 65 were not covered by employment security legislation and were exempted from seniority rules. They were not covered by UI, DI, or the compulsory sick pay insurance. Central and local government employees automatically lost their jobs at age 65. Exceptions from this rule were permitted for one year.

In September 2001, the government started to implement legislation that enabled all employees to remain until age 67. This means that they were now covered by the employment security legislation. The rule that all central and local government employees automatically lost their jobs at age 65 was now postponed to age 67. However, the rules for the income security programs remained at age 65 after the reform. Depending on ongoing collective agreements in some sectors of the labor market, the reform was not fully implemented until 2003.

The reform seems to have had very small effects on the LFP rates of those older than age 65. Going back to figures 10.1 and 10.3, there are no visible changes in the LFP rates or employment in the years following the reform. This reform could, however, have affected the long-term trend toward the increased LFP of 65–69-year-olds.

10.4.4   Stricter Rules for DI Eligibility

The DI program has undergone several changes in recent decades. Before 2003, it was a part of the old-age pension system. It consisted of a basic pension and a supplementary pension. The benefits were related to the insured worker's income from labor and were determined using the same algorithm used for the old-age pension benefits. Since 2003, as a part of the reform of the Swedish pension system, DI is independent of the old-age pension program and is now a part of the social insurance system. The benefits are calculated as 64 percent of the "assumed income" below the social security ceiling. The "assumed income" is the average of the five to eight best years of annual income from labor before the worker became eligible to DI.

In the early 1970s, the eligibility rules for DI were changed from eligibility only due to health problems to include eligibility due to labor market reasons—first in combination with health problems and subsequently for pure labor market reasons for workers older than age 60 who have been unemployed long term. In 1991, the eligibility for DI based on pure labor market reasons was abolished, and in 1997, it was abolished for labor market reasons combined with health deficiencies.

The reform in 2003 also included changes in eligibility rules for DI. The most important change was that the DI benefit was no longer permanent; eligibility would be reconsidered every fifth year. In 2008, the government implemented a new reform of the DI system. The most important element of the new eligibility rules was that the person applying for DI had to show that his or her ability to work was permanently lost. This change was considered to be a very large increase in the stringency of the eligibility rules.

Figure 10.20 shows the development of DI participation between 1962 and 2016 and the development of DI entry between 1971 and 2016 for males and females, respectively. The most striking result in figure 10.20 is the sharp drop in DI entry from the late 1980s to today. The analysis in Jönsson, Palme, and Svensson (2012) indicates that changed eligibility criteria during the 1980s and 1990s clearly affected program caseloads and may also have had an impact on LFP. However, for our purposes, the most interesting change is the decline in DI entry since 2005. It is apparent that the background to the decline is the more stringent eligibility rules following the reforms of the DI system in 2003 and 2008 and the changed implementation of the rules at the Swedish Social Insurance Agency during this period.

10.5 Conclusions

In this chapter, we have investigated the background of the increase in male LFP rates since the mid-1990s. In the first part, we looked at changes in the composition of the population related to the likelihood of being employed. In the second part, we investigated the extent to which institutional changes may have had an effect on the delayed exit from the labor force.

In the first part, we looked specifically at four changes in the Swedish population: (1) the improvement of the population health, (2) the increase in the educational attainment of the labor force, (3) the improved physical

A DI Prevalence 1962–2016, Males

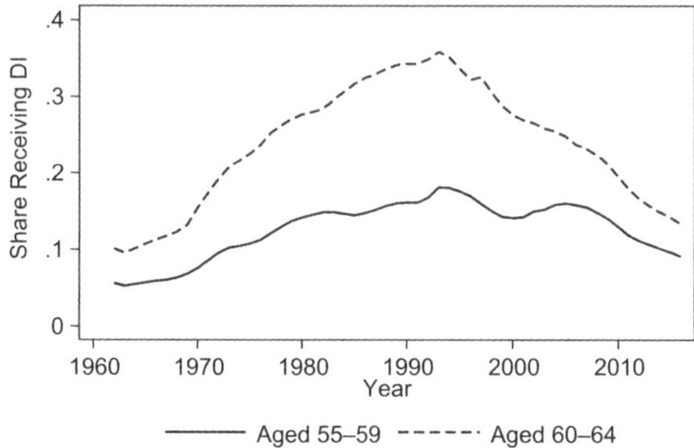

B DI Prevalence 1962–2016, Females

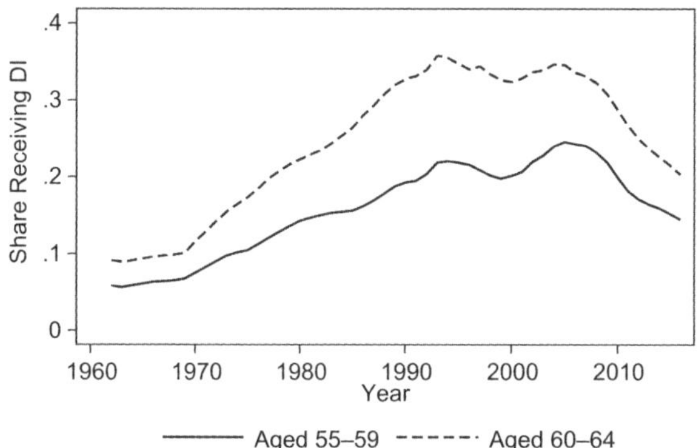

Fig. 10.20 Share of the population receiving DI in different age groups, 1962–2016; and share of DI entry in different age groups, 1971–2016, males and females
Source: Swedish Social Insurance Agency.

work environment, (4) and the increase in female LFP rates. For the first two changes, we found that it is likely that they have contributed to the increase in the LFP of older men. Although there has been a continuous change in mortality rates for men in the 55–59 and 60–64 age groups, it seems like the changes have been stronger in recent years. This picture is confirmed also by the self-assessed measure that we reported. Also, the changes in educational attainment seem to have contributed. Again, there is a trend toward more education across the birth cohorts, but the increase seems to have been stronger—in particular, for higher education—in the cohorts born in the early 1940s, who were in their early 60s at the beginning of the 2000s.

For the second two changes, we found no support that they would have been important for the increased employment rates of older men. The largest improvement in work environment seems to have happened earlier, in the

C DI Incidence 1962–2016, Males

D DI Incidence 1962–2016, Females

Fig. 10.20   (cont.)

1980s, when the LFP rates of men were still decreasing. The same seems to be true for the increased female LFP rates and the joint-retirement-decisions hypothesis: the major increase in the relative LFP rates happened across the cohorts born in the 1930s, for whom the LFP rates in the older age groups were decreasing.

In the second part of the chapter, we studied the effects of four institutional changes that may have led to a delayed exit from the labor market. The stricter rules for DI eligibility and the implementation of these rules at the Social Insurance Agency appear to have had a very strong impact on LFP. Also, the income tax reductions due to the earned income tax credit and payroll tax reduction for older workers seem to have delayed labor force exits, while the 2001 reform of the mandatory retirement age seems to have had a surprisingly small immediate effect on the LFP in the 65–69 age group.

For the most important policy change during the era under study, the major reform of Sweden's public old-age pension system, there are a number of pieces of circumstantial evidence that suggest it actually did affect retirement behavior through changes in the labor supply incentives. First, the staggered implementation of the reform across cohorts coincides with increased LFP rates. Second, a large share—about 45 percent for men and around 67 percent for women—of the delayed exit from the labor market that we observe for the cohorts born between 1935 and 1943 can be attributed to the group that retired through the old-age pension pathway. Third, we observe a smaller average gap between when the workers retire and when they start to claim their benefits from the public old-age pension program, which is consistent with the presumption that the pension reform actually caused changes in labor supply incentives of the elderly.

The research methodology used in this study does not, however, allow us to identify the magnitude of the effects that worked through changes in the labor supply incentives separately from the changes in health status and educational attainment that we also document. This important issue is left for further research.

We have limited this overview to only looking at the supply side of the background of the changes in the LFP of older workers. The demand side—involving the effects of technical change, employers' perception of worker productivity, and age discrimination in work groups—is potentially as important but has also, for now, been left for further research.

References

Gustman, A. L., and T. L. Steinmeier. 2000. "Retirement in Dual-Career Families: A Structural Model." *Journal of Labor Economics* 18 (3): 503–45.

Johansson, P., L. Laun, and M. Palme. 2015. "Pathways to Retirement and the Role of Financial Incentives in Sweden." In *Social Security Programs and Retirement around the World: Disability Insurance Programs and Retirement*, edited by David A. Wise, 369–410. Chicago: University of Chicago Press.

———. 2017. "Health, Work Capacity and Retirement in Sweden." In *Social Security Programs and Retirement around the World: The Capacity to Work at Older Ages*, edited by David A. Wise, 301–27. Chicago: University of Chicago Press.

Jönsson, L., M. Palme, and I. Svensson. 2012. "Disability Insurance, Population Health, and Employment in Sweden." In *Social Security Programs and Retirement around the World: Historical Trends in Mortality and Health, Employment, and Disability Insurance Participation and Reforms*, edited by David A. Wise, 79–126. Chicago: University of Chicago Press.

Laun, L. 2017. "The Effect of Age-Targeted Tax Credits on Labor Force Participation of Older Workers." *Journal of Public Economics* 152:102–18.

Laun, T., and J. Wallenius. 2015. "A Life Cycle Model of Health and Retirement: The Case of Swedish Pension Reform." *Journal of Public Economics* 127:127–36.

Palme, M., and I. Svensson. 1999. "Social Security, Occupational Pensions, and Retirement in Sweden." In *Social Security and Retirement around the World*, edited by Jonathan Gruber and David A. Wise, 355–402. Chicago: University of Chicago Press.

Schirle, T. 2008. "Why Have the Labor Force Participation Rates of Older Men Increased since the Mid-1990s?" *Journal of Labor Economics* 26 (4): 549–94.

Selin, H. 2017. "What Happens to the Husband's Retirement Decision When the Wife's Retirement Incentives Change?" *International Tax and Public Finance* 24 (3): 432–58.

Venti, S., and D. A. Wise. 2015. "The Long Reach of Education: Early Retirement." *Journal of the Economics of Ageing* 6:133–48.

Long-Run Trends in the Economic Activity of Older People in the United Kingdom

James Banks, Carl Emmerson, and Gemma Tetlow

11.1 Introduction

Between the mid-1970s and the mid-1990s, the employment rate of men approaching and just above age 65, the state pension age for men at the time, fell dramatically. Since then, these employment rates have recovered somewhat, but they still remain somewhat below the levels seen 40 years earlier. Employment rates of older women were relatively stable over the second half of the 1970s and the first half of the 1980s but have risen sharply since then and are now at record levels. The net effect of these two offsetting trends has been that aggregate employment rates of 55–74-year-olds are only now broadly comparable to the levels observed in the mid-1970s, albeit with a somewhat different composition across age and sex groups and having displayed a marked U-shaped trend in the intervening period.

In this chapter, we present and examine these trends in employment rates

James Banks is professor of economics at the University of Manchester and a deputy research director of the Institute for Fiscal Studies (IFS).

Carl Emmerson is deputy director of the IFS.

Gemma Tetlow is the chief economist at the Institute for Government.

This chapter is part of the National Bureau of Economic Research's International Social Security (ISS) project, which is supported by the National Institute on Aging (grant P01 AG012810). The authors are grateful to the other participants of the project for useful comments and advice. We are grateful for funding from the Economic and Social Research Council (ESRC) through the "More Years, Better Lives" Joint Programming Initiative (project: "Policies for Longer Working Lives: Understanding Interactions with Health and Care Responsibilities") and through the ESRC Centre for the Microeconomic Analysis of Public Policy (grant reference ES/M010147/1). We are also grateful to Richard Blundell for useful comments. Data from the Labour Force Survey (LFS) were made available by the UK Data Archive. Responsibility for the interpretation of the data, as well as for any errors, is the authors' alone. For acknowledgments, sources of research support, and disclosure of the authors' material financial relationships, if any, please see https://www.nber.org/chapters/c14051.ack.

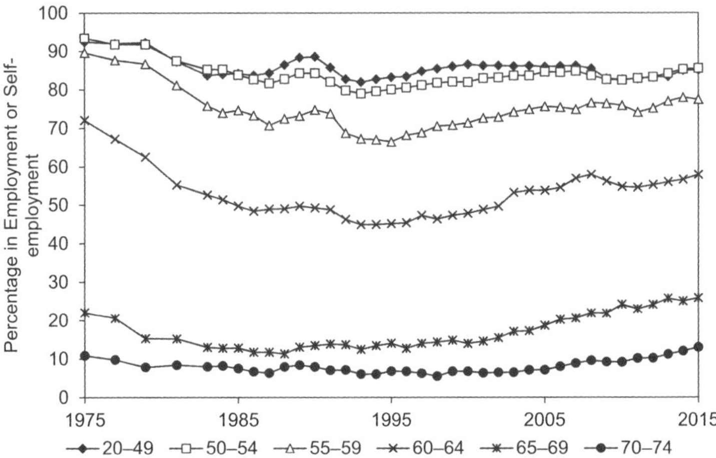

Fig. 11.1   Employment rates of men by age band, 1975–2015
Source: LFS.

of men and women in detail. We document the extent to which they are associated with changes in education levels—as opposed to changes in employment rates within education level—and how they relate to changing employment rates at younger ages of successive birth cohorts, with these also broken down by education level. For the period since the mid-1990s, we compare trends in the employment of older men and women in different occupations to those seen among younger men and women and also describe how wage growth among older workers has, on average, compared to that seen among younger workers.

All the data in this chapter are taken from the UK's LFS. We have data biennially from 1975 to 1981 (inclusive) and then for each single year from 1983 to 2015 (inclusive). These data cover England, Scotland, Wales, and Northern Ireland. The questionnaire contains extensive detail on the labor market activity of respondents, and for a household survey, it has a large sample size; an average of just below 400,000 individuals is observed per year (with a smaller sample size prior to 1992 and a larger sample size from 1992 onward). The key information we use are age, sex, employment status, occupation, and wages.

The headline trends in employment rates, by age, over the 40 years from 1975 are shown for men in figure 11.1 and for women in figure 11.2. Looking first at men, employment rates fell for all age groups between 1975 and the mid-1990s and rose thereafter, with the U shape in employment rates among men aged 50 and older—in particular, those aged between 55 and 69—being more noticeable than that of younger men. By 2015, while the employment rates of 65–74-year-old men were greater than they were 40 years earlier,

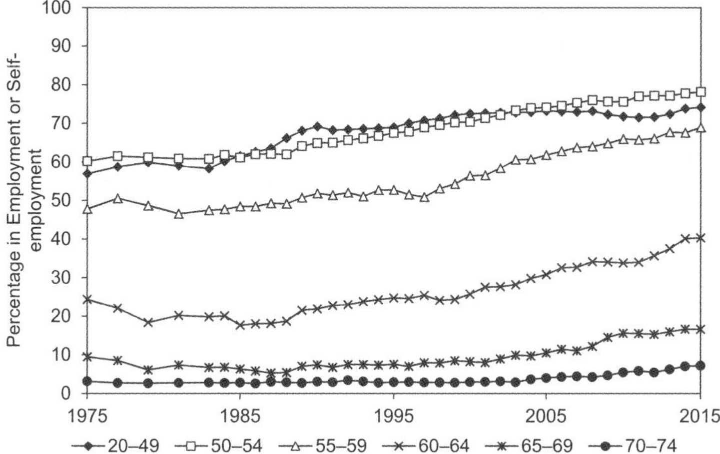

Fig. 11.2   Employment rates of women by age band, 1975–2015
Source: LFS.

among younger age groups, they were still below their mid-1970s level, with this being especially true of men aged 55–59 and 60–64.

A very different pattern over time is seen among women in figure 11.2. Between 1975 and the mid-1980s, employment rates within each age group were generally relatively stable, although there was a fall among women aged 60–69. Since then, employment rates of women have grown strongly, and by 2015, the employment rate within each age group was higher than at any point in the previous 40 years. Indeed, in 2015, the employment rates among women aged 55–59 and 60–64 are considerably higher than those seen at any point previously.

In part, the growth in the employment rates of older men and women over the 20 years since the mid-1990s has occurred alongside growth in the employment rate of younger individuals. But the growth in the employment rates of older individuals has been stronger than that of younger individuals over this period. This is in contrast to the 20 years from the mid-1970s to the mid-1990s (and the first decade of this period in particular), where employment growth was lower among older individuals than younger individuals.

This relative employment growth of older to younger ages is shown in table 11.1. In 1975, the employment rate of men aged 50–64 was 93 percent of the employment rate of men aged 20–49, while the equivalent figure for women was 78 percent. By 1995, these ratios had fallen to 78 percent and 72 percent, respectively. These ratios for both men and women grew over the subsequent 20 years, such that for men the employment rate of the older group reached 88 percent of that of the younger group, whereas among women the employment rate of the older group reached 86 percent of that

Table 11.1   **Employment rate of 50–64 year olds compared to that of 20–49 year olds, by sex, for selected years**

| | Men | | | Women | | |
| | Employment rate | | | Employment rate | | |
	20 to 49	50 to 64	Ratio	20 to 49	50 to 64	Ratio
1975	92.4	85.5	0.93	56.9	44.5	0.78
1985	84.2	69.5	0.83	61.5	41.8	0.68
1995	83.2	65.0	0.78	69.0	49.5	0.72
2005	85.9	72.4	0.84	73.3	56.9	0.78
2015	85.0	74.8	0.88	74.2	64.0	0.86

Source: LFS.

of the younger group. Overall, this means that by 2015, the employment rate of older men—relative to that of younger men—was still lower than it had been 40 years earlier in 1975. In contrast, the employment rate of older women—relative to that of younger women—was greater than it was 40 years earlier. A further consequence of this difference between trends for each gender is that for the first time, the relative employment rates of older to younger adults are now comparable for men and women.

11.2   Background Context

This section sets out some of the background context relating to the employment rates of older individuals that were presented in the previous section. We begin by discussing economic factors—both the macroeconomic situation and changes in the policy environment. We then turn to brief discussions of trends in the education and health of those approaching, or around, retirement age. The combination of these three sets of trends has led to secular cohort effects in terms of the characteristics of those at retirement age, and such trends are important to consider when we look at employment rates by age among different birth cohorts. It also motivates our analysis of cohort trends split by education, which follows in section 11.3.

11.2.1   Macroeconomic and Microeconomic Policy Background

One key factor to bear in mind throughout is the performance of the UK economy over this period. Deep recessions were experienced in the mid-1970s, early 1980s, early 1990s, and late 2000s. In contrast, the second half of the 1980s was a period of very strong growth (with the four years from 1985q1 to 1989q1 seeing average annual growth of 4.5 percent), while the period from the start of 1993 through to the start of 2008 (the eve of the financial crisis) was one of strong and stable growth (averaging 2.9 percent per year from 1993q1 to 2008q1). These ups and downs of economic performance were reflected in the employment rates shown in the previous section: for example, among 20–49-year-old men (figure 11.1), the employment rate fell during the recession of the early 1980s, grew strongly during the boom of the late 1980s, and fell again in the early 1990s recession. It then climbed throughout the period from 1993 through to the end of the 1990s before falling again during the Great Recession of the late 2000s.

In addition to these macroeconomic trends and cycles, however, the UK has been characterized by a huge amount of policy reform. The key sources of income, other than earnings, for older individuals are state pensions, other state benefits targeted at those with lower incomes or those in poor health, and private sources of income including private pensions. Eligibility—or potential eligibility—for many of these can affect incentives to retire. And these sources of income have been subject to many reforms. In some cases, reform has been announcements of future policies to be gradually phased in, and in others, reforms have taken effect immediately. Much has directly affected the incentives to work for those who qualify for the various benefit programs, and in many cases, this was by design. In what follows, we briefly describe the evolving policy context, focusing just on reforms that might be expected to have had impacts on the labor market outcomes of older individuals. The timeline for these reforms is summarized in table 11.2, but further details in each dimension are given in the subsections below (a fully comprehensive description of state pension reforms over the 1948–2010 period can be found in Bozio, Crawford, and Tetlow [2010], while Crawford, Keynes, and Tetlow [2013] discuss more recent changes).

11.2.1.1   *State Pensions*

In terms of marginal financial incentives to retire, the key reform to state pensions was the abolition of the earnings test in 1989.[1] Prior to that date, receipt of the state pension could be reduced if the individual was also earning, whereas since then, individuals could continue with paid work and still receive an unreduced state pension. Some may also find that remaining in paid work up to the state pension age boosts the value of their accrued state pension, with this effect likely to be stronger among women in the past, when more years of contributions were required to qualify for a full state pension and when fewer activities other than being in paid work were counted as a contribution.

The age at which individuals can receive their state pension—the state pension age—may also affect retirement behavior if, for example, it provides a signal about the appropriate age to leave the labor market. Between 1948 and April 2010, this was 65 for men and 60 for women. Since April 2010, the state pension age for women has been rising, reaching male state pension age of 65 in November 2018. Since then, the state pension ages of men and

---

1. For details—and an assessment—see Disney and Smith (2002).

Table 11.2   Key reform dates for policies affecting labor market incentives for older workers

Year	State pensions	Other state benefits	Private retirement income
1975	Increasing generosity		
1981	Indexing made less generous		
1986	Declining generosity		
1988			Introduction of private personal pensions (DC)
1989	Removal of earnings test		
1995	Declining generosity	Reduced generosity, increased stringency	
1999		Other benefits for women over SPA made more generous	
2001		Reduced generosity, increased stringency	
2002	Increasing generosity		
2003		Means-tested pensioner benefits made more generous	
2006			DB plans less restrictive in terms of drawing income while continuing to work
2008		Reduced generosity, increased incentives to move back into work	
2010	Rise in female SPA begins; increasing coverage for some; indexation made more generous		
2016	New state pension introduced: more generous in near term, less generous in long run		

women are being increased together so that they reach age 66 in October 2020. Cribb, Emmerson, and Tetlow (2016) showed that the rise in the female state pension age from 60 to 62, which occurred between April 2010 and April 2014, boosted employment rates among women aged 60 and 61 by 6.3 percentage points (ppt). Some descriptive evidence of this is provided in section 11.3 below.

State pension reforms in 1975 and 2000 made the state pension system significantly more generous, while intermediate reforms—in 1986 and 1995—made it substantially less generous. These changes have generated differences in the state pension entitlements across years of birth, which, in turn, may have affected retirement ages. There has also been variation within individuals born in the same year: the state pension system has been increasingly generous to low earners and some groups not in paid work in more recent years, while the generosity of the system to higher earners peaked among those reaching state pension age around 2000. More recent changes—that came into effect in April 2016—will make the state pension more generous for many individuals (such as the self-employed) but less generous for most individuals over the longer term.

11.2.1.2   Other State Benefits

Other state benefits may also affect retirement behavior, with potentially the most important being out-of-work disability benefits for those deemed to be in poor health. The amount paid to individuals is flat rate—that is, it does not vary with past earnings—and for those who do not meet the contribution requirements, it is means-tested. Thus, for those who could otherwise earn average or above average amounts, the financial incentive to leave paid work in order to receive these disability benefits is relatively weak. But lower earners whose health allows them to qualify for these benefits if they are out of work may face a relatively strong financial incentive to leave the labor market (Banks, Emmerson, and Tetlow 2016).

There have been several reforms to these benefits—in particular, in 1995, 2001, and 2008—all with the intention of reducing the numbers receiving them. The first two of these reforms focused on reducing the inflow to these benefits, while the third also strived to increase the shift from benefits into paid work. Trends in the receipt of benefits are documented in Banks, Blundell, and Emmerson (2015), who show that receipt is less related to age and more related to education levels than it was 20 years ago.

Other out-of-work benefits, which are targeted toward those on lower incomes, also reduce the financial incentive to remain in paid work, with this again being particularly true of lower-wage workers. These are more generous to those who are older than the female state pension age—and those who have a partner older than the female state pension age (regardless of gender)—than they are to younger individuals. For example, in 2015–16, the maximum award of pension credit (for a single person without any disabilities) was £151.20 per week, whereas for a single person older than 25, the maximum rate of Jobseeker's Allowance was £73.10 per week. In addition, the latter would require the recipient to seek work and attend work-focused interviews, whereas pension credit is paid unconditionally. For those older than the female state pension age, these benefits have also been made relatively more generous over time, in particular in 1999 and in 2003.

11.2.1.3   Private Income

By far, the most important source of private income in retirement comes from private pensions: the relatively low level of the state pension (particularly for those "contracted out" of the state earnings-related pension system) has meant that private pensions have always played an important role in providing retirement income. Since 1988, defined-contribution pensions have become more prevalent among private-sector employees, as coverage of defined-benefit pensions has declined sharply. In contrast, among public-sector workers, defined-benefit pension coverage remains very high.

These different types of pensions typically have very different incentives to start drawing at different ages. Defined-contribution pensions would typically be expected to rise in value. Defined-benefit pensions, in contrast, typically provide a strong incentive to draw the pension at the normal pension age, as they often impose an actuarial reduction if they are drawn before this age but do not offer an actuarial increase for delayed drawing. Historically, the normal pension age is 60 for public-sector employees and 65 for private-sector employees (and for many who joined public-sector schemes after 2005).

In individually arranged defined-contribution pensions, any incentive to draw the pension at a particular point in time would not translate into an incentive to leave paid work. In contrast, up until April 2006, for those in employer-provided private pensions, any incentive to draw a private pension translated into an incentive to leave paid work (or at very least to move employers), since up until that point, it was not possible to draw a private pension from an employer and continue to work for that employer. But since April 2006, this restriction has been lifted, and if they wish, employees can draw a pension and continue to work for that same employer.

11.2.1.4   Other

Two other important reforms, which do not fit naturally into table 11.2 or the subsections above, also took place over this period. First, compulsory retirement ages younger than 65 were outlawed in October 2006, and then any compulsory retirement ages regardless of age were outlawed in October 2011. Second, public service pensions have been reformed. The normal pension age in public-sector plans has been increased (often from 60 to 65), with this first affecting new entrants to these schemes in the mid to late 2000s (with the exact date varying from scheme to scheme). Further increases, which were also applied to many existing members, will align it

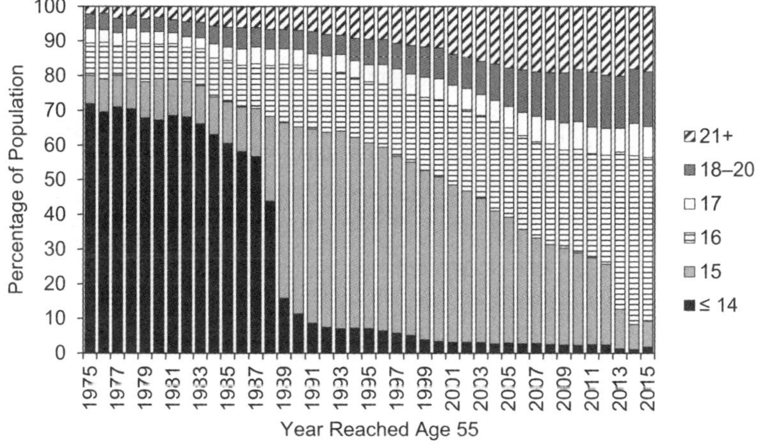

Fig. 11.3   Distribution of age of leaving full-time education by cohort, men
Source: Based on a sample of all individuals aged 55–64 observed in the LFS (1984–2015).

with the state pension age from the mid-2010s (though not for those already within 10 years of their existing normal retirement age). Since April 2011, for deferred members and those receiving these pensions, the indexation has been made less generous, while from the mid-2010s, they were moved from operating on a final salary basis to a career earnings basis (which changes how earnings were uprated and the accrual rate at the same time, with the exact changes varying from scheme to scheme).

11.2.2   Trends in Education

Regardless of how it is measured, education levels in the United Kingdom have been increasing across successive birth cohorts, and this has been particularly true for those cohorts reaching the retirement age over the period since 1999. This section documents two possible measures of education levels—years of school and qualifications received—before documenting trends in employment rates among older individuals split by a measure of education and shown separately for men and women. In each case, we have somewhat incomplete data over the full course of our period. Questions on the age he or she left full-time education were only introduced to the LFS from 1984 onward, and even then, they were included only for those younger than the state pension age or for those still working if older than the state pension age. By choosing a reference age of 55, we are able to get data on years of education back to 1975 for men but only back to 1980 for women. Data on qualifications was introduced to the survey even later, so in that dimension, our series can only go back to 1983 and 1988, respectively.

The evolution of the distribution of school-leaving ages over successive birth cohorts is shown for men in figure 11.3 and for women in figure 11.4. We choose to present these by the age at which the cohort reached age 55

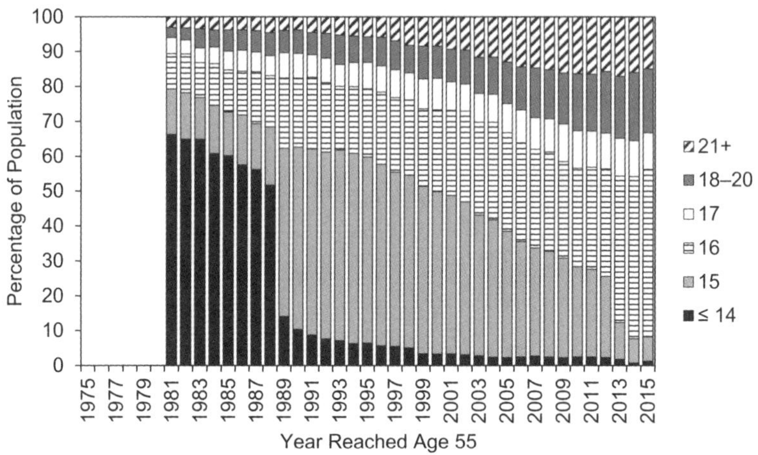

Fig. 11.4   Distribution of age of leaving full-time education by cohort, women
Source: Based on a sample of all individuals aged 55–59 observed in the LFS (1984–2015).

in order to provide a scale that is relevant to the consideration of the group entering the retirement window. In both figures, it is very clear that those reaching age 55 in 1989 were much more likely to have remained in school beyond age 14 than those reaching age 55 a year earlier. This is due to a policy reform: the 1944 Education Act increased the school-leaving age to 15 in April 1947. Those aged 55 in 1989 were born in 1934 and therefore turned age 14 in 1948 and were unable to leave school at that point.[2] In a similar vein, those reaching age 55 in 2013 are much less likely to have left school at age 15 than those reaching age 55 one year earlier. This was driven by the school-leaving age increasing to age 16 in September 1972, and those aged 55 in 2013 were born in 1958 and therefore were aged 15 in 1973 and (typically) unable to leave school at that point.

More generally, there is a noticeable increase in the number of years of full-time education across cohorts over the period, with a general decline in the share of men and women leaving school at or before age 15 and a general increase in the proportion leaving school after age 15. The shares leaving full-time education at ages 18–20 or at ages 21 and older have also increased substantially.

An alternative measure of educational attainment is to look at the qualifications received rather than the years of education attended. Trends in qualifications can be looked at using the LFS, which has recorded these on a consistent basis since 1992. For this analysis, we again look at men aged

2. A small fraction of children can still leave while one year "younger" than the compulsory school-leaving age since the school year ends in July, but it is age on September 1 that determines whether you need to start the next school year.

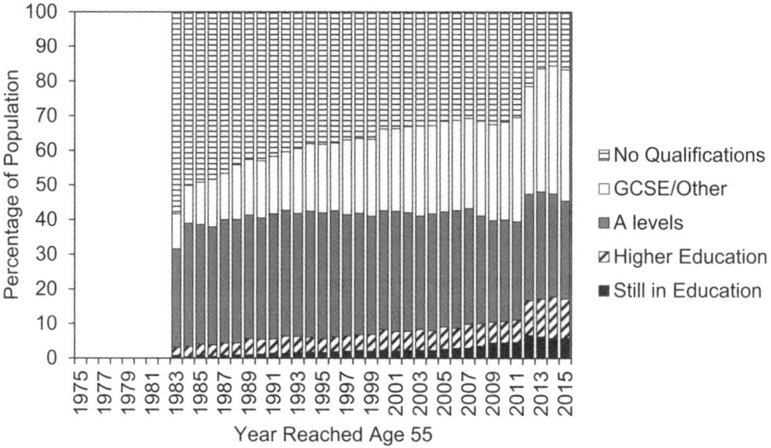

Fig. 11.5   Distribution of qualification among men classified as having "low" education by cohort

Source: Based on a sample of all individuals aged 55–64 observed in the LFS (1992–2015).

between 55 and 64 and women aged between 55 and 59—that is, the same age ranges covered in the previous two figures that examined school-leaving ages (although the data started in 1992 rather than 1984). We then take just the group who left school at or younger than the compulsory school-leaving age—which we can think of as a "low" education group—and show how their levels of qualifications achieved have varied over time. This group is of particular interest, as it is, by definition, the group whose qualifications are more likely to be affected by increases in the school-leaving age. It may also be the group where obtaining some kind of further qualification after leaving formal education may be most prevalent.

The results are shown for men in figure 11.5 and for women in figure 11.6. Several things are apparent from the two figures. First, among this group of "low education" men, there has always been a sizeable group that reports achieving the equivalent of A-level qualifications or greater—that is, qualifications equivalent to those that could typically be attained at age 18 among those who remained in school—despite the fact that these individuals reported leaving school at age 16 at the latest. Indeed, among men who turned age 55 in 1983, the data show that around 30 percent have the equivalent of A-level qualifications or greater despite them having first left school at age 14 (or earlier).

Second, increases in the compulsory school-leaving age did lead to a greater proportion of men and women receiving formal qualifications. This can be seen by the fall in the proportion of men with no qualification between those who were age 55 in 1983 and those who reached age 55 one year later, which coincided with those affected by the compulsory school-

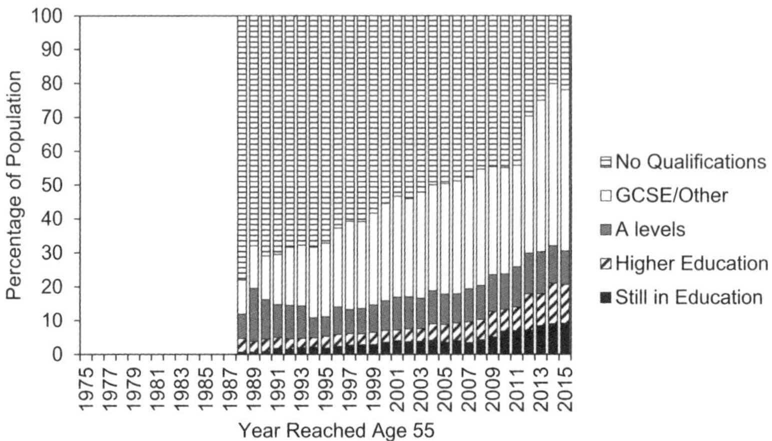

Fig. 11.6   Distribution of qualifications among women classified as having "low" education by cohort

Source: Based on a sample of all individuals aged 55–59 observed in the LFS (1992–2015).

leaving age rising from age 14 to 15. Similarly, a clear effect of the increase in the compulsory school-leaving age from age 15 to 16 on qualifications can be seen in the proportion of both men and women with no qualifications, which fell between those reaching age 55 in 2011 and those reaching age 55 one year later.

Finally, of those who left school at the compulsory school-leaving age, a much larger proportion of women than men have no formal qualifications, although the gap between the two has been falling sharply over time. Between those reaching age 55 in 1988 and those reaching age 55 in 2011 (a period in which the compulsory school-leaving age was 15 throughout), the proportion of men with no formal qualifications fell from 44 percent to 30 percent, while over the same period, the proportion of women with no formal qualifications fell from 78 percent to 44 percent. So the gap between the two genders fell from 34 percentage points to 14 percentage points.

In the remainder of our analysis, we present employment rates for a "low education" group, defined as those who left continuous education at or below the compulsory school-leaving age, and a "high education" group, or those who left continuous education at age 21 or older. (A middle group, comprising those who stayed in continuous education beyond the compulsory school-leaving age but not until age 21 will be omitted from these splits.) The resulting education distribution, as defined by this method, among men aged 55–64 and women aged 55–59, is shown for 1985, 1995, 2005, and 2015 in figure 11.7. This shows that under our classification, the proportion of men and women who are "high education" has been increasing, while the proportion of people who are "low education" has been falling. For men,

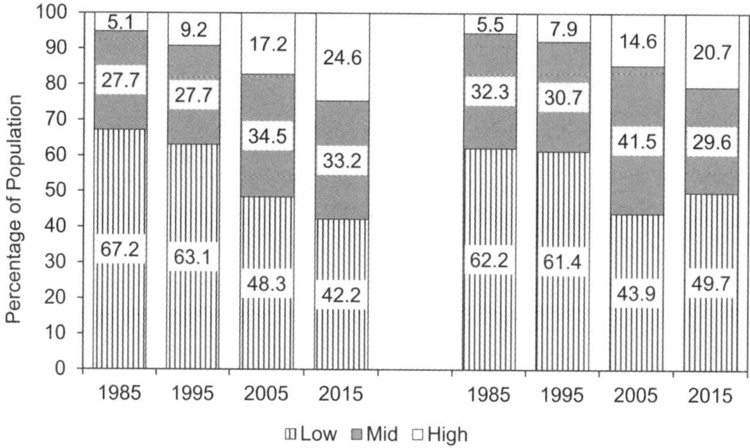

Fig. 11.7   Rising education levels of men aged 55 to 64 and women aged 55 to 59
Source: LFS.

this change is observed between all the years shown in figure 11.7, whereas among women the big shift occurred between 1985 and 1995.

This categorization of education by years of schooling is fairly common in the United Kingdom, particularly in studies that involve analysis alongside other countries, since qualifications are not so easily comparable internationally. Broadly speaking, although the number of years of education may differ, the categorization corresponds conceptually to the split of high school graduates, some college, and college graduates that is frequently used in US analysis. And it has the advantage, when using LFS data, of allowing us to cover the period from 1984 onward. But there are some potential issues with this choice. First, the direct impact of increasing the compulsory school-leaving age for our cohorts will be to increase the proportion of individuals classified as having "low education" within our sample. Second, as the proportion in the "high education" has increased, it is possible that the meaning of "high education" in terms of the labor market could be changing over time. Third, as we have already shown, there is a not-inconsiderable (and increasing) proportion in the "low education" group that has some qualifications. A years-of-education-based split is somewhat crude and cannot capture the changing skills and qualifications of each group conditional on their years of schooling nor any postschooling qualifications (or changes in the rate at which these have been acquired by successive cohorts). On this last point, it is also worth noting that immigration, recall bias, changes to the survey, and differential mortality would be additional reasons the qualifications of a cohort observed at later ages may differ from the degree to which that cohort reports their school-leaving age. These effects may not be negligible and would, again, lead to a qualifications measure (subject to

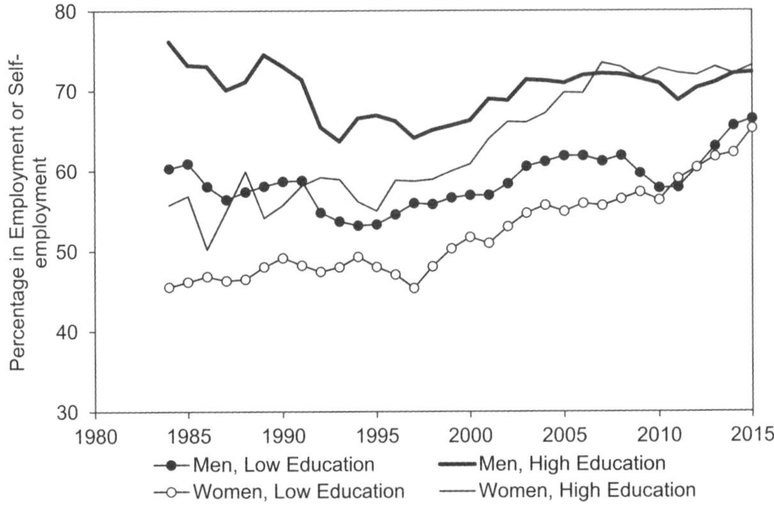

Fig. 11.8   Employment rate among men aged 55 to 64 and women aged 55 to 59 by education
Source: LFS.

sufficient reporting quality) that is superior in terms of corresponding to how the labor market and the technological skills of the cohort may have been changing.

With these caveats in mind, figure 11.8 presents the employment rates of the "low education" and "high education" groups of older men and women over time. Among men, employment rates of both education groups fell between 1984 and the mid-1990s and then rose over the subsequent 20 years. Despite this increase, by 2015, the employment rate of "high education" older men was still below its level in 1984, while the employment rate of "low education" older men was some way above its mid-1980s level. So among men aged 55–64, the education gradient in employment is now less steep than it used to be. Among women aged 55–59, employment rates of those with "high education" and those with "low education" have increased between 1984 and 2015, such that among each group, their employment rates are now at the same level as those seen among men aged 55–64 in the same education category.

The LFS data allow us to carry out a simple shift-share analysis to decompose growth in employment among older individuals over the 20 years from 1995 and 2015, specifying how much is explained by greater levels of education (since, as shown in figure 11.8, individuals with greater levels of education are more likely to be employed and, as shown in figure 11.7, education levels have been increasing over time) and how much is explained by rising levels of employment within each education group.

Among men aged 55–64, employment rates rose by 11.9 percentage points between 1995 and 2015, 2.3 percentage points of which would have occurred had employment rates conditional on education levels (as measured by years of schooling) remained unchanged at their 1995 rates. Among women aged 55–59, employment rates rose by 17.3 percentage points between 1995 and 2015, only 0.8 percentage points of which would have occurred had employment rates conditional on education levels remained unchanged at their 1995 rates. This relatively small effect of rising education levels for women is in part because the increase in education—at least on our measure—has not been as great over this period, and in addition, the gradient in employment by education in the mid-1990s was less steep for women than for men (as shown in figure 11.8).

If we look at the evolution of employment rates among older men and women and instead split the data by our measure of qualifications received (rather than years of schooling), then the decomposition comes out rather differently. Among men, 3.1 percentage points of the 11.9 percentage point increase in employment between 1995 and 2015 would have occurred just from the composition shift if employment rates conditional on qualifications had remained unchanged at their 1995 rates. This is slightly above the 2.3 percentage points reported above when doing the decomposition using years of schooling. Among women, of the 17.3 percentage points increase in employment over the 20 years from 1995, 6.2 percentage points would have occurred had employment rates conditional on qualifications remained at the 1995 rates. This is much larger than the 0.8 percentage points reported above when doing the decomposition using years of schooling. This large difference is due to the proportion of women aged 55 with no qualifications falling sharply over this period (as shown in figure 11.6) and the fact that employment rates among older women with no qualifications are much lower than employment rates among women with some qualifications.

11.2.3   Trends in Health

Perhaps the other obvious secular trend occurring across cohorts in the last 40 years that might be affecting labor market participation has been improvements in health and reductions in mortality. Consistently measured health data over our 40-year period do not exist in the United Kingdom, so we are unable to document this in much detail. What is well known is that life expectancy at older ages has increased rapidly, even more so for males than for females, over the period. While such a trend can be documented in many ways, each telling the same story, a simple indicator of the magnitude of this effect is given in table 11.3, which presents life expectancy at age 60, showing how it has risen by seven years for males and five years for females.

In previous work, we documented these late-life longevity and mortality trends in terms of the underlying one-year mortality probabilities at each age between 50 and 75 (Banks, Emmerson, and Tetlow 2017) and the large

Table 11.3   **Additional years life expectancy at age 60 (period basis) for England and Wales**

	1970–72	1980–82	1990–92	2000–2002	2010–12
Male	15.4	16.4	17.9	19.9	22.4
Female	20.0	20.9	22.1	23.3	25.2

Source: Office for National Statistics, 2015, English Life Tables No. 17, http://www.ons.gov.uk/ons/rel/lifetables/decennial-life-tables/english-life-tables—no-17—2010-12/stb-elt17.html.

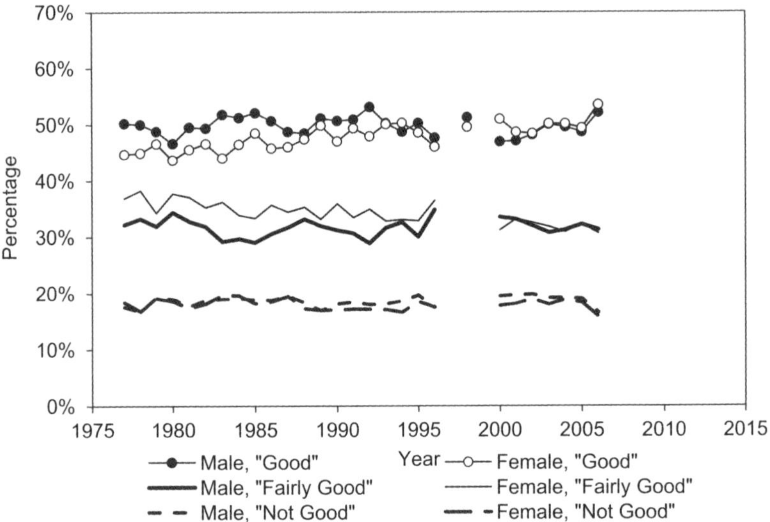

Fig. 11.9   Self-assessed health among 55–69-year-olds, 1975–2015
Source: General Household Survey.

and rapid changes over the period were immediately apparent. Taking the state pension age as a reference point, for example, these fell by a factor of three for a 65-year-old male, from 3.4 percent in 1970 to 1.1 percent in 2015, and they fell by more than a factor of two for a 60-year-old woman, from 2 percent to 0.8 percent.

When it comes to understanding health as opposed to life expectancy, the data in the United Kingdom are considerably more patchy, particularly before the mid-1990s and the advent of the Health Survey for England. Surveys with measures of population prevalence of disease or disability do not exist on a consistent basis over the period since 1975; the best information available comes from crude, self-reported summary health measures of the type available in many general purpose social surveys around the world. Figure 11.9, calculated using data from the General Household Survey, shows that such data only demonstrate a very mild improvement in health over the period, and even this is only really apparent for women, who show an increase in the proportion reporting health as "good" and a reduction in the proportion reporting health as "fairly good." Similar trends would be observed in the Health Survey for England, which measures self-reported health on a more conventional five-point scale over the 1991–2015 period.

Such a trend, or lack of a trend, in self-reported health might seem at odds with such large and rapid improvements in life expectancy and reductions in mortality rates for older working-age cohorts over the period. The measurement of health and disability trends across cohorts is a huge field of research, and it uses various data and methodologies to try to investigate such issues. While there is no consensus to date on exact trends in the United Kingdom, it seems clear that at least some of the extension in longevity has been healthy, but at the same time, there has probably also been some increase in the length of life spent with disease and disability (particularly at older ages). For example, a recent paper calculated that, of the 2.1-year increase in life expectancy of men aged 65 that has occurred over the period from 2000–2002 to 2009–11, 1.2 years has been an increase in years of "good" health and 0.9 years has been an increase in years spent with "not good" health (Government Office for Science 2016).

In order to try to examine the consequences of this for employment rates, in previous work, we looked at various methods aiming to compute the health capacity to work and how it might have changed over time (Banks, Emmerson, and Tetlow 2016), using either time-series variation in mortality or cross-sectional variation in health conditions and disability indicators as a basis for the calculations. In summary, this suggested that there was a substantial capacity to work among the 55–69-year-old population if one was willing to measure capacity to work purely in health terms. Without more definitive data to summarize or quantify this further, we leave the issue here, other than to say that, whatever the cohort trends in health have been, it seems unlikely that they have been a constraint that has been driving employment rates. One caveat to that is that most analysis has looked at health trends on average or rates of health conditions and disabilities calculated for the population of older workers as a whole. If the focus were just on the low educated (as some of our analysis will be in what follows), given what we know about the education health gradient, it might be more important to factor in any education-group-specific trends for health and disability. This is left as a topic for future research.

So far, we have seen that for men, retirement ages are lower than they used to be, while longevity has increased and the number of years of schooling has also increased. Such trends have an immediately apparent impact on the proportion of life individuals spend in the labor market. Banks and Smith (2006) compared men born in 1900 to those born in 1935 and showed that average school-leaving ages rose by 1.8 years, median retirement ages fell by 4 years, and life expectancy at age 55 rose by 2.2 years. As a result, the

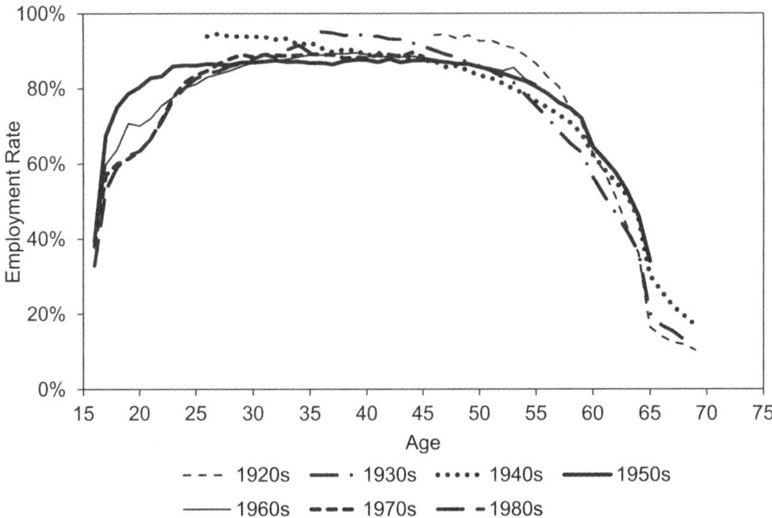

Fig. 11.10   Employment among successive cohorts of men
Source: LFS.

proportion of life spent not working (as a result of either school or retirement) increased from 30 percent to 40 percent. Despite increased retirement ages across later cohorts, the continued increases in schooling and longevity suggest this is unlikely to have been reversed and may well have increased further.

11.3   Trends in Detail

So far, we have documented the trends in employment rates of men and women over time and shown how this varied across different age groups and the extent to which, for those approaching the state pension age, the story changes when accounting for rising levels of education over time among those approaching retirement. In this section, we examine these trends in more detail.

We start by describing differences in employment rates by age for different birth cohorts. Again, we do this separately for men and women. We then turn to examine how these have varied for those with relatively low or high levels of education. Finally, we describe differences in trends in employment for different occupations and how growth in wages has varied between different age groups. Throughout, we highlight policy reforms and other changes to financial incentives to retire, which may help explain the trends that we see.

11.3.1   Trends in Employment: A Birth Cohort Analysis

Differences in male employment rates are shown in figure 11.10 by age and decade of birth. At older ages, two clear differences in employment rates between the different birth cohorts can be seen. First, as expected, there is a much greater rate of employment between ages 50 and 59 among those born in the 1920s (with the bulk of these data relating to the late 1970s and the early 1980s) than for those born in the 1930s, 1940s, 1950s, and—as far as can be seen in the available data so far—1960s. Second, while male employment rates decline sharply with age as individuals move through their late 50s and early 60s, this decline was much sharper among those born in the 1920s and (albeit to a lesser extent) the 1930s than it was among those born in later decades. The combination of these two features means that while those men born during the 1940s were less likely to have paid employment when they were aged between 50 and 59 than those born in the 1920s or 1930s, they were more likely to have paid employment during their late 60s than those born in the previous two decades.

Finally, the figure also shows that employment rates at younger ages fell dramatically for those born between the 1950s and the 1970s, with the main counterpart to this being the expansion of higher education over this period. While not relevant for this study, given that those with higher levels of education are currently more likely to have paid work at older ages than those with lower levels of education (as shown in the previous section), this might be expected to boost the employment rates of older men in the future.

This shift to a more gradual decline in employment rates by age among older men is likely to have been brought about, in part, by policy reforms and other changes affecting the financial incentives to retire at particular ages faced by older workers. Most obviously, the abolition of the earnings test on the state pension in the late 1980s has been found to have increased the labor supply of men aged 65–69 (Disney and Smith 2002). The shift among private-sector employers to providing defined-contribution rather than defined-benefit pensions will also have reduced the financial incentive to retire at a normal pension age rather than at earlier or later ages (Blundell, Meghir, and Smith 2002). Finally, the shift from invalidity benefit (IVB) to incapacity benefit (IB), from April 1995, was designed to reduce the flow to IBs and may have improved financial incentives to work among many of those who might otherwise have been able to qualify for IVB.

The equivalent data for women are presented in figure 11.11. This also shows that there has been a big shift in employment rates at older ages across some successive birth cohorts and also a significant difference in how employment rates vary between, roughly, age 20 and age 35.

First, looking at employment rates of women in their early 50s, these were much higher among those born in the 1950s than the 1940s, 1930s, or 1920s. Rather than leading to a faster drop in employment rates at later ages, this appears largely to have fed into larger employment rates among women from more recent birth cohorts in their late 50s and early 60s. So this suggests that a big part of the rise in employment rates at these older ages is explained by women reaching older working ages with greater attachment to the labor market. So reforms—and other changes—affecting financial incentives to

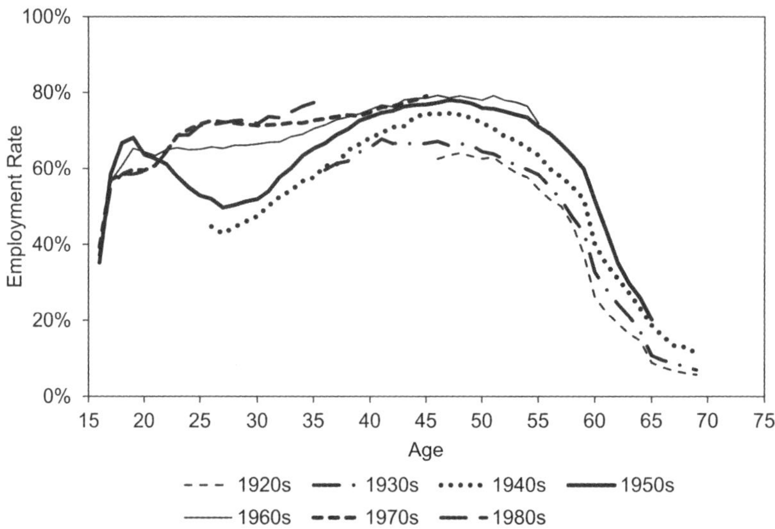

Fig. 11.11   Employment among successive cohorts of women
Source: LFS.

retire are most likely a smaller part of the overall story for women than for men. Looking forward, women born in the 1960s appear to have had slightly higher employment rates in their early 50s than those born in the 1950s did at the same ages. This might suggest we can expect a further increase—albeit slight relative to the large increases seen recently—in the employment of women in their late 50s over the next few years.

The other big difference between the employment rates of women from different birth cohorts can be seen during childbearing ages. For those born in the 1950s, employment rates of women fell from two-thirds during their late teens to half at age 27 before rising again so that they had returned to two-thirds by age 37. In contrast, there was no noticeable dip in the employment rates of women during their 20s among those born in the 1960s and 1970s. This may well have implications for the employment outcomes of older women in the future. As noted above, the employment rate of women in their early 50s who were born in the 1960s is only slightly above what it was for women at the same age who were born in the 1950s, potentially suggesting only a relatively limited increase in employment rates going forward. But because they were more likely to have had paid work through their 20s and 30s, these women will, on average, have a greater amount of accumulated labor market experience than previous generations of women at the same ages. This might help boost their employment prospects at older ages—in terms of not just their employment rate but potentially their hours of work and their hourly wage. While not directly related to the retirement analysis

Fig. 11.12   Employment rate among women by single year of age as state pension age rises
Source: LFS.

here, Blundell et al. (2016) provide a detailed analysis and structural modeling of female life-cycle labor market participation and its relationship to education choices, childbearing, and the incentives in the welfare system.

One policy reform that clearly affected retirement behavior is the rise in the state pension age for women from age 60, which began in April 2010. This increases the age at which women can (and, in the vast majority of cases, do) receive a state pension, although it does not, at least overall, lead to an obvious change in financial incentives to maintain paid work because there is no requirement to retire in order to claim a state pension and no ability to draw a state pension before the state pension age. Exploiting the fact that the state pension age has been increased gradually—and therefore in any time period, there is variation in the state pension age between women born not that far apart—Cribb, Emmerson, and Tetlow (2016) find that increasing this age led to a 6.3 percentage point increase in the rate of employment between the old and new state pension age. Descriptive evidence of this—using the same data as Cribb et al.—is presented in figure 11.12, which shows the employment rate by a single year of age among women aged 56–63 over time. Employment rates are generally higher for younger women than older women and, prior to 2010, tended to increase gradually over time among women of all ages. Marked in black are the employment rates over the window where the state pension age was increased from one age to the next. It is clear from the figure that these periods were associated with particularly rapid increases in employment, relative to what happened among women of that same age both before and after the reform was implemented and also

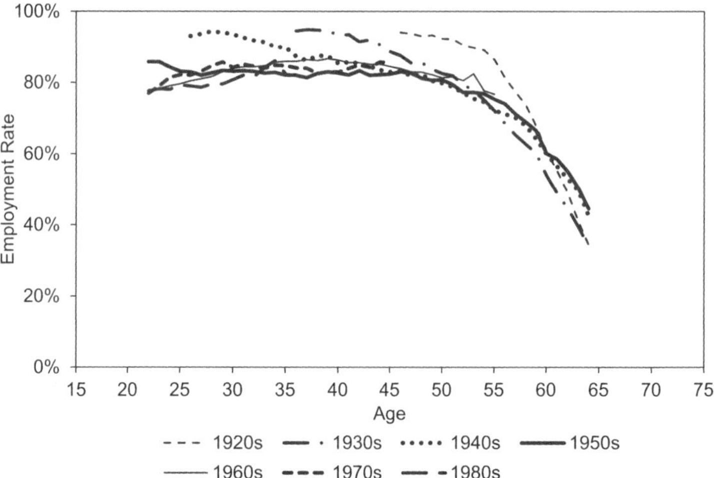

Fig. 11.13   Employment among successive cohorts of low-educated men
Source: LFS.

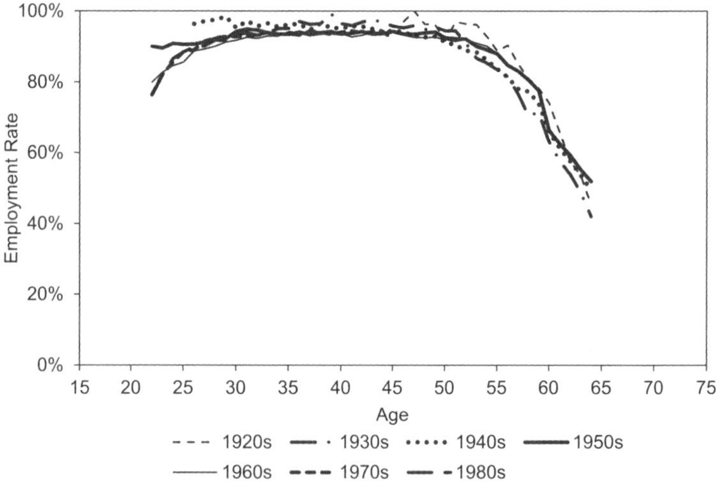

Fig. 11.14   Employment among successive cohorts of high-educated men
Source: LFS.

when compared to what was happening to the employment rate of younger and older women at the same point in time.

Finally, we show how employment rates by age for different birth cohorts have varied by the level of education. This analysis is carried out using the same "high" and "low" education groups (i.e., excluding the "mid" education group) as defined in the previous section. Figures 11.13 and 11.14

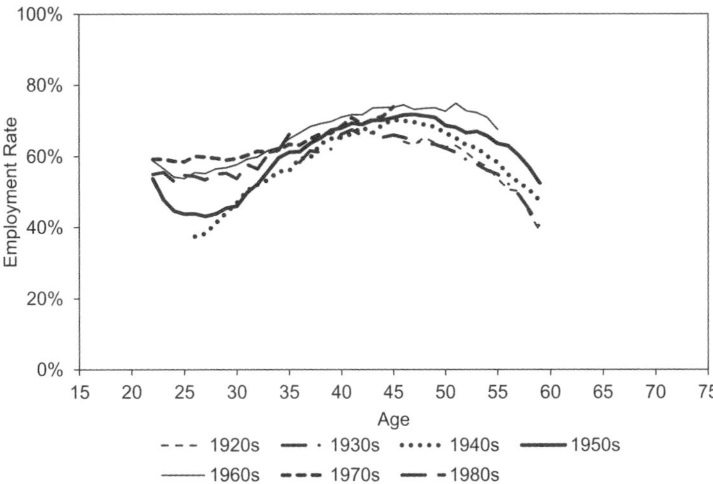

Fig. 11.15   Employment among successive cohorts of low-educated women
Source: LFS.

present the data for men with low and high education, respectively. The two features seen in the aggregate male cohort profiles above—that employment rates during ages 50–59 have fallen sharply from those experienced by those born in the 1920s and that the employment rate of older men now declines more gradually at older ages than it did for those born in the 1920s—are particularly pronounced for those with low levels of education and less visible for those with high levels of education. So these two features of the aggregate profile are not consequences of increasing levels of education over the period and are mainly driven by changes across birth cohorts among those with lower levels of education. This suggests the investigation of institutional explanations for such changes in employment at older ages (as opposed to economic explanations, such as wealth effects or changes in employer demand for certain types of skills) might focus initially on looking at programs or retirement institutions where changes have impacted differentially on different education groups. Examples might be the changing incentives in disability benefits or perhaps the role of cohort changes in the balance (and rules) of defined-benefit versus defined-contribution pensions.

The equivalent statistics for women are presented in figures 11.15 and 11.16. In general, employment rates of high-educated women are greater than those of low-educated women. In contrast to the story for men, the aggregate cohort patterns presented in figure 11.11 can be seen among those with both low levels of education and high levels of education. First, in both cases, employment rates of women in their early 50s were much higher among those born in the 1950s than among those born in the 1940s, 1930s, or 1920s. Second, while there is a dip in the employment rates during child-

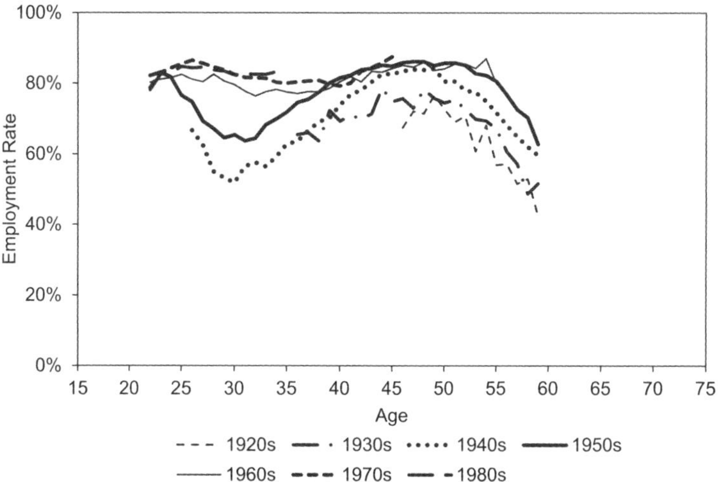

Fig. 11.16   Employment among successive cohorts of high-educated women
Source: LFS.

bearing years among those born in the 1960s and 1970s, this is much less noticeable than it is among those born in the 1950s. In both of these cases, the changes across birth cohorts are more pronounced among those with higher levels of education.

In terms of the outlook for the employment prospects of women in their 60s going forward, two things look likely from these figures. First, the slightly higher employment rate of women in their early 50s who were born in the 1960s (compared to the 1950s) is only present for women with low levels of education. This suggests that the "birth cohort effect" boosting the employment rate of women in their 60s in the near future might be driven by an increase in employment among women with low (as opposed to high) levels of education. Second, the fact that women in their 60s will increasingly have accumulated greater labor market experience over their entire lifetimes is especially true for women with high levels of education, since it is among this group where employment rates during late 20s / early 30s have increased the most. This could be particularly likely to boost the future wages of older women given the evidence that wage returns to labor market experience (and the negative returns to time out of the labor market) are stronger for women with higher rather than lower levels of education (Costa Dias, Elming, and Joyce 2016).

11.3.2   Employment Trends by Occupation

In what follows, we look at employment rates in different occupations over time. In particular, we examine the extent to which the trends seen among older individuals over the period since 1995 are similar to or divergent from

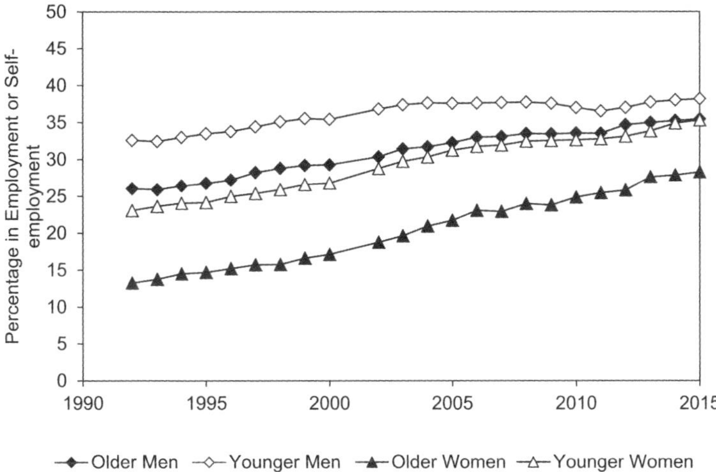

Fig. 11.17   Percentage of older and younger individuals employed in professional, managerial, or technical occupations over time by sex
Source: LFS.
Note: "Older" contains those aged 50–64, and "younger" contains those aged 20–49.

those seen among young working-age individuals. Specifically, the percent of individuals aged 50–64 who are employed in a particular occupation—and how this has changed over time—is compared to the equivalent among individuals aged 20–49. Again, this is done separately by sex. Three broad occupational groups are considered: (1) professional, managerial, or technical; (2) skilled nonmanual; and (3) skilled manual.

Summary data on employment in professional, managerial, and technical occupations are presented in figure 11.17. Over the 20 years from 1995 to 2015, the percent employed in these areas increased among older men, younger men, older women, and younger women. While these increases were very large for those aged 20–49 (at 4.7 ppt and 11.2 ppt for 20–49-year-old men and women, respectively), the equivalent increases seen over the same period for men and women aged 50–64 are even larger (8.7 ppt and 13.6 ppt, respectively). As a result, the employment gap in these occupations between older and younger individuals—seen among both men and women—is now considerably smaller than it was 20 years ago. Thus this is an area where employment growth has generally been favorable in the United Kingdom over the last 20 years, but the increase in the employment rate has been greater for older individuals than for younger individuals.

The equivalent data for employment in skilled nonmanual occupations are shown in figure 11.18. Among men, the employment rate over the period since the mid-1990s in these occupations has been broadly stable, and this is true among ages 50–64 and 25–49. Among women, there is a striking

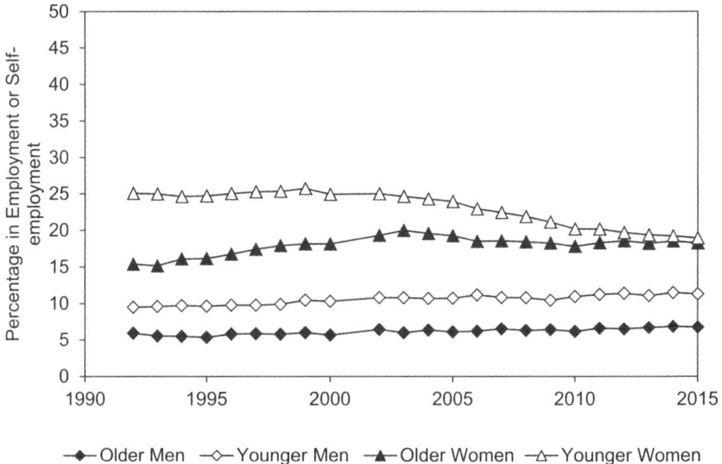

Fig. 11.18   Percentage of older and younger individuals employed in skilled non-manual occupations over time by sex
Source: LFS.
Note: "Older" contains those aged 50–64, and "younger" contains those aged 20–49.

difference in the trends by age. Among those aged 50–64, the employment rate of women in these occupations was greater in 2015 than in 1995, with the decline in employment since 2003 not being sufficient to offset the earlier growth. In contrast, the percentage of women aged 20–49 employed in skilled nonmanual work has declined throughout this period. So among women, this is an area where employment growth among those aged 50–64, albeit slight, has occurred despite employment in these occupations becoming less common among younger women.

Finally, the patterns for employment in skilled manual occupations are presented in figure 11.19. This shows that over the period since 1995, there is little change in the proportion of older men or older women who are employed in skilled manual occupations. This is also true of younger women, despite a reasonably sharp fall (of almost 4 ppt) in the percentage of younger men who are employed in skilled manual occupations. So this is an area where the employment rate of older men (and older women) has held up despite a fall in the employment rate in these occupations among younger men.

11.3.3   Wage Growth among Older Workers

The focus so far has been on trends in employment—both overall and in different types of occupations. This subsection looks instead at the evolution of average hourly wages among older employees and compares these

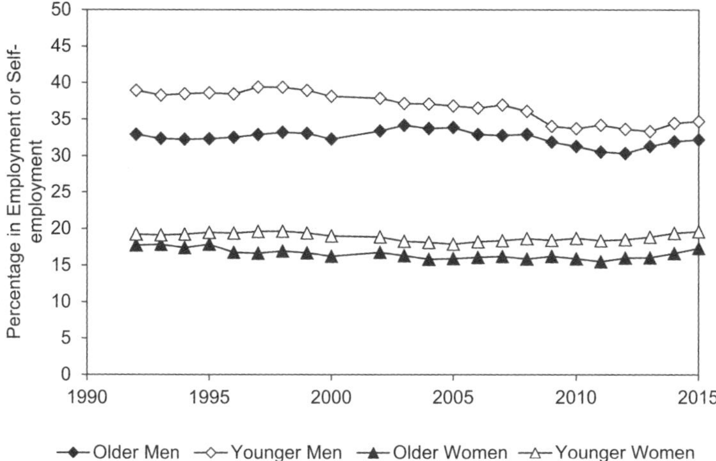

Fig. 11.19   Percentage of older and younger individuals employed in skilled manual occupations over time by sex

Source: LFS.

Note: "Older" contains those aged 50–64, and "younger" contains those aged 20–49.

to both inflation and hourly wage growth among younger employees. This is of interest because it can show how part of the financial incentive to have paid work (the wage) is evolving and also because changes in the observed wage distribution over time for different age groups are informative about the characteristics or skills of the individuals who are choosing to continue paid work.

The data on growth in median hourly wages among men are presented in figure 11.20, with wages indexed to 100 in 2005. Between the mid-1990s and 2003, there was broadly similar growth in hourly wages between different age groups of men. All age groups enjoyed wage growth that exceeded inflation, with those aged 65–69 experiencing slightly higher wage growth than younger age groups. A more diverse pattern can be seen over the period since 2003, with average male wage growth being greater among older age groups than among younger ones. While male wage growth among 65–69-year-olds and, albeit to a lesser extent, 55–64-year-olds has continued to outstrip inflation, the period since 2003 has seen average male wage growth among 20–29-year-olds, 30–39-year-olds, and 40–54-year-olds of less than the rate of inflation.

Trends in hourly wages among women by age group show a fairly similar story to those for men. Over the period from the mid-1990s to 2003, all age groups experienced wage growth in excess of inflation, with not that much dispersion in wage growth between different age groups. Over the period

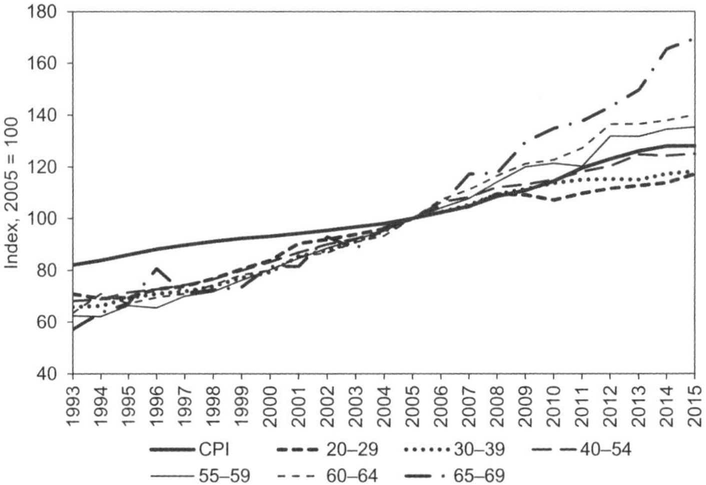

Fig. 11.20   Median wages of men over time by age group
Source: LFS.

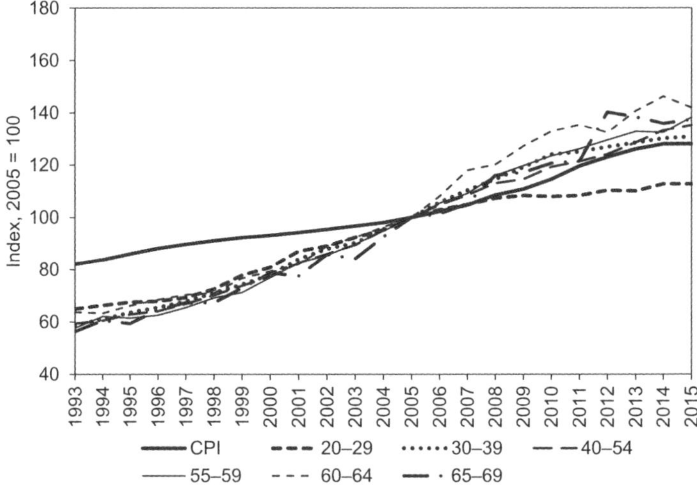

Fig. 11.21   Median wages of women over time by age group
Source: LFS.

from 2003 to 2015, there is more dispersion in wage growth between different age groups with greater average wage growth, as there was for men, among older employees rather than younger ones. Unlike men, however, it is only 20–29-year-old women who, as a group, have experienced wage growth lower than the rate of inflation.

11.4   Conclusions

This chapter has documented employment rates among older men and women over the 40 years from 1975 to 2015. Over the first two decades of this period, employment rates of older men fell, whereas over the subsequent two decades, they rose. In contrast, employment rates of older women were relatively stable over the first decade but have risen sharply since and are now at record levels. The growth in employment of older men and women since the mid-1990s has coincided with a period of increases in the employment rate among younger men and women. In both cases, however, the growth in employment among older individuals over the last 20 years has been stronger than that of the rest of the working-age population.

There have also been differences in these trends by education levels. When taking years of schooling as a measure of educational attainment, the employment rates of older men over the period since 1995 have grown much faster among the "low educated" than among the "high educated." As a result, the gradient in employment among men by education is much less steep than it used to be, with employment rates among "low educated" men now higher than they were in the mid-1970s. In contrast, growth in the employment rate among older women has been similar across the education distribution. But as we have documented, there are some not-insubstantial issues with using years of schooling as a measure of education, not least because a large proportion of men who left school at age 15 or earlier—and therefore without any formal qualifications—have subsequently acquired some. And when using qualifications rather than years of schooling as a measure of education, a much larger proportion of the increase in employment rates of older women over the period since 1995 can be accounted for by increasing education levels across successive birth cohorts.

Of key interest to policymakers is the extent to which reforms have contributed to changes in employment rates that we have documented. In terms of state pensions, there have been many significant reforms over the period since 1975, though many will have had a limited impact on the marginal financial incentive to retire that individuals face. The most important being, perhaps, the removal of the earnings test in 1989, which research has shown increased employment among men aged 65–69 (and will have also limited the extent to which subsequent reforms affected the incentive to work), and the increase in the female state pension age since 2010, which has also been shown to have boosted employment rates of women, who, as a result, now cannot receive a state pension until later. Further increases in the female state pension age—and, from 2018, the male state pension age—are likely to push employment rates of older women and men up further. Other policy reforms since the mid-1990s may have also have had important impacts on employment outcomes, not least the reforms to out-of-work disability benefits in 1995 and 2008, and the more recent outlawing of mandatory retirement ages. A more explicit investigation of the role of these reforms in explaining the overall trend, perhaps in comparison with what has been occurring in other countries over the same time period, is left as an important topic for future research.

It is also clear that the story behind the changes in employment rates cannot fully be told by looking at policy reform alone. Other trends have been important. Among older men—and in particular "low educated" men—we have shown that employment rates at older ages now decline more gradually than they did in the past and this, at least in part, is likely to have been brought about by the shift among private-sector employers from providing defined-benefit pensions to providing defined-contribution pensions. This shift is likely to continue having an effect on retirement behavior for some time—as will, eventually, the reforms to public-service pensions that came into effect in the mid-2000s (for new entrants) and the mid-2010s (for all members more than 10 years from their existing normal pension age).

Among women, differences in employment rates at younger ages are a key part of the story. Women born in the 1950s had much higher employment rates in their early 50s than those born earlier, and this has fed into an increased employment rate at older ages (rather than a faster drop in employment rates in their mid-50s). Among women born in the 1960s, there has been, at least among those with "low" education, a further increase in employment in their early 50s, suggesting that continued increases in employment rates of older women are likely. In addition, employment rates among women at younger ages—in particular among women with higher levels of education—mean that over time, women are approaching their 60s with greater labor market experience, potentially boosting the wage that they can command (especially given the evidence that wage returns to labor market experience are stronger for women with higher rather than lower levels of education), which, in turn, could also encourage them to remain in the labor market for longer.

Economy-wide trends—such as the shift away from physically demanding jobs in primary industry and manufacturing toward service sector roles—might well have affected employment rates at older ages. And as we have shown, the proportion of older men and women employed in professional, managerial, and technical occupations has been particularly strong, outstripping even the strong growth in the employment rate in these roles seen among younger individuals. At the same time, we have seen an increase in the relative wages of older workers that has been particularly apparent for those aged 65 and older. This is a trend that is likely to be related to selection effects as retirement incentives evolve and to cohort effects in education and lifetime occupational choices, feeding through into the employment outcomes of older workers as each successive cohort moves through later life.

Further research—and, indeed, the attention of policymakers—should not only be focused on whether older individuals are working but consider more the nature of their activities in paid work as well as the hours worked and earnings, which will all be key determinants of the living standards of older individuals and are likely to change systematically over time as the pattern of employment participation at older ages evolves.

References

Banks, J., R. Blundell, and C. Emmerson. 2015. "Disability Benefit Receipt and Reform: Reconciling Trends in the United Kingdom." *Journal of Economic Perspectives* 29 (2): 173–90.

Banks, J., C. Emmerson, and G. Tetlow. 2016. "Effect of Pensions and Disability Benefits on Retirement in the United Kingdom." In *Social Security Programs and Retirement around the World: Disability Insurance Programs and Retirement*, edited by D. A. Wise, 81–136. Chicago: University of Chicago Press.

———. 2017. "Health Capacity to Work at Older Ages: Evidence from the United Kingdom." In *Social Security Programs and Retirement around the World: The Capacity to Work at Older Ages*, edited by D. A. Wise, 329–57. Chicago: University of Chicago Press.

Banks, J., and S. Smith. 2006. "Retirement in the UK." *Oxford Review of Economic Policy* 22 (1): 40–56.

Blundell, R., M. Costa Dias, C. Meghir, and J. Shaw. 2016. "Female Labor Supply, Human Capital, and Welfare Reform." *Econometrica* 84:1705–53.

Blundell, R., C. Meghir, and S. Smith. 2002. "Pension Incentives and the Pattern of Early Retirement." *Economic Journal* 112 (478): C153–C170.

Bozio, A., R. Crawford, and G. Tetlow. 2010. *The History of State Pensions in the UK: 1948 to 2010*. IFS Briefing Note 105. London: Institute for Fiscal Studies.

Costa Dias, M., W. Elming, and R. Joyce. 2016. *The Gender Wage Gap*. IFS Briefing Note 186. London: Institute for Fiscal Studies.

Crawford, R., S. Keynes, and G. Tetlow. 2013. *A Single-Tier Pension: What Does It Really Mean?* IFS Report R82. London: Institute for Fiscal Studies.

Cribb, J., C. Emmerson, and G. Tetlow. 2016. "Signals Matter? Large Retirement Responses to Limited Financial Incentives." *Labour Economics* 42:203–12.

Disney, R., and S. Smith. 2002. "The Labour Supply Effect of the Abolition of the Earnings Rule for Older Workers in the United Kingdom." *Economic Journal* 112:C136–C152.

Government Office for Science. 2016. "Future of an Ageing Population." GS/16/10, July. https://www.gov.uk/government/publications/future-of-an-ageing-population.

12

Working Longer in the United States
Trends and Explanations

Courtney C. Coile

In 2016, the share of men in their early 60s who were working or looking for work in the United States was *not* 4 in 10—but it would have been if the trend in earlier decades had persisted. After falling continuously for over a century (Costa 1998), the labor force participation (LFP) rate of older men suddenly began to rise starting in the mid-1990s. Today, more than 6 in 10 men aged 60–64 are in the labor force, a dramatic increase relative to what might have been expected two decades ago. The LFP rates for older women have also been rising for decades, due in part to far-reaching societal changes in the role of women.

Many factors have been proposed to explain the rise in LFP at older ages and the resulting increase in the average age of retirement (Munnell 2015). These include demographic factors like improving health and rising education, shifts in the economy away from sectors with physically demanding work, and changes to employer-sponsored pensions and health insurance benefits and to social security. Rising participation among women may also lead men to work longer if spouses prefer to retire together. While these factors could all plausibly have contributed to the recent trend, it is not clear whether all of them did so nor which factors are the most important.

This chapter aims to begin to fill this gap by providing an analysis of trends in LFP and employment and of factors that may influence these out-

Courtney C. Coile is professor of economics at Wellesley College and a research associate of the National Bureau of Economic Research (NBER).

This chapter was prepared as a part of the NBER International Social Security (ISS) project. The author thanks the members of the ISS team for valuable suggestions and Hero Ashman and Clio Flikkema for excellent research assistance. For acknowledgments, sources of research support, and disclosure of the author's material financial relationships, if any, please see https://www.nber.org/chapters/c14052.ack.

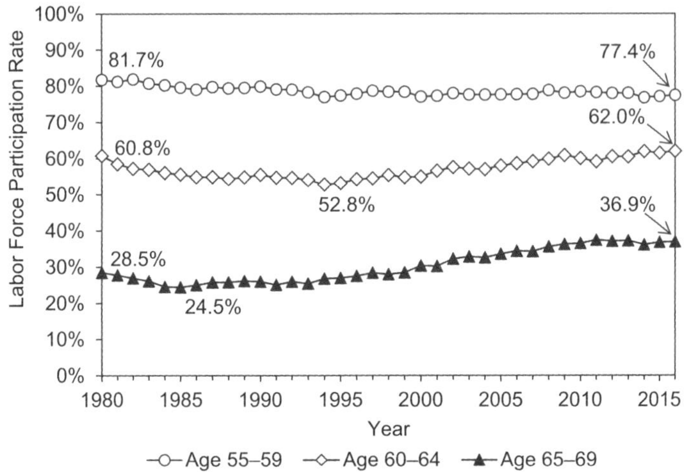

Fig. 12.1   LFP rate for men ages 55–69, 1980–2016
Source: OECD, http://stats.oecd.org (data from US Bureau of Labor Statistics).

comes. The focus is on the years 1980 to the present, a period encompassing both declining and rising participation for men and rising participation for women. The analysis is largely descriptive, examining whether the trends are consistent with the hypothesis that changes in factors such as health or social security may lead to longer work lives and gleaning insights from the literature about the likely role of these factors. This analysis sets the stage for future work that will focus on the role of social security and private pensions, documenting how the financial incentives for retirement have changed over time due to changes in retirement programs and estimating how much of the rise in LFP can be explained by these changes in incentives.

12.1   Trends in Labor Force Outcomes

The rise in LFP at older ages is among the most significant labor market trends in the United States in recent decades. As figure 12.1 illustrates, for men aged 60–64, participation began to increase in the mid-1990s, growing from 53 percent in 1994 to 62 percent in 2016, a 9-point increase. For men aged 65–69, the trend began a decade earlier, and the increase to date was 12 points, from 25 percent in 1985 to 37 percent in 2016. In contrast, there is no U-shaped pattern for men aged 55–59, whose participation declined from 82 percent in 1980 to 77 percent by the mid-1990s and remained flat thereafter.[1]

---

1. Council of Economic Advisors (2016) documents this trend and explores supply and demand factors that may have contributed to this decline, concluding that the decline in real wages of less-skilled workers is an important factor.

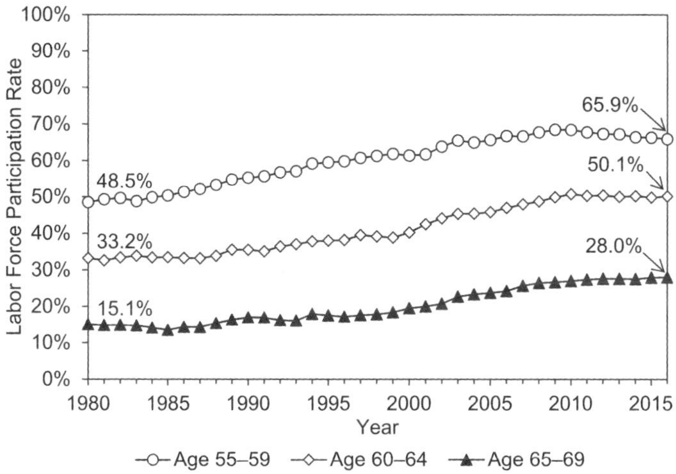

Fig. 12.2   LFP rate for women ages 55–69, 1980–2016
Source: OECD, http://stats.oecd.org (data from US Bureau of Labor Statistics).

The trend for women, shown in figure 12.2, is quite different. In all age groups, participation has risen continuously since 1980, increasing by 17 points at ages 55–59 and 60–64 and by 13 points at ages 65–69. In 2016, nearly two-thirds of women aged 55–59 and half of women aged 60–64 were in the labor force. These numbers are at least partly a reflection of the growing rates of participation (at all ages) among women in more recent cohorts—indeed, Goldin and Katz (2018) show that the cohorts of women who are working longer at older ages had higher rates of participation throughout their life cycle, having invested more in human capital accumulation at younger ages. Women's sustained increases in participation led to a substantial narrowing of the male-female participation gap—for those aged 55–59, the gap fell from 33 points in 1980 to 12 points in 2016. There is some indication in the figure that participation has plateaued for women aged 55–64 since about 2010, though it is not yet clear whether this is a temporary or permanent break from the long-term trend.

The employment rate is also of interest. As shown in figures 12.3 and 12.4, trends in employment are very similar to those in LFP, as unemployment, which is the difference between the two series, is generally quite low in these age groups. The average unemployment rate during the 1980–2016 period is 3.4 percent for men and 2.3 percent for women aged 55–59; rates for the two older age groups are lower. The unemployment rate is affected by the business cycle, reaching highs of 5 to 6 percent for men aged 55–59 in the early 1980s and after the Great Recession of the late 2000s. The official unemployment rate may understate the number of older individuals who would like to work if some discouraged workers do not report themselves

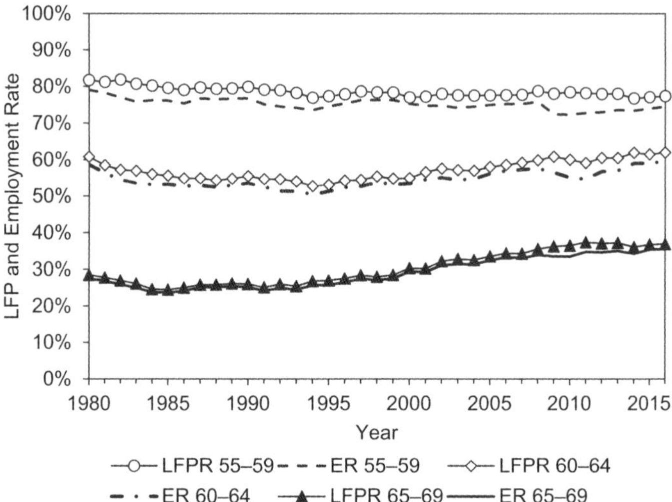

Fig. 12.3   LFP and employment rates for men ages 55–69, 1980–2016

Source: OECD, http://stats.oecd.org (data from US Bureau of Labor Statistics).

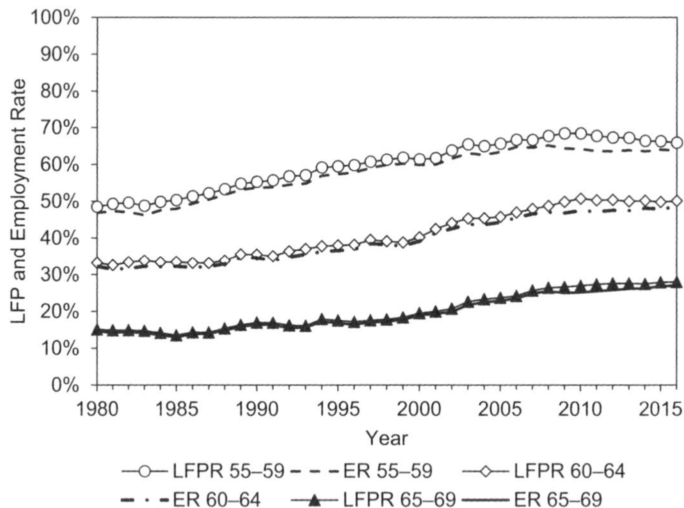

Fig. 12.4   LFP and employment rates for women ages 55–69, 1980–2016

Source: OECD, http://stats.oecd.org (data from US Bureau of Labor Statistics).

to be looking for work. Age discrimination as well as lower labor demand during troughs in the business cycle may impede work at older ages (Lahey 2008; Neumark, Burn, and Button 2015; Coile and Levine 2007).

Population averages may mask substantial heterogeneity in the experiences of different groups. The LFP rates by education are shown in figures 12.5 and 12.6. Rates are reported as a three-year moving average to reduce

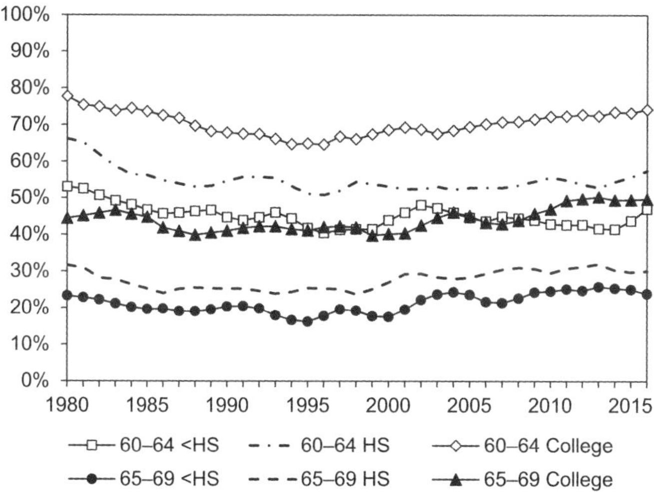

Fig. 12.5   LFP rate by education for men ages 60–69, 1980–2016

Source: March Current Population Survey (CPS). Data are weighted by person weights; rates are a three-year moving average. Those with some college are omitted from the graph.

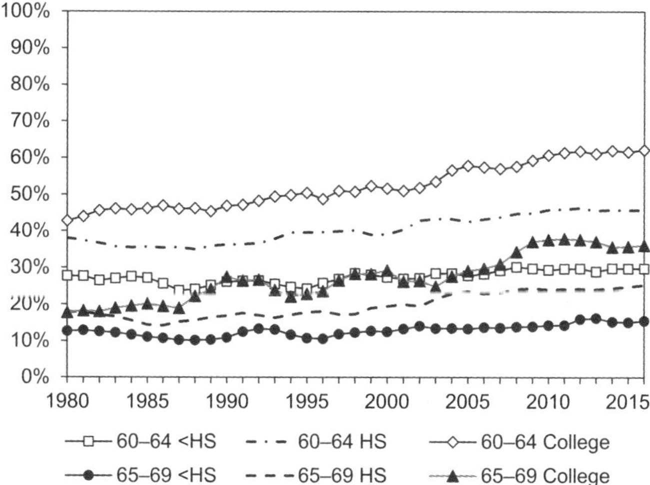

Fig. 12.6   LFP rate by education for women ages 60–69, 1980–2016

Source: March CPS. Data are weighted by person weights; rates are a three-year moving average. Those with some college are omitted from the graph.

sampling variation (here and in similar graphs below), and the youngest age group and those with some college are omitted for clarity of exposition. There are very large differences in participation by education. On average, across all years, the participation of college graduates is 25 points higher than that of high school dropouts for both men and women aged 60–64; at

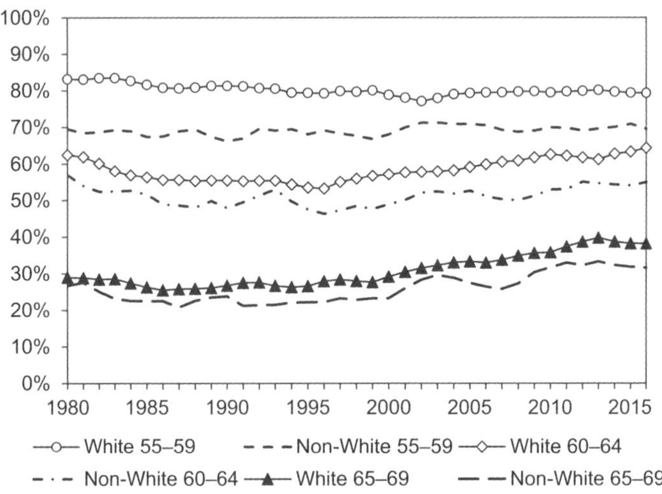

Fig. 12.7   LFP rate by race for men ages 55–69, 1980–2016
Source: March CPS. Data are weighted by person weights; rates are a three-year moving average.

ages 65–69, the participation gap between college graduates and high school graduates is 23 points for men and 15 points for women. For men, patterns over time by education group are fairly similar, though there is some evidence of a widening gap in participation during the past decade, which could reflect a stronger effect of the Great Recession on those with less education. For women, the increases in participation over time are much larger for college graduates than for those with a high school education or less, leading to a substantial widening of the participation gap by education.[2]

The LFP rates by race are presented in figures 12.7 and 12.8. For men, participation rates are consistently higher for whites than for nonwhites, but differences are smaller than those across education groups. At ages 55–59, a gap of 15 points in 1980 declined to 10 points in 2016, due to falling participation of whites. At older ages, the gap held steady or widened slightly over time, reaching 10 points for those 60–64 and 7 points for those 65–69 in 2016. For women, differences in participation by race are smaller, 3–5 points in 2016, though this represents a change from the 1980s, when the participation rate of nonwhites was similar to if not slightly higher than that of whites. As these figures do not control for education, differences in

2. In examining trends in the LFP by education group, it is important to be mindful of the large changes over time in the share of the population in each education group, discussed below. As there are, for example, fewer high school dropouts in recent years, the average characteristics of this group may be somewhat different from the average characteristics of high school dropouts in an earlier era. For a discussion of this issue in the context of trends in mortality by education, see Bound et al. (2014).

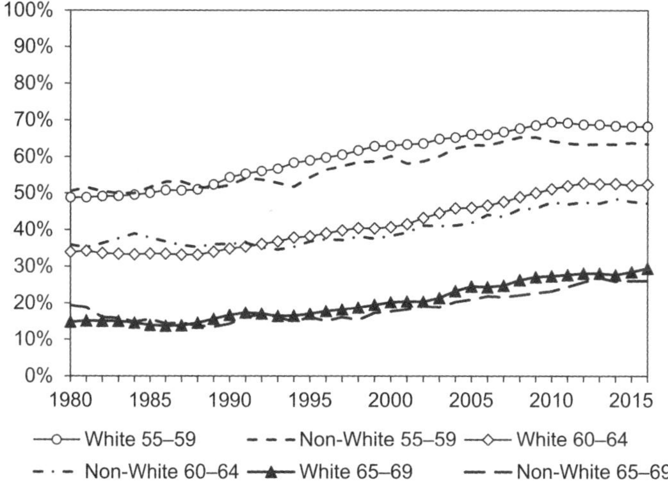

Fig. 12.8   LFP rate by race for women ages 55–69, 1980–2016

Source: March CPS. Data are weighted by person weights; rates are a three-year moving average.

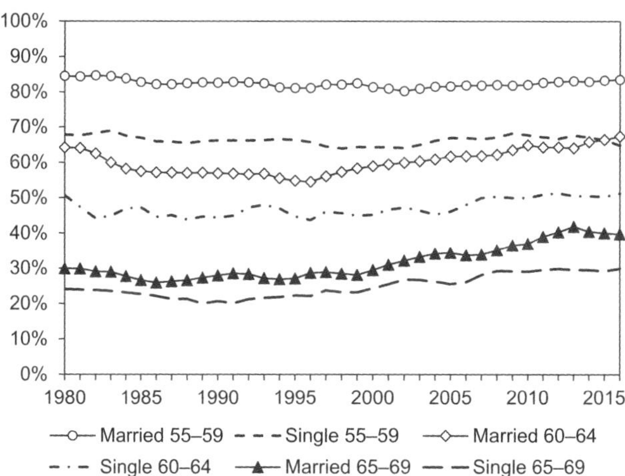

Fig. 12.9   LFP rate by marital status for men ages 55–69, 1980–2016

Source: March CPS. Data are weighted by person weights; rates are a three-year moving average.

participation by race could in part reflect the effect of racial differences in educational attainment.

Participation by marital status, shown in figures 12.9 and 12.10, is markedly different by gender. Single men participate at rates 10–20 points below their married counterparts, depending on the age group, and these differ-

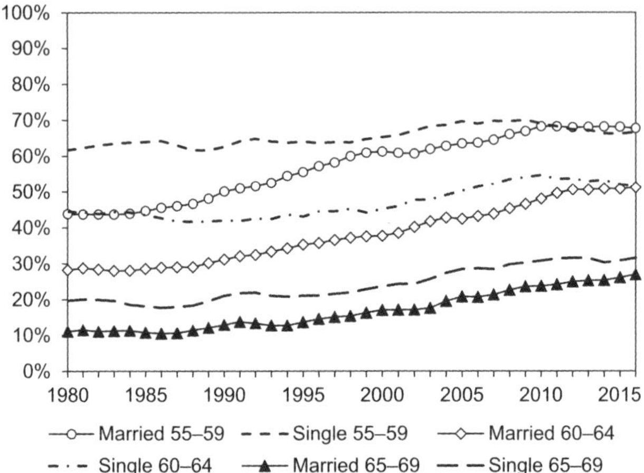

Fig. 12.10   LFP rate by marital status for women ages 55–69, 1980–2016

Source: March CPS. Data are weighted by person weights; rates are a three-year moving average.

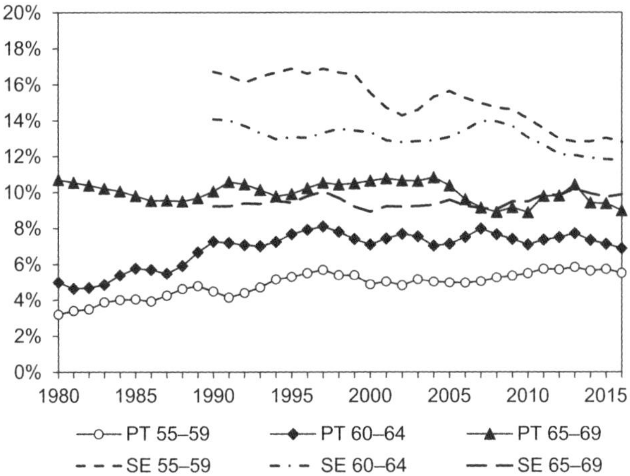

Fig. 12.11   Part-time work and self-employment for men ages 55–69, 1980–2016

Source: March CPS. Data are weighted by person weights; values are a three-year moving average. Self-employment data are shown starting in 1990 due to a change in question.

ences have been stable or widened slightly over time. In the case of women, single women in 1980 had participation rates 16–18 points higher than those of married women at ages 55–64 and 8 points higher at ages 65–69. Over time, this gap was eliminated in the two younger groups and narrowed in the oldest group. Thus much of the rise in women's participation at older ages over the past few decades is the result of an increase in the share of married women who are working.

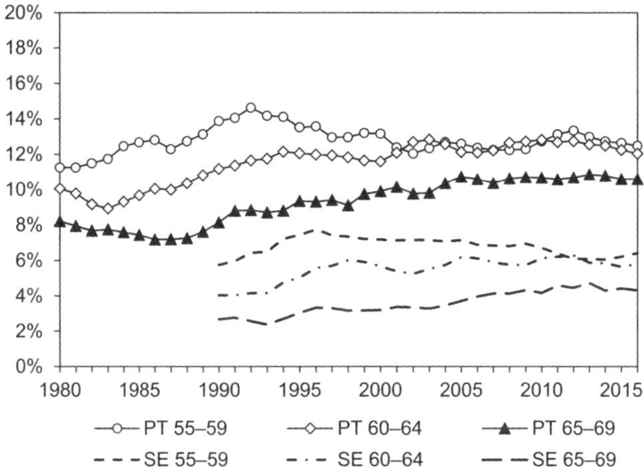

Fig. 12.12   Part-time work and self-employment for women ages 55–69, 1980–2016

Source: March CPS. Data are weighted by person weights; values are a three-year moving average. Self-employment data are shown starting in 1990 due to a change in question.

Work can encompass different kinds of labor market activity, including part-time work and self-employment. Figures 12.11 and 12.12 detail the frequency of these forms of work at older ages. Self-employment is fairly popular among men, with 12–13 percent of men aged 55–64 and 10 percent of men aged 65–69 engaged in such work in 2016; rates of self-employment among women are about half as large. The fraction of men working part time (less than 35 hours per week) is low but increases with age, at about 6 percent for those aged 55–59 and 9 percent for those aged 65–69. Part-time work is more common for women, with 11–12 percent of all age groups working part time in 2016. Part-time work has been essentially flat since 1990, as has self-employment among women, though there is a modest decline in self-employment among men.[3] With employment rate rising over time, the share of workers who are part time has been falling—even so, among those still in the labor force, 25 percent of men and nearly 40 percent of women in the oldest age group worked part time in 2016.

To sum up, the LFP of older men and women has been rising for several decades. The increase began in the mid-1980s for men in their late 60s and a decade later for men in their early 60s, while women's participation has been rising since at least 1980. There are notable differences across groups—

---

3. Data on self-employment from the March Current Population Survey (CPS) are shown starting in 1990 due to a break in the series that appears related to question wording. Beginning in 1988, the survey distinguishes between incorporated and unincorporated self-employment, and there is a roughly 50 percent increase in reported self-employment between 1987 and 1988. As the figure reports three-year moving averages, 1990 is the first year that relies solely on data from 1988 and later.

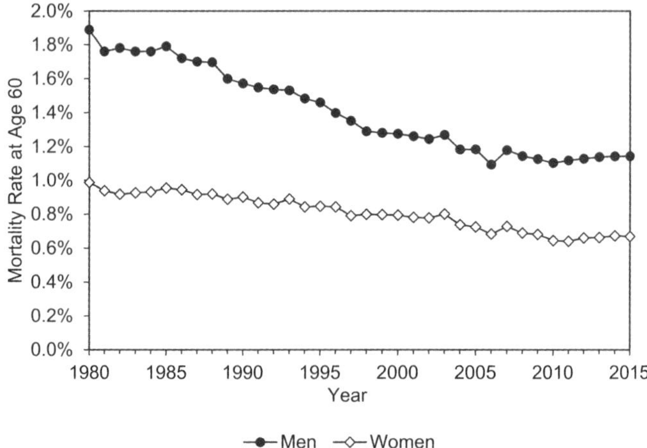

Fig. 12.13   **Mortality rate at age 60 for men and women, 1980–2015**
Source: http://www.mortality.org.

employment at older ages is higher for those with more education, for whites, and for married men. Married women's participation once lagged far behind that of single women, but the gap has largely been eliminated. Part-time work and self-employment are important at older ages, with more women engaged in the former and more men in the latter.

12.2   Trends in Explanatory Factors

These dramatic changes in work at older ages, and in particular the reversal of the century-long decline in participation of older men, naturally raise the question: What are the causes of this trend toward longer work lives? A number of demographic and economic factors are plausible contributors, but it is necessary to examine the trends in these factors and review other relevant evidence to begin to draw conclusions as to the likelihood of their each playing a role.

12.2.1   Mortality and Health

One theory is that improvements in longevity and health have played a key role in rising participation at older ages. Many studies have established that poor health is associated with earlier retirement (e.g., Bound et al. 1999; see Coile 2015 for a review). Health at older ages—as measured by mortality risk—has improved substantially over time. Figure 12.13 shows that the mortality rate at age 60 has declined by 40 percent for men and one-third for women since 1980. As mortality risk may be an imperfect proxy for work capacity, figure 12.14 reports trends in self-assessed health, a frequently used measure of overall health. The share of men and women aged 55–64 report-

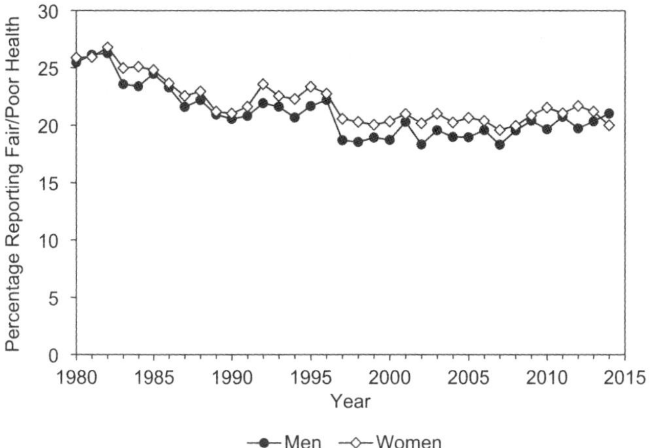

Fig. 12.14   Share reporting fair/poor health at ages 55–64 for men and women, 1980–2014

Source: National Health Interview Survey.

ing fair or poor health fell by 5–7 points between 1980 and the mid-1990s and has been essentially flat thereafter.[4]

A simple juxtaposition of these health and labor force trends is not supportive of the theory that health improvements are driving later retirement. The mortality rate has fallen continuously over time, both during the period that men's participation was falling and during the period when it was rising. Self-assessed health improved from the 1980s through the mid-1990s, while men's participation declined; it was flat thereafter, while men's participation increased. Thus neither of these health trends aligns with the U-shaped trend in men's participation.

One explanation for the lack of time series evidence supporting this theory may be that while poor health is an important determinant of retirement for some, it is not the main reason most people retire. Most people who are in the labor force at age 60 exit it by age 70, yet health declines only slowly with age over this range (Coile, Milligan, and Wise 2017). Moreover, comparing how much older individuals today work relative to either those in the past or slightly younger individuals in similar health suggests that there is significant health capacity to work at older ages (Coile, Milligan, and Wise 2017). In

---

4. Trends in other health measures are also of interest, but obtaining an overall view is complicated by the fact that measures do not necessarily all move in the same direction, at the same time, and equally for all groups (Crimmins 2004). One prominent debate focuses on whether longevity increases are resulting in a compression of disability into a shorter period before death or an increase in the number of years of disability; see Cutler, Ghosh, and Landrum (2014) and Crimmins and Beltrán-Sánchez (2010). For a discussion of other measures of health and disability, see Coile (2018).

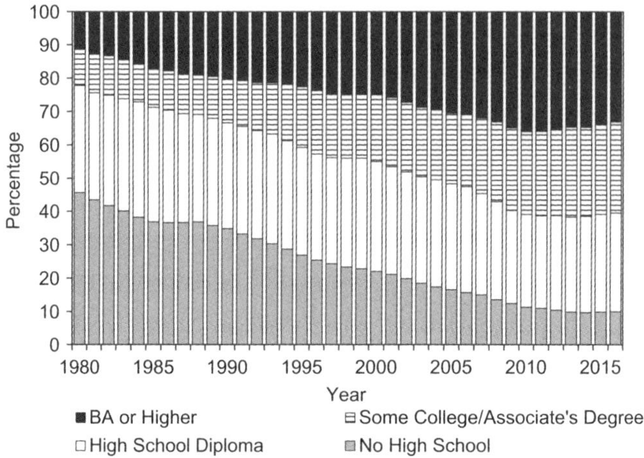

Fig. 12.15   Educational attainment of men ages 60–64, 1980–2016

Source: March CPS. Data are weighted by person weights; values are a three-year moving average.

short, while better health may have supported longer work lives, there is little evidence that it is a primary driver.

12.2.2   Education and Occupation

Another potential candidate is the increase in educational attainment of the near retirement-age population and the shift away from physically demanding jobs. Changes in education since 1980 have been dramatic, as shown in figures 12.15 and 12.16. For men aged 60–64, the share with less than a high school education has fallen by about 30 percentage points, from 40 to 10 percent of the population, while the share with a college degree or some college has grown from one-quarter to half of the population. Patterns for women are largely similar, though the initial share with at least some college was lower than for men. By contrast, changes in broad occupation categories (blue collar, white collar, service, and other) are smaller, as seen in figures 12.17 and 12.18.[5] Between the 1980s and the 2010s, the share of men working in blue-collar jobs fell by 6 percentage points, and the share working in white-collar jobs rose by an equivalent amount. For women, there was a decline in both blue-collar and service jobs and a 12-point increase in white-collar work.

A simple calculation may be useful to begin exploring how much the rise in education may have contributed to the increase in work at older ages. Figure 12.19 simulates the LFP rates that would have occurred in the

---

5. Classification of occupation codes into the categories of blue collar, white collar, service, and other (which includes farm and military) follows Ham et al. (2011).

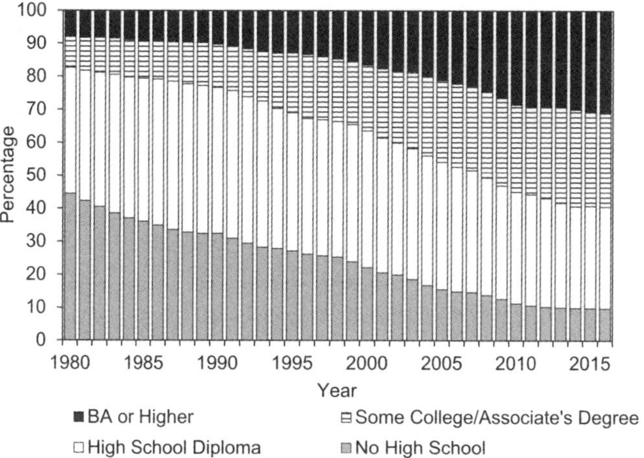

Fig. 12.16   Educational attainment of women ages 60–64, 1980–2016

Source: March CPS. Data are weighted by person weights; values are a three-year moving average.

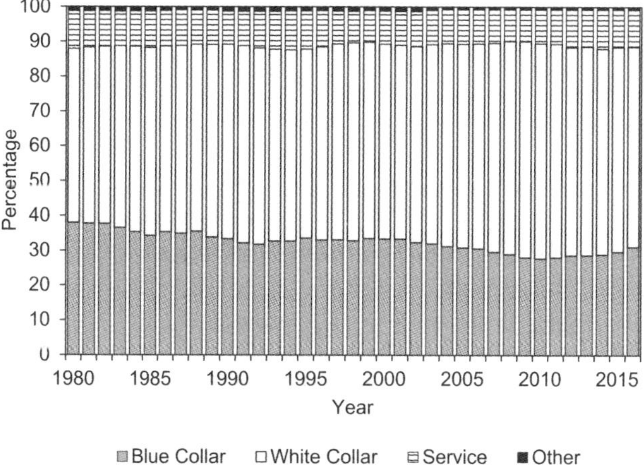

Fig. 12.17   Occupation type of men ages 60–64, 1980–2016

Source: March CPS. Data are weighted by person weights; values are a three-year moving average. See text for definitions of occupation groups.

years 1995–2016 if participation rates by education group (figure 12.5) had remained constant at 1995 levels while the educational composition of the population (figure 12.15) continued to change. In other words, this is an estimate of the rise in work that would be expected simply by having a more educated population, since more educated people tend to retire later. For men aged 60–64, the calculation suggests that participation would have risen

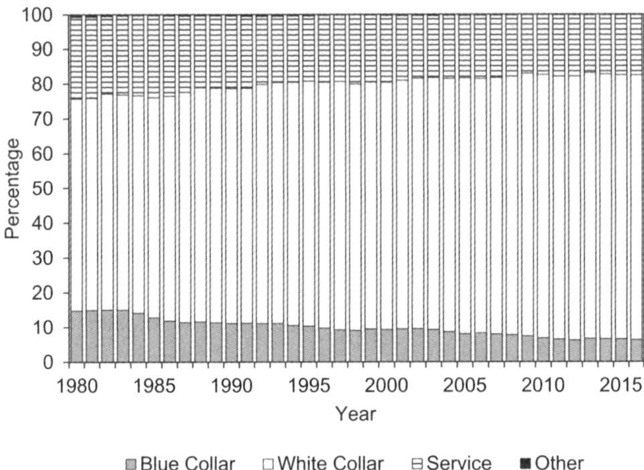

Fig. 12.18   Occupation type of women ages 60–64, 1980–2016

Source: March CPS. Data are weighted by person weights; values are a three-year moving average. See text for definitions of occupation groups.

by 3.5 points between 1995 and 2016 due to the increase in education over this period. Participation actually rose by 9.6 points, suggesting that the increase in education could be responsible for about one-third of the gains. For men aged 65–69, a similar calculation would suggest that increases in education could be responsible for nearly half (44 percent) of the gains.[6] Calculations for women, shown in figure 12.20, suggest that increases in education between 1995 and 2016 could be responsible for 44 percent of the increase in work at ages 60–64 and 30 percent at ages 65–69.

Caution may be warranted in drawing conclusions from such an exercise, however. Repeating this simulation using the participation rates by education group that existed in 1980, one would have predicted that participation would rise by 4.1 points for men aged 60–64 between 1980 and 1995 and by 3.2 points for men aged 65–69; in reality, participation fell by 9.2 and 2.6 points for the two groups, respectively, presumably for reasons unrelated to the change in education. As in the case of health, education has increased during periods of both falling and rising participation; indeed, educational attainment has been fairly flat over the past decade, even as participation

---

6. In a similar analysis, Burtless (2013) projects that slightly over half of the increase in the participation of men aged 60–74 between 1985 and 2010 can be attributed to rising educational attainment. Blau and Goodstein (2007) estimate LFP models using data from the CPS and Survey of Income and Program Participation (SIPP) aggregated by age, calendar year, and education; their estimates suggest that the increase in participation between 1988–92 and 2001–5 can be fully explained by changes in education. Both they and Burtless (2013) estimate that if the educational distribution had been fixed at its 1985 level, the LFP would have continued to decline into the 1990s rather than increasing.

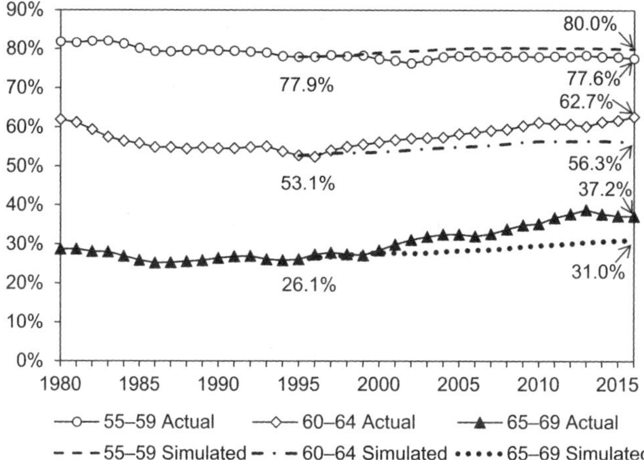

Fig. 12.19   Simulated changes in men's LFP due to changes in education, 1995–2016

Source: March CPS. Data are weighted by person weights; values are three-year moving averages. Simulated rates are weighted averages that combine 1995 participation rates by education group with contemporaneous shares in each education group.

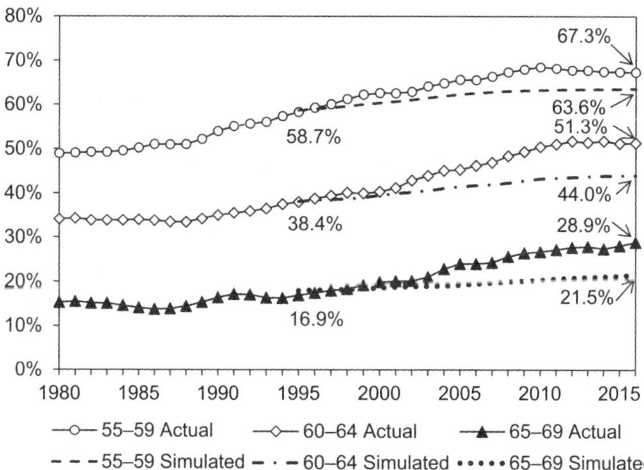

Fig. 12.20   Simulated changes in women's LFP due to changes in education, 1995–2016

Source: March CPS. Data are weighted by person weights; values are three-year moving averages. Simulated rates are weighted averages that combine 1995 participation rates by education group with contemporaneous shares in each education group.

has continued to rise. Moreover, as seen in figure 12.5, the U-shaped trend in LFP for men is also evident within each education group, suggesting that there are factors beyond education that are key to understanding the rise in participation.

12.2.3   Rising Participation among Women

The dramatic increase in women's involvement in the economy during the 20th century has been dubbed a "quiet revolution" (Goldin 2006). As noted earlier, as cohorts of women who have invested more in their education and career reach older ages, older women's LFP rates naturally increase. This trend may also lead to higher participation rates for older men—their husbands—if there are leisure complementarities—that is, if each spouse's enjoyment of leisure time is enhanced when the other spouse is present. Noting that many couples retire together, Gustman and Steinmeier (2000) and Maestas (2001) estimate structural family retirement models and find that complementarity of leisure is a key factor driving joint retirement. Baker (2002) and Coile (2004) find that financial incentives for retirement from public pensions have spillover effects on the retirement decision of the spouse, which is also consistent with leisure complementarities.

Estimating the causal effect of increasing women's participation on men's participation is challenging given the strong possibility that other factors, such as changes to social security, may affect the participation of both men and women. Schirle (2008) overcomes this obstacle by using the women's LFP rate at age 40—which will reflect women's changing role in the economy but will not be affected by factors such as social security—to predict their participation at older ages. Figure 12.21 shows that the LFP rate of women aged 35–44 lagged by 20 years, which roughly corresponds to the share of older men in a given year whose wives were working two decades earlier. This series grew by 35 points, from 43 percent in 1980 to 78 percent in 2016. Using this approach, Schirle (2008) estimates that the increase in older women's participation can explain one-quarter of the increase in older men's partici-pation in the United States.[7]

12.2.4   Employer-Provided Benefits

Employer-provided benefits including pensions and retiree health insur-ance may influence retirement decisions, and thus changes in these benefits may contribute to retirement trends. One significant change in employer benefits has been the shift from defined-benefit (DB) to defined-contribution (DC) pension plans.[8] As shown in figure 12.22, the share of private-sector

---

7. Schirle (2008) estimates that changes in US men's education and age explain about one-third of the increase, leaving 40 percent unexplained by the combination of women's participa-tion and these other factors.

8. In terms of the factors behind this shift, Friedberg and Webb (2005) point to the impor-tance of regulatory changes since 1974 that have tightened funding standards for DB plans,

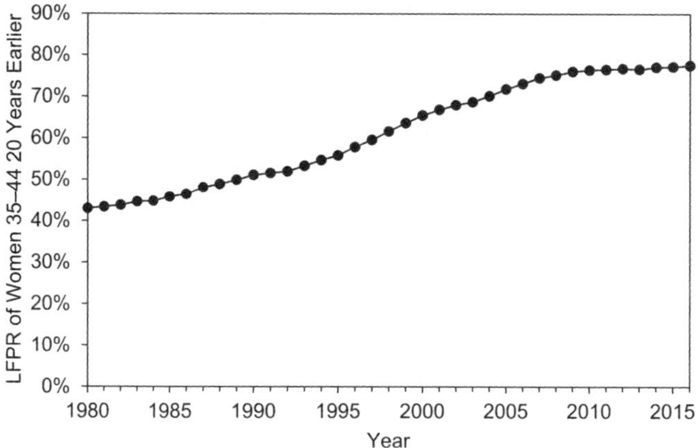

Fig. 12.21   LFP of women ages 35–44, lagged by 20 years, 1980–2016
Source: OECD, http://stats.oecd.org (data from US Bureau of Labor Statistics).

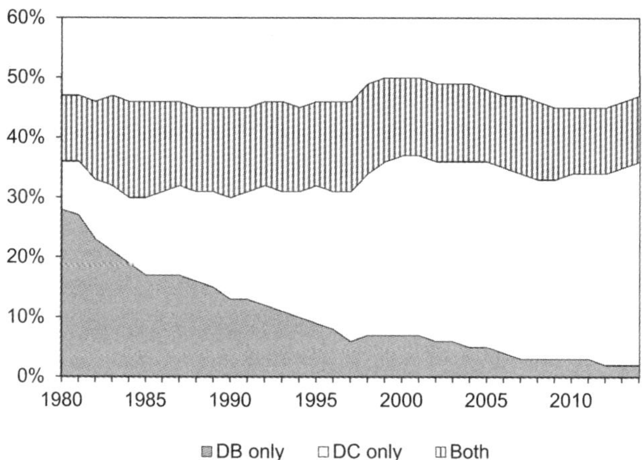

Fig. 12.22   Share of private-sector workers participating in an employer-sponsored pension plan by plan type, 1980–2014
Source: EBRI, http://www.ebri.org/publications/benfaq/index.cfm?fa=retfaqt14fig1.

workers participating in an employer-sponsored pension plan has remained relatively constant over time, at just under half the workforce. The share of workers with a DB plan only, however, fell from 28 percent in 1980 to 2 percent in 2014, while the share with a DC plan rose by a similar amount, from

---

constrained the structure of both DB and DC plans, and extended tax breaks for DC contributions. Poterba et al. (2007) note that firms in rapidly expanding industries have chosen to rely on DC rather than DB plans.

6 to 34 percent. The share with both a DB and DC plan remained roughly flat, averaging 13 percent over the period.[9]

DB and DC plans offer very different financial incentives for continued work at older ages. In DB plans, pension wealth typically grows until the plan's early or normal retirement age and declines thereafter; DC plans, in contrast, lack age-specific retirement incentives. Friedberg and Webb (2005) estimate that their absence leads workers with a DC plan to retire nearly two years later.[10] A simple calculation suggests that the shift from DB to DC plans might have led to a roughly five-month increase in the median retirement age, corresponding to nearly one-fifth of the increase for men since 1995 (Munnell 2015).[11]

Another important change in employer-sponsored benefits has been the decline in the share of firms offering health insurance to retirees. By one estimate, the share of private-sector workers employed by firms offering health insurance to their pre-Medicare-age retirees fell from 29 percent in 1997 to 18 percent in 2011 (Fronstin and Adams 2012).[12] A number of studies suggest that the availability of retiree health insurance benefits leads workers to retire at least several months and potentially more than a year earlier (Madrian, Burtless, and Gruber 1994; Nyce et al. 2013). Using the midpoint of these estimates suggests that the decline in retiree health insurance coverage between 1997 and 2011 might have led to an increase in the median retirement age of about one month.[13]

9. The vast majority of public-sector workers continue to be covered by DB plans. Among state and local workers in 2012, for example, only 2 percent had a DC plan while 7 percent had a hybrid (DB and DC) plan (Munnell, Aubry, and Cafarelli 2014). Most federal workers are covered by both a DB and a DC plan.

10. While this study is one of the few to estimate the effect of the shift from DB to DC pensions on retirement, many previous studies find that DB pension incentives have strong effects on retirement decisions—see, for example, Stock and Wise (1990a, 1990b) and Samwick (1998).

11. Friedberg and Webb (2005) estimate that moving from a DB to a DC plan is associated with a 21-month increase in the median retirement age. Given a 26-point decline in the share of private-sector workers with DB plans between 1980 and 2014 (figure 12.22) and an estimated 84 percent of workers in the private sector (Mayer 2014), this suggests that the shift from DB to DC plans led to a 4.5-month decline in the median retirement age. Munnell (2015) calculates that the median age of retirement for men rose by 26 months between 1995 and 2013, so 4.5 months represents 18 percent of that increase. Friedberg and Webb (2005) forecast a somewhat larger (9–13 month) increase in the median retirement age between 1983 and 2015, based on projections of future age-specific rates of DB coverage with the data then available.

12. Trends in this statistic prior to 1997 are more difficult to discern. The Employee Benefit Research Institute (1996) reports that the share of full-time workers in firms with 100 or more employees who have access to retiree health benefits remained constant between 1988 and 1993, even as a 1990 regulatory change required companies to record unfunded benefit liabilities on their financial statements, potentially causing employers to reexamine their role in providing these benefits. However, the number of large employers offering retiree health insurance benefits has been declining since at least 1991 (Fronstin 2001).

13. Estimates of the effect of retiree health insurance access on retirement vary. Madrian et al. (1994) report an effect of 5–16 months, while Nyce et al. (2013) find an effect of 3–13 months, depending on the employee's length of service and the share of premiums covered by the firm. Using 9 months as an approximate midpoint of these estimates, an 11-point decrease in coverage for private-sector workers (who make up 84 percent of the workforce, as discussed above) yields an estimate of 0.8 months.

12.2.5   Social Security Reforms

While public pension reforms in the United States in recent decades have not been as frequent or dramatic as those in some other countries, there have nonetheless been meaningful changes that have significantly impacted the incentive to work at older ages and likely contributed to longer work lives.

The 1983 amendments to the Social Security Act made a number of changes that collectively were designed to put the system on firmer financial footing for coming decades. One such change was an increase in the full retirement age (FRA), which is the age at which beneficiaries receive their full monthly benefit amount without a reduction for early claiming. The FRA has historically been age 65, but it has risen over time to age 67 in a series of steps, with the first increase for those born in 1938 (who turned 65 in 2003).[14] The increase in the FRA may affect the decision of when to retire for two reasons. First, an FRA increase is effectively a benefit cut for any given claiming age. For example, a worker claiming at age 65 whose primary insurance amount (PIA) is $1,000 would be entitled to a monthly benefit of $1,000 if her FRA is 65 versus $933 per month if her FRA is 66, a decline of 6.67 percent. Economic theory suggests that she will respond to this negative wealth shock by reducing consumption of leisure (and other normal goods), and postponing retirement is one means of doing so. Second, the FRA may play an important role in establishing a focal point for retirement, affecting social norms.

Mastrobuoni (2009) examines the effect of the FRA increase using data for the 1928 through 1941 birth cohorts, covering the first four steps in the FRA increase (from 65 to 65 and 8 months). He shows that the average age of retirement was rising quite gradually across birth cohorts until the FRA increases began and then rose more rapidly thereafter. He concludes that each two-month increase in the FRA is associated with a one-month increase in the average age of retirement.[15] Song and Manchester (2007a) show that the spike in claiming at age 65 for men and women moved in lockstep with the FRA as it increased, though changes in claiming behavior may not necessarily reflect changes in retirement. Extrapolating from these results suggests that the one-year increase in the FRA to date (from 65 to 66) may have increased the average age of retirement by six months.

A second key change in social security provisions is the increase in the delayed retirement credit (DRC) for claiming after the FRA. Workers may claim social security benefits starting at age 62, but they receive a larger monthly benefit amount the longer they wait to claim. Delayed claiming may

---

14. Specifically, the FRA is 65 for those born in 1937 or earlier, rises by two months per birth cohort for the 1938–42 cohorts, is 66 for those born in 1943–54, rises again by two months per birth cohort for the 1955–59 cohorts, and is 67 for those born in 1960 and later.

15. Mastrobuoni (2009) notes that Blau and Goodstein (2007) reach a different conclusion about the effect of social security reform on the LFP; however, their approach does not isolate the change in benefits that results solely from reforms.

increase or decrease lifetime social security benefits, depending on whether the adjustment is more or less than actuarially fair. Historically, benefits have been reduced by 6.67 percent per year for claiming before the FRA and raised by 3 percent per year of delay after the FRA. Coile et al. (2002) show that with these rates of adjustment, many types of worker can maximize the financial or utility value of benefits by waiting until the FRA to claim, but no types gain from delay beyond the FRA.[16]

The 1983 amendments raised the DRC from 3 to 8 percent per year in a series of steps.[17] This change has increased the value of delay beyond the FRA; Sun and Webb (2009) report that for cohorts exposed to the higher DRC, there are many worker types for whom delay beyond the FRA is optimal. An increase in the DRC may encourage individuals to delay their benefit claim without changing their retirement decision or to delay both retirement and claiming if they tend to treat these decisions as linked (though they need not be). Pingle (2006) estimates the effect of the DRC on employment in a model that includes age and year fixed effects and a polynomial in birth year, using the step increases in the DRC for identification. He finds that each one percentage point increase in the DRC is associated with a roughly one percentage point increase in the employment rate of men aged 65–69. This estimate suggests that the five-point increase in the DRC since 1990 could explain up to half of the increase in participation of men aged 65–69 over this period, reported in figure 12.1.

A final change relates to the social security retirement earnings test (RET). Those who claim social security retired worker benefits but continue to have earnings are potentially subject to the RET. Workers below the FRA face a benefit reduction of $1 for each $2 of earnings above an exempt amount ($15,270 in 2016, though this amount is higher for those reaching the FRA during the year). Workers above the FRA were historically subject to the RET with a somewhat higher exemption amount. In 1990, the tax rate on those above the FRA was lowered to $1 of benefit reduction per $3 of earnings, and in 2000, the RET was eliminated for those above the FRA. Benefits lost through the RET are subsequently credited back to workers in the form of an increased actuarial adjustment, but this appears to be a little-understood provision.

An existing literature has explored the effect of the RET on both the extensive and the intensive work margins; the former is more relevant here.[18]

---

16. Shoven and Slavov (2014) show that the value of delaying from age 62 to the FRA has increased since the 1960s, with most of the increase due to improvement in mortality and declining real interest rates, though a social security rule change that affects survivor's benefits has also increased the benefit of delay for husbands. They do not report the gains (or losses) from delay beyond the FRA in their analysis.

17. Specifically, the DRC is 3 percent per year for those born in 1924 or earlier, then increases by 0.5 percent every other year (e.g., to 3.5 percent for the 1925–26 cohorts and to 4 percent for the 1927–28 cohorts), reaching 8 percent for those born in 1943 and later.

18. See Friedberg (2000) and Gelber, James, and Sacks (2013) for evidence of the effect of the RET on the intensive margin.

A number of studies employ a differences-in-differences approach to explore the effect of changes to the RET over time and conclude that the test has little effect on employment (see Gruber and Orszag 2003; Haider and Loughran 2008; Song 2004; Song and Manchester 2007b).[19] In contrast, Friedberg and Webb (2009) find that the RET affects employment in some of their specifications and conclude that its elimination above the FRA increased employment at ages 66–68 by 0.5–2 percentage points. Gelber et al. (2017) also identify an extensive margin response to the RET using a regression discontinuity approach based on changes in the employment levels of 63- and 64-year-olds with earnings near the RET threshold; the authors estimate that eliminating the RET would cause an increase in employment of 1.4 points among workers at those ages with earnings near the threshold. While these results are not directly informative regarding the effect of eliminating the RET above the FRA, they may suggest that a modest increase in employment was likely.

Overall, these three changes to social security—the increase in the FRA, the increase in the DRC above the FRA, and the elimination of the RET above the FRA—seem likely to have contributed substantially to the increase in employment at older ages, particularly at ages 65 and older. As the literature on the FRA and DRC increases is fairly limited and the results of different studies are not necessarily reported in a way that allows easy comparison of the effects of these policy changes on employment, additional work examining how social security policy changes have affected the return to work at older ages would be helpful.

12.3 Discussion

Men and women in the United States are working substantially longer than their counterparts of a few decades ago, a phenomenon with profound implications both for the workers themselves and for the economy as a whole. Many theories have been put forth to help explain this trend. Improving health is one such theory. Yet while good health is certainly a necessary ingredient for a longer career, there is little evidence that changes in health are driving rising participation. Education is another likely candidate, given the steep participation gradient with respect to education and the dramatic increases in the educational attainment of the older population in recent decades. Although simple calculations suggest that this factor could have played a key role, there is as yet no test of this hypothesis based on a compelling empirical strategy.

More persuasive evidence appears to exist with respect to several other hypotheses: Rising women's participation in the economy has encouraged

---

19. Gustman and Steinmeier (2008) employ a different methodology, estimating a structural model of retirement and wealth; they conclude that the RET reduces participation between ages 62 and the FRA by 4 percentage points.

older husbands to work longer due to leisure complementarities. A shift in employer-provided pensions from DB to DC plans has reduced the share of workers facing strong incentives to retire at particular ages, while a decline in retiree health coverage has left some workers with no means of obtaining health insurance other than through their job until the Medicare eligibility age of 65; both changes contributed to longer work lives. Finally, changes to the social security FRA, DRC, and RET have strengthened the incentive for work past the FRA, contributing to the increase in participation at older ages.

The estimates from the existing literature may be combined to get some sense of the share of the increase in work that is explained by these various factors, although the results this exercise should be treated very cautiously given that they are projections based on findings from different studies that may not be directly comparable. Using Munnell's (2015) estimate of a 26-month increase in men's average retirement age since 1995, Schirle's (2008) estimate that the rise in women's participation accounted for one-quarter of the increase in men's participation would suggest a 6.5-month increase in men's average retirement age from this factor. In the discussion above, the effects of the DB to DC shift and the decline in retiree health insurance coverage were estimated to be 4.5 months and 0.8 months, respectively, while the effect of the FRA increase was estimated to be 6 months. Making a projection of the effect of the rising DRC and elimination of the RET is more difficult. Pingle (2006) suggests that the DRC increase led to a 5-point increase in participation at ages 65–69 while the findings of Friedberg and Webb (2009) might suggest a further 1–2-point increase from the elimination of the RET. Together, these would account for roughly half the increase in participation since 1995 in the 65–69 age group. Given that the participation rate of this group is roughly half that of men aged 60–64, this might be seen as the equivalent to one-sixth of the overall increase in the retirement age, or 4.3 months. Together, these factors account for an estimated 22-month increase in the average retirement age for men, or about 85 percent of the total increase since 1995. Social security is the single largest factor, with all the changes combined accounting for perhaps 10 months of the increase, although the calculations with respect to the DRC and RET are particularly speculative. The average age of retirement for women rose by 24 months between 1995 and 2013, indicating that changes in social security can account for a large share of the increase in women's work over this period as well.

Several potentially fruitful directions for future analysis are suggested from this analysis. First, there is some evidence of a slowdown or even an end to the trend toward longer work lives for men and women, as seen in figures 12.1 and 12.2, although this period coincides with the recovery from the Great Recession and so trends could reflect business-cycle effects. It will be important to monitor these trends to see how retirement behavior continues to evolve in the future. Second, trends by socioeconomic status merit further attention. There is clear evidence of a widening gradient in participation by education for women (figure 12.6) and some evidence of this for men as well (figure 12.5), although the changing distribution of educational attainment complicates the evaluation of trends over long periods of time. It would be useful to explore trends in retirement and benefit claiming by other key measures of socioeconomic status, such as lifetime income group. In addition, as noted earlier, better evidence regarding the effect of increasing education on participation at older ages is needed.

Finally, this discussion highlights the need for more analysis of how changes to social security since 1980 have affected the incentives for work at older ages and how much these reforms have contributed to the increase in work at older ages. Making projections based on results from different studies, as has been done here, necessarily provides only tentative answers to these important questions. Future work on these questions will not only provide a better understanding of past reforms but also lay the groundwork for projecting the effect of future reforms as well.

References

Baker, Michael. 2002. "The Retirement Behavior of Married Couples: Evidence from the Spouse's Allowance." *Journal of Human Resources* 37 (Winter): 1–34.

Blau, David M., and Ryan Goodstein. 2007. "What Explains Trends in Labor Force Participation of Older Men in the United States?" IZA Discussion Paper No. 2991, Institute for the Study of Labor (IZA), Bonn, Germany.

Bound, John, Arline Geronimus, Javier Rodriguez, and Timothy Waidmann. 2014. "The Implications of Differential Trends in Mortality for Social Security." Retirement Research Center Working Paper No. 2014 314, University of Michigan, Ann Arbor.

Bound, John, Michael Schoenbaum, Todd R. Stinebrickner, and Timothy Waidmann. 1999. "The Dynamic Effects of Health on the Labor Force Transitions of Older Workers." *Labour Economics* 6 (2): 179–202.

Burtless, Gary. 2013. "Can Educational Attainment Explain the Rise in Labor Force Participation at Older Ages?" Center for Retirement Research, Boston College, Issue Brief No. 13-13.

Coile, Courtney C. 2004. "Retirement Incentives and Couples' Retirement Decisions." *B. E. Journal of Economic Analysis and Policy* 4 (1): 1–30.

———. 2015. "Economic Determinants of Workers' Retirement Decisions." *Journal of Economic Surveys* 29 (4): 830–53.

———. 2018. "The Demography of Retirement." In *Future Directions for the Demography of Aging: Proceedings of a Workshop*, edited by Mark D. Hayward and Malay K. Majumdar. Washington, DC: National Academies Press.

Coile, Courtney, Peter Diamond, Jonathan Gruber, and Alain Jousten. 2002. "Delays in Claiming Social Security Benefits." *Journal of Public Economics* 84 (3): 357–85.

Coile, Courtney C., and Phillip B. Levine. 2007. "Labor Market Shocks and Retirement: Do Government Programs Matter?" *Journal of Public Economics* 91 (10): 1902–19.

Coile, Courtney, Kevin S. Milligan, and David A. Wise. 2017. "Health Capacity to Work at Older Ages: Evidence from the U.S." In *Social Security Programs and Retirement around the World: The Capacity to Work at Older Ages*, edited by David A. Wise, 359–94. Chicago: University of Chicago Press.

Costa, Dora. 1998. *The Evolution of Retirement: An American Economic History, 1880–1990*. Chicago: University of Chicago Press.

Council of Economic Advisors. 2016. "The Long-Term Decline in Prime-Age Male Labor Force Participation." https://obamawhitehouse.archives.gov/sites/default /files/page/files/20160620_cea_primeage_male_lfp.pdf.

Crimmins, Eileen M. 2004. "Trends in the Health of the Elderly." *Annual Review of Public Health* 25:79–98.

Crimmins, Eileen M., and Hiram Beltrán-Sánchez. 2010. "Mortality and Morbidity Trends: Is There Compression of Morbidity?" *Journal of Gerontology: Social Sciences* 66B (1): 75–86.

Cutler, David M., Kaushik Ghosh, and Mary Beth Landrum. 2014. "Evidence for Significant Compression of Morbidity in the Elderly U.S. Population." In *Discoveries in the Economics of Aging*, edited by David A. Wise, 21–51. Chicago: University of Chicago Press.

Employee Benefit Research Institute. 1996. "Retiree Health Benefits: What the Changes May Mean for Future Benefits." Employee Benefit Research Institute, Issue Brief No. 175, July.

Friedberg, Leora. 2000. "The Labor Supply Effects of the Social Security Earnings Test." *Review of Economics and Statistics* 82:48–63.

Friedberg, Leora, and Anthony Webb. 2005. "Retirement and Evolution of the Pension Structure." *Journal of Human Resources* 40 (2): 281–308.

———. 2009. "New Evidence on the Labor Supply Effects of the Social Security Earnings Test." In *Tax Policy and the Economy*. Vol. 23, edited by Jeffrey R. Brown and James M. Poterba, 1–35. Chicago: University of Chicago Press.

Fronstin, Paul. 2001. "Retiree Health Benefits: Trends and Outlook." Employee Benefit Research Institute, Issue Brief No. 236, August.

Fronstin, Paul, and Nevin Adams. 2012. "Employment-Based Retiree Health Benefits: Trends in Access and Coverage, 1997–2010." Employee Benefit Research Institute, Issue Brief No. 377, October.

Gelber, Alexander M., Damon James, and Daniel W. Sacks. 2013. "Earnings Adjustment Frictions: Evidence from the Social Security Earnings Test." NBER Working Paper No. 19491, National Bureau of Economic Research, Cambridge, MA.

Gelber, Alexander M., Damon Jones, Daniel W. Sacks, and Jae Song. 2017. "Using Kinked Budget Sets to Estimate Extensive Margin Responses: Method and Evidence from the Social Security Earnings Test." NBER Working Paper No. 23362, National Bureau of Economic Research, Cambridge, MA.

Goldin, Claudia. 2006. "The Quiet Revolution That Transformed Women's Employment, Education, and Family." *American Economic Review* 96 (2): 1–21.

Goldin, C., and L. F. Katz. 2018. "Women Working Longer: Facts and Some Explanations." In *Women Working Longer: Increased Employment at Older Ages*, edited by C. Goldin and L. F. Katz, 11–53. Chicago: University of Chicago Press.

Gruber, Jonathan, and Peter Orszag. 2003. "Does the Social Security Earnings Test Affect Labor Supply and Benefits Receipt?" *National Tax Journal* 56:755–74.

Gustman, Alan L., and Thomas L. Steinmeier. 2000. "Retirement in Dual-Career Families: A Structural Model." *Journal of Labor Economics* 18 (3): 503–45.

———. 2008. "Projecting Behavioral Responses to the Next Generation of Retirement Policies." *Research in Labor Economics* 28:141–96.

Haider, Steven J., and David S. Loughran. 2008. "The Effect of the Social Security Earnings Test on Male Labor Supply: New Evidence from Survey and Administrative Data." *Journal of Human Resources* 43 (1): 57–87.

Ham, D. Cal, Thomas Przybeck, Jaime R. Strickland, Douglas A. Luke, Laura J. Bierut, and Bradley A. Evanoff. 2011. "Occupation and Workplace Policies Predict Smoking Behaviors: Analysis of National Data from the Current Population Survey." *Journal of Occupational and Environmental Medicine* 53 (11): 1337–45.

Lahey, Joanna N. 2008. "Age, Women, and Hiring: An Experimental Study." *Journal of Human Resources* 43 (1): 30–56.

Madrian, Brigitte, Gary Burtless, and Jonathan Gruber. 1994. "The Effect of Health Insurance on Retirement." *Brookings Papers on Economic Activity* 1994 (1): 181–252.

Maestas, Nicole. 2001. *Labor, Love, and Leisure: Complementarity and the Timing of Retirement by Working Couples.* Berkeley: University of California, Berkeley (Department of Economics).

Mastrobuoni, Giovanni. 2009. "Labor Supply Effects of the Recent Social Security Benefit Cuts: Empirical Estimates Using Cohort Discontinuities." *Journal of Public Economics* 93 (11–12): 1224–33.

Mayer, Gerald. 2014. "Selected Characteristics of Private and Public Sector Workers." Congressional Research Service report 7-5700, Washington, DC.

Munnell, Alicia H. 2015. "The Average Retirement Age: An Update." Center for Retirement Research, Boston College, Issue Brief No. 15-4.

Munnell, Alicia H., Jean-Pierre Aubry, and Mark Cafarelli. 2014. "Defined Contribution Plans in the Public Sector: An Update." Center for Retirement Research, Boston College, State and Local Pension Plans No. 37, April.

Neumark, David, Ian Burn, and Patrick Button. 2015. "Is It Harder for Older Workers to Find Jobs? New and Improved Evidence from a Field Experiment." NBER Working Paper No. 21669, National Bureau of Economic Research, Cambridge, MA.

Nyce, Steven, Sylvester J. Schieber, John B. Shoven, Sita N. Slavov, and David A. Wise. 2013. "Does Retiree Health Insurance Encourage Early Retirement?" *Journal of Public Economics* 104:40–51.

Pingle, Jonathan F. 2006. "Social Security's Delayed Retirement Credit and the Labor Supply of Older Men." Federal Reserve Board Finance and Economics Discussion Series, Working Paper No. 2006-37, Washington, DC.

Poterba, James, Joshua Rauh, Steven Venti, and David Wise. 2007. "Defined Contribution Plans, Defined Benefit Plans, and the Accumulation of Retirement Wealth." *Journal of Public Economics* 91 (10): 2062–86.

Samwick, Andrew A. 1998. "New Evidence on Pensions, Social Security, and the Timing of Retirement." *Journal of Public Economics* 70:207–36.

Schirle, Tammy. 2008. "Why Have the Labor Force Participation Rates of Older Men Increased since the Mid-1990s?" *Journal of Labor Economics* 26 (4): 549–94.

Shoven, John B., and Sita Slavov. 2014. "Does It Pay to Delay Social Security?" *Journal of Pension Economics and Finance* 13 (2): 121–44.

Song, Jae. 2004. "Evaluating the Initial Impact of Eliminating the Retirement Earnings Test." *Social Security Bulletin* 65 (1): 1–15.

Song, Jae, and Joyce Manchester. 2007a. "Have People Delayed Claiming Retirement Benefits? Responses to Changes in Social Security Rules." *Social Security Bulletin* 67 (2): 1–23.

———. 2007b. "New Evidence on Earnings and Benefit Claims following Changes in the Retirement Earnings Test." *Journal of Public Economics* 91:669–700.

Stock, James H., and David A. Wise. 1990a. "Pensions, the Option Value of Work, and Retirement." *Econometrica* 58:1151–80.

———. 1990b. "The Pension Inducement to Retire: An Option Value Analysis." In *Issues in the Economics of Aging*, edited by David A. Wise, 205–30. Chicago: University of Chicago Press.

Sun, Wei, and Anthony Webb. 2009. "How Much Do Households Really Lose by Claiming Social Security at Age 62?" Center for Retirement Research, Working Paper No. 2009-11, Boston College, Chestnut Hill, MA.

Contributors

James Banks
Department of Economics
School of Social Sciences
University of Manchester
Manchester M13 9PL UK

Paul Bingley
VIVE—The Danish Centre for Social
  Science Research
Herluf Trolles Gade 11
1052 Copenhagen K Denmark

Didier Blanchet
INSEE-CREST
15 Blvd. Gabriel Péri BP 100
92244 Malakoff Cedex France

Axel Börsch-Supan
Munich Center for the Economics of
  Aging
Max Planck Institute for Social Law
  and Social Policy
Amalienstrasse 33
80799 Munich Germany

Antoine Bozio
Paris School of Economics
48 Bd Jourdan
75014 Paris France

Agar Brugiavini
Department of Economics
Ca' Foscari University of Venice
Cannareggio 873
30121 Venice Italy

Courtney C. Coile
Department of Economics
Wellesley College
106 Central Street
Wellesley, MA 02481

Klaas de Vos
CentERdata
Tilburg University
Warandelaan 2
5037 AB Tilburg The Netherlands

Carl Emmerson
Institute for Fiscal Studies
7 Ridgmount Street
London WC1E 7AE UK

Irene Ferrari
Munich Center for the Economics of
  Aging
Max Planck Institute for Social Law
  and Social Policy
Amalienstrasse 33
80799 Munich Germany

Pilar García-Gómez
Erasmus School of Economics
P.O. Box 1738
3000 DR Rotterdam The Netherlands

Nabanita Datta Gupta
Department of Economics and
    Business Economics
Aarhus University
Fuglesangs Allé 4
8210 Aarhus V Denmark

Sergi Jiménez-Martín
Department of Economics
Universitat Pompeu Fabra
Ramon Trias Fargas 25-27
08005 Barcelona Spain

Alain Jousten
University of Liège
Law Faculty, HEC-ULg and Tax
    Institute
Place des Orateurs 3
4000 Liège 1 Belgium

Adriaan Kalwij
Utrecht University School of
    Economics
Adam Smith Hall
Kriekenpitplein 21-22
3584 EC Utrecht The Netherlands

Arie Kapteyn
University of Southern California
Center for Economic and Social
    Research
635 Downey Way Suite 312
Los Angeles, CA 90089-3332

Lisa Laun
Institute for Evaluation of Labour
    Market and Education Policy
    (IFAU)
Box 513
SE-751 20 Uppsala Sweden

Mathieu Lefebvre
BETA, University of Strasbourg
61, avenue de la Forêt Noire
67085 Strasbourg Cedex France

Kevin Milligan
Vancouver School of Economics
University of British Columbia
6000 Iona Drive
Vancouver, BC V6T 1L4 Canada

Takashi Oshio
Institute of Economic Research
Hitotsubashi University
2-1 Naka, Kunitachi
Tokyo 186-8603 Japan

Mårten Palme
Department of Economics
Stockholm University
SE-106 91 Stockholm Sweden

Giacomo Pasini
Department of Economics
Ca' Foscari University of Venice
Cannaregio 873
30121 Venice Italy

Peder J. Pedersen
Department of Economics and
    Business Economics
Aarhus University
Fuglesangs Allé 4
8210 Aarhus V Denmark

Corinne Prost
INSEE-CREST
15 Blvd. Gabriel Péri
B.P. 100
92244 Malakoff Cedex France

Muriel Roger
CES—Université Paris 1 Panthéon-
    Sorbonne
106-112 boulevard de l'Hôpital
75013 Paris France

Tammy Schirle
Department of Economics
Wilfrid Laurier University
75 University Avenue West
Waterloo, ON N2L 3C5 Canada

Satoshi Shimizutani
Ricoh Institute of Sustainability and
  Business
20th Fl., Marunouchi Kitaguchi
  Building
1-6-5 Marunouchi, Chiyoda-ku
Tokyo 100-0005 Japan

Gemma Tetlow
Institute for Government
2 Carlton Gardens
London SW1Y 5AA UK

Emiko Usui
Institute of Economic Research
Hitotsubashi University
2-1 Naka, Kunitachi
Tokyo 186-8603 Japan

Judit Vall Castelló
Department of Economics and IEB
Universitat de Barcelona
John M. Keynes, 1-11
08034 Barcelona Spain

Guglielmo Weber
Department of Economics and
  Management
University of Padua
Via del Santo 33
35123 Padua Italy

David A. Wise
NBER
1050 Massachusetts Avenue
Cambridge, MA 02138

<h1 align="center">Subject Index</h1>

Note: Page numbers followed by "f" or "t" refer to figures or tables, respectively.